INDUSTRIAL RELATIONS RESEARCH

ASSOCIATION SERIES

Theoretical Perspectives
on Work and the Employment Relationship

EDITED BY

Bruce E. Kaufman

First Edition

ISBN 0-913447-88-9

Price: $29.95

INDUSTRIAL RELATIONS RESEARCH ASSOCIATION SERIES:
Proceedings of the Annual Meeting
Annual Research Volume
IRRA 2002 Membership Directory (published every four years)
IRRA Newsletter (published quarterly)
Perspectives on Work (published biannually)

Inquiries and other communications regarding membership, meetings, publications, and
general affairs of the association, as well as notice of address changes, should be addressed
to the IRRA office.

INDUSTRIAL RELATIONS RESEARCH ASSOCIATION
University of Illinois at Urbana-Champaign
121 Labor and Industrial Relations Building
504 East Armory Avenue
Champaign, IL 61820
Telephone: 217/333-0072   Fax: 217/265-5130
Internet: www.irra.uiuc.edu   E-mail: irra@uiuc.edu

To Jack Barbash, John Dunlop, and Noah Meltz,
leaders in the development of industrial relations theory

CONTENTS

Preface

Most of the research volumes published by the Industrial Relations Research Association (IRRA) over the years have been on relatively applied, problem-driven topics. This orientation reflects both the nature of the field and the IRRA's mix of academic and practitioner members.

In something of a departure, I proposed to the association's Executive Committee that the 2004 volume pursue a more overtly theoretical and academic topic. The topic proposed was industrial relations theory—rephrased for sake of generality and broad acceptance to "theoretical perspectives on work and the employment relationship."

The motivations for proposing this theme were threefold. The first was that the topic has considerable intrinsic interest and presents great opportunities for further advance. Ever since the industrial relations (IR) field coalesced into its modern form after World War II, leading thinkers in the field have sought to develop an integrative theory of industrial relations—or at least an overarching conceptual framework—in order to tie the disparate branches of the field together and guide empirical work and policy debate. The intrinsic interest of this project arises from the fact that theorizing gets to the core of what science is about, and few subjects are as important or interesting for theorizing in the social sciences as work and employment. Success in this endeavor, however, has been only partial and piecemeal, despite the best efforts of some of the field's leading thinkers, and thus many exciting new ideas and theoretical insights remain to be discovered and developed. Since the IRRA was founded to promote research on all aspects of labor, a volume on IR theory seemed both highly relevant and timely.

The second motivation came from the long-term decline in the academic fortunes of industrial relations and my desire to reverse this trend. As numerous people in the field have observed, industrial relations in this country—and to some substantial degree in many other countries of the world—has in the last two decades suffered a significant loss of intellectual energy and scholarly participation. The root causes are diverse, but surely one is the failure to develop a more substantial, integrative theoretical base for the field. To survive and prosper, an academic field must attract a critical mass of "paying customers" through one or a combination of three routes: by providing a body of theory or set of tools that attracts scholars because these ideas or methods are highly productive in the conduct of scientific research, by addressing a real-world practice area or set of applied problems that is of sufficient breadth and depth of interest that it attracts a sizable body of students and considerable attention from policy makers, or by focusing on a subject that for ethical, ideological, or other normative reasons is deemed sufficiently important that numerous universities are moved to include it in their academic programs. The latter two have been the primary base of support for industrial relations in American universities in the post–World War II period but have weakened considerably in recent decades with the substantial decline in the power and size of the labor movement. Thus, one strategy for renewal of the IR field is to turn to the theory and methods dimension and work to strengthen it, which is in part what this volume seeks to accomplish.

The third reason for undertaking this volume was suggested by Kurt Lewin's well-known aphorism "There is nothing as practical as a good theory." On the face of it, academic theorizing can be a highly esoteric and sometimes eye-glazing exercise of seemingly little relevance or applicability to people with practical problems to solve in the real world of industry and government. Recognizing this side of the matter, another far more positive side to theorizing also exists. The job of theory is to explain why A leads to B and under what conditions. A moment's reflection reveals that without a backbone of theory, every recommended workplace practice and employment policy is, at the end of the day, no more than someone's opinion or informed conjecture. A specific practice or policy may work in one situation, but we cannot be sure why it works or whether it will work in a different situation. In other words, practice and policy without theory are essentially ad hoc and always in danger of confusing correlation with causation. A theory, even if couched in a few words or a simple diagram, helps turn opinion and educated guesses into scientific propositions that have greater reliability, explanatory insight, and predictive power. Does higher pay elicit more work effort from employees? Should more firms adopt "high-performance" work practices? Do unions hinder or promote firm performance? A plausible, well-constructed theory is essential to answering all these types of questions—questions, I note, that are of great practical importance.

The IRRA's Executive Committee accepted these arguments and approved the volume. As part of the proposal, I pledged to include a mix of chapters that would be both inclusive and diverse: inclusive of the numerous disciplines, fields of study, and points of view that are contained within industrial relations and diverse with respect to subject areas and authors' backgrounds. Another goal was to attract a complement of well-recognized, leading scholars but also to open the door to younger, less-established researchers doing significant work in the area of IR theory.

For the most part these goals have been met. I sent out a call for papers using the IRRA newsletter and various Web sites and e-mail distribution lists, explicitly aiming to reach not only IRRA members but also nonmembers in North America and other countries around the world. (Nonmembers are always potential new members!) A number of telephone calls soliciting author suggestions and commitments from prominent people in the field were also made.

The result of these efforts is the 11 chapters contained in this volume. I believe readers will find these chapters to be a high-quality, insightful, and welcome contribution to the literature on IR theory. I also think they are fitting tribute to the legacy of Jack Barbash, John Dunlop, and Noah Meltz, three longtime IRRA members who made major contributions to IR theory and to whom this volume is dedicated. (Meltz passed away while his chapter in this volume was at a preliminary stage of development.)

The 11 chapters are inclusive and diverse in that they span the gamut of subjects related to the employment relationship and provide a wide range of perspectives and theoretical orientations. The chapter topics extend, for example, from the micro or individual level to the macro or nation-state level; include fields such as organizational behavior, human resource management, economics, sociology, comparative politics, and history; and include various perspectives ranging from Marxist to managerialist and institutional to neoclassical.

In several respects the authors are also quite diverse. People from five countries (Australia, Britain, Canada, Germany, United States) are represented, as are authors from management departments, business schools, industrial relations departments, economics departments, and law schools. Two dimensions of diversity are less well met: female authors and younger authors. Despite concerted efforts to obtain more of both, success was modest. Very few of either write on IR theory, and an even smaller number answered the call for papers. Also unfortunate, one of the chapters commissioned for the volume written by both a female and younger author could not be completed.

One final aspect of the chapter lineup deserves brief mention. Two chapters were commissioned but for regrettable reasons could not be completed. One was a survey of regulation theory (the French regulation school); the second was on theory in human resource management (HRM). I deemed the latter chapter to be crucial but did not learn that the original authors would be unable to complete it until very close to the publishing deadline. I immediately asked two other well-known scholars in the HRM field to take over the chapter, but when they learned that it had to be finished in a very short time period and had to contain new, original research, both demurred. Rather than have no chapter on HRM, I took a deep breath and wrote the chapter myself.

In closing, I wish to thank all the authors for their patience, cooperation, and hard work; Paula Wells of the IRRA for her unflagging dedication and valuable help and advice in all phases of this project; and Karen Bojda for excellent copyediting.

BRUCE E. KAUFMAN

CHAPTER 1

Theoretical Approaches to Industrial Relations

WALTHER MÜLLER-JENTSCH
Ruhr-Universität Bochum

It is common knowledge that social sciences intend to not only describe and classify empirical facts but also to explain them with recourse to their underlying causes. Although social sciences have these goals in common with natural sciences, their epistemologies and logics of research differ considerably. More explicitly, I do not believe in the Popperian unity of sciences but prefer the Weberian approach, which postulates that social and cultural sciences deal with those subjects that can be explained only via interpretative understanding (Weber [1922] 1964:3). Following Habermas (1970), social sciences can be understood as hybrids of cultural and natural sciences. Accordingly, social behavior can be conceptualized as an intentional human action *(participant's perspective)* on the one hand and as an outcome determined by structural constraints[1] *(observer's perspective)* on the other. This ambivalence calls for different epistemologies: analytical theory of science for the latter, hermeneutics (theory of interpretation) for the former. Social sciences require a combination of both perspectives, a synthesis of "structural analysis" and "strategic analysis" (Giddens 1984:327ff), in other words, a "hermeneutically informed social theory" (Giddens 1982:5).

Explanations can be only as good as the theories we deploy. In the subject area of industrial relations there are several impediments to the development of good theories. Two of these should be mentioned here. First, industrial relations is an interdisciplinary field of study, and the individual disciplines contributing to it (sociology, business studies, labor economics, political science, labor law, social psychology, etc.) provide scholars with divergent analytical tools. Second, because of the complexity of the subject area, specific theories exist for different institutions, actors, and issues that are tailor-made for their respective explanatory domains (e.g., collective bargaining, trade unions, industrial conflict, industrial democracy). It is impossible to integrate them into a unified theory because their premises and frameworks, their levels of analysis, and their disciplinary traditions are too disparate. Thus, theoretical pluralism prevails and finds its justification in the different analytical foci and objectives. The spectrum of theories applied in industrial relations consists of grand theories as well as middle-range theories and ad hoc approaches. I will review the array of theories, schools, and approaches and assess their strengths and weaknesses before outlining my own proposal for a theory designed particularly for the subject matter of industrial relations: *actor-centered institutionalism.*[2]

The earliest scientific work on industrial relations was undertaken by Lujo Brentano in Germany, by Sidney and Beatrice Webb in England, and by John R. Commons in the United States. These authors viewed laissez-faire capitalism with skepticism and were sympathetic to labor organizations and their members. With their analytical focus on the role and functions of trade unions in the economy, their main concern was the character of labor as a commodity. Whereas Brentano and Commons directed their attention toward the asymmetrical and conflictual relationship between capital and labor and the resulting particularities of the employment contract, the Webbs explored the differences between individual and collective contracts. Actually, it was Beatrice Webb (née Potter) who first used the term *collective bargaining* (see Potter 1891:217, cited in Webb and Webb [1897] 1902:173).

Systems Theory

Dunlop and His Critics

The first systematic attempt to formulate a theoretical framework of industrial relations was John Dunlop's *Industrial Relations Systems* ([1958] 1993). With several direct references to Parsons's theory of social systems, Dunlop defined the industrial relations system (IRS) as an analytical subsystem of industrial societies and located it "at the same logical plane as an economic system" (p. 45). But following Parsons's assumption of functional differentiation of modern societies into four particular subsystems (economy, polity, law and social control institutions, family and cultural system), the IRS can be a subsystem of a subsystem only in Parsons's frame of reference.

The conceptual framework of Dunlop ([1958] 1993) had two specific merits: First, it moved the rules and norms of industrial relations into the center of the analysis, whereas previous accounts had regarded industrial conflict or collective bargaining as the essence of industrial relations. Second, it identified the elementary components of which each IRS is composed.[3]

Dunlop ([1958] 1993) defined the core or internal structure of the IRS as "a web of rules." By this he meant in particular the institutions and norms that frame the IRS and its outcomes, including substantive norms (e.g., wage rates, working hours) and procedural institutions (e.g., conciliation and arbitration boards). Thus, the IRS was conceptualized in terms of both process and product: as a rule-guided *process* generating as its *product* other rules governing the actors and administered by systems of industrial relations at the national, industry, or plant level. Dunlop identified as the basic components of an IRS three groups of actors (managers, workers and their respective representatives, and government institutions dealing with industrial relations), three different environmental contexts (technologies, markets, and power distribution), and an ideology "that binds the IRS together"([1958] 1993:47).

If we ask for the causal relationship between the core and the components of IRS, we get the following explanation: the internal structure—norms and rules that govern the IRS and that are generated and altered in the IRS—is the dependent variable (R = rules). The interplay of actors (A), contexts (T, M, P), and ideology (I) is the independent variable. We can formalize this result in the following functional equation:

$$R = f(A, T, M, P, I)$$

But this is simply a formal explanation without information on how and why rules are made. Because of this deficiency, Dunlop's ([1958] 1993) approach cannot pretend to present a general theory of industrial relations. As a friendly critic mentioned, it is solely "a general framework to organize a description of the interaction between the actors, the environmental contexts and the ideologies" (Meltz 1991:14). Thus, the theoretical status is reduced to a taxonomy or a matrix listing, an ordering of the key elements and components that have to be taken into account when analyzing an IRS.

Two further points of critique are usually made:

1. The dimension of conflict and change is underrated. According to the premise of the older systems theory, Dunlop ([1958] 1993) regarded stability ("unity") as a structural essential of an IRS. He stipulated that the actors who produce the rules do this under a normative consensus; if they do not share a common ideology, their respective ideologies must at least be compatible. Finally, little attention was paid to

the internal dynamics and conflicts of the constituent parts of the IRS; they were treated as unitary elements.

2. The IRS is not a subsystem at the same level as the economic system, as Dunlop asserts. Wood, Wagner, Armstrong, Goodman, and Davis (1975) convincingly argued that the IRS is a subsystem with regulative functions for the production system and that both IRS and production system are subsystems of the economic system.

Nevertheless, the two merits mentioned earlier and the heuristic potential of the theory remain undisputed. One further advantage is its ability to connect with other theoretical approaches, as was shown by Kochan, Katz, and McKersie (1986) with their concept of "strategic choice" (discussed later).

Luhmann and His Disciples

An interesting attempt to conceptualize the IRS in the framework of Luhmann's autopoietic systems theory[4] has been undertaken by Ralf Rogowski (2000) and Wil Martens, Ad Nagelkere, and Willem de Nijs (2001). Even though Luhmann made no direct contributions to industrial relations as a field of reasoning, his paradigm shift from a structural-functionalist view to an autopoietic understanding of social systems provided these authors with new intellectual tools to analyze systems of industrial relations.

Rogowski (2000) argued in favor of a full-fledged autopoietic IRS that reproduces itself through collective communications, especially negotiations. By analogy to the legal system, he treats it as a functionally differentiated societal subsystem with a specific societal function. "It serves to continue communication in the case of collective conflict. It provides procedures that transform violent collective conflicts into negotiations" (p. 113). "Industrial relations have developed from a conflict system into a societal subsystem, which defines itself with respect to fulfilling a function in society at large," namely, "to manage collective violence, which can occur in the relations between industrial interest groups" (p. 116). Managing conflicts between collective actors through "procedures of conflict resolution," "collective agreements," "joint decision making," "industrial democracy," and so on has contributed to a transition from external regulation (e.g., state intervention) to self-regulation. Having transcended the stage of a mere conflict system, industrial relations are no longer adequately described by the semantic of *capital* and *labor.*

The mode of communication in the IRS is *negotiation:* "Negotiations within an industrial relations system can be called 'industrial relations acts,' in analogy to 'legal acts'" (Rogowski 2000:118). Such acts are, in particular, negotiations in collective bargaining. To distinguish its elementary communications—in other words, to select them from societal communications—an autopoietic system operates along a binary code, which Rogowski proposed to call "negotiable or nonnegotiable between collective industrial actors" (p. 120). That means anything that is negotiable can become part of the IRS. Finally, autonomous functional systems do "relate to each other 'horizontally' through performances" (p. 121). The particular intersystemic exchange relations of an IRS are performance relations with the political and legal systems, and these systems reciprocally benefit from each other; they "are often tripartite in nature with the two industrial actors interacting with state officials" (p. 122).

Taking up Rogowski's theoretical challenge, Martens, Nagelkere, and de Nijs (2001) modified the binary code to "agreeable–nonagreeable in relation to work–nonwork" (p. 242) and defined the societal function of a *labor relations system* more broadly as "handling the problem of lasting usability of persons for an organized instrumentalization for other societal problems (e.g., scarcity of goods and services, production of new knowledge)" (p. 247). Put in less abstract terms, IRSs are necessary to develop patterns for education, selling, and application of labor.

The theoretical endeavors of the disciples of the autopoietic systems theory might open our eyes to some new insights into industrial relations, but they also leave us with the general suspicion that systems theory is rephrasing well-known phenomena in a new language.

Marxist Approaches

Neither the notion *labor relations* nor the term *industrial relations* belongs to the vocabulary of Karl Marx. The reason is simply that regulation of the class struggle via institutionalized channels of conflict resolution—the very subject matter of industrial relations—was still unknown at his time. On the other hand, the core institutions underlying industrial relations—*free labor markets* and the *factory system*—were main components of Marx's analysis of industrial capitalism, and he was also a keen observer and intellectual supporter of workers' early efforts to build trade unions. But his analytical focus was less on their role as agencies of collective regulation of wage and labor conditions than on their historical mission as organizers of workers' resistance against exploitation, estrangement, and impoverishment, leading to the eventual overthrow of the capitalist wage system.

After the relationship between capital and labor had undergone profound changes during the late 19th and early 20th centuries, with improvements in the living and working conditions of the "laboring poor" and the recognition of labor organizations, Marxist theoreticians interpreted these changes as achievements of the class struggle and the unions' exercise of organized power. They concluded from those historical movements that the struggles must go on until the final victory of full industrial democracy, either by revolutionary actions (as Rosa Luxemburg and Karl Korsch thought) or by social reforms (as Eduard Bernstein assumed).

It took quite some time before Marxist theorists overcame their ignorance of the emerging practice of day-to-day industrial relations and instead discovered it as a serious subject for their analyses. The current spectrum of theories on industrial relations that can be traced to Marxist origins includes three schools of thought: the political economy of industrial relations, labor process analysis, and the French regulation school.

Political Economy of Industrial Relations

An early systematic Marxist tableau of industrial relations was Richard Hyman's textbook *Industrial Relations: A Marxist Introduction* (1975). His later collection of essays was published under the programmatic title *Political Economy of Industrial Relations* (1989).

Attacking the theoretical mainstream dominated by Dunlop and Flanders, he first questioned their narrow and one-sided definition of industrial relations:

> to define the subject *exclusively* in terms of rules and regulation is far too restrictive, and has unfortunate evaluative overtones. The implication is that what industrial relations is all about is the maintenance of stability and regularity in industry. The focus is on how any conflict is contained and controlled, rather than on the processes through which disagreements and disputes are generated. From this perspective, the question whether the existing structure of ownership and control in industry is an inevitable source of conflict is dismissed as external to the study of industrial relations. (Hyman 1975:11)

He argued that "order" and "regulation" were only one side of industrial relations; instability and disorder must be evaluated as of "equal significance as 'system outcomes'" (Hyman 1975:12). This led him to conclude that industrial relations were not to be defined as "the study of job regulation" but rather as "the study of processes of control over work relations" (1975:12). But those processes can be theoretically explained only with recourse to class structure and the capitalist environment, in particular the capitalist accumulation and crisis processes as well as political, social, and ideological power relations.

In an article published in 1994, Hyman (1994:177) affirmatively quoted Shalev (1992) in characterizing industrial relations as an "intervening variable," specifying in a footnote its dual meaning: its role as a "passive transmission belt from cause to effect" on the one hand and the fact that it "actively conditions the causal consequences" on the other (Hyman 1994:178).

A different Marxist approach to the political economy of industrial relations was elaborated by John Kelly (incidentally now Hyman's colleague at the London School of Economics) in his book *Rethinking Industrial Relations* (1998). In his theoretical synopsis Kelly combined a social-psychological mobilization theory with the economic long-wave theory. The argument starts with what the author regarded as the intellectual core of his approach: *injustice.* By taking the Marxist interpretation of the employment relationship for granted, he recognized exploitation and domination as its main elements. However, he did not ignore that only perceived injustice is relevant for stimulating an opposing response or—even more important—collective resistance against it. Thus, workers' interests and their collective identity are the real forces to be mobilized. In this context, militant activists play a key role; they act as catalysts who help spread the feeling of injustice and elevate the collective identity of workers. According to this theory, however, the employers are not idle but embark on countermobilizations against organized labor with the support of the capitalist state. This makes it difficult for workers to achieve the status of a class-conscious collectivity, in Marx's term, a "class for itself."

Kelly (1998:128) rigorously asked: "How do workers come to define dissatisfaction as injustice" and "how do they come to acquire a shared identity with their fellow employees that divides them from their employer?" He found the theoretical answer in the long-wave theory: "Each turning point between upswing and downswing is associated with an upsurge of mobilization, epitomized by heightened strike activity" (p. 86). The workers' mobilization triggers a period of countermobilization by employers and the state, resulting in a period of intensified class struggle. The consequence for industrial relations is "a more or less far-reaching reconstruction of the relations between labour, capital and the state" (p. 86). During the following long wave, the new patterns of industrial relations are gradually consolidated until the next transition.

Focusing on exploitation, conflict, power, and collective mobilization, Kelly's (1998) approach provides a framework to explain change
and long-run trends in the unequal exchange between capital and labor,
but it tells us little about the nature and functioning of the institutions
and procedures of industrial relations.

Labor Process Debate

Another strand of Marxist reasoning on industrial relations is the
debate on the character of the labor process. The nub of the debate is
the so-called transformation problem, which Marx had already defined
as the transformation of (bought) labor power into performed work, or
in a more common term, the problem of managerial control of labor.

The debate was triggered by Harry Braverman's book *Labor and
Monopoly Capital* (1974). The author's main argument was that the key
task of capitalist management is the control of the labor process in order
to extract a maximum of surplus value by transforming labor power into
work performance. Equipped with Taylor's "scientific management" and
the advanced machinery of industrial technology, management com-
mands the optimal means and methods of a nearly complete control of
the labor process. Since management follows Taylor's recipes—that is,
rigid separation between planning (management) and implementation
(workers), together with progressive division and dissection of labor and
progressive mechanization and automation—the process of degradation
of work should accelerate not only in factories but also in offices. This is
the recognized general tendency of monopoly capital (hence the subtitle
of the book: *The Degradation of Work in the Twentieth Century*).

This strong thesis provoked productive opposition among industrial
relations experts and social scientists. The accusation that Braverman
argued in the framework of technological determinism was unjust, since
he explicitly stated: "In reality, machinery embraces a host of possibilities, many of which are systematically thwarted rather than developed by
capital" (1974:230). Nonetheless, his argument entails an *economic
determinism* with the underlying assumption that the logic of capital sub-
jugates technology and shapes it into an instrument of intensification and
objectivization of capitalist power and exploitation. According to this
understanding, technology and machinery are elastic potentials that can
be used to systematically deprive the workers of their control of the job.

The main criticism (see Friedman 1977; Littler 1982; Wood 1982)
was launched against Braverman's (1974) construction of a linear process
of progressive degradation of labor and intensification of managerial

control over the labor process. The critique accepted neither that managerial strategies were treated as roughly equivalent with Taylorist strategies nor that managerial practices could simply be understood as emanations of strategic concepts. Instead, it was argued that hardly any strategy could be implemented without serious changes because practice is a product of conflict, bargaining, and compromise between two or more parties. It is worth mentioning that Braverman did not deal with phenomena like industrial conflict, trade unions, or other institutions of industrial democracy.

Arguably, the main merit of the labor process debate was that it broadly engaged sociologists, industrial relations experts, political scientists, economists, and labor historians and generated a deeper understanding of managerial strategies and practice and their constraints. Together with the increased knowledge of the dynamics of the labor process, old and new concepts (e.g., negotiation of order, micropolitics) became more elaborate and sophisticated.

Regulation Theory

Following Marx's theory of political economy, the French regulation school (founded by Aglietta 1979, 1982; Boyer 1990; Lipietz 1991) regards industrial relations as a key component in a comprehensive net of societal relations and institutions, in fact as an essential variable for identifying specific modes of regulating capitalist societies.

Their general object of analysis is the conditions and requisites of normal reproduction of the societal form of capitalism. Marx understood *reproduction* as the permanent reestablishment of capitalist production and capitalist relations between classes by objective processes of production, distribution, and accumulation. The regulation theory replaces reproduction by *regulation,* a term that indicates the regularity of the social practices of individual and collective actors and the governing effects of social, economic, and political institutions that are the fabric for reestablishing and changing societal formations. In other words, the proponents of this school of thought ask: How does capitalism function? They find the answer in societal relations and their manifestations in institutions on the one hand and in the clash between social actors (class conflicts, competition) on the other hand. Prominent among such societal relations is the wage relation.

Regulation theoreticians are particularly interested in long-term changes in capitalist economies and societies. Unlike followers of Marxist orthodoxy, they divide capitalism into periods according to specific regimes of accumulation and modes of regulation. These key categories are not always stringently defined. *Regime of accumulation* stands for conditions of surplus value production such as forms of transformation of labor power, factors and mechanisms of wage determination, and reproduction of the working class. *Modes of regulation* is the label for the historical patterns of institutions and social practices that foster, underpin, and sustain the respective regime of accumulation.

Fordism is the preferably analyzed mode of regulation, ironically called the "golden age of capitalism." Lipietz (1991) identified these characteristic components of Fordism:

- Fordism is a specific form of work organization, namely, Taylorism (with its clear-cut separation between conceptualization and performance) *plus* mechanization (e.g., conveyer belt).
- The macroeconomic accumulation regime, characterized by the steady increase of labor productivity, allows the financing of accumulation out of profits as well as expanding mass purchasing power. Thus, a stable rate of profit goes hand in hand with increasing sales of productive goods and consumer goods.
- The "rules of the game" (i.e., the mode of regulation) comprise collective bargaining over wages, relative employment security, regular wage increases, and social security. In return the trade unions accept managerial prerogatives and the organizational principles of the labor process.

According to the regulation school, the model or paradigm of Fordism was the prevailing societal compromise between capital and labor, supported by an active state, in the developed capitalist countries during the postwar period. Since the late 1970s, however, the retardation of the productivity rate on the one hand and the augmenting of total labor cost on the other led to a crisis of Fordism. The shift of economic policy from demand to supply management and the accompanying institutional changes of industrial relations were political strategies to convert the rigid rules of Fordism into a flexible, neoliberal regime of governance. Flexible regulation, first introduced in the United States and the United Kingdom and later in most OECD countries, is central to a new mode of regulation that is referred to as *post-Fordism.* But this term is a misnomer because it indicates only negatively that it is different from the former mode of regulation.

So far the contours of post-Fordism have remained vague, in spite of Lipietz's (1991) attempt to evade the agonies of decision by distinguishing between three different variants of post-Fordism:

- *Neo-Taylorism* means a return to pre-Fordist flexibility (e.g., low wages, high job insecurity) with external labor market flexibility and internal hierarchical control of the workforce, particularly prevalent in the United States and the United Kingdom.
- *Kalmarism* (named after the Swedish city of Kalmar, site of a Volvo plant) implies the collectively negotiated participation of the workforce in a process whereby social guarantees and profit sharing are exchanged for a willingness to contribute to improvements in quality, productivity, and the optimization of new technology. It is widespread in the Scandinavian countries and with some qualifications in Germany.
- *Toyotism* is a mixture of the two other variants. Flexibility is achieved by the dual labor market structure (core and peripheral workforce); workers' participation is restricted to the employees of big companies. This is the predominant pattern of industrial relations in Japan.

Assessment of the Marxist Approaches

The theoretical approaches discussed have their respective strengths and weaknesses. Without doubt, Hyman's books and articles are lucid analyses of historical and present problems of industrial relations. However, his concept of political economy of industrial relations constitutes an obstacle to the establishment of a proper industrial relations theory since it demands the embedding of industrial relations in a comprehensive Marxist theory of relations of production and capitalist accumulation. Hyman himself (1989:ix, 138) denies the possibility of elaborating a viable theoretical account inside the narrow confines of industrial relations.

Kelly's approach has the capacity only to explain changes in industrial relations systems. It explains neither their institutions nor the national differences among industrial relations systems. It merely reflects the changes in power relations between industrial relations actors, which in turn depend not only on the occurrence of long waves (whose theoretical status is highly controversial) but also on the fragile notion of justice as an indispensable substratum for collective action and on the assumption of a revival of the labor movement.

The regulation school, too, is primarily interested in macroeconomic and macrosociological analyses of society. Its ideal models of Fordism and post-Fordism have no solid empirical footing. Lipietz's (1991) attempt to bridge the gap between regulation theory and industrial relations empiricism became possible only by introducing ad hoc categories. Nevertheless, both modes of regulation are meaningful heuristic models that can—like Dunlop's systems model—be used as interpretive frameworks. Last but not least, labor process analysis is limited to microsociological analysis (despite Braverman's [1974] and Littler's [1982] regard of some supra-firm dimensions). But it has contributed to refining analyses of the control aspects at the workplace level and thereby has forged valuable links to other microlevel approaches, especially to micropolitics.

Institutionalism

Institutions are an essential ingredient of regulation theory, although this grand theory fails to elaborate a substantial concept of institutions. It incorporates a much more detailed exposition of the accumulation regime and the mode of regulation than of the institutional setting that acts as the intermediating variable between these two categories. In contrast, institutions are the explicit focus of the theoretical frameworks used by the following approaches.

Institutions structure the field of actions. We realize the presence of institutions while acting. The intention as well as performance of actions is regulated by institutions. The less spontaneous our acting, the more we are being guided by institutions. According to Durkheim ([1895] 1938), they are social facts (*faits sociaux*), which are external to individuals and impose constraints on them. Naturally, institutions not only restrict our behavior but also allow us to economize on our actions and interactions. More specifically, they relieve us from inventing each action anew. Sociologists such as Gehlen (1956) and Berger and Luckmann (1966) already regard as institutions those actions that are performed in a regular, standard, or routine manner. For our purposes, however, this is too broad an understanding of the term. We regard institutions as programs of actions that are robust enough to make them anticipatory for other actors. They do not rigidly determine individual actions but rather establish corridors for possible actions. Those corridors have conditioning effects on the goals, strategies, and interest definitions of the respective actors as well as on the power relations between them. It would be wrong to perceive them only under the aspect of restraint, for they also open options and offer resources for actions within defined boundaries. This duality of function was recognized by Commons (1934) when he defined an institution as "collective action in restraint, liberation, and expansion of individual action." Instead, institutions can be conceptualized as "filters" through which some strategies and goals are promoted and others are restricted. Following Giddens's (1984) structuration theory,[5] which states that *rules* and *resources* are inherent to institutions, they confront actors with restrictions and opportunities for their social interactions.

Historical or Evolutionary Institutionalism

Historical and evolutionary institutional theories link the emergence of and changes in institutions and practices of employment relations with developments in society and the nation-state at large. Fundamental is the embeddedness of institutions in the political, economic, and societal processes that give birth to and shape a separate sphere of industrial relations.

An early example of an evolutionary institutionalist explanation is Karl Korsch's ([1922] 1968) historical profile of the development of *industrial democracy*, a term that he adopted from the Webbs ([1897] 1902) and literally translated into German. Inspired by Hegel and Marx, he understood history, on the one hand, as a history of class struggles and, on the other hand, as a process of the development and gradual expansion of human freedom (Korsch [1922] 1968:35). This led him to the following historical analogy: Like the bourgeois class (the "third estate"), whose struggle against aristocracy and absolutism gradually secured democratic institutions in the polity, the working class (the "fourth estate"), with its class struggle against the bourgeoisie, gradually achieved codetermination rights in the "community of work." Korsch delineated the historical development of the constitution of work starting with the feudal-paternalistic period that endowed the capitalist entrepreneur with absolute, despotic power over the wage worker. Due to the struggles of the labor movement, legal restrictions and rights have successively established a state of "industrial constitutionalism" stretching from the employment relationship to the broader economy.

Korsch distinguished three categories of workers' participation rights:

- Rights of the worker as a citizen (e.g., social policy, worker protection law)

- Rights of the worker as a seller of his or her labor power: combination rights

- Rights of the worker as a member of a work organization: codetermination in labor relations

According to his theory, the three categories also signify three different and unsynchronized paths of institutional development or paths toward industrial democracy. The first category relates to state intervention in the economic sphere, the second to the process of legalizing trade unionism and collective bargaining, and the third to the workers' move-ment for works councils and codetermination in the factories. Being a revolutionary socialist, he regarded the institutions of industrial consti-tutionalism (social policy, collective bargaining, joint regulation, co-determination) as important but only transitional steps toward full industrial democracy.

T. H. Marshall, the British sociologist, identified another evolution-ary track. In his seminal article "Citizenship and Social Class" (1963), he explained the emergence of a separate sphere of "industrial citizenship rights" as a by-product of a long evolutionary process characteristic of industrial societies. His concept of citizenship is the following: "Citizen-ship is a status bestowed to those who are full members of a community. All who possess the status are equal with respect to the rights and duties with which the status is endowed" (Marshall 1963:87). As a system of equality, citizenship mitigates the inequality of the societal hierarchy of social classes. Obviously, in view of British social history, Marshall (1963:73) recognized "continuous progress for some 250 years" in the development of citizenship rights.

The historical pattern in the development of citizenship is the suc-cession of the following rights by special institutions, each serving as a platform for the development of the next:

- Civil rights: rights necessary for individual freedom, that is, liberties concerning the person (institutions: courts of justice)
- Political rights: rights to participate in political power (institutions: parliament, local government)
- Social rights: economic welfare and security (institutions: educational system, social services)

The civil rights of citizenship gradually added new rights to a status that already existed. They were a cornerstone for the foundation of the mar-ket economy and the contractual system. The political rights of citizen-ship granted old rights to new sections of the population. Since they "were full of political danger to the capitalist system" (Marshall 1963:96), they were only cautiously extended during the 19th century. They enabled the working class to achieve political power and led to the recognition of the right of collective bargaining. Marshall described this as "an extension of the civil rights in the economic sphere" (1963:97), for trade unions collectively exercise civil rights on behalf of their members. He concluded: "Trade unionism has . . . created a secondary system of industrial citizenship parallel with and supplementary to the system of political citizenship" (1963:98). With the creation of the welfare state after World War II, all three rights have been fully established.

Giddens (1982:171) has rightly criticized Marshall for understanding the evolution of citizenship rights as "a natural process of evolution, helped along where necessary by the beneficent hand of the state" without taking into regard that they had been the result of the efforts and struggles of the underprivileged.

Whereas Korsch and Marshall located the driving forces of institutional development in the political sphere, Kerr, Dunlop, Harbison, and Myers (1960) believed them to be in the economic system. In their view the inherent logic of industrialism leads to a *convergence* of different industrialized countries toward a pluralistic industrial society. The secular tendencies are the growing importance of the educational system, an expanding role of the state, growth of large companies with paid managers, and a differentiated, highly qualified, and disciplined working class. The inevitably increasing complexity of production affords decentralization of the control functions in the labor process, which in turn requires the consensus, responsibility, and cooperation of the employees. A pluralist balance of power and institutionalized procedures between the industrial elites and other corporate actors of industrial relations regulate their interests and conflicts.

We find a rather new subspecies of historical institutionalism in comparative political economy (Hall 1986; Thelen and Steinmo 1992; among others). So far it has only partially been applied to the analysis of industrial relations; therefore I confine myself to a short account, particularly as I shall take up some of its assumptions in my own theoretical project.

The proponents of this brand of historical institutionalism[6] place institutions and relations of power at the center of their analyses. They are interested predominantly in the state, but also in other social and political institutions. A central question is how institutions structure political interactions, with a focus on the quality of institutions to distribute power among political actors and societal groups. In the words of Thelen and Steinmo (1992:2): "[Historical] institutionalists are interested in the whole range of state and societal institutions that shape how political actors define their interests and that structure their relations of power to other groups." We further learn that the existing institutions embody asymmetries of power and—since institutions also reflect particular "world views" (Max Weber)—that actors' interests and objectives are shaped in institutional contexts.

In general, historical institutionalism provides analytical tools for a better understanding of the qualities and the origins of institutions as well as the interactions between institutions and human agency. Thus, institutions are defined as "formal rules, compliance procedures, and standard operation practices that structure the relationship between individuals in various units of the polity and the economy" (Hall 1986:19). As for the formation and development of institutions, Kathleen Thelen (1999) has elaborated the concept of *path dependency*. According to her, institutions, once founded, "continue to evolve in response to changing environmental conditions . . . but in ways that are constrained by past trajectories" (Thelen 1999:387). In other words, the existing institutions structure the process whereby new institutions are adopted, without excluding the possible departure from established patterns at "critical junctures" (Hall 1986:19). Finally, the approach bears certain affinities with the governance approach of neocorporatism (discussed later), as the title of the school's founding document, *Governing the Economy* (Hall 1986), itself indicates.

New Sociological Institutionalism

Sociological neo-institutionalism (Meyer and Rowan 1977; Walgenbach 1995, 2002) is a more recent influential theory that opposes the economic approach of institutionalism. Whereas institutional economics (discussed later) is interested in the genesis of institutions and organizations, sociological institutionalism focuses on their effects on organizational behavior. The structure of organizations is explained through isomorphic processes, that is, conforming to the normative demands, expectations, and behavioral patterns demanded by institutional environments, or rather *organizational fields*.[7] It is in this sense that organizations are to be seen as institutions, the genesis of which cannot be explained by the concept of the (limited) rational behavior of the actors. The rationality of decisions, according to the argument of Meyer and Rowan (1977), is a façade, primarily serving the cause of legitimacy. It is not the optimization of input–output relationships but the norms and models of the institutional environment that determine good, efficient, and successful rules of conduct for management action. The decoupling theory (Meyer and Rowan 1977:356), which states that enterprises display the rationality façade on the "front stage" but "back stage" pursue quite different practices according to the technical demands of the task, secretly reintroduces the rational actor—something that the basic theory suppositions exclude (Müller-Jentsch 2002).

From an action theory standpoint the argument is undifferentiated because it ignores the categorical difference between strategic (i.e., calculated rational) and norm-regulated action (Habermas 1981:chap. 3). New sociological institutionalism, just like role theory, assumes only norm-regulated actions. Behavior in organizations is, according to this standpoint, determined more by rules (conventions, routines, customs) and less by the interests and rational choice of actors. This is reflected by a concern with legitimacy rather than with efficiency.

At least the core statements of the theory arose from research on nonprofit organizations (health organizations, universities, schools, etc.). The absence of market feedback enables such organizations to conceal at least part of their performance and build up rational façades of legitimacy. This explains the plausibility of this approach with regard to such institutions. However, its most important tenets are not independent of these types of organization, even if this approach has since been applied to business organizations too with some plausible results. But in general, the effects of market environment are systematically played down in favor of the impact of the institutional environment.

A much more serious objection is that institutions of industrial relations that are not organizations (collective bargaining, codetermination, etc.) cannot be explained by this theory. These institutions usually involve a bilateral procedure that has been established by strategically acting parties during and after conflictive interactions between them. Their outcomes are compromises that mostly differ from the original, strategically pursued plans of the individual parties.

Governance Approach: Neocorporatism and Beyond

Evolutionary institutionalism focuses on the function of achieving social integration of conflicting interests by means of the institutional system of industrial relations. In contrast, the governance approach puts the steering potential of institutions and organizations, or in other words, their political and economic effects on performance, at the center of its analysis. Starting with the fundamental sociological question of the possibility of social order in the face of a plurality of interests and conflicting strategies, this approach focuses on the mechanisms and processes of forming, aggregating, negotiating, and implementing interests.

Streeck and Schmitter (1985) have coined a specific term for this mode of associational self-regulation: *private interest government.* They interpret it as "an associative model of social order" besides community, market, and state (p. 14). According to this view, intra- and interorganizational harmonization of intermediary associations shape and coordinate private interests, as opposed to spontaneous solidarity *(community)*, dispersed competition *(market)*, or hierarchical control *(state)*. Being a "mixed mode of policy making" (p. 14), private interest government does not replace the other three modes of social order. Instead, the latter "constitute important limiting and facilitating conditions for and inside of any given associative arrangement" (1985:14). Where public policy is implemented through intermediary associations, these are "to some important extent dependent on community values and cohesion, kept in check by economic and political market forces, and subject to hierarchical control, political design and the pressure of possible direct state intervention" (1985:28).

We have to thank theorists of neocorporatism (e.g., Schmitter and Lehmbruch 1979) for the insight that governance functions can be carried out by nonstate ("private") institutions and intermediary associations. They have drawn our attention to the concerted coordination of interests between state, trade unions, and employers' associations (tripartism) and to the institutional systems, often created and changed with aid from the state, without which the associative arrangement of relevant interests would not work. After all, the central question remains: What are the institutional conditions under which corporatist arrangements of interest representation and mediation can emerge and endure? (See, for example, Streeck 1981; Traxler 1982, 1986.)

As various authors have established, corporatism or tripartism at the macroeconomic level requires, inter alia, a state that engages in active economic policy and that has the ability to act at the national level, social democratic parties that are at least part of the government and that are supported by the trade unions, and encompassing interest organizations that have bargaining power and centralized representation structures. These preconditions are present in only a few countries today. Theorists of neocorporatism have thus reacted to the demise of their subject matter by extending their theoretical concept: they nowadays differentiate between macro-, meso-, and microcorporatism.

A more recent governance approach was outlined by Hall and Soskice (2001) in their well-received volume *Varieties of Capitalism*. It combines several approaches (game theory, transaction costs, governance- and actor-centered institutionalism) with a "firm-centered political economy" (Hall and Soskice 2001:6). The basic contention is that companies are the main actors in the capitalist economy and that they establish their relationships with other actors by strategic interaction.

Institutions enter the analysis because firms have to solve several coordination problems, internally and externally. Their success depends substantially on the "ability to coordinate effectively with a wide range of actors" (Hall and Soskice 2001:6) in five spheres: industrial relations, vocational training and education, corporate governance, interfirm relations, and the workforce. Institutions and organizations (themselves regarded as institutions) provide support for resolving these coordination problems. The authors identified a whole array of institutions that serve this function besides markets and hierarchies, which the transaction-cost approach (discussed later) exposed as the main coordinating institutions in the capitalist economy.

Building on the distinction between two ideal types—"liberal market economies" and "coordinated market economies"—Hall and Soskice (2001) argued that firms solve their coordination problems with different sets of institutions. In market economies, firms coordinate their activities mainly via market relations and hierarchies, whereas in coordinated economies, firms depend more heavily on additional institutions and organizations. These provide "capacities for the exchange of information, monitoring and the sanctioning of defections relevant to cooperative behavior" (p. 10). Also relevant is the capacity for deliberation, not only in terms of formal rules and organizations.

Since the firm is at the center of the analysis, industrial relations represents only one of several dimensions in the institutional matrix of this approach.[8] For our purposes, however, we need a conceptual framework that focuses on industrial relations as a societal subsystem with its own dynamics and distinctive actors.

Action Theory

Institutionalism examines the action program of structures—institutions and organizations—and the logic of their evolution, their effects on social integration, and their steering achievements. In contrast, proponents of the action theory focus their analysis on the interaction of strategically operating actors. The reference is therefore to actor-centered approaches and strategic organization analysis.

In contrast to deterministic approaches (systems theory, Marxism) and concepts of the "one best way" (classical organization theory), these approaches draw attention to the "political" processes in organizations resulting from the incompleteness of the employment contract and the "power games" between actors in the company. Contingency (i.e., everything is also possible in a different way) is of programmatic significance for this school of thought. Despite this common perspective, we are dealing with a heterogeneous group of theoretical approaches. Four of these approaches are briefly outlined in the following sections.

Micropolitics

The term *micropolitics*, coined by the British sociologist Tom Burns (1961/1962), applies to the approach that regards the micro level of companies and working processes as a political field of action. Companies and establishments are seen not as planned, cooperative systems of organization nor as a mere *"Herrschaftsverband"* (Max Weber) but rather as the "totality of micropolitical games" (Ortmann 1995:33) involving actors with varying degrees of power potential and conflicting strategies. The genuine political aspect is to be found in the dimension of power as an exchange relationship between the actors. According to Crozier and Friedberg (1993), there is no situation in any given organization that places an actor under a complete and deterministic type of pressure. The space left to the actor in which to maneuver and negotiate presents the opponent with "a source of uncertainty"; the actor's power increases depending on the relevance of the source of uncertainty for the other (Crozier and Friedberg 1993:56).

The proponents of the micropolitical approach do not deny that the actors in organizations, and organizations as a whole, act under structural pressures, but these only limit the free choice of the actors ("lock-ins"); they form a "decision corridor," the barriers of which are defined by previous organizational and technological decisions, pure economic compulsion, and so on (see Ortmann 1995:39).

Labor Politics

Regarding the apparently politically neutral area of labor and production, the labor politics approach emphasizes the political dimension even more than the micropolitical approach does. Naschold (1985:10) speaks of "the endogenising of politics," of the necessity to anchor it systematically as an "element of the technical-economic context." Politics is defined as "the regulation (constitution, reproduction and transformation) of social relations" (p. 9), and labor politics as the regulation of social relations in the process of work and production. The concept of regulation, at the same time synonymous for labor politics, remains strangely indefinite. Jürgens (1984) speaks of labor politics in terms of power, dominance, and control. Power is "characteristic of social relations within the company" (p. 61). It appears as "primary power" (power that grows from the "dependent relationships arising from the power positions held by the actors in the company") and "secondary power" (based on "regulations and institutions set up by the state or achieved through collective bargaining," p. 61). In contrast to micropolitics, labor politics does not restrict itself to the micro level of the company; it brings in actors not only at the company level, but also at the association and state levels, who then in turn influence labor and production processes. Moreover, being a "fragmented field of politics, situated at the point where state, association, and company come together" (Naschold and Dörr 1990:12), labor politics is the macropolitics of state and para-state institutions and the micropolitics of the enterprise. This approach was elaborated by the working group at the *Wissenschaftszentrum* (Science Center) in Berlin (Jürgens and Naschold 1984; Naschold 1985; Naschold and Dörr 1990) and has affinities with the regulation theory and the labor process debate. Furthermore, it corresponds with Burawoy's (1979) analysis of political and ideological processes in production, which he coined "power games" and "politics of production."

Negotiation of Order

Negotiation and negotiation-like interaction between actors in industrial relations are the thematic focus of another strand of action theory. The spectrum ranges from formal negotiations to the "shadow area of informal rules and relations" (Trinczek 1989:43), from *collective bargaining* and *labor negotiation* to *silent bargaining, tacit agreement,* and *implicit negotiation.*

For the area of formal negotiating processes, Walton and McKersie (1965) have put forward a "behavioral" theory of labor negotiations. They draw attention to the multifunctionality of negotiations, which they split up into four parts, each having a special function:

1. *Distributive bargaining.* This means hard bargaining with the function of solving conflicts of interest according to the pattern of zero-sum games: what one side wins, the other loses. A typical example for this is the wage conflict resolved by collective bargaining.

2. *Integrative bargaining.* This type of negotiation is based on the mutual efforts to mobilize joint interests toward cooperative problem solving according to the model of positive-sum games. A typical example for this is the company-level negotiations between management and works council regarding the introduction of teamwork, which is intended to both increase productivity and reduce work stress.

3. *Attitudinal structuring.* This means influencing the attitude and position of the opposition, for example, in order to dismantle resistance or create willingness to cooperate.

4. *Intraorganizational bargaining.* This includes harmonization between results attained, or rather attainable results, in the negotiation process on the one hand and the aims and interests of those for whom negotiations were carried out on the other.

Weitbrecht (1974) draws attention to the linkages between inter- and intraorganizational bargaining processes by bringing into the discussion the power variables established in organizations. He demonstrates, with the example of agreement tactics and concession processes, the interplay between organizations and the negotiating table: "The organization requires signs and signals from the negotiating table in order to be able to steer the concession and ratification process. On the other hand, the person leading the bargaining discussion at the negotiating table requires signs from the organization in order to be able to exercise bargaining power" (Weitbrecht 1974:229).

At the other end of the negotiating spectrum, so to speak, we find the *negotiated order* approach (Strauss, Schatzmann, Ehrlich, Bucher, and Sabshin 1963; Strauss 1978; Edwards 1993). According to this approach, any type of social order, even the most repressive, is to a certain degree a negotiated order. It springs from the interaction of the individual and collective actors; they produce and reproduce social order in organizations—either implicitly through tacit agreements and silent bargaining or explicitly through formal negotiations. Negotiated social order can achieve relative stability and duration—for example, in the form of an unwritten works constitution or of organizational culture—and thereby sets limits and guidelines for future negotiations. Strauss (1978:6) terms the more stable elements of social order "the background" and the daily bargaining processes "the foreground."

Strategic Choice

This approach, developed by American scholars of industrial relations (Kochan, Katz, and McKersie 1986), represents an action theory extension of Dunlop's systems approach. It deals with a combination of systems and action theory elements, but—as analysis of the material shows—the authors mostly use the action theory dimension for their explanations. The justification for this is that the profound historical transformation of American industrial relations has rendered the systems approach less relevant. Collective bargaining no longer has the central significance given to it by the traditional approach, and thus the preconditions for the consensual creation of rules has ceased to exist. This can be seen in the efforts of many executives of enterprises to keep trade union representatives out, or even to force them out (union avoidance policy). Moreover, the frequently observed proactive role of management forces a reassessment of *strategic choice.*[9] Kochan, Katz, and McKersie (1986) pleaded for the relative autonomy of strategic decisions not only on the part of the management but also on the part of trade unions and the state. Those decisions count as strategic that influence the role and scope of action of an actor in his or her relationship to other actors within industrial relations.

Kochan, Katz, and McKersie (1986) elaborate a three-tier institutional structure. Below the level of strategic decisions, they identify further levels of action: the middle level of collective bargaining and personnel policy and the lowest level of the workplace and the individual. This explanatory approach had some impact on American industrial relations research (see Chelius and Dworkin 1990). But the empirical backdrop against which it must be seen is the U.S. system, for which state abstinence from issues of industrial relations is as characteristic as the existence of company-level trade unions and widespread use of human resource management, which prefers individual solutions to collective ones. As a result of its focus on the firm's strategy, the analytical framework has attracted some British authors (Boxall and Purcell 2003) specialized in human resource management. To date, however, it has seldom been applied to the analysis and explanation of industrial relations outside the United States and Britain (the exception is Rojot 1990).

Economic Approaches

It is economic theory that provides models defining rational behavior as that which maximizes individual benefit with respect to the attainment of individual preference. Two of these models that are relevant for industrial relations analyses are the *rational choice* approach and the *transaction costs* approach.

Rational Choice

At the basis of the rational choice (RC) paradigm is the supposition that individuals faced with a range of alternative actions will always choose those that most readily conform to their preference and from which they expect to derive the greatest utility. This axiom is employed by various strands of economic and social theory (game theory, theory of collective goods, new microeconomics, new political economy, but also the game theory variant of American Marxism). It should be stressed, however, that these modern approaches do not imply complete decision-making and operational rationality. Since Herbert A. Simon's ([1945] 1976) survey that analyzed administrative decision-making processes, the assumption of hyperrationality has been increasingly replaced by the concept of "bounded rationality."[10] It is conceded that individuals tend to be aware of only some of their possible courses of action and in turn the consequences of only some of these actions. Within such informational constraints, economic agents decide rationally. One of the main drawbacks is that preferences are not explained by this approach but regarded as extrinsically given and independent of the alternative actions.

Analysts working with the model of the *rational choice of alternatives* (Kirchgässner 1991:12) are less interested in explaining the specific behavior (or actions) of individuals than in the behavior of larger groups (e.g., consumers, voters, employers, employees) and the explanation of social interaction (and some of its unintended consequences) resulting from individual rational behavior. It is primarily macrophenomena that are to be explained with the aid of individual decision-making processes. While the RC approach is sometimes seen as reducing social interaction to rational bartering, it has yielded a range of useful analytical tools for the analysis of social structures and processes.

A central emphasis in the analysis is the so-called rationality traps and dilemmas between individual and collective rationality. Examples that can also apply to industrial relations are the problematic nature of *collective goods* and the *prisoner's dilemma*. The problematic nature of collective goods results from the possibility of being able to benefit from public or collective goods (e.g., clean air, collective agreements) without having to contribute to the production of such goods (the so-called free-rider effect). Mancur Olson's *The Logic of Collective Action* (1965) is regarded as the classical analysis dealing with the production of collective goods and the free-rider problem. Many publications in economics and social science are based on these analytical insights (e.g., in the area of industrial relations, Crouch 1982; Offe and Wiesenthal 1980). Olson had decisive influence on investigations into membership recruitment and the organizational security of trade unions. The prisoner's dilemma is a game theory version of the problematic nature of collective goods: it exposes a structure of conflict and a constellation of interests that leave "players" who consistently follow their egoistic interests worse off than those assuming a cooperative attitude. In addition to the prisoner's dilemma, which holds as paradigmatic for the analysis of strategic behavior in game theory, further game concepts (e.g., the "chicken game" and "battle of the sexes") find application in investigations into strategic games between capital and labor (see Elster 1989).

Transaction Costs

In contrast to neoclassical economics, which focuses predominantly on markets and production costs and leaves the theoretical analysis of the embedding institutions to other sciences, the *new institutional economics* (Williamson 1985) tries to establish an endogenous economic explanation of institutions and organizations. As in the neoclassical approach, the analysis takes as its axiom rational choice (here, the choice between alternative institutions), for which the decision-making criterion is the minimization of transaction costs (TC), which—according to a general definition by Arrow (1969)—are understood to be the "operating costs of the economic system." These include search and information costs, negotiating and decision-making costs, and controlling and monitoring costs.

The TC approach was put on a systematic theoretical footing by Williamson (1981, 1985). His model of the contractual exchange of performance takes as its starting point the specific features of the transaction object (given location, capital stock, human resource specifications) and looks at two types of behavior: (1) actors are limited in their ability to acquire and process information *(bounded rationality)*, and (2) they pursue their own interests with the aid of cunning, shirking, and so on *(opportunism)*. The resulting conflicts, uncertainty, and other transaction costs make it necessary to have institutions to control and monitor contractual relationships primarily through out-of-court regulations. The initial consideration is that wherever an exchange of goods and services (i.e., a transaction) takes place, the need to determine the joint duties and responsibilities causes conflict and friction—in short, TC. In many cases the coordination and directing of transactions can be carried out far more cost-effectively by nonmarket institutions than through market mechanisms. The specific framework conditions for economic transactions determine the optimal (efficient) boundaries and structures of institutions. Their existence is explained in a purely functional manner by the need for a minimization of TC. According to Williamson (1981:574), coordination and directing structures with a high saving effect displace those with low saving effects, a course of "natural selection."

Two typical areas of application for TC analysis are the (incomplete) employment contract and the company. In the presence of information asymmetries, an alignment between the interests of the employer (principal) and the actions of the employee (agent) through contracts would entail high TC (a complex document would be necessary to take account of all possible eventualities). As a result, the work contract remains unspecific, and the transactions are instead governed by hierarchy, bureaucratic organization, and the prerogative of the management. More generally, in his classical analysis "The Nature of the Firm" (1937), Coase raised the question of why transactions are carried out via orders and execution within the framework of the firm's organization rather than via the market. His answer was that company decisions pertaining to the extent of vertical integration are determined by considerations of TC savings. In other words, if the costs for the use of the market and price mechanisms for certain economic activities are higher than coordination costs within a company, those activities will be integrated; otherwise, they will be externalized.

An interesting attempt to explain codetermination through TC savings is given by Schmidtchen (1987). He interprets codetermination as a contribution to coordination efficiency in a company. With a supposition of the specialization of resources (or rather factor specificity), limited rationality, and opportunism, codetermination as interpreted in terms of TC savings can function as a protective measure against the negative consequences of vaguely formulated labor contracts where rules and working conditions are sketchily outlined. Nevertheless, Schmidtchen (1987) had some difficulties with a plausible explanation for why codetermination does not occur spontaneously and why it is not widespread.

The RC and TC economic approaches have limited explanatory power for many phenomena that are of interest to industrial relations experts. They pay for their methodological rigor by forgoing the social context in which rational behavior is embedded. It is exactly this point that a sociologically oriented theory would not want to forgo.

An Extended (Actor-Centered) Institutional Approach

Since the 1950s, when Dunlop put forward his concept of systems theory, social scientists have sought a theoretical conceptualization of industrial relations. As shown earlier, this has led to a great variety of theoretical approaches. Given the evolution of the scientific discipline and the inherent complexity of its subject matter, it is not surprising to find substantial differences among these approaches. Grand theories, such as systems theory and Marxist theory, coexist with specific analytical models that have limited explanatory domains. Between these two are the "middle-range" theories, which are specifically tailored to the analysis, explanation, and evaluation of an issue, area, or event, for example, intermediate institutional systems, negotiating processes, and corporate actors in industrial relations. Their power of explanation varies with the type of research question posed and the object of analysis: explanations of concrete bargaining processes or specific conflict constellations cannot be assessed with the same conceptual tools as explanations of the genesis of institutions, organizational and institutional change, or the stability and efficiency of national industrial relations systems.

In my view, institutions ought to be the main focus of industrial relations analyses, but without actors they can be only insufficiently understood. Culturally based ideas and actors' interests are the building blocks of institutions. As outcomes (conscious or unintended) of mainly strategic interactions between actors, they recursively shape further interactions. Regarding institutions and agency, rules, and strategies as the core elements of industrial relations, I propose an extended, actor-centered institutional approach,[11] a synthesis of historical and governance approaches and theoretical concepts of action (mainly negotiation) theory.

This approach comprises three analytical layers:

- The historic-constitutional analysis of actors and institutions
- The arena concept
- The negotiation concept

Their (interrelated) theoretical ingredients are the following:

1. *Action and structure.* Following Giddens's (1984) insight into the interplay (recursiveness) of action and structure, I postulate that actors act in institutional and organizational contexts that they themselves produce, reproduce, and modify.

2. *Strategic actors and resources.* The individual and corporate actors are able to learn and to act strategically; they possess resources that constitute their power base since other actors are essentially interested in those resources.

3. *Power.* Contrary to strategic calculation and economic efficiency, the factor of power has often been underestimated as an institution-building and institution-preserving force. In particular, the building of institutions by two or more actors in conflictive interactions cannot be explained without the notion of power and counterpower.

4. *Role of the state.* Equally underestimated is the role of the state as medium and midwife in institution-building processes, particularly between parties with diverging interests, for their capacities to build *intermediating* institutions (i.e., ones that bridge conflicting interests) are limited.

5. *Path dependency and path change.* The evolutionary process of building, selection, and change of institutions is path dependent. Institutions created in early formative periods lay the base for further institutional development. Path change occurs only at historic turning points (critical junctures) that disrupt and reconfigure the power relation between capital and labor.

6. *Emergence and learning process.* Evolving systems of industrial relations have a tendency to develop new capacities to govern interests and to resolve conflicts, due to the interactive learning processes between actors.

Historic-Constitutional Analysis

The historical analysis of organizations and institutions of industrial relations follows the concept of "analytic narrative" (*rationale Nachkonstruktion* [Habermas 1976:184]) of an evolutionary process. A structural conflict constellation (starting situation) releases a dynamic social process, in the course of which new collective actors constitute themselves, build new institutions through their strategic, interest-motivated actions, and are in turn influenced by these with regard to their own future goals and strategies. The process of *coevolution* of collective actors and institutions—which grew into different national systems of industrial relations—is neither consciously planned nor structurally determined but rather emerges out of the interplay between the actors, who themselves gain their identity during these recursive interactions. Emergence actually means that the actors strategically pursue divergent goals but have ultimately to find a compromise, that is, to build institutions that, mathematically speaking, are a kind of resultant of their individual plans and deliberate strategies.

What are here abstractly described in terms of evolution and social momentum, as feed-back processes forming actors and creating institutions, can, in historical terms, be outlined as follows.

The starting point (which cannot be theoretically explained by this approach) is characterized by a constellation typical for early industrial capitalism: *free labor markets* and a *factory system.* The pauperized masses of craftsmen and former agricultural workers have to submit to "objective" economic laws and social pressures. From this results a dual conflict structure:

- on the one hand, the antagonistic exchange relation between labor and capital, signified by the rude fact of exploitation (Marx), and
- on the other, the prevalent contradiction in civil society between the status of citizenship with equal rights and duties, and the subordinated status as wage earner being a disadvantaged participant in the market and a servant of the factory regime (Marshall 1963).

Social misery, spontaneous rebellion, and political protest are the direct consequences: they become the motor of social dynamics, which during the early days of industrialization led to the development of civil reform movements that tried to solve the "social question." They contributed to the formation of a self-organizing working class through the establishment of trade unions and workers' parties. Through industrial action and right-to-vote movements, they achieved both social and political rights and forced the setting-up of welfare state institutions, including those that were anticipatorily conceded by the ruling elite (e.g., Bismarck's social reforms). Responding to the trade union offensive, employers formed their own associations to mobilize their economic and political resources with the objective of curtailing the spread of the workers' movement.

Out of the principally conflictive class relations with their asymmetrical distribution of power originate institutions (conscious or unintended) that "freeze" interest configurations and compromises to regulate the precarious exchange relations (wage for labor power). Geiger (1949) aptly called this development "institutionalization of class conflict." From the initially antagonistic but later counteracting and cooperative interactions between the collective actors developed a system of complementary institutions for the labor market and the (formerly despotic) factory regime. Their function was "decommodifying" labor by addressing social vulnerability, market risks, and other hazards arising within the employment relationship.

The spectrum of labor institutions covers a broad variety, among them the employment contract, the labor market (including employment service), the occupation, the establishment (factory, work organization), the work constitution, collective bargaining, arbitration and conciliation, human resource management, and organizations of the parties to collective bargaining.

With regard to their genesis, they can be classified into three categories:

- Unilaterally originated institutions, formed by one actor through repeated practice, a conscious exercise of power, or a formal act of foundation. These include many of the industrial relations phenomena labeled as "custom and practice" as well as permanent organizations.
- Bilaterally founded institutions, created jointly by two (or more) nongovernment actors. They include many institutions concerned with joint job regulation, such as collective bargaining, arbitration, and so on.
- Institutions formed through the rule of law, which are also described as legal institutions (e.g., regulating safety and health at work, works constitution).

In practice, these three categories of institutions overlap and interact. An institution based on custom and practice by one side, for instance, can be turned into a subject for negotiations by the opposing side and thus later be accounted for bilaterally. In other cases, institutions created bilaterally by autonomous associations can later become codified by law (as, for example, the *Tarifautonomie* in Germany).

The evolutionary process leading to the creation and modification of labor institutions is determined less by the logic of rational calculation and transaction costs savings than by the logic of power and counterpower of the participating actors. This process follows the nation-specific *development paths* of each industrial society (the course of which is influenced by, inter alia, the political and legal traditions of the country and the political-ideological orientation of the actors, as well as the specific configurations of interests and power relationships among actors). Once the formative period in which specific institutions are created has concluded, self-reinforcing mechanisms of feedback reproduce the institutional arrangement and keep its evolution on a particular path. Those feedback mechanisms are incentives for the actors; distribution of power; and interdependency, aptness, and affinity of (old and new) institutions. Path dependency also implies that institutional change and the recasting of industrial relations take place primarily at points of historic upheaval. Examples of critical junctures that can shift the balance of power between actors and thus trigger changes in the institutional framework are wars, economic crises, large-scale labor struggles, power changes in the political domain, and explicit government interventions. An "ideal-type" evolution in the West can be identified, with common features that have been observed across industrial capitalist countries. For instance, workers everywhere gained the right to form trade unions that are independent of the state and managed to extract social concessions from their employers by means of industrial action. At the same time, systems of regulation developed that ensured their participation—usually representative—in the regulation of labor relations. Stated in a more general manner: social protest, class struggle, and social politics allowed unleashed economic liberalism to be controlled by sustainable institutionalizing processes. System-threatening forces could thus be productively integrated.

The evolving system of industrial relations developed new mechanisms to govern conflictual labor–management relations. The evolutionary "gains" were the following:

- Social aggregates (classes) gained the ability to act through organizations. (In this way, the Marxist "class for itself" became a tangible historic player through the organization of trade unions and workers' parties.)
- The organizations themselves constituted and developed "management of interests," meaning that they took over the task of forming, aggregating, intermediating, and implementing members' interests.
- Unilateral conflict strategies were extended and overarched by bilateral regulations. (Neumann [(1935) 1978] speaks of "the victory of parity"; Flanders [1968] of "joint regulation.")
- With organizational support by the government, institutional systems—*arenas*—eventually emerged with specific instruments for interest mediation and conflict resolution.

The Arena Concept

The functional differentiation of specific subsystems, described here as *arenas*, can be regarded as a qualitatively new step in the evolution of industrial relations. By the term *arena* we understand a "forum" where conflicts can be regulated and problems solved institutionally, but also a "battlefield" on which actors not only pursue their interests but also strive to change the procedural framework conditions ("the rules of the game"). In this sense the arena is a complex institutional system that determines which interests and actors are to be admitted but also an enclosed area of conflict that sets boundaries for the courses of action open to the actors when they seek solutions to specific problems. Prototypical arenas of German industrial relations are the regulatory systems of the works constitution *(Betriebsverfassung)* and collective bargaining

(Tarifautonomie); they prescribe a selective representation of interests for employees through works councils and trade unions. In other countries, specialized arenas include shop-floor bargaining, workplace representation, sectoral and national bargaining, wage councils, social pacts, joint committees, grievance procedures, human resource management, and so on. They are not always so distinctly separate from each other as the two German arenas mentioned.

The most important structural effect of arena building manifests itself in the curbing and channeling of conflicts through the disaggregation of conflict issues and decentralization of the locations where the conflicts are solved. The more clearly established the arena boundaries are, the stronger the barriers to a shift of locations and to a cumulation of conflict potential. If the individual arenas are governed by *different rules,* if *other actors* are responsible and if *other interests* determine the agenda, the "flash-over" and fusion of conflicts become less probable and the coexistence of conflict in one arena with cooperation in another arena becomes possible.

In most continental European countries, the establishment of system boundaries for arenas is the task of the state. Although the state mostly codifies autonomously developed bilateral regulation systems of the social parties, it gives them the character of legally binding institutions. It thus inhibits attempts of the original creators to change the rules of the game, for example, in times of intensified interest struggles. Furthermore, characteristic for a range of legally codified institutions is that the coordination and governing programs follow an "intermediary agenda." In other words, they create linkages between opposing logics of actions and conflicting interests. Typical of such an institution is the works council, which represents not only the interests of the employees but also the "welfare of the company." It is difficult to conceive of setting up institutions with intermediary programs without assistance from the state, because the parties involved tend to create institutions according to their own respective interests and the logic of their strategic choices.

The Negotiation Concept

Negotiation has become the typical manifestation of the exchange relation between industrial relations actors who are mutually dependent on their respective resources. Their strategic interaction is structured by institutions and takes place in the context of an asymmetrical distribution of power. We do not need to develop a new concept of negotiation since we find genuine ones in two classics: Anselm Strauss's negotiation of order (Strauss et al. 1963; discussed earlier) and Walton and McKersie's *A Behavioral Theory of Labor Negotiations* (1965; discussed earlier).

Strauss's *negotiated order approach* postulates that all social order is, in a certain way, a negotiated order. As far as our subject is concerned, it means that the actors involved in industrial relations both implicitly and explicitly are, in their cooperative and conflictive interactions, producing, reproducing, and transforming social order and systems of rules according to custom and practice, in muted agreement and through silent bargaining or by way of formal agreements and contracts (collective bargaining). For the extended area of formal negotiations, the most appropriate analytical instrument still seems to be the *negotiation theory* of Walton and McKersie (1965)—particularly the authors' differentiation between distributive and integrative bargaining.

That negotiating processes take place at all is based on the fact that actors have specific resources at their disposal. Mutual resource dependency does not imply the equality of power between actors (the structural dominance of capital over labor remains). But as the negotiations take place in an arena, as described earlier, the possibilities for and restrictions on the institutionalized actions can compensate (at least in part) for the given power asymmetry. In the negotiating process we are dealing with actors who are not only equipped with specific resources but also capable of learning and of carrying out strategic actions. Their aims, strategies, and decisions cannot be explained merely by their "objective" interests (or that of their clients). They are "socially constructed," that is, influenced by their (historically developed) normative and political-ideological orientations as well as by the institutional framework that determines their room to maneuver and the chances of success for their respective strategies. Structurally determined approaches to the analysis of industrial relations are not compatible with actor-centered institutionalism. Contingencies can be limited by the boundaries of the particular arena—but they cannot be eliminated altogether. The power based on resources remains indispensable as an explanatory variable for the behavior of actors driven by interests and strategic action.

Conclusion

It has been my intention to review theories and analytical approaches that help us *to understand and to explain* a particular segment of capitalist societies. This segment has come to be called an industrial relations system. The frequent usage of this term shows that Dunlop's ([1958] 1993) idea of industrial relations as a societal subsystem is still an indispensable category. We do not need to accept the analytical rigor of systems theory à la Parsons or Luhmann to construe industrial relations as a system embedded in but relatively autonomous from broader society. However, we can say—with Rogowski (2000)—that its societal function is to canalize violent forces resulting from the employment relationship and—with Martens, Nagelkere, and de Nijs (2001)—to develop patterns for education, selling, and application of labor. It fulfills this function by institutionalizing rules and procedures that, generally speaking, moderate the perils of the commodification of labor in capitalist societies.

Being primarily interested in the understanding and explanation of the emergence, evolution, and functioning of industrial relations systems, I have outlined an analytical framework—the *actor-centered institutional approach*—that attempts to establish theoretical links between historical processes of industrial relations on the one hand and present-day institutional structures and negotiation processes on the other. It takes account of the fact that institutions and arenas (as complexes of institutions) are the outcome of interactive learning processes by strategically operating actors. The evolution of institutions is conditioned by path dependency. This implies that the way the actors once chose to "freeze" their settled interest compromise into institutions also regulates their future interactions. In other words, the institutional system that emerged from the actors' interactions conditions further negotiation processes in the dual sense of "limiting" and "enabling." And these, in turn, affect the institutional framework by contributing to its further development. Even if it is only a current conflict over collective agreements that is to be explained, it is important to have a historical understanding of institutions. This will help the analysis of how strategies and interactions of the actors are filtered and conditioned and how their actions follow historically prepared paths of institutional change.

No doubt, the theoretical framework is a middle-range approach, tailored to a specific explanatory domain. Nonetheless, I hope it provides analytical tools that yield additional empirical information, beyond that of other approaches, and deepens our theoretical understanding of the intricate subject matter of industrial relations.

Notes

[1] In Giddens's (1979:56) terms, the acting subject has control of neither "unacknowledged conditions" nor "unintended consequences" of his or her actions.

[2] Although I use the same term as Scharpf (1997), the theoretical architecture of my approach is a different one, mainly because of the different field of analysis.

[3] Usually the Oxford school (Allan Flanders, Hugh Clegg, Alan Fox), which stands for "pluralism" in industrial relations, is also treated under the heading of systems theory.

[4] Autopoietic systems operate self-referentially according to their special codes; that is, they reproduce themselves by the elements of which they consist and transform anything from the environment into their own mode of operations or communications. Autonomous functional systems of society (e.g., economy, polity, science, legal system) operate under a specific binary code that separates them from other systems. For example, communications in the science system proceed under the binary code of *true* and *false*.

[5] I eclectically adopt only some insights from Giddens's work without taking on his general theory. Recently, however, some German social scientists have made initial attempts to rigorously apply the structuration theory to organizational studies (Ortmann, Sydow, and Windeler 1997), to labor–management relations (Weitbrecht and Braun 1999; Braun 2002), and even to the industrial relations system on the whole (Sydow and Windeler 2001). The explanatory productiveness of the latter application has still to be tested by empirical studies.

[6] For the sake of terminological clarity, we might label the three previously discussed kinds of institutionalism as *evolutionary* and the one currently under review as *historical* institutionalism proper.

[7] A term coined by DiMaggio and Powell (1983:148) that includes organizations "which take each other's behavior into consideration" (Windeler 2001:58), for example, rival organizations, suppliers, customers, but also state institutions and professional bodies.

[8] Although Kathleen Thelen's (2001) chapter on labor politics in the same volume takes into account the institutional settings of different industrial relations systems and their effects on firms' strategies, she treats them within the given analytical framework of firm-centered institutionalism.

[9] Herewith proponents take up criticism made by Child (1972) of the traditional organizational theory (contingency theory), which understood organizational structures as being determined solely by environmental factors, whereas Child recognized in the relatively autonomous strategic decisions of management an intervening variable between environmental conditions and enterprise structures.

[10] Contrary to the traditional concept that an individual provided with complete information will permanently seek maximal utility, the concept of bounded rationality lets individuals search among the accessible alternatives until finding a "sufficiently" acceptable one. Kirchgässner (1991) sees both models as "special cases of a general concept" (p. 31), of which he considers bounded rationality to be "empirically perhaps the most significant variety" (p. 33).

[11] See note 2.

References

Aglietta, Michel. 1979. *A Theory of Capitalist Regulation: The US Experience.* London: NLB.

————. 1982. *Regulation and Crisis of Capitalism*. New York: Monthly Review Press.

Arrow, Kenneth J. 1969. "The Organization of Economic Activity: Issues Pertinent to the Choice of Market vs. Nonmarket Allocation." In U.S. Joint Economic Committee, ed., *The Analysis and Evaluation of Public Expenditures: The PPB-System*, Vol. 1, Washington, DC: Government Printing Office, pp. 59–73.

Berger, Peter L., and Thomas Luckmann. 1966. *The Social Construction of Reality*. Garden City, NY: Doubleday.

Boxall, Peter, and John Purcell. 2003. *Strategy and Human Resource Management*. Basingstoke, U.K.: Palgrave Macmillan.

Boyer, Robert. 1990. *The Regulation School: A Critical Introduction*. New York: Columbia University Press.

Braun, Wolf Mattias. 2002. *Strategisches Management der industriellen Beziehungen*. Munich: Hampp.

Braverman, Harry. 1974. *Labor and Monopoly Capital: The Degradation of Work in the Twentieth Century*. New York: Monthly Review Press.

Burawoy, Michael. 1979. *Manufacturing Consent*. Chicago: Chicago University Press.

Burns, Tom. 1961/1962. "Micropolitics: Mechanism of Institutional Change." *Administrative Science Quarterly*, Vol. 6, pp. 257–81.

Chelius, James, and James Dworkin, eds. 1990. *Reflections on the Transformation of Industrial Relations*. Metuchen, NJ: Institute of Management and Labor Relations Press.

Child, John. 1972. "Organizational Structure, Environment and Performance: The Role of Strategic Choice." *Sociology*, Vol. 6, no. 1, pp. 1–22.

Coase, Ronald H. 1937. "The Nature of the Firm." *Economica*, New Series, Vol. 4, no. 16 (November), pp. 386–405.

Commons, John. 1934. *Institutional Economics: Its Place in Political Economy*. New York: Macmillan.

Crouch, Colin. 1982. *Trade Unions: The Logic of Collective Action*. London: Fontana.

Crozier, Michel, and Erhard Friedberg. 1993. *Die Zwänge kollektiven Handelns: Über Macht und Organisation*, 2nd ed. Frankfurt: Athenäum.

DiMaggio, Paul J., and Walter W. Powell. 1983. "The Iron Cage Revisited: Isomorphism and Collective Rationality in Organizational Fields." *American Sociological Review*, Vol. 48, pp. 147–60.

Dunlop, John T. [1958] 1993. *Industrial Relations Systems*, rev. ed. Boston: Harvard Business School Press.

Durkheim, Emile. [1895] 1938. *The Rules of Sociological Method*. Chicago: University of Chicago Press.

Edwards, Paul K. 1993. "Konflikt und Kooperation: Die Organisation der betrieblichen industriellen Beziehungen." In Walther Müller-Jentsch, ed., *Konfliktpartnerschaft: Akteure und Institutionen der industriellen Beziehungen*, 3rd ed., Munich: Hampp, pp. 33–64.

Elster, Jon. 1989. *The Cement of Society: A Study of Social Order*. Cambridge, MA: Cambridge University Press.

Flanders, Allan. 1968. "Collective Bargaining: A Theoretical Analysis." *British Journal of Industrial Relations*, Vol. 6, no. 1, pp. 1–26.

Friedman, Andrew L. 1977. *Industry and Labour: Class Struggle at Work and Monopoly Capitalism*. London: Macmillan.

Gehlen, Arnold. 1956. *Urmensch und Spätkultur. Philosophische Ergebnisse und Aussagen.* Bonn: Athenäum.

Geiger, Theodor. 1949. *Die Klassengesellschaft im Schmelztiegel.* Cologne: Kiepenheuer.

Giddens, Anthony. 1979. *Central Problems in Social Theory: Action, Structure and Contradiction in Social Analysis.* London: Macmillan.

———. 1982. *Profiles and Critiques in Social Theory.* London: Macmillan.

———. 1984. *The Constitution of Society: Outline of the Theory of Structuration.* Cambridge: Polity Press.

Habermas, Jürgen. 1970. *Zur Logik der Sozialwissenschaften.* Frankfurt: Suhrkamp.

———. 1976. *Zur Rekonstruktion des Historischen Materialismus.* Frankfurt: Suhrkamp.

———. 1981. *Theorie des kommunikativen Handelns.* 2 vols. Frankfurt: Suhrkamp.

Hall, Peter A. 1986. *Governing the Economy: The Politics of State Intervention in Britain and France.* Cambridge: Polity Press.

Hall, Peter A., and David Soskice, eds. 2001. *Varieties of Capitalism: The Institutional Foundations of Comparative Advantage.* Oxford: Oxford University Press.

Hyman, Richard. 1975. *Industrial Relations: A Marxist Introduction.* London: Macmillan.

———. 1989. *Political Economy of Industrial Relations: Theory and Practice in a Cold Climate.* London: Macmillan.

———. 1994. "Theory and Industrial Relations." *British Journal of Industrial Relations,* Vol. 32, no. 2, pp. 165–80.

Jürgens, Ulrich. 1984. "Die Entwicklung von Macht, Herrschaft und Kontrolle im Betrieb als politischer Prozeß—Eine Problemskizze zur Arbeitspolitik." In Ulrich Jürgens and Frieder Naschold, eds., *Arbeitspolitik, Leviathan,* Sonderheft no. 5/1984, pp. 58–91.

Jürgens, Ulrich, and Frieder Naschold, eds. 1984. *Arbeitspolitik, Leviathan,* Sonderheft no. 5/1984.

Kelly, John. 1998. *Rethinking Industrial Relations: Mobilization, Collectivism and Long Waves.* London: Routledge.

Kerr, Clark, John T. Dunlop, Frederick H. Harbison, and Charles A. Myers. 1960. *Industrialism and Industrial Man: The Problems of Labor and Management in Economic Growth.* Cambridge, MA: Harvard University Press.

Kirchgässner, Gebhard. 1991. *Homo oeconomicus: Das ökonomische Modell individuellen Verhaltens und seine Anwendung in den Wirtschafts- und Sozialwissenschaften.* Tübingen, Germany: Mohr.

Kochan, Thomas A., Harry C. Katz, and Robert B. McKersie. 1986. *The Transformation of American Industrial Relations.* New York: Basic Books.

Korsch, Karl. [1922] 1968. *Arbeitsrecht für Betriebsräte.* Frankfurt: Europäische Verlagsanstalt.

Lipietz, Alain. 1991. "Die Beziehungen zwischen Kapital und Arbeit am Vorabend des 21. Jahrhunderts." *Leviathan,* Vol. 11, no. 1, pp. 79–101.

Littler, Craig R. 1982. *The Development of the Labour Process in Capitalist Societies.* London: Heinemann.

Marshall, Thomas H. 1963. "Citizenship and Social Class." In Thomas H. Marshall, *Sociology at the Crossroads and Other Essays,* London: Heinemann, pp. 67–127.

Martens, Wil, Ad Nagelkere, and Willem de Nijs. 2001. "Das gesellschaftliche System der Arbeitsbeziehungen. Bemerkungen zu Ralf Rogowskis 'Industrial Relations as a Social System.'" *Industrielle Beziehungen*, Vol. 8, no. 3, pp. 229–53.

Meltz, Noah M. 1991. "Dunlop's *Industrial Relations Systems* after Three Decades." In Roy J. Adams, ed., *Comparative Industrial Relations*, London: HarperCollins Academic, pp. 10–20.

Meyer, John W., and Brian Rowan. 1977. "Institutionalized Organizations: Formal Structure as Myth and Ceremony." *American Journal of Sociology*, Vol. 83, no. 2, pp. 340–63.

Müller-Jentsch, Walther. 2002. "Organisationales Handeln zwischen institutioneller Normierung und strategischem Kalkül." In Georg Schreyögg and Peter Conrad, eds., *Theorien des Managements: Managementforschung*, Vol. 12, Wiesbaden, Germany: Gabler, pp. 203–9.

Naschold, Frieder, ed. 1985. *Arbeit und Politik. Gesellschaftliche Regulierung der Arbeit und der sozialen Sicherung.* Frankfurt: Campus.

Naschold, Frieder, and Gerlinde Dörr. 1990. "Arbeitspolitik—Thesen und Themen." *WZB-Mitteilungen*, no. 50, pp. 12–14.

Neumann, Franz L. [1935] 1978. "Die Gewerkschaften in der Demokratie und in der Diktatur." In Franz L. Neumann, *Wirtschaft, Staat und Demokratie. Aufsätze 1930–1954*, Frankfurt: Suhrkamp, pp. 145–222.

Offe, Claus, and Helmut Wiesenthal. 1980. "Two Logics of Collective Action." *Political Power and Social Theory*, Vol. 1, pp. 67–115.

Olson, Mancur. 1965. *The Logic of Collective Action.* Cambridge, MA: Harvard University Press.

Ortmann, Günther. 1995. *Formen der Produktion: Organisation und Rekursivität.* Opladen, Germany: Westdeutscher Verlag.

Ortmann, Günther, Jörg Sydow, and Arnold Windeler. 1997. "Organisation als reflexive Strukturation." In Günther Ortmann, Jörg Sydow, and Klaus Türk, eds., *Theorien der Organisation: Die Rückkehr der Gesellschaft*, Opladen, Germany: Westdeutscher Verlag, pp. 315–54.

Potter, Beatrice. 1891. *The Cooperative Movement in Great Britain.* London.

Rogowski, Ralf. 2000. "Industrial Relations as a Social System." *Industrielle Beziehungen*, Vol. 7, no. 1, pp. 97–126.

Rojot, Jacques. 1990. "A View from Abroad." In James Chelius and James Dworkin, eds., *Reflections on the Transformation of Industrial Relations*, Metuchen, NJ: Institute of Management and Labor Relations Press.

Scharpf, Fritz W. 1997. *Games Real Actors Play: Actor-Centered Institutionalism in Policy Research.* Boulder, CO: Westview Press.

Schmidtchen, Dieter. 1987. "'Sunk Costs,' Quasirenten und Mitbestimmung." *Jahrbuch für Neue Politische Ökonomie*, Vol. 6, pp. 139–63.

Schmitter, Philippe C., and Gerhard Lehmbruch, eds. 1979. *Trends toward Corporatist Intermediation.* London: Sage.

Shalev, Michael. 1992. "The Resurgence of Labour Quiescence." In Marino Regini, ed., *The Future of Labour Movements*, London: Sage, pp. 102–32.

Simon, Herbert A. [1945] 1976. *Administrative Behavior: A Study of Decision-Making Processes in Administrative Organization*, 3rd ed. New York: Free Press.

Strauss, Anselm. 1978. *Negotiations: Varieties, Contexts, Processes, and Social Order.* San Francisco: Jossey-Bass.

Strauss, Anselm, Leonard Schatzmann, Danuta Ehrlich, Rue Bucher, and Melvin Sabshin. 1963. "The Hospital and Its Negotiated Order." In Eliot Freidson, ed., *The Hospital in the Modern Society.* New York: Free Press, pp. 147–69.

Streeck, Wolfgang. 1981. *Gewerkschaftliche Organisationsprobleme in der sozialstaatlichen Demokratie.* Königstein, Germany: Athenäum.

Streeck, Wolfgang, and Philippe C. Schmitter. 1985. "Community, Market, State—and Associations? The Prospective Contribution of Interest Governance to Social Order." In Wolfgang Streeck and Philippe C. Schmitter, eds., *Private Interest Government: Beyond Market and State,* London: Sage, pp. 1–29.

Sydow, Jörg, and Arnold Windeler. 2001. "Strukturationstheoretische Analyse industrieller Beziehungen—Soziale Praktiken der Arbeitsregulation im Fokus." In Jörg Abel and Hans Joachim Sperling, eds., *Umbrüche und Kontinuitäten. Perspektiven nationaler und internationaler Arbeitsbeziehungen.* Munich: Hampp, pp. 31–48.

Thelen, Kathleen. 1999. "Historical Institutionalism in Comparative Politics." *Annual Reviews of Political Science,* Vol. 2, pp. 369–404.

———. 2001. "Varieties of Labor Politics in the Developed Democracies." In Peter A. Hall and David Soskice, eds., *Varieties of Capitalism,* Oxford: Oxford University Press, pp. 71–103.

Thelen, Kathleen, and Sven Steinmo. 1992. "Historical Institutionalism in Comparative Politics." In Sven Steinmo, Kathleen Thelen, and Frank Longstreth, eds., *Structuring Politics: Historical Institutionalism in Comparative Politics,* Cambridge: Cambridge University Press, pp. 1–32.

Traxler, Franz. 1982. *Evolution gewerkschaftlicher Interessenvertretung.* Vienna: Braumüller.

———. 1986. *Interessenverbände der Unternehmer. Konstitutionsbedingungen und Steuerungskapazitäten.* Frankfurt: Campus.

Trinczek, Rainer. 1989. "Betriebliche Mitbestimmung als soziale Interaktion." *Zeitschrift für Soziologie,* Vol. 18, pp. 444–56.

Walgenbach, Peter. 1995. "Institutionalistische Ansätze in der Organisationstheorie." In Alfred Kieser, ed., *Organisationstheorien,* 2nd ed., Stuttgart: Kohlhammer, pp. 269–302.

———. 2002. "Neoinstitutionalistische Organisationstheorie—State of the Art und Entwicklungslinien." In Georg Schreyögg and Peter Conrad, eds., *Theorien des Managements: Managementforschung,* Vol. 12, Wiesbaden, Germany: Gabler, pp. 155–202.

Walton, Richard E., and Robert B. McKersie. 1965. *A Behavioral Theory of Labor Negotiations: An Analysis of a Social Interaction System.* New York: McGraw-Hill.

Webb, Sidney, and Beatrice Webb. [1897] 1902. *Industrial Democracy,* new ed. London: Longmans.

Weber, Max. [1922] 1964. *Wirtschaft und Gesellschaft: Grundriss der verstehenden Soziologie.* Studienausgabe, Erster Halbband. Cologne: Kiepenheuer & Witsch.

Weitbrecht, Hansjörg. 1974. "Das Machtproblem in Tarifverhandlungen." *Soziale Welt,* Vol. 25, pp. 224–34.

Weitbrecht, Hansjörg, and Wolf Matthias Braun, 1999. "Das Management als Akteur der industriellen Beziehungen." In Walther Müller-Jentsch, ed., *Konfliktpartnerschaft: Akteure und Institutionen der industriellen Beziehungen,* 3rd ed., Munich: Hampp, pp. 79–101.

Williamson, Oliver E. 1981. "The Economics of Organization: The Transaction Cost Approach." *American Journal of Sociology,* Vol. 87, pp. 548–77.
————. 1985. *The Economic Institutions of Capitalism: Firms, Markets, Relational Contracting.* New York: Free Press.
Windeler, Arnold. 2001. *Unternehmungsnetzwerke: Konstitution und Strukturation.* Wiesbaden, Germany: Westdeutscher Verlag.
Wood, Stephen, ed. 1982. *The Degradation of Work? Skill, Deskilling and the Labour Process.* London: Hutchinson.
Wood, S. J., A. Wagner, E. G. A. Armstrong, J. F. B. Goodman, and J. E. Davis. 1975. "The 'Industrial Relations System' Concept as a Basis for Theory in Industrial Relations." *British Journal of Industrial Relations,* Vol. 13, no. 3, pp. 291–308.

CHAPTER 2

Employment Relations and the Employment Relations System: A Guide to Theorizing

BRUCE E. KAUFMAN
Georgia State University

The essays in this volume are about industrial relations theory. The preceding review chapter by Müller-Jentsch ably documents the large theoretical literature that explores various facets and dimensions of industrial relations. To date, however, no one has discovered what may be considered the holy grail of industrial relations: an integrative theory that binds the field together and gives it intellectual coherence.

Some scholars claim that the search for the theoretical holy grail is a hopeless or misguided venture. One point of view, for example, is that industrial relations comprises a polyglot of disconnected subjects having nothing more in common than some relation to labor (Chamberlain 1960). Others claim that a search for an integrative theory misconstrues the raison d'etre of the field, which is to borrow theories and research methods developed in the basic disciplines and use them to address practical employment problems and policy issues (Shultz 1968). A third point of view holds that the distinctive feature of industrial relations is a set of normative principles about labor and the employment relationship (Kochan 1998)—a perspective that seems de facto to preclude an integrative theory since normative principles are subjective individual beliefs and inherently nonscientific. Lastly, in his essay in this volume, Hyman clearly demonstrates how even the most basic ideas, practices, and institutions in industrial relations change shape and meaning across countries, making the theorist's quest for a unifying explanatory model problematic indeed.

One or all of these positions may well be correct. With perhaps considerable overoptimism, however, I believe that an integrative theory of industrial relations may in fact be attainable. Certainly, in my view, more progress and insight are possible and well worth the effort, even if we

41

don't entirely accomplish the mission. But, having said this, the following question immediately arises: Why, despite a half century of work by some of the field's most able scholars, has the attempt to construct an integrative theory of industrial relations so far borne relatively modest results?

Building an integrative theory of industrial relations rests on both a *necessary* and a *sufficient* condition, to use the terminology of economics. The necessary condition is that scholars correctly define and conceptualize the object of study, that is, What is the subject we are theorizing about? What should the theory try to explain? and What are the key relationships and components that the theory must contain? The answers to these questions provide a guide or road map for the next step—actually constructing the theory. The sufficient condition for an integrative theory of industrial relations is that the object of study and, in particular, the key components and features to be explained are in some significant way related to each other through a web of cause-and-effect relationships. If no such relationships exist across the domain of the subject, then theorizing will never progress beyond the realm of descriptive frameworks and conceptual taxonomies.

My contention is that one reason theorizing in industrial relations has made only modest progress is that researchers have not yet gotten right the necessary condition, or at least have not reached a needed degree of consensus on it. Indeed, as I shall document later, modern-day scholars still cannot agree on what industrial relations *is*, while numerous contending opinions exist about what the central object of study and the key processes and conceptual constructs that should form the inputs for an integrative theory are. Whether getting these matters right will allow us to go the next step and actually build an integrative theory remains an open question, but what can be said with confidence is that *not* doing so necessarily dooms the effort.

Thus, the purpose of this chapter is not to build an integrative theory of industrial relations but to address the necessary condition just outlined. That is, this chapter addresses the following three central questions: What is the object of study in industrial relations? What are the major outcomes and behaviors to be explained (the dependent variables)? and What are the key explanatory components (independent variables) and processes that must be included in the theory?

The Subject Domain: What Is Industrial Relations?

Self-evidently, to construct a theory of industrial relations, we must specify the subject of industrial relations. Since the field of industrial relations is more than 80 years old, one might think that this issue was settled years ago. Surprisingly, this is not the case. Revealingly, Strauss and Whitfield (1998:6) state: "There is considerable disagreement as to what the field of industrial relations comprises." The validity of this assertion is readily indicated by a review of some of the alternative definitions of industrial relations found in the literature.

The broadest definition was offered by Chamberlain (1960:103), who equated industrial relations with "all aspects of labor." Also quite broad is the definition offered by Cox (1971:139): "industrial relations are defined . . . as the social relations of production." A somewhat less expansive but nonetheless broad definition was given by Heneman (1969:4), who defined industrial relations as the study of "employment relationships in an industrial economy."

In the middle are some more specialized definitions of the subject of industrial relations. Barbash (1993:67), for example, defined industrial relations as "the resolution of tension and conflict among the contending interests in the employment relationship," while Hyman (1995:10) defined it as "the social regulation of market forces." Another perspective was given by Clegg (1972:1): "Industrial relations could be briefly defined as the study of job-regulation," while Hills (1993:191) suggested along somewhat similar lines, "Industrial relations is the study of negotiation between the firm and groups of individuals (or their agents) about control over the employment relationship."

On the narrow side are several other definitions of industrial relations. Laffer (1974:72), for example, contended that the core subject of industrial relations is the "study of bargaining relations between employers and employees." A popular but more narrowly focused definition of industrial relations is the study of union–management (or collectively organized) employment relationships. Thus, Richard Marsden (1982:232) stated, "Everyone, instinctively it seems, knows what industrial relations is about, even those who have never studied the subject. It is 'about' trade unions, managers, and collective bargaining."

Amidst this welter of conflicting definitions a person could legitimately demand, "Will the real industrial relations please stand up?" More to the point, the job of the industrial relations theorist is made difficult and problematic by the plethora of alternative conceptualizations of the field's subject domain. Obviously, if the field is defined as "all aspects of labor," one theory is required (if a theory of such a broad domain as "labor" is even imaginable), while if it is about collective bargaining and union–management relations, an entirely different theory is required.

Is there any way to determine the "true" subject domain of industrial relations? One method is to look back in history and examine how the field of industrial relations was defined in the 1920s by the people who first developed it (Kaufman 1993, 2004). A historical definition is not the last word on the subject, but it does carry the authority of precedent.

The earliest document known to me on this matter is a pamphlet published in 1919 by the Russell Sage Library titled *Industrial Relations: A Selected Bibliography*. The reading list is divided into two major parts: *employment management* and *participation in management*. The former covers various subjects related to labor or personnel management; the second covers what today would be called methods of workforce governance. The latter includes readings on trade unionism, shop committees, plans for guild socialism, and wartime joint labor–management committees.

A second piece of evidence comes from a survey of the industrial relations field written by Herman Feldman in 1928 for the Social Science Research Council. The report states that "the focal point of the field [labor/industrial relations] is the *employer-employee relationship*" (p. 19, emphasis added). Amplifying on the subject area of industrial relations, Feldman went on to say that the field deals with five principal topics: factors in human behavior with special reference to industry, the worker in relation to his work, the worker in relation to his fellow worker, the worker in relation to his employer, and the worker in relation to the public.

A third piece of evidence comes from university curricula. The first program of study in industrial relations was established at the University of Wisconsin in 1920. It contained four areas of coursework: labor legislation, labor management (personnel management), labor history and industrial government (including trade unionism), and causes and remedies of unemployment. This pattern was widely repeated, with variations. The industrial relations program at Columbia University, for example, required coursework in law of the employment of labor, labor administration, adjustment of labor disputes, and personnel and employment problems (U.S. Bureau of Labor Statistics 1930). Yet another indicator comes from the industrial relations course that Sumner Slichter taught at Harvard University in the early 1930s. The lecture notes survive and reveal that approximately one half of the course was devoted to employers' labor policies (personnel management, employee representation, benefits programs, etc.) and one half to trade unionism and labor policy (Kaufman 2003b).

A final testament on the subject matter of industrial relations comes from the report *Industrial Relations: Administration of Policies and Programs* (1931) by the National Industrial Conference Board. The report declares: "In the broadest sense, the term 'industrial relations' comprises every incident that grows out of the fact of employment" (p. 1).

Summing up, one may conclude from these four sources that industrial relations as an intellectual enterprise circa the 1920s covered the subjects of *work, labor,* and the *employment relationship;* gave particular attention to *relations* in the work world; subsumed both *employers' methods of work organization and personnel management* and *employees' individual and collective responses* to the work experience, including *strikes, trade unions,* and *collective bargaining;* took a *multidisciplinary* perspective, including attention to legal, psychological, technical, sociological, economic, ethical, historical, and administrative forces; and focused on both *public policy issues* concerning labor and *workplace practices and outcomes.*

This list of topics is quite broad and covers the entire world of work. Taking the word "relations" seriously suggests, however, that the fundamental construct that underlies the field is the *employment relationship,* while a definition of the broad content area of industrial relations might be stated as *the study of the employment relationship and all the behaviors, outcomes, practices, and institutions that emanate from or impinge upon the employment relationship.* Given the centrality of the employment relationship to the study of industrial relations, the name of the field could thus be more accurately called *employment relations.* The term employment relations was in fact also used in the early 1920s to describe the field but never achieved popular usage (Kaufman 1993; Morris 1997).

The Facts to Be Explained: The Employment Relations System

To say that the employment relationship is the subject of industrial relations (or employment relations, the term used hereafter) is similar to saying that the subject of economics is the economy and the subject of sociology is society. This type of statement focuses attention on a particular dimension of human activity but gives little guidance regarding the important features and processes of the employment relationship, economy, or society that a theory should seek to explain. To make progress, we have to fill in the picture by giving more structure and substance to the employment relationship.

Dunlop's Industrial Relations System Theory

Just as many alternative definitions of the subject domain of employment relations exist, so too are there numerous alternative ways to organize and delineate the key features and processes of the employment relationship. The picture can be drawn many different ways. To proceed, I again appeal to precedent. In looking for an organizing concept for employment relations, the one that has without doubt been most popular and widely cited for the last half century is Dunlop's notion of an *industrial relations system.*

The concept of an industrial relations system comes from Dunlop's seminal book *Industrial Relations Systems* (1958). A number of people (e.g., Bellace 1994) consider it to be the single most influential book in industrial relations published in the post–World War II period. In the book Dunlop claimed to do what no one else had previously even tried; in his words, "The present volume presents a *general theory of industrial relations*" (emphasis added). He went on to say:

> This view of an industrial relations system permits a distinctive analytical and theoretical subject matter. To date the study of industrial relations has had little theoretical content. . . . It has been a cross-roads where a number of disciplines have met—history, economics, government, sociology, psychology, and law. Industrial relations requires a theoretical core in order to isolate facts, to point to new types of inquiries, and to make research more additive. The study of industrial relations systems provides a genuine discipline. (p. 6)

For us to proceed, several concepts appear to require definition. For example, we need to be clear on what constitutes a general theory. Dunlop did not provide an explicit statement on this matter but at one place equated a general theory with "tools of analysis to interpret and to gain understanding of the widest possible range of industrial relations facts and practices" (1958:vii). Elsewhere he suggested that a general theory is "an analytical framework" and "a systematic body of ideas . . . and concepts fitted together" (p. 380). In an in-depth review of theorizing in industrial relations, Adams (1993:334) offered this alternative statement of what constitutes a theory: "any empirically grounded conceptual system containing two or more variables connected by one or more rules of interaction whose intention it is to represent a regularity in nature." Using this definition, presumably a general theory is a conceptual system and set of variables and interactions that explain and predict regularities at the highest and broadest level of the subject domain (i.e., the systemwide level).

The next concept inviting definition is that of an industrial relations system. It has two parts: "system" and "industrial relations." On the concept of a system, Dunlop (1993:13) stated in the "Commentary" section of the revised edition, "[T]he central notion of a system is that the parts and elements are interdependent and each may affect other elements and the outcomes of the system as a whole." He then quoted Slichter (from a 1955 address), who said, "Our arrangements in the field of industrial relations may be regarded as a system in the sense that each of them more or less intimately affects each of the others so that they constitute a group of arrangements for dealing with certain matters and are collectively responsible for certain results."

On the concept of "industrial relations," Dunlop (1958:v) stated in the original book only that it comprises "the complex of interrelations among managers, workers, and agencies of government." (In the "Commentary" of the 1993 revised edition, Dunlop devoted the first section to "The Discipline of Industrial Relations" but nowhere defined the concept or subject domain of industrial relations.)

Dunlop then proceeded to fill in the structure of an industrial relations system by outlining its key features and processes. In the preface to the 1958 edition, Dunlop provided in one paragraph as compact a statement of the structure of his theory as is available:

> Every industrial-relations system involves three groups of actors: (1) workers and their organizations, (2) managers and their organizations, and (3) governmental agencies concerned with the work place and the work community. Every industrial-relations system creates a complex of rules to govern the work place and work community. These rules may take a variety of forms in different systems—agreements, statutes, orders, decrees, regulations, awards, policies, and practices and customs. The form of the rule does not alter its essential character: to define the status of the actors and to govern conduct of all the actors at the work place and work community. The actors in an industrial-relations system are regarded as confronting an environmental context at any one time. The environment is comprised of three interrelated contexts: the technology, the market or budgetary constraints, and the power relations and statutes of the actors. The system is bound together by an ideology or understandings shared by all the actors. The central task of a theory of industrial relations is to explain why particular rules are established in particular industrial-relations systems and how and why they change in response to changes affecting the system. (pp. viii-ix)

Dunlop's theoretical model has been the subject of considerable commentary, criticism, and debate over the years. I do not wish to go into an extensive review and repetition of this discussion (see Meltz 1993, Adams 1997, and Kaufman 2004 and the extensive citations contained therein). Several salient points deserve mention, however, as they bear on the subject of this essay.

- A widely shared opinion (e.g., Adams 1997; D. Kelly, in press) is that Dunlop did not succeed in constructing a general theory. The sine qua non of a theory, as noted earlier, is specification of one or more cause-and-effect relationships. Dunlop's model does not specify any such relationship. Rather, he provided a useful conceptual framework that helps identify key features and processes of the industrial relations system.

- The concept of an industrial relations system does appear useful, however, as a basis for theory construction. The purpose of the systems concept is to organize and represent the key elements (structures, actors, processes) that make up the world of industrial relations, to delineate the interdependencies and lines of causation between them, and to suggest the important outcomes that require theoretical explanation. It thus serves as a helpful organizing framework and guide for theorizing.

- The historical citations provided earlier suggest that the central construct underlying the field of industrial relations is (or should be) the employment relationship. Presumably this construct would also be a central variable in the industrial relations system. Dunlop, however, gave almost no attention to the employment relationship in his model. Rather, he defined industrial relations more expansively to include all the relations between workers, managers, and government agencies, and the central construct was the web of rules.

- Although insightful, Dunlop's model of the industrial relations system leaves out a number of important elements. He did not, for example, model the *process* by which the rules of the industrial relations system are determined nor give but passing attention to the role of the state in this matter. Dunlop also provided no theoretical representation of the human agent ("model of man") or of the key institutional actors, such as firms and unions. The role of social and behavioral forces in the industrial relations system, as investigated in psychology, sociology, and organizational behavior, is also largely omitted.

- Dunlop's claim that the rules of the workplace and work community represent the dependent variable in a theory of industrial relations is problematic. Most industrial relations researchers would maintain that the objects of interest are various outcomes and behaviors, such as wage rates, strikes, work effort, and union organizing success. The rules of the industrial relations system would be an appropriate dependent variable if they completely determined these outcomes. Obviously, however, in most cases they do not, suggesting that rules are usually better represented as independent or mediating variables (depending on the level of analysis).

The Employment Relations System

Because of these and other shortcomings, Dunlop's industrial relations system model has not proven to be a fruitful source for an integrative theory of industrial relations. Since the systems idea appears to be a useful way to think about institutional structure and behavioral interdependencies in the world of work, I propose to keep it as the overall organizing framework. But the specific features of Dunlop's model need revision and further development. With this in mind, I start at the ground level and construct an alternative model (or picture) of the industrial relations system. It is entirely descriptive, in the same sense as a road map is. For the sake of parallelism with the term *employment relations*, I henceforth refer to this model as the *employment relations system* (ERS). The complete representation of the employment relations system is presented in figure 1. I proceed to describe and develop it step by step, starting at the most micro level and working up to the broadest macro level.

The beginning point for the ERS is the rectangle at the bottom center of the diagram. It is the only part of the ERS that is generic (common) across all historical time periods and all industries, economies, and societies. The rectangle depicts the *production process,* where factor inputs of labor (L), capital (K), and natural resources (N) are transformed via the production function into outputs (Q) of goods and services. This transformative activity, often called in the industrial relations literature the *labor process* (see the chapter by Thompson and Newsome in this volume), is where the laborer is motivated or induced to work, that is, to apply physical, mental, and emotional energy or effort to the act of production, along with the cooperating factor inputs. All types of economies—primitive and advanced, capitalist and socialist—have a labor process. The scope and scale of the labor process vary greatly, however, as do the possible methods for providing labor input to the production function.

One common method of operating the labor process is to establish an *employment relationship.* The employment relationship is a legal creation in which one person (the employee) agrees for a sum of money specified

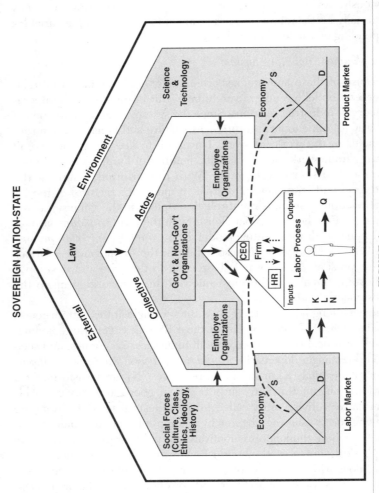

FIGURE 1

The Employment Relations System

over some time period to provide labor to another person (the employer) and follow the employer's orders and rules regarding the performance of work, at least within limits (Simon 1951). With an employment relationship, therefore, the labor process involves at a minimum two people—a boss and a worker, involves an open/incomplete form of contract, invests in the boss the legal authority to control and command the worker in the operation of the labor process, and provides an opportunity for either party to sever the relationship under specified conditions (see the Wachter chapter in this volume). Typically, the employment relationship is established through voluntary agreement mediated by a labor market (a negotiation between a buyer and seller of labor), but at least in theory, this need not be the case. In a socialist economy, for example, labor markets in a capitalist sense may not exist, and the state planning agency may instead coordinate the matching up of labor demand and supply. Workers can still be employees in this system as long as they have a private property right in their labor, are paid based on some measure of work input or output, and are free to change enterprises. Whatever the system, the employment contract is akin to a rental contract in that the employer rents the employee's labor services for a period of time, subject to the ongoing mutual consent of both parties.

An employment relationship is not generic even in capitalist economies, however, as labor can be provided to the production function in other ways. One example is an economy where all "firms" (production units) are one-person establishments, such as the family farm, the self-employed artisan, or the independent contractor. In this case the functions of boss and worker are combined in the same person. Another example is a slave economy, where law or custom permits certain people to own not only the inanimate factor inputs of capital and natural resources but also the physical bodies of the people providing labor. (Serfdom is a close permutation.) A slave relation thus transforms labor from a service that is rented by an employer to an asset that is the property of the person running the business. Whereas an independent contractor or farmer is self-managed, however, a slave has a boss, perhaps in this respect putting the slave relation somewhere in the middle between the employed and self-employed. (The independent contractor has a boss, too, but it is the purchaser of the good or service in the product market.)

If employment relations is defined as "all aspects of work" or "all aspects of labor," then forms of economic organization that involve the self-employed and independent contractors are included within the field. Thus, employment relations would subsume farmers and peasants in the agricultural sector and self-employed artisans and service vendors in the informal sector. Since one half or more of the workforce in some underdeveloped countries earn a living from agriculture and the informal sector, some rationale exists for including them in the domain of the field. If, however, we take the employment relationship to be the central characteristic that defines the subject matter of the field, then these alternative forms of labor are excluded or at least treated as of secondary importance. One way to rationalize this dividing line is to note that the self-employed and independent contractors exchange labor services more as a species of *commercial relations* than of employment relations since the exchange takes place through contracting in the product market rather than employment contracting in the labor market.

A pragmatic position on the matter holds that the subject domain of the field depends in part on the objective of the analyst. If the objective is the applied practice of solving labor problems, then all forms of labor should be included. But when the object shifts to theory building, success requires that attention be focused on a central analytical construct. History suggests that the founders of the field intended this construct to be the employment relationship. As I argue later in this chapter, prospects for developing a theory of the employment relationship also appear promising due to recent advances in institutional economics, lending further support to making the employment relationship the field's core object of study. If this proposition is accepted, then the ERS in figure 1 depicts that subset of production processes for which an employment relationship exists. Indeed, without an employment relationship, much of the ERS superstructure above the production process in both the diagram and real life disappears, as do many of the most interesting conceptual and empirical issues in the field.

Moving on, the next element of the industrial relations framework is the formal, hierarchical *organization* that contains and coordinates the production process and sells or otherwise distributes the produced goods and services. It is depicted in the diagram as the pyramid that rests on the rectangular production process. Formal, hierarchical organization is not generic, for, as noted earlier, a significant amount of production activity is carried out by the self-employed. But in all modern economies the great bulk of goods and services comes from large, formally structured organizations, comprising various types of for-profit and not-for-profit enterprises.

These formal organizations have several features that are fundamental to employment relations. One is that ownership of the organization gives to the entrepreneur and delegated managers decision-making rights over resource allocation and utilization—including labor and the operation of the labor process. Thus, at the apex of the organization is the chief executive officer (CEO), followed by gradations of upper, middle, and lower managers. Although the line can be fuzzy in practice, conceptually there is a fundamental split in the organization between people who are managers (order givers) and those who are production workers (order takers). The former are in the cone part of the pyramid; the latter are in the rectangle containing the production process. Stretching from the top of the pyramid to the bottom is a hierarchy of authority relations, job responsibilities, organizational rewards (compensation), and status positions.

A second feature is that the owners of organizations use them to achieve specific goals. Among private business organizations in a capitalist economy, the dominant (though not necessarily only) goal is maximum profit. Other organizations, such as those in the public sector or socialist economies, have different goals that leaders strive to reach, such as maximum output, rapid growth, or personal enrichment. Regardless of specific goal, most organizations are under considerable pressure to be efficient and yield a surplus of revenue over cost.

A third feature of formal organizations is that they are coordinated and controlled through the exercise of command by management decision makers. They are, in effect, a micro version of a centrally planned economy. Organizations are thus fundamentally different from the markets that are external to them, since the latter are to varying degrees coordinated by supply and demand and price. Organizational coordination thus depends on the exercise of authority, represented in the diagram by the downward-pointing solid arrow, and flows of information up and down the hierarchy, denoted by the upward and downward dashed arrows.

A fourth feature of organizations is distinct patterns of internal structure with respect to jobs—how they are grouped together, the vertical and lateral movement between jobs, the degree of linkage to external market forces, and the manner in which jobs and job clusters are coordinated and managed. Generically, these different patterns are called *employment systems* (Begin 1991; Lepak and Snell 1999; the Marsden chapter in this volume). One important form of employment system in the ERS is the internal labor market, a term that is clearly a misnomer since no market per se exists inside firms but nonetheless usefully captures the idea that the pricing and allocation of labor inside firms are to some extent often administered by management rather than set by supply and demand.

A fifth feature of organizations is that they perform more effectively when the goals and behaviors of all participants are aligned and united in a common cause. Diversity in people's skills, experiences, perspectives, and demographic characteristics can be productive for organizations, but alignment of goals and behaviors facilitates cooperation and reduces performance-sapping intraorganizational conflict and principal–agent problems.

A final feature of organizations important for employment relations is the existence of discrete management departments or functional areas created to coordinate and control specific parts of the operation. One such functional area is the industrial relations, personnel, or human resource (HR) department. It is denoted in figure 1 by the box labeled "HR" in the management pyramid. The HR department's core responsibility is the labor input and, in particular, acquiring, developing, motivating, and disposing of the labor input so that the labor process most effectively meets the organization's goals (see the other Kaufman chapter in this volume). Subsumed within these tasks are issues of compensation, benefits, selection, training, termination, employee relations, and collective bargaining.

Organizations are not self-contained but interact with and are influenced by their external environment. The *external environment* has a variety of dimensions, including economic, social, legal, and technological dimensions. It also transmits the influence of other organizations.

Economic forces, operating through markets, are one important dimension of the external environment that forms part of the employment relations system. Organizations in modern economies typically obtain the labor input from the labor market. The *labor market* is denoted in the left-hand portion of figure 1. The demand (D) for labor comes from all the organizations in the market; the supply (S) of labor comes from individuals who desire gainful employment. Organizations with a demand for labor input can obtain it by paying the market-determined rate of pay, along with market-determined hours, benefits, and working conditions.

Several points about labor markets deserve brief mention. First, the existence of a labor market is a sufficient condition for the existence of an employment relationship, given that the fundamental purpose of a labor market is to match up job seekers with organizations that have job openings. When a match is made, the organization becomes the employer, the job seeker becomes the employee, and an employment relationship comes into being.

Second, the employment relation is established through some form of explicit or implicit negotiation, culminating in an agreement (often unwritten and perhaps even tacit) between the two parties as to the terms, conditions, and performance expectations to be fulfilled. The employment relation is thus a contractual one, and the terms of the contract reflect the relative bargaining power and market position of each party. Tight labor markets, for example, give employees greater leverage, while slack markets (or lack of other employers) give the individual organization the advantage.

Third, labor markets place upper and lower limits on the terms and conditions that employers and employees can negotiate. The more competitive labor markets are, the more organizations are constrained to adopt market-set wages and cost-competitive terms and conditions of employment; the more imperfect labor markets are, the greater the discretion organizations have in these matters. The very fact that multiperson organizations exist, however, is a sign that markets are less than perfect (in the economist's sense) due to positive transaction costs.

Fourth, the employment relation fosters an adversarial relationship between the employer and employee. The tendency is to see the employment contract as a zero-sum game; what one party gains in wages, hours, or working conditions comes at the expense of the other.

Fifth, due to imperfect information and the bounded rationality of human agents, employment contracts are necessarily incomplete. Not all terms, conditions, and performance requirements can be anticipated and set down in writing *ex ante* to the start of work. The employment relation thus requires ongoing administration, negotiation, and adjustment, while the incomplete nature of the employment contract opens the door for conflict, misunderstanding, and opportunistic behavior as the employer and employee seek to exploit contractual gaps and holes to their advantage (Williamson 1985).

Finally, it must be noted that organizations can also sometimes influence labor markets, as in the case of monopsony and other forms of imperfect competition. To indicate this reverse line of causation, a solid arrow is drawn in figure 1 going from the organization to the labor market. (The individual business organization may likewise influence other elements of the external environment and also the collective actors, but to avoid cluttering the diagram, these arrows of causation are omitted.)

Organizations and employment relations are also affected by product markets, depicted on the right-hand side of figure 1. The *product market* is where the organization sells its good or service, denoted by a solid arrow going from the organization to the product market. The more competitive the product market, the greater is the pressure on the organization to minimize cost, the smaller are profit margins, and the less stable are sales. All these pressures feed back into the organization's employment relations practices, such as the terms and conditions of employment and the nature of the employment system; this feedback is indicated by the solid arrow going from product market to the organization. Macroeconomic conditions in product markets, such as the rate of economic growth, extent of cyclical booms and busts (and associated amount of involuntary unemployment in labor markets), and degree of global market integration, have a similar impact.

Product and labor markets determine prices and wages, which provide information to managers about relative productivity, value, and scarcity of goods and factor inputs. These information flows to organizational controllers are marked by the dashed arrows going from the labor and product markets to the management pyramid in figure 1. The employment relations system thus uses a mix of coordination and control mechanisms—markets and organizations—and information is passed to organizational controllers through two alternative channels—market-determined prices and wages and written and verbal messages or directives passed up and down the internal organizational hierarchy.

The employment relations system contains and is shaped by a variety of institutions, some of which are formal and others informal. An "institution" is a collective entity that "expands, liberates, and controls" the behavior of individuals (Commons 1934). An institution is synonymous with a "governance structure": a set of explicit or implicit rules that delimit the rights, responsibilities, and duties of all parties, as well as penalties for violations of these rules (Williamson 1985). Examples include formal organizations, such as governments, corporations, political parties, families, and churches, and informal collective entities, such as national or ethnic cultures, social norms and customs, and ethical belief systems. A market is also an "institution." Individuals create institutions, but once established, institutions have an existence and influence that transcend the will of individual participants.

Two of the principal institutions of the employment relations system—firms and markets—have already been introduced. Next to be considered are the *collective actors* in the ERS: employer organizations, employee organizations, and various governmental and nongovernmental organizations. These are located in figure 1 in the middle block above the organization. From the individual firm's perspective, the collective actors represent part of the external environment that conditions the internal practice of employment relations.

Employers and employees enter the employment relations system as individual entities (at least in the legal sense) but frequently conclude that they can promote attainment of their self-interested objectives through combination and collective action with others of their kind. The motivations, conditions, and constraints that influence the decision of individuals to mobilize for collective action and institution building are thus an important conceptual and practical issue in industrial relations (Olson 1965; J. Kelly 1998). Likewise, once institutions are established, their operation, structure, and impact on individual and collective behavior in the work world are equally important subjects.

Central in this regard is the decision of workers to organize collective organizations. A particularly important form of worker collective organization is the independent *labor union*. Other forms include employee professional associations; lobbying, advocacy, and civil rights groups; and welfare, beneficial, and church-based associations. Labor unions and other collective employee entities are formal organizations that speak for and represent groups of workers on subjects of common interest. In this respect, they are institutions or governance structures in their own right, since they establish rules and sanctions governing the rights and behaviors of members.

Workers are motivated to form and join labor unions for a variety of reasons, but a generic reason is that collective action is frequently more effective in advancing their common interests than is individual action (Wheeler and McClendon 1991; Bennett and Kaufman 2002). Collective action by labor unions takes three principal directions in the employment relations system. The first is to use collective bargaining to influence the economic terms of the employment contract, such as wages, hours, work speed, and so on. This method involves changing the rules and operation of both external markets (the arrows to the labor and product markets) and internal human resource practices of firms (the arrow to the producing organization). The second is to use collective bargaining to change the internal governance structure of firms, typically from some form of employer unilateralism (or "autocracy") to a more "democratic" model featuring expanded joint decision making, formalized due-process protections, and balanced methods for resolving disputes (also depicted by the arrow going to the producing organization). The third channel of influence exercised by labor unions is to use collective action in the political sphere (national, state or province, local) to bring about improved terms, conditions, and governance of employment through legislation and government edict (not indicated in figure 1).

Employers also have incentives to combine efforts for mutual protection and advancement of their interests. Companies may, for example, form an *employers' association* to present a common front in collective bargaining with labor unions. Employers also combine to influence demand, supply, or wage determination in labor markets; to regulate and restrict competition in product markets; to provide training, recruitment, and professional development services in the employment area; and to promote their employment-related interests in the political process.

Although employee and employer organizations are central to the study of employment relations, the ERS also contains a variety of other important organizations that bear on work and the employment relationship. These are denoted in figure 1 by the box for *governmental and nongovernmental organizations.* Examples of the former include government regulatory agencies (e.g., the National Labor Relations Board), courts, and supranational organizations such as the World Bank and the International Labor Organization; examples of the latter include civil rights organizations, community and religious groups, and political parties.

The labor and product markets and the workers', employers', and private and public organizations are part of the external environment, seen from the perspective of the individual employer and employee inside the organization. But there are also other components of the external environment. The three most important are portrayed in figure 1 in the arched area above the markets and collective actors: social forces, law, and science and technology. Each in some way affects the structure, activities, or behavior of the actors and institutions in the employment relations system.

An important influence on industrial relations is the *social forces* of culture, class, ethics, ideology, and history. *Culture,* for example, is a social influence on behavior, operating through social norms, shared ideals, and widely accepted customs and conventions. Culture helps structure people's goals and preferences, such as the saliency of money and work, the appropriate role of women in the workplace, and the value of individual versus collective action. Culture also defines rules for social behavior in the industrial relations arena, such as standards for work effort and punctuality, acceptable forms and expressions of competition among workers, and the degree of acceptance of authority.

Class is a closely related social force in the external environment. Social classes are broad, relatively well-identified strata in society that determine one's position in the economic and social hierarchy. Class affects industrial relations by separating employers and employees, or occupational and social groups within the workforce, into distinct groups with divergent, sometimes conflicting interests and outlooks. Countries that have a more rigid and well-defined class system are also more likely to feature highly developed forms of collective action, such as extensive trade unionism and corporatist forms of economic organization.

A third social force is *ethics*, representing the influence of moral principles, religious precepts, and ethical values (Budd 2004). Like culture, ethics affects behavior in industrial relations by shaping goals and preferences and laying down rules governing what is right and wrong. It is an ethical principle, for example, that human life is sacred, and thus workers' labor should not be treated as a commodity. Likewise, ethical principles of truth, fairness, and respect help restrain numerous antisocial behaviors in the work world, such as cheating, opportunism, exploitation, and injustice, that would otherwise arise from unalloyed pursuit of self-interest.

A fourth social force is *ideology*. Ideology is a shared belief system based on some doctrine, theory, or set of ideas that influences how people regard the legitimacy of the ERS and its appropriate structure and operation. Ideology, for example, influences workers' sense of class identity and solidarity, whether trade unions pursue reform or revolution, and the degree of employers' hostility toward unions. A shared ideology, as Dunlop emphasized, can provide an important element of stability and consensus in an ERS, while strongly opposed ideologies can create deep fissures and instability in an ERS and even its complete collapse.

The fifth social force in employment relations is *history*. History reflects the influence of past events. The ERS is not re-created every day but is built incrementally on the foundation of what preceded. Thus, if one country has a history of class consciousness, industrial unionism, and frequent strike activity, while another has an individualistic culture, a system of individual bargaining, and low strike frequency, it is likely that these historical features will be reproduced in future years (i.e., the ERS is path dependent).

A completely different influence on industrial relations in the external environment is *science and technology*, positioned opposite social forces in the diagram. Science and technology is a broad category that subsumes both the state of scientific knowledge and its embodiment in machines, products, and processes. Science and technology affect employment relations through several channels. Inside firms, for example, technology heavily influences the operation and structure of the production process and the work experience of employees. To illustrate, technology substantially influences whether a product is produced through a continuous assembly-line process or through small-batch custom-order methods, as well as the extent of division of labor, the work skills required, and room for autonomy and creativity. Another route of influence for technology is its influence on organizational and market structure. Economies of scale, for example, favor large organizations and oligopolistic product markets, while computers, telecommunications, and the Internet promote organizational decentralization, rapid change, and increased competition in markets. Finally, advances in the general state of scientific knowledge open up new ideas and processes in the world of work, such as new management methods (e.g., high-performance work systems) and ways of organizing and controlling work (e.g., telecommuting, electronic monitoring of employees).

The third environmental force depicted at the top of figure 1 is *law*. Law is also a social force since it is human-created and defines the nature of the legal relation between people, institutions, and things. In a generic sense, law is simply one other form of social rule making and regulation in the ERS. In a practical sense, however, law is a more authoritative and powerful social force than the others since it is laid down by formal units of government; embodied in written statutes, court decisions, and regulations; and enforced through the very tangible presence of police, courts, and threats of physical confinement and violence. To represent this superior position symbolically, law is placed at the top of the arch of environmental forces.

Law influences industrial relations through a variety of routes. Law, for example, determines property rights of owners of labor and capital and their legal obligations under an employment contract. Whether employers can terminate employees at will or only for just cause is one illustration. Law also determines the extent to which employees can organize for collective bargaining, the structure and operation of the bargaining process, and the use of economic weapons. Illustrations include permissible union security arrangements (e.g., a closed shop), methods for determining union recognition (e.g., secret-ballot election), the duties of the employer in collective bargaining (e.g., whether plant shutdowns must be negotiated), and permissible use of economic weapons (e.g., secondary boycotts). A third dimension of law is legislation and court decisions aimed at protecting or enhancing the rights and security of employees. Examples include protective labor laws, such as those addressing minimum wages and workplace safety, and social insurance programs, such as unemployment and old age insurance.

The external environment of employment relations in its totality is thus composed of five broad human-created forces: economic, organizational, social, technological, and legal. Together, these forces create a complex array of formal and informal constraints, or *web of rules*, that guide and shape individual and collective action. These rules may also be thought of as a *governance structure* in that they define the rights, duties, liberties, and resources of the parties in an employment relation.

Two elements of the ERS remain to be introduced. At the apex of the ERS is the *sovereign nation-state*, located at the very top of the ERS in figure 1 (Commons 1950; Kaufman 2003a). Sovereignty refers to the supreme decision-making power of the nation-state and its rulers. Thus, the nation-state and its leaders have the ultimate authority to decide how the ERS is structured and operated, although in a democratic political system, the people (and organizations) exercise a large degree of influence through their ability to replace and reward or punish the leaders. (An arrow denoting this upward line of influence is omitted from the figure.) The sovereign decides, for example, whether the economy is socialist or capitalist and whether political and economic governance structures are democratic or autocratic. Likewise, the sovereign determines whether trade unions are independent or government controlled and whether workers can freely decide to go on strike. In large measure the decisions of the sovereign on these matters are expressed in formally constituted law, but the sovereign power can also determine these matters through command and coercion. Viewed from this perspective, employment relations cannot be separated from broader issues of political economy.

The final element in the employment relations system is really the first: its *people*. The people of the ERS are depicted by the human figure in the center of the production process box in figure 1. This placement is meant to emphasize that the labor input into production comes from human beings. The explicit inclusion of a person in the diagram also calls attention to the fact that the employment relations system is human-made and all institutions, practices, and behaviors are the result of human action.

Deeper reflection reveals that the human essence of labor is, in fact, the core characteristic of the labor process and the ERS that gives employment relations a compelling claim to stand as an independent field of study. After all, if we have employment relations, then why not capital relations and land relations? The obvious but profoundly important answer is that capital and land are inanimate objects and have no independent welfare claim above and beyond their instrumental economic value. Labor, on the other hand, is embodied in human beings, and thus the employment of human beings carries a higher moral significance (Budd 2004). This fact represents one of the great dividing lines between the discipline of economics (in its modern neoclassical guise) and the field of employment relations. The former gives labor no different status from capital and land and argues that all three factor inputs should be utilized in the manner that maximizes economic efficiency and consumer welfare. Employment relations, however, takes seriously the human essence of labor and argues that the quest for efficiency and consumer welfare must be balanced against society's interest in the workers' welfare and, in particular, the attainment of equity, voice, and human self-development in the workplace (Barbash 1984; Meltz 1989; the chapter by Budd, Gomez, and Meltz in this volume; Kaufman 2004).

With regard to a theory of the ERS, an implication of the human essence of labor is that principles of psychology and sociology are central to understanding and predicting the performance of work, the operation of business organizations, and the relations between employers and employees. Employment relations thus requires for theory building a "model of man" in order to predict behavioral relations and derive hypotheses (the Kelloway, Gallagher, and Barling chapter in this volume; Kaufman 1989, 1999). More so than economics, employment relations—by the nature of its subject matter—has to give greater recognition to psychological and sociological considerations, such as bounded rationality, theories of motivation, emotional states, and principles of group behavior (Wheeler 1985). Without these factors, a theory of employment relations would have considerable difficulty explaining and predicting, for example, effective leadership practices, the persistence of discrimination, and the role of injustice in sparking union organizing and strikes. Indeed, the very concept of "relations" when applied to the work world seems to demand a sociologically informed theory.

Implications for Theorizing

The portrait of the employment relations system presented in the preceding section is intended as a road map to help guide researchers in the development of an integrative theory. Whether such a theory can be constructed remains an open question. But the purpose of the ERS model is to clear the way for a more sustained and fruitful attack on this matter by at least getting right what I have called the *necessary condition*.

The necessary condition is to correctly identify the central object of study, the outcomes and behaviors the theory should explain, and the key institutions, actors, and processes that must be built into the theory. In thinking further about this matter, two preliminary but important questions seem to be (1) Why is an integrative theory needed? and (2) What should it integrate?

The answer to the first question has two parts. The first is that an integrative theory gives the field greater intellectual coherence and unity by demonstrating how all the pieces of the ERS fit together and operate as an interconnected system. Such a theory should also illuminate the variation in employment relations systems across time, industries, and countries, thus providing a theoretical foundation for comparative and international employment relations (see the Godard and the Martin and Bamber chapters in this volume). The second part is that an integrative theory provides a productive tool for better explaining and predicting key outcomes and behaviors in the world of work.

And what should such a theory integrate? Up to the present time, researchers in employment relations have examined in a relatively fragmented and disconnected fashion various parts of the ERS and have developed equally fragmented and disconnected theories and models about them borrowed largely from other surrounding disciplines and fields of study. Sometimes these theories are called middle-range theories (Kochan 1993), suggesting that they cover an important component part of the ERS but do not generalize to the system as a whole. Examples cited by Adams (1988) include collective bargaining theory, conflict theory, job satisfaction theory, internal labor market theory, and union-joining theory; to this list might be added high-performance work systems theory, exit-voice theory, organizational commitment theory, and employment regulation theory. The job of an integrative theory of employment relations is to find some conceptual common denominator or "intellectual thread" that shows how each of the various parts of the ERS fit together and interact and why they take the form and perform the function they do.

Given these considerations, how would a person go about constructing an integrative theory of employment relations? One approach is to first identify the central construct around which all phenomena in the ERS revolve. This construct then becomes the core component of the theory and the foundation of the field. Based on earlier discussion, for the field of employment relations the obvious choice of a central construct is the employment relationship. The virtues of the employment relationship for theorizing are that it effectively encompasses the field of inquiry and all the phenomena to be studied, it is an objective and value-free entity, and it is found in a generic form (if not always a capitalist form) in all present-day countries regardless of culture, political system, or form of economy.

If the employment relationship is accepted as the central construct for an integrative theory, the next step is to determine the key outcomes and behaviors that the theory should endeavor to explain. These become, in effect, the dependent variables in employment relations research. In approaching this matter, it is useful to start at the highest level of generalization and work down.

What question is antecedent to all others in employment relations? That question seems to be: Why is there an employment relationship, and under what conditions will societies choose to use an employment relationship in the production of goods and services? Any theory that claims to be integrative in the field of employment relations must provide an answer to this baseline question, otherwise it is partial in nature and falls in the middle range.

To inquire about the existence of the employment relationship is to ask, in terms of figure 1, why the ERS has a labor market, for without a labor market (or some other external coordinating mechanism for providing labor to the organization) an employment relationship is impossible. Immediately at this step the field of employment relations is differentiated from the field of labor economics, since the latter takes the existence of a labor market as an exogenously determined given, while the former treats the existence of a labor market as an endogenous variable to be explained. By the same token, when an employment relationship exists, the field of employment relations is also differentiated from the field of management and organization theory, since the operation of the labor market is central to the former while often treated as a given in the latter.

The field of employment relations thus serves as an intellectual bridge between economics (the study of resource allocation and production and distribution through price coordination in markets) and the study of management and organization theory (the study of resource allocation and production and distribution through command coordination in hierarchical organizations), since both forms of coordination and economic organization are present and work interactively when an employment relationship exists (Coase 1937). A theory of employment relations is thus a form of "general equilibrium theory" in the sense that labor economics theory and management and organization theory are partial theories and the integrative theory of employment relations brings the two together and endogenously explains their interface and respective domains in the ERS. (For an example, see the other Kaufman chapter in this volume.)

In passing, we can note that this way of looking at the ERS also raises a question about a key part of Dunlop's formulation of an industrial relations system. He stated (1958:5), "An industrial relations system is not a subsidiary part of an economic system but is rather a separate and distinctive subsystem of the society, on the same plane as an economic system." Figure 1 suggests, however, that the industrial relations system is not analytically separate and distinct from the economic system but rather represents one sector of the economic system, the labor or "employment" sector, assuming that the concept of *economic system* is defined broadly in a political economy sense and includes both the market (price) and organizational (command) components. If *economic system* is instead treated conceptually and theoretically to include in a substantive sense only the operation of demand and supply in markets (the product and labor market portions of figure 1, which essentially represent the economic system in neoclassical models of general equilibrium and most microeconomics textbooks), then the ERS in fact subsumes the relevant portions of the economic (market) system and adds to them the organizational and political parts.

Once an integrative theory has determined that an employment relationship exists, a number of otherwise blank spots in figure 1, metaphorically speaking, are filled in with institutions and people. That is, with an employment relationship, not only does a labor market appear in figure 1, but so also do the management hierarchy (including the HR function) in the organizational triangle of the business firm and the trade unions, employers' associations, and various governmental and nongovernmental organizations in the collective actors block of the ERS. These institutions help define the *architectural structure* of the ERS and give rise to different ERS typologies and configurations.

Thus, at the second level of theorizing, an employment relationship is assumed to exist, and the purpose of an integrative theory is to then explain within this context why these institutions arise, why they take the forms and functions they do, and how they collectively give rise to different ERS architectures. An important, concrete question asked in employment relations is why workers form labor unions, why some unions are organized along craft lines and others along industrial lines, and why some unions emphasize political action and others emphasize economic gains. In terms of ERS architecture, one can distinguish between an organized (unionized) and unorganized (nonunion) ERS. Alternatively, one can ask why some firms have human resource management departments and others do not, or why some firms choose to join an employers' association for collective bargaining but others prefer individual bargaining. Another important dimension of ERS architecture concerns the structure and performance of labor and product markets and, in particular, why markets take different forms (e.g., competitive, dual or segmented, monopsonistic) and the impact these different forms have on terms and conditions of employment. All these questions invite theoretical explanation, but to date, researchers in employment relations have largely contented themselves with pulling disparate middle-range theories from surrounding disciplines to explain them. The task of an integrative theory of employment relations is to find a common intellectual link that provides some unity of cause and effect between and among these objects of study.

Moving down another step in the ERS hierarchy of analysis, we come to the level of the individual organization. Here too are numerous interesting questions for the field of employment relations. As with the other institutions of the ERS, we wish to know why firms exist; why they come in different sizes, forms, and structures; and how they operate. Also subsumed in the internal study of organizations is the employment function of human resource management. An integrative theory of employment relations should shed light, for example, on why firms choose alternative human resource strategies and adopt different configurations of individual human resource practices. Finally, an integrative theory should also provide insight on the conditions that lead to the adoption of alternative internal organizational architectures. In each case, the sine qua non of an integrative theory is to bring to these questions some common analytical tool or concept that provides both unity and insight to the process of understanding and explanation.

As it does for other areas of the ERS, an integrative theory allows the field of employment relations to serve as a valuable intellectual bridge between other surrounding disciplines and fields of study for understanding organizations and their relationship to the external environment. As earlier noted, the study of business organizations has traditionally been the special province of scholars in management and organization theory, while the structure and operation of labor markets have been the province of economists. Left to themselves, these fields tend to develop partial theories that focus on either organizations or markets but without due consideration to the interactive effect of the other. The field of labor economics, for example, is prone to model wage determination as an auction market process in which wage rates are determined by supply and demand, similar to commodity prices. Employment relations, because it spans both markets and organizations, valuably demonstrates that when hierarchical organizations are introduced into the picture, the economist's model and predicted results are seriously compromised because they ignore the motivational aspect of wages. For example, wage cuts or wage differentials predicted by a supply–demand model may so harm morale or feelings of equity within organizations that they are counterproductive and thus not adopted (Levine 1993; Bewley 1999). Employment relations also valuably broadens the partial theories of management and organization theory. Certain theories of strategic human resource management predict, for example, that all firms would gain greater profits by adopting a high-performance work system (Delery and Doty 1996). But this conclusion is immediately called into question when macroeconomic conditions in product and labor markets are introduced (see the other Kaufman chapter in this volume). For example, fostering trust, unity of interest, and a win-win culture is difficult during a recession or depression when layoffs and wage cuts are made necessary, while motivating employees through the threat of dismissal becomes both cheaper and more effective than trying to accomplish this through high morale and esprit de corps.

Descending further in the level of analysis brings theorizing to the next-to-lowest level in the ERS: the labor process. Everything already discussed in the ERS now becomes superstructure, and the object of study is the individual employment relationship at the point of production. As was asked for other parts of the ERS, a baseline question to be answered by an integrative theory is why a labor process exists. Answering that, attention then turns to the structure, performance, and outcomes of the labor process. One aspect of the structure of the labor process is fundamental to the field of employment relations: the mix of conflicting and shared interests between the employee and employer. The labor process juxtaposes management's goal of maximum output at least cost with the worker's goal of reasonable work effort, high wages, and good benefits and conditions. To some degree the employment relationship thus places the two parties in an inevitably conflicting position, and out of this conflict arise many of the most important objects of study in the field, such as strikes, turnover, and protective labor laws. To date this conflict of interest has been largely assumed and stipulated rather than subjected to theoretical analysis. An integrative theory of employment relations should address this issue, explaining why a conflict of interest exists in the employment relationship, the extent to which it can be changed into a unity of interest, and the factors that determine the mix between conflict and cooperation. Also of interest are other issues such as the alternative control systems used by management to regulate the labor process and the counterstrategies used by workers to shift conditions in their favor.

We come, finally, to the lowest level of analysis in the employment relations system: the individual person, depicted by the human outline in figure 1. An integrative theory of employment relations requires a representation of the external environment that in various ways influences the employment relationship, such as the collective actors and social, economic, legal, and technological forces. But also required is a representation of the human beings who work and manage in the employment relationship and perform functions in all the other levels of the ERS. The challenge, however, is to construct a model of the human agent that is analytically tractable but also has good powers of explanation and prediction. One possibility is the rational actor model from economics, but while it passes the first test (analytical tractability) in many cases it fails or falls short in the second (explaining important outcomes and behaviors), at least without modification and extension. Examples of such modifications include incorporation of bounded rationality, interpersonal status and welfare comparisons, principles of fairness and justice, other self-concepts besides self-interest (e.g., self-esteem, self-efficacy), and a broader range of emotions than egoistic greed and desire (e.g., security, envy, hate, love). An integrative theory in employment relations thus requires a model of humanity that is more realistic and expansive than that used in economics, which is to say more congruent with and informed by theories and empirical evidence in psychology, sociology, and organizational behavior.

To summarize, I began this essay by stating that the model of an employment relations system presented here is intended to provide a guide to theorizing and, in particular, to answer three important questions that form the necessary condition for development of an integrative theory.

The first question is: What is the central object of study that an integrative theory should be built around? The answer is the employment relationship.

The second question is: What should the theory try to explain, or alternatively stated, what are the dependent variables in a theory of employment relations? The answer to this question depends on the level of analysis. At the highest level of analysis, the dependent variable is the existence and extent of the employment relationship; the explanatory variables are the exogenous social, legal, economic, technological, and state sovereignty forces in the external environment and the psychological and sociological properties of the human agent. Then cascading down to lower levels of analysis are other dependent variables. At the next lower level of analysis, for example, the dependent variable is the institutional structure and configuration of the employment relationship, while at the next lower level the dependent variables are the form, operation, and performance of individual institutions and functional areas in the employment relations system. Here, for example, relevant dependent variables are the existence and extent of trade unions or, alternatively, human resource management departments and their architecture and key outcomes and behaviors. The set of relevant independent variables likewise expands at successively lower levels of analysis, since factors that are endogenous at a higher level are predetermined and thus exogenous at a lower level. Finally, at the lowest level of analysis are all the individual personal and organizational outcomes and behaviors that emanate from the employment relationship, such as job satisfaction, work effort, plant-level productivity, extent of high-performance work practices, compensation and benefit levels, worker desire for union representation, and many others. Broadly stated, therefore, the dependent variables in employment relations are all the endogenously determined institutions, structures, outcomes, practices, and behaviors that emanate from or impinge upon the employment relationship.

Finally, the third question is: What are the key components and relationships that an integrative theory should include? The most compact answer would be "see figure 1." Expanding on this modestly, the most significant insight from the model presented in figure 1 concerns the relationship between organizations and markets. The employment relationship is the subject domain of industrial relations, and the employment relationship spans both markets and organizations. Organizations and markets, however, have heretofore been largely treated as exogenous and separate entities in the employment relations system. As a result, the management field and business schools have carved out theorizing about organizations, and the labor economics field has carved out theorizing about markets, while industrial relations—spanning the two—has been left with what appears to be a theoretical hollow spot. Forced to find some subject area that it might claim as its own for theorizing (and abetted by ideological commitments), the field has retreated to unionized employment relationships and labor–management relations, self-evidently only a part—and in many countries a small and declining part—of the employment relations system.

The solution to industrial relations' theory problem suggested here is to endogenize the boundary between organizations and markets, thus opening up a cause-and-effect relationship over which the boundary-spanning field of industrial relations can legitimately claim jurisdiction. At one extreme, for example, all economic activity takes place through single-person firms and is entirely coordinated by price and markets (an economy of "perfect decentralization"), giving rise to a complete absence of employment relationships (Kaufman 2003a). At another extreme, the economy is one giant organization with no private property rights, such as a pure socialist, centrally planned economy (an economy of "perfect centralization"), and again no employment relationship exists. In between are a multitude of permutations of markets and organizations and a multitude of alternative employment relations systems—all representing dependent variables for a theory of employment relations.

Conclusion

The field of industrial relations is currently in a state of decline and even crisis in the United States. A similar if less dire trend is also evident in many other countries. To secure its future, the field must attract a sufficient body of participants and "paying customers" through one of three routes. The first is to provide a body of theory or methods that are productive in research and science building; the second is to address an important and widespread body of applied problems; the third is to cover a subject deemed important for political or ideological reasons. In past decades the industrial relations field based its claim for a place in the social sciences largely on the second and third options. With the substantial decline of the labor movement and organized sector of the economy, these legs of support have noticeably weakened, leaving the field in an increasingly marginalized and threatened position.

One strategy to turn around the fortunes of the field is to take up the first option and develop a theoretical base for industrial relations. This suggestion is not a new one, as an earlier generation of industrial relations scholars invested considerable ingenuity and effort in endeavoring to construct industrial relations theory. This project produced relatively modest results, however, and at least in the United States most industrial relations scholars seem to have given up on the task of developing industrial relations theory.

The proposition advanced in this chapter is that some of the roadblocks and meager results in industrial relations theorizing stem from failure to correctly conceptualize the object of study, to identify the important questions and dependent variables, and to formulate the key processes and features to be modeled. My purpose has thus been to reconsider these matters and offer a new perspective. The new perspective begins with the very definition and conceptualization of the subject of industrial relations. On the basis of historical evidence, I contend that the central construct and object of study in industrial relations is the employment relationship. To more accurately convey this subject domain, a good case can be made that a better name for the field is *employment relations*. Next I developed a new version of Dunlop's concept of an industrial relations system, called an *employment relations system* (ERS). The ERS is a descriptive and taxonomic device that illustrates the subject domain covered by the field of employment relations and, more importantly, points out the key environmental forces, institutions, processes, and relationships that an integrative theory must include. The ERS was then used to draw out a variety of implications for an integrative theory of employment relations. The most important insight is that a theory of the employment relationship must necessarily explain the juxtaposition of organizations and markets, as this connection influences both the existence and configuration of the employment relationship. The virtues of this theoretical project are twofold. First, it gives theoretical substance to the field's claim to a unique and independent position in the social sciences as the "study of the employment relationship," and second, it carves out an area of theorizing that is currently not addressed in a significant way by any of the other work-related disciplines and fields of study.

In closing, the reader may agree with all that has been said to this point but still believe that little has been accomplished. After all, what this chapter has done is only to address the necessary condition for the development of a theory of employment relations theory—to identify the subject domain, dependent variables, and important components of an integrative theory. The hard, perhaps impossible, next step is to actually construct such a theory. Quite possibly, the road map of this chapter notwithstanding, the holy grail of an integrative theory will remain frustratingly out of reach.

I am optimistic, however, that the basis for an integrative theory exists. Indeed, the important concepts and ideas have already been developed and have merely to be refined, extended, and creatively put together. These intellectual threads are contained, I believe, in the field of institutional economics and, in particular, the theoretical writings of the academic father of the American field of industrial relations, John R. Commons, and other institutional economists such as Coase and Williamson.

Four of the central constructs needed for a theory of employment relations come from the work of these men: bounded rationality, the transaction and transaction cost, the incomplete nature of the labor contract, and the economy as a governance system (Medema 1996; Kaufman 2003a). Modern institutional economists have used these concepts to explain the existence of the employment relationship, the organizational structure of firms, and the decision to internalize or externalize production (Williamson 1985; Furubotn and Richter 1997). The fruitful application of these ideas to theorizing about employment relations systems is also gathering momentum, as illustrated in recent books by Hollingsworth and Boyer (1997), Marsden (1999), and Hall and Soskice (2001). (Also see the reviews by Godard and by Marsden in this volume.) It is beyond the scope of this chapter to go further into these matters, but I remain confident that through institutional economics we may yet discover the holy grail of industrial relations: an integrative theory of the employment relations system.

References

Adams, Roy. 1988. "Desperately Seeking Industrial Relations Theory." *International Journal of Comparative Labour Law and Industrial Relations*, Vol. 4, no. 1, pp. 1–10.

―――. 1993. "Theory Construction and a Checklist." In R. Adams and N. Meltz, eds., *Industrial Relations Theory: Its Scope, Nature, and Pedagogy.* Metuchen, NJ: Scarecrow, pp. 333–54.

―――. 1997. "Integrating Disparate Strands: An Elaborated Version of Systems Theory as a Framework for Organizing the Field of Industrial Relations." In J. Barbash and N. Meltz, eds., *Theorizing in Industrial Relations: Approaches and Applications.* Sydney: University of Sydney, pp. 29–56.

Barbash, Jack. 1984. *The Elements of Industrial Relations.* Madison: University of Wisconsin Press.

―――. 1993. "The Founders of Industrial Relations as a Field of Study: An American Perspective." In R. Adams and N. Meltz, eds., *Industrial Relations Theory: Its Nature, Scope, and Pedagogy.* Metuchen, NJ: Scarecrow, pp. 67–80.

Begin, James. 1991. *Strategic Employment Policy: An Organizational Systems Perspective.* Englewood Cliffs, NJ: Prentice Hall.

Bellace, Janice. 1994. "The Role of the State in Industrial Relations." In J. Niland, R. Lansbury, and C. Verevis, eds., *The Future of Industrial Relations: Global Change and Challenges.* London: Sage, pp. 19–40.

Bennett, James, and Bruce Kaufman. 2002. "The Future of Private Sector Unionism—Assessment and Forecast." In J. Bennett and B. Kaufman, eds., *The Future of Private Sector Unionism in the United States.* Armonk, NY: Sharpe, pp. 359–86.

Bewley, Truman. 1999. *Why Wages Don't Fall during a Recession.* Cambridge, MA: Harvard University Press.

Budd, John. 2004. *Employment with a Human Face: Balancing Efficiency, Equity, and Voice.* Ithaca, NY: Cornell University Press.

Chamberlain, Neil. 1960. "Issues for the Future." In *Proceedings of the Thirteenth Annual Meeting,* Madison, WI: Industrial Relations Research Association, pp. 101–9.

Clegg, Hugh. 1972. *The System of Industrial Relations in Great Britain.* Totowa, NJ: Rowman and Littlefield.

Coase, Ronald. 1937. "The Nature of the Firm." *Economica,* New Series, Vol. 4, no. 16 (November), pp. 386–405.

Commons, John. 1934. *Institutional Economics: Its Place in Political Economy.* New York: Macmillan.

———. 1950. *Economics of Collective Action.* Madison: University of Wisconsin Press.

Cox, Robert. 1971. "Approach to the Futurology of Industrial Relations." *International Institute for Labour Studies, Bulletin,* Vol. 8, pp. 139–64.

Delery, John, and D. Harold Doty. 1996. "Modes of Theorizing in Strategic Human Resource Management: Tests of Universalistic, Contingency, and Configurational Performance Predictions." *Academy of Management Journal,* Vol. 39, no. 4, pp. 802–35.

Dunlop, John. 1958. *Industrial Relations Systems.* New York: Holt.

———. 1993. *Industrial Relations Systems,* rev. ed. Cambridge: Harvard Business School Press.

Feldman, Herman. 1928. *Survey of Research in the Field of Industrial Relations.* New York: Social Science Research Council.

Furubotn, Erik, and Rudolph Richter. 1997. *Institutions and Economic Theory.* Ann Arbor: University of Michigan Press.

Hall, Peter, and David Soskice. 2001. *Varieties of Capitalism: The Institutional Foundations of Comparative Advantage.* Oxford: Oxford University Press.

Heneman, Herbert, Jr. 1969. "Toward a General Conceptual System of Industrial Relations: How Do We Get There?" In G. Somers, ed., *Essays in Industrial Relations Theory.* Ames: Iowa State University Press, pp. 3–24.

Hills, Stephen. 1993. "Integrating Industrial Relations and the Social Sciences." In R. Adams and N. Meltz, eds., *Industrial Relations Theory: Its Scope, Nature, and Pedagogy.* Metuchen, NJ: Scarecrow, pp. 183–226.

Hollingsworth, J. Rogers, and Robert Boyer. 1997. *Contemporary Capitalism: The Embeddedness of Institutions.* Cambridge: Cambridge University Press.

Hyman, Richard. 1995. Editorial. *European Journal of Industrial Relations,* Vol. 1 (March), pp. 9–16.

Kaufman, Bruce. 1989. "Models of Man in Industrial Relations Research." *Industrial and Labor Relations Review,* Vol. 43 (October), pp. 72–88.

———. 1993. *The Origins and Evolution of Industrial Relations in the United States.* Ithaca, NY: ILR Press.

———. 1999. "Expanding the Behavioral Foundations of Labor Economics." *Industrial and Labor Relations Review,* Vol. 52 (April), pp. 361–92.

———. 2003a. "The Organization of Economic Activity: Insights from the Institutional Theory of John R. Commons." *Journal of Economic Behavior and Organization,* Vol. 52, no. 1, pp. 71–96.

———. 2003b. "Sumner Slichter on Personnel Management and Employee Representation before the New Deal." In D. Lewin and B. Kaufman, eds., *Advances in Industrial and Labor Relations,* Vol. 12, New York: Elsevier, pp. 223–69.

————. 2004. *The Global Evolution of Industrial Relations: Events, Ideas, and the IIRA.* Geneva: International Labor Organization.

Kelly, Diana. In press. "The Transfer of Ideas in Industrial Relations: Dunlop and Oxford in the Development of Australian Industrial Relations Thought, 1960–85." In D. Lewin and B. Kaufman, eds., *Advances in Industrial and Labor Relations,* Vol. 13, New York: Elsevier.

Kelly, John. 1998. *Rethinking Industrial Relations: Mobilization, Collectivism and Long Waves.* London: Routledge.

Kochan, Thomas. 1993. "Teaching and Building Middle Range Industrial Relations Theory." In R. Adams and N. Meltz, eds., *Industrial Relations Theory: Its Nature, Scope, and Pedagogy.* Metuchen, NJ: Scarecrow, pp. 353–80.

————. 1998. "What Is Distinctive about Industrial Relations Research?" In G. Strauss and K. Whitfield, eds., *Researching the World of Work: Strategies and Methods in Studying Industrial Relations.* Ithaca, NY: ILR Press, pp. 31–50.

Laffer, Kingsley. 1974. "Is Industrial Relations an Academic Discipline?" *Journal of Industrial Relations,* Vol. 16 (March), pp. 62–73.

Lepak, David, and Scott Snell. 1999. "The Human Resource Architecture: Toward a Theory of Human Capital Allocation and Development." *Academy of Management Journal,* Vol. 24, no. 1, pp. 31–48.

Levine, David. 1993. "Fairness, Markets, and Ability to Pay." *American Economic Review,* Vol. 83 (December), pp. 1241–59.

Marsden, David. 1999. *A Theory of Employment Systems.* Oxford: Oxford University Press.

Marsden, Richard. 1982. "Industrial Relations: A Critique of Empiricism." *Sociology,* Vol. 16 (May), pp. 232–50.

Medema, Steven. 1996. "Ronald Coase and American Institutionalism." In *Research in the History of Economic Thought and Methodology,* Greenwich, CT: JAI Press, pp. 51–92.

Meltz, Noah. 1989. "Industrial Relations: Balancing Efficiency and Equity." In J. Barbash and K. Barbash, eds., *Theories and Concepts in Comparative Industrial Relations,* Columbia: University of South Carolina Press, pp. 109–13.

————. 1993. "Industrial Relations Systems as a Framework for Organizing Contributions to Industrial Relations Theory." In R. Adams and N. Meltz, eds., *Industrial Relations Theory: Its Scope, Nature, and Pedagogy,* Metuchen, NJ: Scarecrow, pp. 161–82.

Morris, Richard. 1997. "The Old Concept of Employment Relations and Its Modern Renaissance." In R. Morris, ed., *Essays in Employment Relations Theory,* Nepean, Australia: Centre for Employment Relations, University of Western Sydney, pp. 67–86.

National Industrial Conference Board. 1931. *Industrial Relations: Administration of Policies and Programs.* New York: National Industrial Conference Board.

Olson, Mancur. 1965. *The Logic of Collective Action.* Cambridge, MA: Harvard University Press.

Russell Sage Foundation. 1919. *Industrial Relations: A Selected Bibliography.* New York: Russell Sage Foundation.

Shultz, George. 1968. "Priorities in Policy and Research for Industrial Relations." In *Proceedings of the Twenty-first Annual Winter Meeting,* Madison, WI: Industrial Relations Research Association, pp. 1–13.

Simon, Herbert. 1951. "A Formal Theory of the Employment Relationship," Vol. 19 (July), pp. 293–305.

Strauss, George, and Keith Whitfield. 1998. "Research Methods in Industrial Relations." In G. Strauss and K. Whitfield, eds., *Researching the World of Work: Strategies and Methods in Studying Industrial Relations,* Ithaca, NY: ILR Press, pp. 5–30.

U.S. Bureau of Labor Statistics. 1930. *Personnel Research Agencies.* Bulletin no. 518. Washington, DC: Government Printing Office.

Wheeler, Hoyt. 1985. *Industrial Conflict: An Integrative Theory.* Columbia: University of South Carolina Press.

Wheeler, Hoyt, and John McClendon. 1991. "The Individual Decision to Unionize." In G. Strauss et al., eds., *The State of the Unions,* Madison, WI: Industrial Relations Research Association, pp. 47–83.

Williamson, Oliver. 1985. *The Economic Institutions of Capitalism.* New York: Free Press.

CHAPTER 3

Employment Systems: Workplace HRM Strategies and Labor Institutions

DAVID MARSDEN
London School of Economics

For many years, our thinking about employment relations and human resource management (HRM) has been conditioned by collective bargaining and its presumed opposite, individual bargaining by workers with their employers. Whereas collective bargaining has been overtly concerned with the joint making of institutional rules, HRM has often been associated with individual bargaining and with workers' being faced with a take-it-or-leave-it offer of management-determined rules. According to this perception, one is faced with a contrast between joint governance and unilateral management action. In the latter, management is often seen as having a more or less free hand in the design of work rules and workplace administrative systems. Using the typology of workplace HRM systems compiled by Sherer and Leblebici (2001; see table 1 on page 84), for example, we might consider managers as being largely free to choose between the different models according to their commercial objectives.

In this paper, I should like to argue that this conception is mistaken and that we need to pay more attention to the dynamics of the employment relationship, treating it as a social institution that has to satisfy the joint requirements of those who adopt it, both firms and workers. In the first section of the paper, I examine the structure of the employment relationship and the requirements that it must satisfy to be viable. In the next two sections, I trace out how this view affects our understanding of the dynamics of different kinds of HRM systems at the workplace level and how it should refocus our approach to labor institutions, and in doing so, I also explore how the analysis can be applied to some of the emerging employment patterns, such as project-based employment, which at first sight might appear to challenge its foundations.

The need to refocus our analytical lens is highlighted by the shrinking coverage of collective bargaining across much of the industrial world and the consequent need to reexamine our theories of formal labor institutions. For many years, the "nonunion" sector could be treated as governed by spillover effects from the organized sector or by recalcitrant employers who treated their workers harshly and quite logically sought to keep unions out. Often, it was just ignored. More recently, it has been described by some prominent industrial relations scholars as a "black hole" (see Guest and Conway 1999). This intellectual blind spot is no longer defensible. The decline of union strength in the United States and Britain has been well-known for some years. However, even in Germany, long the exemplar of organized corporatist relations between employers and employees, observers have become increasingly aware of the shrinking coverage of the traditional pillars of the German model and the emergence of a large "codetermination free zone"; nearly half of all West German workers are in plants with no works councils (Addison, Bellmann, Schnabel, and Wagner 2002), and the share of West German workers outside the coverage of industry agreements grew from 28% to 36% between 1995 and 2001 (Kohaut and Schnabel 2003). A good deal of the decline in coverage of established labor institutions has occurred at the same time as a major economic expansion, and one in which skill requirements, and hence skilled workers' individual bargaining power, have been increasing in a great many jobs. Long-term jobs remain a prominent feature of advanced industrial economies and outside certain sectors (Organisation for Economic Co-operation and Development [OECD] 1997:chap. 5). Although low-wage employment has increased in a number of countries, such as the United States and the United Kingdom, its growth across countries does not coincide neatly with declines in collective regulation. The decline in coverage of established forms of collective representation does not therefore appear to have led to a rise in industrial disorder. To understand why, we need to look more closely at the employment relationship.

The Employment Relationship and Work Rules

The employment relationship is the central social and economic institution in labor markets and is the foundation of the modern firm as an employing organization. It solves a very difficult coordination problem: how to achieve the gains from cooperation between self-interested parties, given that each knows more than the other about important aspects of their joint work and that separation is costly.

For much of the 19th century, subcontracting had worked well when the outcomes could be easily defined and monitored.[1] But it reached its limits as technical change and increasing complexity of production meant that firms wanted more direct control over the work process and wanted to tailor work tasks more closely to their own organizational needs. This meant becoming able to redefine workers' assignments without renegotiation or with greatly reduced negotiation. To do this, firms needed a new contractual form: the open-ended employment relationship.

For workers who distrusted the intentions of potential employers, an open-ended contract would have seemed a recipe for exploitation, and so it would become attractive only as various protections were integrated. Coase (1937) captured its essence: it gives employers the authority to define workers' tasks *ex post* "within certain limits." These limits cannot be set by exhaustive job descriptions with complex contingency clauses (Williamson 1975). Apart from the cost of writing such contracts, they would not work because their very detail would create endless scope for job-level bargaining. The solution that gradually emerged was to use certain kinds of transaction rules, or work rules, to identify the limits of managerial authority and the limits of employees' obligations. To be effective, such rules have to be simple enough to be applied by ordinary workers and their line managers, far from the help of personnel departments and legal advice. The earliest such rules tended to identify certain kinds of work tasks, either by their complementarity, as in the case of the "work post" rule common in French and U.S. forms of Taylorism, or by the tools and materials associated with certain tasks, as was common under British and U.S. craft demarcation rules ("job territory" rules). Although Taylorism was originally a management invention—as Crozier's (1963) and Slichter, Healy, and Livernash's (1960) field studies illustrate so well—the work posts very quickly transformed into a defensive mechanism for workers. Defining their jobs also delimited their obligations. In more recent years, work rules have developed that focus on functions rather than individual tasks. Although they are more flexible, they also require higher levels of trust and more complex relationships between work groups and management. Well-known examples can be found in the flexible work organization of large Japanese firms, where, as discussed later on, the "competence rank" rule often guides the distribution of tasks within work groups (Koike 1997; Yamanouchi and Okazaki-Ward 1997). Similarly, in Germany, the "qualification" rule commonly assigns work according to its skill requirements (Sengenberger 1987). Both of the latter rules establish a much looser relationship between tasks and workers' jobs, improving task flexibility.

They do so by focusing on functions related either to production needs or to workers' skills. Labor law and collective agreements have helped reinforce these work rules.

A *Typology of Transaction Rules*

The same four broad types of employment rules can also be derived logically from the requirements for a viable form of contracting. They therefore have the special status of "constitutive rules." To derive this typology, we need to consider the sufficient and necessary conditions such rules must fulfill if there is to be a viable relationship over time. I assume that firms and workers are basically self-interested and subject to bounded rationality. There are also important informational asymmetries between the two parties; both parties face costs if they break off the relationship, and each knows that the other's interests overlap but are not identical with their own. There is therefore scope for either party to behave opportunistically once the relationship has started, and both are aware of this.

The key to the relative economic advantages of the employment contract lies in the scope of the *ex post* definition of a worker's duties within the employment relationship compared with the *ex ante* specification of work outcomes or tasks required in the case of self-employment. Enforcing open-market contracts, such as in self-employment, is made relatively easy because the terms of the contract are agreed on in advance and the parties have an interest in ensuring that the degree of ambiguity is small. The situation is quite different with the open-ended employment relationship, which is more like an agreement to work together, albeit under the employer's direction, than a market exchange. Sunk costs can be considerable on both sides: at a minimum, job search and recruitment are expensive, and the sunk costs rise if there is significant investment in firm-specific skills and such. There are great potential gains, particularly for employers, from the open-ended nature of the relationship. The costs and rigidities of defining tasks or outputs *ex ante* are avoided, and firms do not need to know the precise timing with which they will need certain kinds of work. Coase (1937) and Simon (1951) developed the different aspects of these benefits in their two famous articles. Slichter, Healy, and Livernash (1960) and Williamson (1975), in different ways, showed the costs of trying to work with tightly defined tasks and work assignments, and Crozier (1963) showed the perverse effects of defining work tasks in too much detail. This helps explain why, even though there is real choice, nine out of ten workers are engaged as employees in the advanced industrial economies (OECD 1992:chap. 4).

Limits to managerial authority are essential, and they can be most effectively provided by some kind of rule. We therefore need to consider what the *sufficient* and *necessary* attributes of such rules are for a viable employment relationship, a relationship that will be freely chosen over its main alternative: self-employment governed by a sales contract. Taken together, these are represented by the *efficiency* and the *enforceability* constraints.

A *sufficient* condition for workers and firms to choose to cooperate through an employment relationship is that the relationship be mutually beneficial compared with the alternatives. The arguments of Coase (1937) and Simon (1951) take us part of the way by showing the overall gains that can arise as compared with the main alternative, some kind of sales contract. However, this argument is not sufficient because it is possible that one party will try to appropriate all the gains. Given the costs each has sunk in the relationship, the losing party may often be worse off if this happens. A *necessary* condition, therefore, is the existence of a rule that ensures that both parties gain, in other words, a rule that clarifies the extent of employees' obligations to their employers in a way that can be enforced. Unless this can be done, one or other party will refuse to engage in the relationship. However, enforceability is not enough on its own. Work assignments could be determined by the color of an employee's eyes. Enforceable rules must also be productively efficient and must define obligations in such a way that employees' competencies match employers' job demands. Indeed, by aligning these, the rule boosts the "added value" of the employment relationship by organizing the training process and job classification systems.

Satisfying the enforceability and efficiency constraints together is necessary and sufficient to ensure a viable employment relationship. As a result, one can regard the two constraints as the basis for an exhaustive classification of employment rules, given the basic assumptions of the Coase–Simon approach. Broadly speaking, employment rules can satisfy each constraint in one of two ways, and this founds the typology of rules shown in figure 1.

There are two broad approaches by which employment rules establish the enforceability of work assignments. They may focus either directly on attributes of individual work tasks or indirectly on functions within the production or service process. A famous example of the first, widely found in craft work environments, is to identify the tasks belonging to

FIGURE 1

Contractual Constraints and Common Employment Rules

| | | Efficiency constraint Job demands identified by: | |
		Production approach	Training approach
Enforceability constraint The focus of enforcement criteria:	Task-centered	Work post rule	Job territory or "tools of trade" rule
	Function- or procedure-centered	Competence rank rule	Qualification rule

particular "job territories" by the tools or materials used: the tools of the trade. Such simple rules provide a very robust way of delimiting the boundaries of the jobs of one group of workers and determining where those of another begin. In professional work, where distinctive tools figure less prominently, boundaries are often drawn by identifying key operations that must be undertaken only by those holding a particular qualification. Another famous rule, common in both blue- and white-collar environments, is that of the "work post," under which tasks are grouped according to complementarities in production and assigned exclusively to individual work stations for which individual workers are responsible. Usually, neither of these rules is enforced rigidly, but the important thing is that everyone knows they may be invoked should work relations deteriorate. Likewise, management tends to enforce work rules strictly only in periodic crackdowns when effort seems to be drifting in the wrong direction. "Working to rule" is a pressure tactic and not usually the normal method of working.

The other approach to enforceability is to assign work tasks on the basis of functions. Mostly, these transcend the jobs of individual workers and so rely heavily on stable dynamics within work groups. It can be shown that a seniority- or competence-based ranking rule can enable a flexible allocation of tasks within a work group (Marsden 1999:chap. 2). Similarly, recognized qualifications can be used to assign types of work that pose similar technical demands. Enforcement is trickier for function-centered rules than for task-centered rules and depends on a higher degree of cooperation between workers and management. Function-centered rules are vulnerable to a breakdown in trust, there being no safety net of minimal compliance as under task-related rules, and this vulnerability is a strong incentive for employers to behave cooperatively.

To satisfy the efficiency constraint, work assignments can be organized according to complementarities either in production or in training.

These are the *production* and *training* approaches. They diverge mainly because of the different cost structures of informal on-the-job training (OJT) and formal off-the-job instruction. The first has low setup costs, but costs rise steeply as the share of trainees increases. The second has high setup costs because of the investment in special training facilities, but falling average costs per trainee. Organizing work according to production complementarities leads to what Williamson (1975) called "idiosyncratic" jobs, whereas seeking to maximize the utilization of expensive training causes firms to group tasks according to their training requirements. Intermediate forms, between the production and training approaches, tend to be unstable, gravitating to one or other form over time (Marsden 1999).

Employment Rules and Workplace HRM Strategies

In their survey of strategic HRM research, Sherer and Leblebici (2001) sketched out a number of common types of workplace HRM systems that can be identified in the literature: low-wage, HRM/high-commitment, Japanese-oriented, and joint team-based systems. In doing so, they drew heavily on the international survey by Katz and Darbishire (2000) and U.S. work by Baron, Burton, and Hannan (1996, 1999). In their study, Katz and Darbishire (2000) also identified a bureaucratic model that can be either union or nonunion. One can construct an additional type of system, based on research on project-based work in the media and information technology sectors (e.g., Tolbert 1996; Baumann 2003; Haunschild 2003). These systems are summarized in table 1. In terms of the analysis of the employment relationship, they fall into two broad categories, depending on whether management's authority to assign tasks is determined in relation to individual jobs, as is commonly the case in the low-wage and bureaucratic systems, or whether it is defined in more abstract functional terms, as in the case of high-performance systems. I shall argue that the former group belongs to the task-centered approach and the latter to the function-centered approach.

A key feature of the bureaucratic system is that work tasks are divided up between a set of jobs and workers are assigned to these individually, each one accountable for performance at a given work post. Maurice, Mannari, Takeoka, and Inoki (1988) described this one-to-one accountability as one of the defining features of Taylorist work organization in France, and the same is true of Taylorist work organization in many other countries, such as the United States (Cole 1994). This approach provides one solution to the problem of establishing recognizable limits

TABLE 1

Examples of Workplace Human Resource Management Systems

Model	Low-wage	Bureaucratic/ mass production	HRM	Japanese-oriented	Joint team-based	Network/ project employment
Performance type	Cost-minimizing	Managerial discretion with formal management set procedures	High-performance	High-performance	High-performance	High-performance
Nature of authority	Managerial discretion with informal procedures	Hierarchical, unilaterally decided work patterns organized around the "job"	Corporate culture and extensive communication	Standardized procedures	Joint decision making	Likely to be agreed; reputation a key to future work
Nature of work coordination	Hierarchical work relations	Pay for the job or grade	Directed teams	Problem-solving teams	Semi-autonomous work groups	Project team
Reward systems	Low wages with piece rates	Promotion systems based on management appraisal in internal labor markets and some job security	Above-average wages with contingent pay	High pay linked to seniority and performance appraisals	High pay with pay-for-knowledge	Base pay for job plus "royalties" and enhanced reputation
Learning and careers	High turnover	Seniority by custom or agreement	Individualized career development	Employment stabilization	Career development	Boundaryless career, professional qualifications, and progression to more demanding work
Employment security	None, based on management	Seniority rules common	Some, based on rules	Long-term, based on formal rules (in U.S.)	Long-term, jointly determined	Duration of project
Basis for selection	Availability	Standardized criteria	Skill	Cultural fit	Potential	Informal contacts (weak ties)
Basis for attachment	Money with piece rates	Money with fixed pay-progression rules	Money with contingent pay	Loyalty with identification	Challenging work	Occupational community
Nature of union organization	Strong anti-union bias	Union rules solidify management practice	Union substitution	Enterprise unionism	Union and employee involvement	"Hiring hall" as labor market intermediary
Where found?	Most countries	Many countries	U.S.	Japan, U.S.	Germany, Sweden	Media, high tech, universities

Based on Katz and Darbishire (2000), Baron, Burton, and Hannan (1996, 1999), Sherer and Leblebici (2001), Baumann (2003), and Haunschild (2003).

to management's authority to assign work. By having a series of work posts, each with its own discrete set of tasks, workers know where their own jobs and obligations to their employer end and those of other workers begin. In a study of the introduction of new flexible methods of working in such an environment, Clark (1993) found that many workers were unhappy with the new arrangement because the loss of clear job boundaries left them exposed to the threat of sanctions from management for not doing their jobs properly. Likewise, in a study of flexible work systems in France, Dugué (1994) reported that the new ambiguity about work roles and their related competencies left workers feeling exposed to arbitrary sanctions from management for poor performance. Koike (in a conversation about his fieldwork in Japanese and U.S. manufacturing plants at a seminar in Tokyo, June 2000) also stressed workers' fears of exposure to management favoritism under more flexible systems.

The bureaucratic system also simplifies the monitoring of worker performance by management. As Reynaud (1992) remarked, simplifying and codifying jobs mean that outputs can be more easily defined and quantified. As is well-known, when jobs involve multiple tasks, some of which are easily quantified and monitored and others not, there is a built-in bias toward performance of the former at the expense of the latter (Holmstrom and Milgrom 1991).

It is easy to see that one consequence of organizing jobs in this way is a dualism between tasks of conception and those of execution. Because each worker has a discrete area of accountability, experience and skills developed on the job develop as a mirror reflection of the job, and workers do not usually develop a holistic understanding of the overall objectives of their work, be it a production or a service activity. On the basis of Holmstrom and Milgrom's (1991) analysis of multitasking, an optimal solution for top management is to separate routine production tasks from those of coordination and quality control. Thus, a common solution is to have specialist line managers and specialist quality inspectors whose performance can be evaluated and rewarded separately.

Although this analysis has focused on a somewhat stylized description, we can see quite easily how key features of the bureaucratic system of HRM fit around one means of limiting management's authority to regulate the content of the employment contract *ex post*.

At first glance, we might think that high-performance work systems, especially those with well-developed patterns of flexible work, defy this rule. Because there is some debate about how far North American models of Japanese-oriented work systems have really broken with the bureaucratic model—some writers describe it as "team Taylorism"—I propose to address Japanese-oriented systems as they occur in Japan. The greater agreement about the high degree of task flexibility there makes it a stronger test of the argument about the limits to management's authority within the employment relationship.

A widely noted feature of Japanese work organization in private manufacturing firms is the substitution of the work area or function for the job or work post as the basic organizational unit (Coriat 1991; Koike 1997). Rather than assigning jobs to individual workers, groups or teams assume responsibility for a certain area of work. A number of key features contribute to restricting management bad faith over work assignments. The first of these is the greater risk or moral hazard to which *both* parties are exposed. Unlike strict job boundaries, work groups provide no safety net of minimum prescribed performance or maximum demands. Moreover, management now has to deal with teams of workers that provide a basis for work-group power, which the individualized jobs and performance monitoring of the older Taylorist system were believed to undermine. This increases management's dependence on cooperative work relations. Thus, one element in stability arises from increasing the likely costs to management from a breakdown of cooperation.

A second feature that restricts management bad faith is work rules that give a stable structure to the work group and its relations with management. This structure is necessary to sustain the work group's internal coherence, which is the foundation for both flexible work and the group's relations with management. A widespread practice is to rank members of the work group according to the competencies that they have acquired, which are a function of the range of tasks management recognizes that they can undertake. Thus, senior workers can undertake a wider range of tasks than more junior ones. This ranking protects senior workers against replacement by junior ones and provides junior workers with an incentive to develop their skills with the help of senior ones. Koike (1994) described a common practice used in Japanese plants to underpin this exchange: the publicly displayed job grade matrix. In this matrix, each worker can see what skills management has recognized in him or her and how he or she is ranked vis-à-vis fellow workers. An additional protection against managerial favoritism, which is a particular danger when heavy reliance is placed upon judgmental appraisals of employees, is the rotation of line managers among groups, which enables the personnel department to monitor consistency of evaluations of individual employees.

In this particular type of high-performance work system, workers are given incentives to progressively enlarge the range and complexity of tasks that they undertake over time, which brings management a benefit in terms of job flexibility. By encouraging work-group formation, management creates a potentially more powerful basis for opposition and gives workers enhanced means to monitor and control how its authority over work assignments is exercised, in contrast to the individualistic focus of Taylorism.

Thus, the success of this strong example of a high-performance work system hinges on its ability to provide a functional equivalent to the protections for employees under the bureaucratic model. Management's choice of HR practices in other areas is constrained once this solution has been adopted. If a team organization is adopted and there are no individual work posts, then line management's role is changed. Performance management also changes. One cannot measure individual outputs in team production, although one can evaluate individual workers' team-related behavior, such as how cooperative they are and how willing they are to share knowledge and skills with their fellow workers and management. Likewise, rewards tied to individual output make little sense if that output cannot be easily measured, so rewards might be tied to other aspects of performance, as appraised, or to group outcomes. Thus, one can trace many of the linkages between different HR practices that belong to the different models outlined in table 1.

The discussion so far has focused on the way solutions to the enforceability constraint influence the choice of related HR practices. A second axis of differentiation can be found in the way the efficiency constraint is handled. This concerns the distinction between organizing work around the demands of the production system and organizing it around the skills that workers bring with them: respectively, the production and the training approaches. The training approach introduces a new dimension because of the additional criterion of establishing employees' task areas in relation to the skills they have acquired, particularly occupational or professional skills. Craft work organization, as is common in the construction trades in many countries, and professional bureaucracies follow the task-centered approach, defining the boundaries of the work undertaken by skilled and professional workers by certain key types of tasks. Work involving the tools or the materials of the trade has long been used in blue-collar craft work as the criterion for job boundaries. Similar distinctions exist between the work of different professional employees and between professional and nonprofessional employees.

Again, because of the debate about the degree of differentiation in the United States among the models outlined in table 1, it is better to take a strong example of an environment in which occupational skills are widely recognized as limiting management's powers to assign work flexibly. Sherer and Leblebici (2001) and the authors whose work they reviewed cited GM as an example of a U.S. firm adopting the joint team-based approach to workplace HRM, whereas Katz and Darbishire (2000) stressed Germany and Sweden in their international study. If one uses occupational skills to determine job boundaries, a number of consequences follow for the structure of workplace HRM. Line management relations are often determined by the asymmetry of technical competence between principal and agent. This often precludes close supervision unless the line manager also possesses the same skills. In any case, it is usually more economic for management to delegate a certain amount of decision making because workers have the necessary technical skills to make the appropriate choices. Seniority is unlikely to play a key role in work allocation and progression because of the emphasis on peer-recognized training and work experience as criteria for access to skilled work. Unlike the stylized Japanese work system, where the work group was relatively homogeneous and structured on the basis of progression in seniority and task competencies, reliance on occupational skills tends to segment the workforce along occupational lines, restricting upgrading opportunities for the less qualified and restricting rewards for firm-specific as opposed to occupational skills.

There has been growing interest in project-based employment and in the so-called network economy as a new variant of high-performance HR systems, as signaled by the keynote theme of the International Industrial Relations Association's Berlin Conference in 2003. Thus, any theory of the employment relationship should have some analytical purchase on this kind of contractual arrangement. The key difference between this kind of employment and the established employment relationship is its transient nature, defined by the expected duration of a particular project, such as making a film, a CD, or an advertisement in the media industries. One important characteristic of such activities—distinguishing them from more traditional forms of self-employment where there is a specific product whose delivery can be agreed upon in advance, as in freelance translation work (e.g., Fraser and Gold 2001)—is that the workers involved are expected to cooperate flexibly. Project-based employment also shares this feature with high-performance work systems. Although the relationship is temporally defined, it remains open-ended in terms of the work to be undertaken (Baumann 2003; Haunschild 2003). Might we not argue that this demonstrates that firms are able to contract for the provision of specific labor services on the open market and still retain the flexibility to adapt the content of these services as management deems necessary?

Closer scrutiny of the available evidence indicates that these project-based employment relationships are built on protections that are functionally equivalent to those identified in the mainstream employment relationship. These protections provide incentives and means of enforcing good faith cooperation equivalent to those in indefinite-duration employment. Indeed, Haunschild (2003) characterized the project-based employment relations he observed in the German theater industry as governed by an "inter-organisational employment system." Baumann (2003) made similar observations in his comparison of the British and German film industries. As did Tolbert (1996) in her study of high-tech sectors, they note the importance of occupational norms in guiding the organization of work and the importance of "occupational communities" as a key source of sanctions against noncooperative behavior. Reputation on its own is inadequate because people may provide false information on others' past performance in order to denigrate their competitors, whereas within an established social network one has better means to judge the reliability of the source of such information. In addition, social and professional norms among members often help to underpin reliable behavior. In this kind of employment, there are often also alternative financial incentives to deferred salary, such as royalty-type payments that accrue from the additional commercial use of film rights (Paul and Kleingartner 1994) and stock options, which also enable the project coordinator to translate current performance into future rewards.

Thus, the way in which flexibility within the employment relationship is regulated can be seen to have a major influence in shaping the workplace human resource strategy. In *A Theory of Employment Systems* (Marsden 1999), I argued that satisfying the two contractual constraints provides a necessary and sufficient condition for a viable employment relationship that is acceptable to both firm and worker. If these conditions are not satisfied, then at least one of the parties would be better off to opt for an alternative contractual framework. Being necessary and sufficient means that, given the basic assumptions, an exhaustive typology can be based on these two constraints, so that, in theory, other typologies should be able to fit into this one.[2] In the augmented typology of strategic HRM models in table 1, it seems that the low-wage and bureaucratic models belong within the task-centered production approach, and the

Japanese-oriented model belongs within the function-centered production approach. The team-based model belongs under the training approach, and depending on how flexibly job boundaries are regulated, it belongs in either the task- or the function-centered approach. The HRM model, on account of its strong degree of management control, seems to belong to the task-centered production approach. The tensions reported within it seem to indicate that although management would like to obtain the flexibility of the function-centered approach, the strong degree of control pulls it back toward the task-centered approach (e.g., Baraldi, Dumasy, and Troussier 1995 on experiments in France). Finally, many versions of project-based employment as practiced in the media sectors appear to combine function-centered control and the training approach.

Regulating the Employment Relationship: The Role of Labor Institutions

Turning to the contribution of labor institutions to the employment relationship, I should like to focus on the way in which their presence helps to reinforce the effectiveness of the employment rules underpinning it. I shall focus especially on the way in which interfirm institutions enrich the range of sanctions either party may apply to enforce its understanding of employment rules. Renegotiation is an especially problematic time because the sunk costs in the relationship have made the exit option expensive. However, this is only one of a range of problems in which interfirm institutions can boost the flexibility of the employment relationship. I shall consider first some of the common problems that arise under microlevel bargaining and then some that arise especially under the training approach. In both cases, collective action plays a key role by involving actors that are external to the immediate transaction, and through their involvement, these actors contribute to both the individual and the collective benefits from an effective coordination mechanism: the employment relationship.

The Control of Externalities in Microbargaining

Although the work rules outlined earlier solve the problem of defining the limits of managerial authority over work assignments, the rules themselves can become the object of moral hazard, which can take several forms:

- Either party may take advantage of information asymmetries to impose their interpretation of a given rule.

- There may be mutual gains from a flexible application of the rule, provided that this is not used to redefine the rule itself.

- Changing economic circumstances require that work rules be adapted periodically, and this has to be achieved without opening up every-thing for renegotiation.

- Work rules function more stably if their broad principles are codified in some kind of collective agreement (e.g., in a classification agreement).

Most social rules create scope for individuals to find shortcuts that are attractive precisely because everyone else is observing the rule. Lying and queue jumping are good examples. Thus, workers may enter an employment relationship in the expectation that management will respect the spirit of certain employment rules, only to find all sorts of pretexts being used to justify different tasks or higher work loads. Like-wise, workers may take advantage of their greater job knowledge to try to pull the wool over the eyes of their managers (for some good examples see Roy 1952 and Burawoy 1979). How can individual workers or managers enforce what they believe to be the fair interpretation? Often it is difficult within the confines of an individual workplace. On the other hand, if either side can call on the support of an outside organiza-tion, a union or an employer's association, then there is scope for esca-lating the dispute. This has two important implications. First, it increases the ability of individual work groups and managers to draw on additional support and so raises the potential sanctions against oppor-tunistic application of work rules. This in itself can increase the readi-ness of workers and managers to accept particular work rules, because they are more confident that a fair interpretation can be enforced. Sec-ond, any outside coalition would quickly dissipate its strength if it sup-ported every grievance, so it must be selective. Thus, unions and employer organizations have every reason to judge which of their mem-bers' grievances should be backed up and which refused. They there-fore usually wish to discourage opportunistic claims. Brown (1973) gave some apt examples of how workplace shop steward committees refused to back what they felt were opportunistic claims of workplace custom by some groups that threatened to undermine their overall bargaining rela-tionship, which benefited all work groups in the firm. Thus, interfirm coalitions of workers and firms can contribute to the greater effective-ness of employment rules in two ways. They increase the confidence of individual groups that they can resist unfair action by the other party, and they can police the actions of their own members and so discourage action in bad faith.

Support of interfirm institutions also facilitates flexible application of rules in the workplace. One of the problems of the flexible application of rules in a decentralized environment, especially when the rules are only partially codified, is that this can cause the actual content of the rule to drift over time as today's flexibility becomes tomorrow's norm. If the rule's point of reference is embedded in current work-group relations, it is hard to resist this process. On the other hand, if there is a collective agreement or an informal norm that applies across workplaces, as can be found in craft demarcation rules, then there is an external point of comparison. If people know that the baseline of their cooperation will not be compromised by working flexibly, then it is easier to envisage doing so.

Institutions external to the firm can also assist with adapting employment rules to changing economic and technical circumstances. It is very difficult for the parties to engage in such negotiations at the workplace level because the outcome affects the applicability of the employment rules, and this affects the power of either side to sustain its position. It is therefore much safer for individual groups to refuse negotiation or to stall and thus to slow change. It is much easier to renegotiate employment rules when supported by such institutions. A striking example of this can be found in the Dutch flexibility agreements, which, once agreed at the highest level, created a framework for change at the local level. Visser (1998) argued that this enabled the very rapid spread of new practices across firms in the Netherlands, whereas relying on decentralized renegotiation of employment terms had proved very slow and uneven.

Finally, job classification rules, especially when applied across firms, aid the transparency of job regulation. They respond to one of the fundamental problems of economic organization highlighted by Simon (1951) and Williamson (1975). When economic agents are only boundedly rational, they need a language with which to handle the complexity of job information. This is provided by job classifications. In effect, these serve as the agreed-upon criteria for comparing jobs within and between firms. They are used for determining pay rates for different kinds of work, and they can be used to determine work standards by fixing the qualification required on hiring. They can also guide people within organizations regarding work demands and performance standards.

In his very perceptive study, Jacoby (1985) showed how central job classification was to the development of modern pay and performance management systems in the United States and in particular how they served to replace the internal contract system. This gives a clue to their wider significance, which has not been fully appreciated. Except for auction markets, where people are trading unique goods, one cannot have a set of prices without an equivalent set of categories to which they apply. What job classifications do in the first instance is to establish such categories. However, as Jacoby (1985) showed, they also play a critical role in personnel administration. They enable management to coordinate the work of the diverse range of employees within the organization and to know what kinds of tasks different employees can be expected to perform, to what standards of performance they can be expected to perform them, and at what rate of pay.

The Control of Externalities under the Training Approach

The training approach to work organization and identifying legitimate work assignments takes employee skills as given and organizes jobs and work assignments around them. Using occupational skills simplifies a number of job regulation problems as compared with the production approach, because the training process helps to socialize workers and line managers to accepted norms of work distribution and job performance.[3]

On the other hand, the training approach and the occupational markets associated with it are vulnerable to various types of free-rider actions that need to be controlled by interfirm institutions. As is well known, Becker (1975) predicted that trainees would bear the cost of training for transferable skills because their very transferability means that employers cannot be sure of any return on their investment. Nevertheless, most of the empirical research on training costs for blue-collar apprenticeships shows that, overall, the costs borne by employers are considerable, even when low rates of apprentice pay and their productive contribution during training are taken into account. Becker would predict that under such conditions employers would cut back on such training and one would see a decline as has occurred in British apprenticeship training in recent decades.

Most of the arguments advanced by economists to explain why employers nevertheless pay for general or transferable training depend on the existence of some kind of "stickiness," mostly attributed to informational problems. However, these are absent in the case of certified skills. Hence, the critical role of institutional regulation of occupational markets lies in the control of any tendencies by individual employers to "defect" (e.g., by cutting their training budgets and cherry-picking workers trained by others). Without institutional support, occupational markets are unstable because the greater the shortage of skills, the greater the incentives to poach and the fewer the incentives to provide general training. The decline of apprenticeship training in Britain compared with its continued vitality in Germany illustrates this process (Marsden 1995).

Employer provision of training for occupational skills incurs a competitive disadvantage only if some firms train and others do not. As a result, if the high involvement of firms is maintained, the temptation to free-ride is correspondingly weaker. Likewise, it is easier to sanction a small number of free riders than a large number. Hence, provided that a high overall rate of training can be sustained, it is possible to avoid entering a vicious circle in which employer cutbacks on training cause skill shortages, which then raise the incentive to free-ride, engendering further shortages.

Occupational markets also require other forms of institutional support to function. If costs are to be shared, then trainees need to be sure that employers will provide suitable vacancies for them, and there also needs to be sufficient standardization of training contents and standards. Thus, from both the employers' and the employees' sides, we arrive at the need for an institutional infrastructure to support the working of occupational markets and thus the training approach within the employment relationship.

The evidence on project-based employment suggests that it is best thought of as subject to the pressures of the training approach because of the weakness of the attachment to any single firm or organization. This emerges clearly from Tolbert's (1996) contribution to *The Boundaryless Career*. She and subsequent writers have stressed the role of "occupational communities," which perform functions similar to those of more formal organizational bodies. In essence, these are social networks of individuals bound by a shared occupational attachment, bonds of socialization, and often economic interest also. Where members have a shared set of skills, they have a shared interest that their collective reputation for competence and trustworthiness be sustained and not undermined by free riders (Marsden, in press). One has only to open the trade section of a telephone directory to see the large number of special trade associations, such as the Guild of Master Craftsmen, and hence the importance that suppliers of these services attach to reassuring their potential customers of the quality and reliability of their work. The role of occupational communities in the media industry also stands out clearly in research in Germany (e.g., Sydow and Staber 2002).

The Behavior and Structure of Labor Institutions

I shall now explore how collective action supports the two contractual constraints: the enforceability of transaction rules and the efficiency of matching skills and job demands. Because one of the key goals of labor institutions is to further their members' employment interests, they can be expected to evolve in ways that support the needs of the employment relationship.

The most important contributions of the wider, interfirm institutions discussed so far are the ways that they

- provide collective sanctions to help enforce transaction and classification rules within the enterprise, thus making them more predictable;
- provide channels for renegotiation;
- contribute to workplace trust; and
- support occupational and, to a lesser degree, internal labor markets.

What kinds of institutional structures can provide this support?

If we combine the two contractual constraints, we can trace out the patterns of worker–employer representation that best support each of the HRM strategies outlined earlier (see table 2). The demands for strong workplace representation are greatest for the two function-based rules. In fact, strong workplace guarantees for workers seem to be a necessary condition for the success of function-based rules, and under most circumstances, strong interfirm coordination is necessary for the success of the training approach.[4] The greater specification of boundaries in the task-centered production approach means that although collective action may be beneficial, it is not essential. Thus, in large Japanese firms, which combine the function-based and production approaches, a very active form of enterprise unionism predominates. In large German firms, works councils play a key role dealing with a large number of job-related issues. French works councils provide an interesting counterexample. Using the task-centered work post rule, French firms have had less need for close workplace cooperation. Also, for much of the postwar period, political competition among the unions and a weak membership base have meant that works councils have not been able to play the same role in France as in Germany. So, as Lorenz (1995) observed, French works councils have been more adversarial and less effective than their German counterparts.

Turning to the production versus the training approach, strong interfirm coordination plays a key role in containing the pressures from free

TABLE 2

The Four Transaction Rules and Patterns of Worker–Employer Representation

| | | Interfirm representation | |
		Weak	Strong
Workplace	Weak	Work post rule	Job territory rule
representation	Strong	Competence rank rule	Qualification rule

riders. Unregulated occupational markets are always exposed to the risk of free riding because of the common pressures that induce employers to bear part of the cost of providing training for occupational skills. This often happens because of the supply constraints when employers rely on training financed by trainees and their families, especially those from poorer households. Once employers shoulder a substantial part of this cost, other firms have an incentive to free-ride by poaching those trained by their competitors. Collective regulation by the interested parties provides a common solution to this problem. Thus, local employer organizations provide much support to Germany's blue- and white-collar apprenticeship systems. Britain provides an interesting counterexample here. For decades it had a successful apprenticeship system and lively occupational markets, but their decline in the 1970s and 1980s owes much to the weakness of the institutional framework on which they depended (Marsden 1995). Weak employer coordination led to greater reliance on task-centered rules to keep the system going. These were keenly defended by craft union organizations, albeit increasingly from special occupational sections within more general unions. These rules constrained many employers to train apprentices because they could not easily substitute other workers for apprentice-trained skilled workers. This economically handicapped the firms considerably, so their interest in apprenticeship declined, leading to its virtual collapse after the mid-1980s.

At first sight, the industrial pattern of German union organization might also seem to be at odds with the argument. However, as Sengenberger (1987) showed, a great many occupational skills covered by apprenticeship are specific to certain industries, particularly in view of the very broad scope of industries and sectors in German union and employer organization. Thus, although German unions are "industry" unions in terms of their scope, unlike unions with similar coverage in other countries, they give remarkable power to occupationally skilled workers whose special status is enshrined in classification and in wage agreements. The agreements are very specific about just how far workers without an apprenticeship may progress toward skilled status on the basis of on-the-job training. Although German unions nominally have similar membership coverage to that of French industrial unions, they represent skilled workers in a completely different way, stressing occupational principles in contrast to the strong internal labor market logic found in France.

Finally, although interfirm representation may not be essential to the workings of the production approach, there are good examples of how it can improve its flexibility. In France, where the work post system has wide currency, industry classification agreements have provided a framework for renegotiating skill norms in the enterprise (Eyraud, Jobert, Rozenblatt, and Tallard 1989). Cole's (1989) study of the spread of quality circles in Japan as a result of coordinated action between firms likewise illustrates how such action can promote greater job flexibility. Although the movement was led by employers, Cole argued that it developed many aspects of a "mass movement" as a result of informal coordination among firms, which was not achieved in the United States.

The Work Post Model and "Nonunion" Workplaces

I now turn to look at employment relationships in the weakly institutionalized environment of nonunion firms. Because of its lesser need for collective action, the work post model is the one most likely to flourish in weakly institutionalized and nonunion workplaces. There the problems of asymmetric information, bounded rationality, and partially divergent interests still need to be resolved, and transaction rules remain essential to the employment relationship.

The likely dominance of the work post system rests on two observations. One would expect task-centered rules to be the type preferred by workers. These provide more clearly defined job responsibilities and work roles and so enable workers more easily to identify potential pressures from their line managers to extend their jobs. It is also easier for workers to monitor performance management if work obligations are relatively codified. Function-centered rules are unlikely to appeal because employees' work obligations are too open-ended. In addition, the absence of collective organization among both employers and employees makes it less likely that stable occupational markets will emerge. This pushes firms toward the production rather than the training approach. Because of these factors together, the work post rule can be expected to predominate. It is the one that best handles the problems of opportunism within the employment relationship in the absence of strong labor and employer institutions. Thus, the absence of a suitable collective framework can help explain the uneven development and slow diffusion of American models of high performance and the persistence of Taylorist models of organization there (Appelbaum and Batt 1994; Katz and Darbishire 2000).

Like the other types of employment rules, the work post system can be administered with varying degrees of flexibility. I argued earlier that collective action can facilitate flexible working and, most importantly, assist with renegotiation of work organization principles. In its absence, firms and workers still have to adjust to shifting markets, so what mechanisms are open to them?

First, we can expect employees to minimize their investments in the firm because these tie them and expose them to opportunistic renegotiation by their employers. If they cannot afford to quit, they are in a weak bargaining position. In the absence of collective bargaining, a worker's best protection is a job offer from a rival employer. As a result, workers can be expected to let firms shoulder a greater part of investments in skill development, and firms therefore to privilege firm-specific skills.

Second, there are alternative individual routes to renegotiating work assignments. Firms can link this renegotiation to promotion for career workers, using it as an opportunity to alter work assignments, but they must also increase pay. Firms may also have to be more specific about promotion opportunities when they hire workers into such an environment because workers are less likely to believe open-ended promises when the employer faces fewer checks and balances. In this respect, it is significant that Baron, Davis-Blake, and Bielby (1986) found that nonunion firms had more structured job ladders than union ones.

Third, firms can use the process of labor turnover to adjust work roles by individual negotiation: such negotiation occurs through the arrival of new hires. This can be important because careers provide incentives to only a small percentage of workers. According to Layard, Nickell, and Jackman (1991:222), nearly 30% of employees in the United States had been hired during the previous year, as against about 20% in the United Kingdom and around 10% in France.[5] A year's figures provide only a rough indication, and we need to remember too that the U.S. economy also contains a significant proportion of long-term jobs. Nevertheless, it does suggest that heavy reliance on individual negotiation may lead to more rigid job assignments, which in turn lead to shorter job tenures and associated recruitment and training costs for employers.

Finally, generalized individual renegotiation of jobs may require the firm to periodically declare a "state of emergency," for example, downsizing in response to bad stock market performance. However, this can prove to be a double-edged sword. As Bewley's (1999) study showed, even in the United States many employers are reluctant to announce job cuts because, although they may generate concessions, they may also cause employee morale to collapse.

Conclusion

This paper has sketched out the argument that the focus of both industrial relations and human resource management needs to be refocused around central features of the employment relationship, notably, the conditions that need to be satisfied for both firms and workers to benefit from this flexible framework for cooperation. The empirical impetus for this exercise stems from two sources. The first is the decline and reshaping of the collective representational institutions in labor markets, even in countries where they have until recently been strong, such as in Germany, but also Japan and a number of other E.U. countries. The second is the increasing evidence that, just as there was no universal model of Taylorist organization, so now there is no universal pattern of high-performance work system. Indeed, recent research on workplace "strategic human resource management," such as that by Sherer and Leblebici (2001), indicates an enduring diversity.

The first part of this essay set out the main elements of the employment relationship as a social institution. It highlighted the range of different solutions that limit management's control of work flexibility sufficiently for workers to find employment attractive and for both parties to benefit from this contractual framework. I argued that satisfying the two fundamental contractual constraints—that work rules delimiting management's authority should be both enforceable and efficient at matching workers' skills with employers' job demands—gives rise to four basic types of work rules. These, I argued, are the foundation of the different types of work systems associated with different models of strategic human resource management. This is because delimiting management authority shapes the workplace managerial hierarchy, performance management, jobs, skill formation, and the nature of interdependency among workers.

The second part of this paper identified the kinds of interfirm institutional arrangements that can make work rules function more effectively within the workplace and so enhance the gains to both workers and their employers. One might think of the externalities associated with each of the rules—the different ways in which they are vulnerable to breaking down—as a factor generating the demand by workers and firms for different kinds of collective organization.

An important question remaining is the degree of influence exercised by these work rules on the evolution of patterns of HRM and on labor institutions more generally. Clearly, there are important historical influences, and the law and other social institutions can embody other principles of social and economic organization. It is also clear that the open-ended employment relationship is itself a historically contingent framework for economic cooperation. As shown in the masterful historical survey by Mottez (1966), the employment relationship emerged as the dominant form only in the late 19th and early 20th centuries. Moreover, work by the OECD (1992) showed that both firms and workers move between employment and self-employment, which demonstrates the continued presence of choice in this respect. In my theory of employment systems, I argue that the different patterns of employment relationship can diffuse in a totally decentralized manner, even though this may not always be how they spread. They can do so because once a particular rule becomes predominant in a particular environment, it is easier to use it to govern coordination than to try to impose a different rule. Once people are familiar with a rule and trust it, outcomes become more predictable, and enforcement becomes easier. Thus, we could say that the stronger these gains are, the greater the pressure toward some kind of isomorphism within a particular sector or region, and hence the greater the influence exerted on the evolution of the HRM systems adopted in firms and on the evolution of the structure of labor institutions.

Notes

[1] There were, of course, other moral-hazard problems, notably overworking the entrepreneur's capital equipment, skimping on quality, and frequent disputes over use of raw materials. On the other side, employers were frequently reluctant to provide training (e.g., Slichter 1919).

[2] In essence, these assumptions concern the choice between employment and self-employment, bounded rationality, imperfect information, and at least partially divergent interests.

[3] The training approach is not logically dependent on the prior existence of occupational markets; this was demonstrated by the way large German firms in the late 19th century organized their own internal apprenticeship training systems to make up for the inadequacies of the existing apprenticeship system (Lutz 1975). However, its effectiveness is greatly enhanced by the establishment of occupational markets, not least because they help to establish familiarity with certain types of work rules, thus making the rules more robust.

[4] Logically, the training approach can exist within a single firm, as appeared to be the case when the large industrial firms in Germany took over and modernized the apprenticeship system in the late 19th century. However, the model soon extended across firms.

[5] The data are for 1988, which was a period of low unemployment between the peaks of 1982–83 and the early 1990s.

References

Addison, John T., Lutz Bellmann, Claus Schnabel, and Joachim Wagner. 2002. *German Works Councils Old and New: Incidence, Coverage and Determinants*. IZA Discussion Paper 495. Bonn: Forschungsinstitut zur Zukunft der Arbeit [Institute for the Study of Labor].

Appelbaum, Eileen, and Rosemary Batt. 1994. *The New American Workplace: Transforming Work Systems in the United States*. Ithaca, NY: Cornell University Press.

Baraldi, L., J.-P. Dumasy, and J.-F. Troussier. 1995. "Accords salariaux innovants et théorie du salaire." *Économie Appliquée*, Vol. 48, no. 4, pp. 105–37.

Baron, J. N., M. D. Burton, and M. T. Hannan. 1996. "The Road Taken: The Origins and Evolution of Employment Systems in Emerging High-Technology Companies." *Industrial and Corporate Change*, Vol. 5, pp. 239–76.

———. 1999. "Engineering Bureaucracy: The Genesis of Formal Policies, Positions, and Structures in High Technology Firms." *Journal of Law, Economics and Organization*, Vol. 15, pp. 1–41.

Baron, J., A. Davis-Blake, and W. Bielby. 1986. "The Structure of Opportunity: How Promotion Ladders Vary within and among Organizations." *Administrative Science Quarterly*, Vol. 31, no. 2 (June), pp. 248–73.

Baumann, Arne. 2003. "Path-Dependency or Convergence? The Emergence of Labour Market Institutions in the Media Production Industries of the UK and Germany." Diss., European University Institute, Florence, Italy.

Becker, G. S. 1975. *Human Capital: A Theoretical and Empirical Analysis, with Special Reference to Education*. Chicago: University of Chicago Press.

Bewley, Truman. 1999. *Why Wages Don't Fall During a Recession*. Cambridge, MA: Harvard University Press.

Brown, W. E. 1973. *Piecework Bargaining*. London: Heinemann.

Burawoy, M. 1979. *Manufacturing Consent: Changes in the Labor Process under Monopoly Capitalism*. Chicago: University of Chicago Press.

Clark, J. 1993. "Full-Flexibility and Self-Supervision in an Automated Factory." In J. Clark, ed., *Human Resource Management and Technical Change*, London: Sage.

Coase, Ronald H. 1937. "The Nature of the Firm." *Economica*, New Series, Vol. 4, no. 16 (November), pp. 386–405.

Cole, R. E. 1989. *Strategies for Learning: Small Group Activities in American, Japanese, and Swedish Industry*. Berkeley: University of California Press.

Cole, R. 1994. "Different Quality Paradigms and Their Implications for Organisational Learning." In M. Aoki and R. Dore, eds., *The Japanese Firm: The Sources of Competitive Strength*, Oxford: Oxford University Press, pp. 66–83.

Coriat, B. 1991. *Penser à l'envers*. Paris: Christian Bourgois.

Crozier, M. 1963. *Le phénomène bureaucratique.* Paris: Seuil.

Dugué, E. 1994. "La gestion des compétences: Les savoirs dévalués, le pouvoir occulté." *Sociologie du Travail,* no. 3, pp. 273–92.

Eyraud, F., A. Jobert, P. Rozenblatt, and M. Tallard. 1989. *Les classifications dans l'entreprise: Production des hiérarchies professionnelles et salariales.* Document Travail Emploi. Paris: Ministère du Travail, de l'Emploi et de la Formation Professionnelle.

Fraser, Janet, and Michael Gold. 2001. "'Portfolio Workers': Autonomy and Control amongst Freelance Translators." *Work, Employment and Society,* Vol. 15, no. 4, pp. 679–97.

Guest, D., and N. Conway. 1999. "Peering into the Black Hole: The Downside of the New Employment Relations in the UK." *British Journal of Industrial Relations,* Vol. 37, no. 3 (September), pp. 367–89.

Haunschild, Axel. 2003. "Managing Employment Relationships in Flexible Labour Markets: The Case of German Repertory Theatres." *Human Relations,* Vol. 56, no. 8 (August), pp. 899–929.

Holmstrom, B., and P. Milgrom. 1991. "Multitask Principal–Agent Analysis: Incentive Contracts, Asset Ownership, and Job Design." *Journal of Law, Economics and Organization,* Vol. 7, no. 2, pp. 24–53.

Jacoby, S. M. 1985. *Employing Bureaucracy: Managers, Unions, and the Transformation of Work in American Industry, 1900–1945.* New York: Columbia University Press.

Katz, H., and O. Darbishire. 2000. *Converging Divergencies: Worldwide Changes in Employment Systems.* Ithaca, NY: ILR Press/Cornell University Press.

Kohaut, Susanne, and Claus Schnabel. 2003. "Zur Erosion des Flaechentarifvertrags: Ausmass, Einflussfaktoren und Gegenmassnahmen." *Industrielle Beziehungen,* Vol. 10, no. 2, pp. 193–219.

Koike, K. 1994. "Learning and Incentive Systems in Japanese Industry." In M. Aoki and R. Dore, eds., *The Japanese Firm: The Sources of Competitive Strength,* Oxford: Oxford University Press, pp. 41–65.

———. 1997. *Human Resource Development.* Japanese Economy and Labor Series, no. 2. Tokyo: Japan Institute of Labour.

Layard, R., S. Nickell, and R. Jackman. 1991. *Unemployment: Macroeconomic Performance and the Labour Market.* Oxford: Oxford University Press.

Lorenz, E. 1995. "Promoting Workplace Participation: Lessons from Germany and France." *Industrielle Beziehungen,* Vol. 2, no. 1, pp. 46–63.

Lutz, B. 1975. *Krise des Lohnanreizes: Ein empirisch-historischer Beitrag zum Wandel der Formen betrieblicher Herrschaft am Beispiel der deutschen Stahlindustrie.* Frankfurt: Europäische Verlagsanstalt.

Marsden, D. W. 1995. "A Phoenix from the Ashes of Apprenticeship? Vocational Training in Britain." *International Contributions to Labour Studies (Supplement to the Cambridge Journal of Economics),* Vol. 5, pp. 87–114.

———. 1999. *A Theory of Employment Systems: Micro-foundations of Societal Diversity.* Oxford: Oxford University Press.

———. In press. "The 'Network Economy' and Models of the Employment Contract: Psychological, Economic, and Legal." *British Journal of Industrial Relations.*

Maurice, M., H. Mannari, Y. Takeoka, and T. Inoki. 1988. *Des entreprises françaises et japonaises face à la mécatronique: Acteurs et organisation de la dynamique industrielle.* Aix-en-Provence, France: Laboratoire d'Economie et de Sociologie du Travail (CNRS).

Mottez, B. 1966. *Systèmes de salaire et politiques patronales: Essai sur l'évolution des pratiques et des idéologies patronales.* Paris: Centre National de la Recherche Scientifique.

Organisation for Economic Co-operation and Development. 1992. *Employment Outlook 1992.* Paris: Organisation for Economic Co-operation and Development.

———. 1997. *Employment Outlook 1997.* Paris: Organisation for Economic Co-operation and Development.

Paul, A., and A. Kleingartner. 1994. "Flexible Production and the Transformation of Industrial Relations in the Motion Picture and Television Industry." *Industrial and Labor Relations Review,* Vol. 47, no. 4 (July), pp. 663–78.

Reynaud, B. 1992. *Le salaire, la règle et le marché.* Paris: Christian Bourgeois.

Roy, D. 1952. "Quota Restriction and Goldbricking in a Machine Shop." *American Journal of Sociology,* Vol. 67, no. 2, pp. 427–44.

Sengenberger, W. 1987. *Struktur und Funktionsweise von Arbeitsmärkten: Die Bundesrepublik Deutschland im internationalen Vergleich.* Frankfurt: Campus Verlag.

Sherer, P. D., and H. Leblebici. 2001. "Bringing Variety and Change into Strategic Human Resource Management Research." *Research in Personnel and Human Resources Management,* Vol. 20, pp. 199–230.

Simon, H. A. 1951. "A Formal Theory of the Employment Relationship." *Econometrica,* Vol. 19, no. 3 (July), pp. 293–305.

Slichter, S. 1919. *The Turnover of Factory Labor.* New York: Appleton.

Slichter, S., J. Healy, and E. Livernash. 1960. *The Impact of Collective Bargaining on Management.* Washington, DC: Brookings Institution.

Sydow, Jörg, and Udo Staber. 2002. "The Institutional Embeddedness of Project Networks: The Case of Content Production in German Television Regional Studies." *Regional Studies,* Vol. 36, no. 3, pp. 215–27.

Tolbert, P. 1996. "Occupations, Organizations, and Boundaryless Careers." Chap. 20 in M. Arthur and D. Rousseau, eds., *The Boundaryless Career: A New Employment Principle for a New Organizational Era,* New York: Oxford University Press, pp. 331–49.

Visser, J. 1998. "Two Cheers for Corporatism, One for the Market: Industrial Relations, Wage Moderation and Job Growth in the Netherlands." *British Journal of Industrial Relations,* Vol. 36, no. 2 (June), pp. 269–92.

Williamson, O. E. 1975. *Markets and Hierarchies: Analysis and Antitrust Implications.* New York: Free Press.

Yamanouchi, T., and L. Okazaki-Ward. 1997. "Key Issues in HRM in Japan." In S. Tyson, ed., *The Practice of Human Resource Strategy,* London: Pitman.

CHAPTER 4

Work, Employment, and the Individual

E. KEVIN KELLOWAY
Saint Mary's University

DANIEL G. GALLAGHER
James Madison University

JULIAN BARLING
Queen's University

It is not from the benevolence of the butcher, the brewer or the baker that we expect our dinner, but from their regard to their own interest.

—Adam Smith, *The Wealth of Nations*

With these words, Adam Smith ([1776] 1976:119) formulated the most influential psychological hypothesis of all time. Although rarely tested (Furnham and Argyle 1998), or even recognized as a psychological hypothesis, Smith's conceptualization of economic man has had a dramatic impact on our understanding and management of work and employment. Smith's views became the basis for the classical school of organizational theory (Shafritz and Ott 1996) and found a well-known expression in the scientific management movement (Taylor 1911), which is often identified as the beginning of modern behavioral theories of management. Indeed, given an absence of alternative theories, Smith's views became the dominant model of motivation until well into the 20th century. More than 200 years after his original formulation, the suggestion that individuals work solely or primarily as a function of economic self-interest would now go unremarked upon in a class on human resource management, and discussions of how to structure economic rewards that appeal to an individual's economic self-interest permeate the contemporary literature on employee compensation (e.g., see Rynes and Gerhart 2000; Thierry 1992).

This is not to say that Smith's views have been universally accepted. Both economists and researchers in organizational behavior have repeatedly challenged the formulation of economic man. Stagner (1950) referred to the suggestion that individuals work only for money as the "dollar fallacy," while Harrell (1949) argued that a purely economic view demeaned workers, reducing them to "rabble." Economists such as Polanyi (2001) objected to the commodification of labor implicit in Smith's model and mounted a rigorous attack on the notion of economic man, pointing out that Smith's original formulation of the "bartering savage" bore little resemblance to actual human societies and that individual economic behavior is embedded in social contexts. The human relations movement beginning with the Hawthorne studies (Roethlisberger and Dickson 1939) and expressed through the works of Whyte (1948), Maslow (1943), McGregor (1960), and others, identified a multiplicity of motives for working that either supplanted or supplemented economic self-interest as a reason for working. Indeed, for the most part, behavioral theories of work rarely discuss money or its role in employment (Furnham and Argyle 1998).

Although both the economic and behavioral perspectives have taken different approaches, both are attempting to deal with the fundamental question, Why do people work? (Lea, Tarpy, and Webley 1987). Answering this question from the perspective of the individual is the goal of this chapter. Before we attempt to do so, it is instructive to consider and clarify exactly what we mean by *work* and *employment*.

The Definitions of Work and Employment

Arguably one of the most influential accounts of the origin of our species, the Genesis creation narrative is in many ways a story about work and the role of work in human lives. Work is metaphorically presented as the purpose of creation (i.e., "to keep the garden and till it," Genesis 2:15) as well as a punishment (i.e., "in the sweat of thy face shalt thou eat bread," Genesis 3:17). Indeed, in highlighting the act of creation, the narrative depicts God as a worker (Fox 1994).

The anthropological record parallels the theological. Major steps in evolution have been almost uniformly associated with, if not caused by, changes in the nature and organization of work (see Donkin 2001). The shift from a hunting-gathering society to a primarily agrarian one is clearly a shift in the type of "work" performed by individuals. The growth of the market economy was made possible by the efficiencies of agrarian labor, allowing the development of specific skills and specialization of individual tasks that eventually evolved into waged labor. It is not an overstatement to claim that work and employment have been central aspects of the human experience throughout the development of civilization (see Applebaum 1984, 1992; Pahl 1988). Although our species has adopted the taxonomic category of "thinking man," it is clear that "working man" would be an equally good choice.

From a very broad perspective, employment and its associated income are often cited as aggregate measures of the changing economic health of a nation or region. However, within contemporary society, work and employment can also have tremendous importance at the individual level in terms of how people perceive themselves and are perceived by others. Work, as actualized in the form of employment, serves as a vehicle through which individuals realize such outcomes as income, status, identity, and social opportunities (Jahoda 1982; Roberson 1990). Conversely, the absence of paid employment has been linked to deleterious consequences for individuals and society since at least the beginning of the Industrial Revolution (Burnett 1994; Feather 1990; Jahoda 1982).

Work

Although there is little argument about the importance of work in individuals' lives, it is surprising to note that there is no widely agreed-upon definition of *work*. As Neff (1977; also see Thomas 1999) noted, the dictionary contains many definitions of the word *work* (over 30 definitions of the verb and 20 definitions of the noun). In one of the first attempts to deal with this issue, Arendt (1959) distinguished between labor and work. The former was a function of biological and economic necessity, while the latter was an act of creation. Distinguishing labor from work, or work from employment, is a necessary first step. It is clear that not all work occurs in the context of a formal employment relationship (Ferman 1990; Pahl 1988).

At least two definitions predominate in our understanding of work. First, there is a physical definition of work that emphasizes the notion of purposive activity (Brief and Nord 1990). Second, there is an economic definition that emphasizes the role of work in "earning a living" (Polanyi 2001) or sustaining oneself (Neff 1977). While both definitions are limited, both offer some essential meaning of the term *work*.

The physical definition of work (emphasizing the role of activity) is appealing because it corresponds to the precise definition of work contained in physics (i.e., the use of force to move mass). Moreover, we commonly use the term *work* to describe strenuous physical or mental activity. Following in the tradition of the biblical narrative of Creation, work is viewed as an activity that is exhausting or onerous. In this sense, the physical definition captures some essence of what is meant when people say that they are working. At the same time, reliance solely on the physical definition of work would result in considerable confusion. In particular, emphasizing the role of purposive activity would result in almost all human endeavors being defined as work (Brief and Nord 1990). By doing so, this definition fails to differentiate between the contexts in which activities are performed. For example, a strenuous physical activity (e.g., cross-country skiing) would be considered work under this definition, while thinking about a work-related problem might not. In this example, it would be impossible to distinguish between the work of a professional golfer and the recreation of the weekend golfer. Moreover, defining work in terms of exhausting or onerous activities belies the observations that (a) much of the work in today's societies places minimal physical demands on workers (e.g., see Sohn-Rethel 1978) and (b) there are numerous individuals who enjoy their work and do not find it to be onerous (Freidson 1990). Clearly then, one must move beyond the nature of the activity to define work adequately (Freidson 1990).

Rather than focusing on the nature of the activity, the economic definition of work emphasizes the economic function of work (i.e., to make a living, to produce the means of survival; Brief and Aldag 1989; Neff 1977). Indeed, this economic definition is probably the most common definition of work and is adopted by many authors mainly because of the lack of viable alternatives (see Brief and Nord 1990). In accepting this definition, theorists have, however unwittingly, accepted Smith's view of labor as a commodity. The economic definition defines work as that which is produced for economic gain and leaves little room for alternative explanations of work-related behaviors.

The economic definition of work is also problematic. If the physical definition is inadequate because it fails to distinguish between activities, the economic definition is limited in that it introduces seemingly arbitrary distinctions. Following this definition, any given activity is work if one is paid to do it, and it is not work if it is not associated with remuneration. Thus, a domestic worker who provides cleaning and childcare services for a salary is engaging in work, but a homemaker who provides these same services for free is not working, according to the economic definition of work (Jahoda 1982). Several authors have noted the political and social consequences of defining work purely in terms of economic reward and thereby devaluing unpaid labor (see Brief and Nord 1990).

If both the physical and the economic definitions contain some truth and some limitations, then perhaps the route to an acceptable definition of work is to combine the two definitions, thereby offsetting the weaknesses of each. An acceptable definition of work as we commonly use the term is *purposeful activity directed at producing a valued good or service*. Note that the emphasis of the definition is on economic value rather than on direct compensation (see Freidson 1990 for a similar approach). Unlike the physical definition, this definition offers a distinction between similar activities. To return to the earlier example, professional golfers are working when they are on the course because someone is willing to pay them to do so.

Unlike the economic definition of work, our definition limits the arbitrariness of the distinction between work and nonwork. Again, to follow up on our earlier example, full-time homemakers are working when they clean the house or care for the children because these activities have direct economic value. That is, people are willing to pay to have these services performed. Should the full-time homemaker return to the paid workforce, for example, a portion of the income thus obtained would typically be directed into purchasing alternative child-care or domestic services.

Employment

If work is viewed as the production of a valued good or service, then what is employment? As noted by Marie Jahoda in her classic work *Employment and Unemployment: A Social-Psychological Analysis* (1982:8), "in common parlance as well as in the social science literature, work and employment are often used interchangeably." The difference between work and employment can be demonstrated indirectly by the fact that being without employment (i.e., unemployed or not participating in the labor market) does not equate with not being engaged in a *purposeful activity directed at producing a valued good or service*. In contrast, it appears reasonable to suggest that employment can most appropriately be viewed in the context in which individuals perform work. Based on components of both Jahoda's perspective and frequently applied governmental measures, employment can be more specifically defined as *work that is performed under contractual arrangements and that involves material rewards*.

This definition encompasses both contractual and economic components. The contractual aspect of employment introduces the presence of a second entity (i.e., contractor, employer, or user) who is willing to become a party in an exchange relationship. The second aspect of employment is the presence of an economic or material reward or payment as part of the contractual exchange relationship. In essence, employment can be viewed as an individual's contractual exchange of work with another individual or organization for economic reward. It can also be argued that the contractual nature of the exchange can vary in formality and explicitness (Rousseau 1989). Furthermore, the material reward can extend beyond currency and might also include bartered goods. These last two points are particularly important, since they would allow employment arrangements to be viewed in a broader scope than those included in many formally constructed governmental definitions of employment or unemployment.

From a definitional perspective, it is also useful to recognize that just as work and employment have mistakenly been treated as synonymous, a distinction exists between work, employment, and jobs. In the context of our definitions, a job is most properly understood as the intersection of work and employment, comprising a set of tasks undertaken in a specific context. For example, a person may be *employed* in a dental practice in the *job* (or position) of dental hygienist. This distinction is important because people's perception of the value of employment (or work) may reflect the type of job that they are performing. Furthermore, individuals may remain continuously employed (and working) but move between different jobs in the same or different employment arrangements. In times of economic restructuring, this distinction becomes more important, as employees may be offered employment security but not necessarily job security (see Pfeffer 1998a for an explication of employment insecurity).

In a popular press book titled *Job Shift: How to Prosper in a Workplace without Jobs*, Bridges (1994) contended that organizations were moving away from the traditional concept of jobs. In particular, Bridges suggested that employee activities were being driven more by project teams and the accomplishment of objectives than by fulfilling the requirements of job descriptions. According to Bridges (1994), this trend toward "dejobbing" was motivated by two major factors. First was the desire for organizations to have greater flexibility in staffing and enhancing the movement of workers among assignments within the organization. Second, many organizations found that using jobs as the focal point for employees' activities was not very effective. Stated differently, workers may "do their jobs" but accomplish very little.

In addition to the so-called dejobbing of work, there has been a documented trend in most postindustrial societies toward a change in the nature of the employment contract. In particular, as a means of building greater flexibility into their staffing arrangements as well as making labor more a variable cost, many employers have turned to the increased utilization of workers in various forms that have been referred to as *contingent, temporary,* or *fixed-term* contracts.

Contingent employment contracts are actualized in a number of formats or structures. One of the most recognizable and fastest-growing forms of contingent employment is organizational reliance on temporary help firms (e.g., Manpower, Adecco, Accutemps) as a vehicle for short-term staffing needs. For the most part, temporary help firms have been associated with the short-term (days, weeks, months) placement of clerical support staff and unskilled laborers. Unlike traditional employer–employee relationships, the nature of the contractual arrangement for workers employed through temporary help firms is more triangular in form. More specifically, temporary workers are not actually employed by the organization at which they are performing a job but rather by the temporary or brokerage firm that has contracted the worker's services to a client organization. With few exceptions, the temporary worker's employment with the temporary firm is concurrent with the client assignment. When the temporary assignment ends, so does the formal employment relationship with the temporary firm. A new contractual arrangement is established when the temporary worker receives a new assignment with a subsequent client organization (Gallagher 2002).

An increasingly popular form of contingent work arrangement is the organizational use of independent contractors. In most countries, independent contractors or freelance workers are legally defined as self-employed individuals who contract or sell their services to a client organization on a fixed-term or project basis. Once the project or assignment is completed, the contractual relationship is terminated unless a decision is made by both parties to enter into a subsequent contract. Typically, independent contractor or freelance arrangements assume that the worker has considerable discretion and independence as to how the work is performed, and the emphasis is often on outcomes rather than process. In recent years, there has also been growing evidence of workers' being terminated from more traditional or ongoing employment contracts and being "rehired" by the same organization in the classification of a non-employee, or independent contractor.

What is viewed today as a traditional or ongoing employer–employee relationship is, in fact, a fairly new phenomenon. In fact, as noted by Cappelli (1999), most work prior to the beginning of the 20th century tended to be contingent or based on short-term delivery or service contracts. Hence, the gradual emergence of contingent or short-term employment contracts may actually be better characterized as a devolution back to contractual work arrangements that were not specifically long term or ongoing. However, one of the most important issues that confronts virtually all behavioral theories of work and almost all theoretical (and legal) perspectives in the field of industrial relations developed in the 20th century is the assumed presence of an identifiable and ongoing employer–employee relationship (Beard and Edwards 1995; Pfeffer and Baron 1988). Not only did behavioral researchers approach the study of work theoretically from the perspective of an identifiable traditional employer–employee relationship, but many of the research questions being examined are inherently or frequently tied to the presence of an ongoing employment contract (commitment, turnover, etc.).

The growth or reemergence of temporary contracts and independent contractor arrangements raises some important issues pertaining to the meaning and level of focus that should be attached to jobs. For example, in the case of workers hired out through intermediate or temporary help firms, the meaning and context of "the job" may be extremely variable. In fact, each client assignment may represent a different or modified set of role-related duties and responsibilities and occur in a different work context as the worker shifts from one client organization to another. Research by Gallagher and McLean Parks (2001) has also raised the question of temporary workers' own notions of the jobs they perform. More specifically, do workers dispatched to different client organizations through the services of a temporary help firm define their job as being a "temporary worker"? Or alternatively, is the work (job) defined in terms of the tasks they are hired to perform for the client organization? Or, in the case of more professional workers, can work be defined as characteristic of the "occupation" they labor within? Furthermore, issues of job context become more variable, as previously noted, for the simple reason that temporary or contingent workers may have similar sets of responsibilities in very different client environments. In the case of growing legions of independent contractors, the understanding of work also shifts away from the presence of the employer–employee or master–servant relationship and, as in the case of temporary help workers, shifts to consideration of the characteristics of the client organizations. Among independent contractors, the role that the client organization plays in shaping the context of work is further complicated by the fact that independent contractors may be employed simultaneously by multiple clients. The fact that being an independent contractor represents a form of self-employment raises questions of the relevance of any theoretical perspective on work that is fundamentally based (explicitly or implicitly) on the presence of an identifiable employer–employee relationship. Furthermore, by legal definition, independent contractors are in the position of exercising a great deal of personal autonomy over where and how their work is performed. Unlike more traditional employment relationships, the independent contractor arrangement represents a shift in direct control away from the employer and to the individual worker. From a theoretical perspective, it is also possible to suggest that the motivations and interests of workers who gravitate toward self-employment arrangements may, in fact, be different from those of workers who express a preference for the traditional employer–employee relationship.

Summary

The question "Why do people work?" is really a question about both work (i.e., purposeful activity directed toward the production of a valued good or service) and employment (i.e., the context of work based on both contractual arrangements and material rewards). This distinction is frequently overlooked in the literature, but it is not unique to our presentation. Polanyi (2001:185) quotes Mises as saying "It has occurred to no one . . . that lack of wages would be a better term than lack of employment for what the unemployed person misses is not work but the remuneration of work." Over 100 years earlier, Bishop Whately said, "When a man begs for work he asks not for work but wages" (Polanyi 2001:185). We suggest that this distinction is critical to resolving the debate between economic and behavioral perspectives.

As the historical record attests, work has assumed a central position in human history and has been clearly linked to individual well-being throughout the ages. Societies at various times have devalued certain forms of employment relationships, but work, as the production of valued goods and services, is held in high esteem. This form of work ethic seems to be alive and well. In evaluating her experiences with low-wage employment in the United States, Ehrenreich (2001:213) observed, "On the contrary, I was amazed and sometimes saddened by the pride people took in jobs that rewarded them so meagerly, either in wages or in recognition."

This is a distinctly non-economic view of work. Work is more than just a means to an end; rather, work is intimately related to individual well-being. In this sense, work (but not necessarily employment) is a good in and of itself. Anecdotal reports suggest that if employers design poor work (e.g., routine, nonchallenging jobs), employees will go to considerable lengths to change their tasks into "good work" (see Garson 1994). Moreover, individuals deprived of employment are not necessarily bereft of work. Rather, unemployed and non-employed individuals invest considerable energy in producing economically valuable goods and services. Seen in this light, claims that we are witnessing the "end of work" (Rifkin 1995) are premature at best and can be seen as gross exaggerations at their worst. Indeed, at least one theorist has suggested that the essential meaning of work has not changed in at least the last 50 years (O'Brien 1992).

Having said that, it is equally true that we do seem to be witnessing a fundamental reshaping of employment relations. Although frequently seen as a dramatic restructuring, the emergence of contingent work and portfolio jobs (e.g., see Handy 1984) may be more accurately viewed as a correction of the historically minor trend to full-time, waged employment. Indeed, for most of recorded history and for most individuals, contingent work was the norm, with our current notion of "normal" employment being a relatively recent emergence.

Work as an Instrumental Activity

Perhaps the most common answer to the question of why people work is that work is an instrumental activity. Therefore, individuals engage in work to obtain valued outcomes. Although this perspective is similar to Adam Smith's ([1776] 1976), viewing work as instrumental does not necessarily limit consideration to economic outcomes.

Jahoda (1982) took the view that we could learn about the functions or instrumentalities of paid work by examining the experience of those deprived of employment. In her model, the manifest function of employment is the accumulation of sufficient financial resources to meet individual needs, while the latent functions are more psychological. Latent functions of work include the enforcement of a time structure for life that provides people with a link to reality. Other latent functions of employment include the provision of social contact, a sense of purpose, and a sense of social status and personal identity. Jahoda argued that the unemployed are deprived of these functions and it is this deprivation that explains the negative consequences of unemployment.

Subsequent research has both supported and refined Jahoda's (1982) model. The functions of employment that she identified appear to be related to well-being and mental health in a variety of samples (e.g.,

Grant and Barling 1994; Higginbottom, Barling, and Kelloway 1994). However, it appears that these latent functions may originate in work rather than employment. Both unemployed (Grant and Barling 1994) and retired (Higginbottom, Barling, and Kelloway 1994) individuals are able to obtain the latent consequences identified by Jahoda even though they are "unemployed."

Conceptually, Jahoda may have confounded the consequences of employment with the causes of employment (Lea, Tarpy, and Webley 1987). The observation that one obtains money through paid employment does not mean that individuals work solely or primarily for money. Indeed, a very old line of inquiry using some variant of the "lottery question" (i.e., If you won the lottery, would you continue to work?) suggests that money may not be a very important rationale for working. Morse and Weiss (1955) found, for example, that 80% of their respondents would continue to work if they inherited enough money to live comfortably. Findings such as these suggest that monetary factors are insufficient to explain the meaning of and motivation for work.

A Framework for Work Values

A more comprehensive attempt to understand the instrumental nature of work was presented by Nord and his colleagues. Nord, Brief, Atieh, and Doherty (1988, 1990) proposed an extremely useful two-dimensional framework for the categorization of work values and meaning. Although limited by their treatment of work and employment as a unitary construct, Nord et al.'s framework is an attempt to elucidate the multiple meanings of work.

The first dimension of the framework is the extent to which the meaning or values of work are seen as relating to either *secular* or *non-secular* (primarily religious) outcomes. While the secular outcomes of work are well understood in organizational behavior and management theory, it is also the case that much of the history of work beliefs and values has been intertwined with religious teachings. In the Judeo-Christian tradition, these teachings range from those of Jewish belief through those of the early Christian Church, the monastic movement, and, of course, the Protestant work ethic.

Given repeated Old Testament metaphorical references to God as a worker, Geogheghan (1945:60) noted that "surely if the Most High is described as the Divine Laborer, it cannot be dishonorable for man to work." Indeed, in this tradition, work assumes a spiritual dimension; by working, individuals both atone for original sin and emulate their God.

Given this set of beliefs, there was a tradition of manual labor among the rabbis. For example, Hillel worked as a woodcutter, Joshua made charcoal. Thus, the rabbis both taught and lived respect for the worker.

To some extent, early Christians followed in the steps of the rabbis by holding occupations. Jesus was a carpenter, although he abandoned his trade to begin his ministry. St. Paul was a tent maker who frequently addressed his contemporaries as "my fellow worker" (e.g., Romans 16:21). As Geogheghan (1945) noted, early Christian teachings about work focused on three themes. First, work was seen as a means of atonement for original sin and as the path to salvation. Second, St. Paul emphasized the moral nature of work. For Paul, work was both a means of attaining independence and, perhaps more importantly, a means of providing charity for others. Finally, although early Christians valued spiritual work more than manual labor, the early writings emphasized the importance of combining both types of work. Thus, a Christian was obligated to work and to contribute to the community. One of the tasks of community support was the responsibility of finding work for individuals who were without work.

These early Christian beliefs carried on during the formation and rise of the monasteries. The monastic movement assumes special importance in the study of work beliefs in that many authors have traced the beginning of Western attitudes toward work back to the monastic movement (e.g., Weber 1952). Perhaps most characteristic of the monastic movement was the importance placed on work for both material and spiritual gain. St. Basil held that work was necessary to support oneself and to provide the means for charity and mortification of the spirit. However, he also held that work was the purpose of Creation and that humans were morally bound to use the faculty for work that was provided by God (Geogheghan 1945). The Rule of St. Benedict, which established the mode of life for Benedictine monks, also enshrined the value of labor in spiritual life (e.g., Farago 2002). All were expected to work, and every minute of the day was assigned a task.

Although the rise of monasticism through the Middle Ages has been identified as a time of great economic development, the Protestant Reformation is typically identified as the precursor to modern views about work (Applebaum 1992). In particular, the teachings of Martin Luther and John Calvin laid the groundwork for what would become known as the Protestant work ethic (Weber 1952).

Weber's (1952) classic thesis was that it was the teachings of the Protestant Reformation that led to the growth of capitalism, hence the title of his work, *The Protestant Ethic and the Spirit of Capitalism.* While this thesis still generates considerable debate, there is little doubt that the teachings of Luther and Calvin were in accord with the times and the growing spirit of capitalism. As Brief and Nord (1990) point out, Luther's view was essentially content-free. It did not matter what one did for a living, only that one did it to the best of one's ability. Tilgher (1930:50) commented that "Luther placed a crown on the sweaty forehead of labor. From his hands work came forth endowed with religious dignity."

Thus, the teachings of early Christians, the monastic communities, and the leaders of the Protestant Reformation all emphasized the spiritual values to be obtained through work. This focus has seen a resurgence of interest as writers focus on the spiritual aspects of modern work (e.g., see Allegretti 2000; Briskin 1996; Nash, McLennan, and Blanchard 2001; Richmond 2000). Despite this focus on spiritual values, there is also recognition that individuals work for material gain as well. Eventually, these views coalesced into the belief that material gain is a mark of spiritual favor.

The second dimension of the Nord, Brief, Atieh, and Doherty (1988) typology is whether beliefs and values focus on *extrinsic* or *intrinsic* features of work. That is, given some form of either secular or nonsecular outcomes from work, are these outcomes obtained from the act of working (extrinsic) or from the nature or content of the work itself (intrinsic)? While the terms are difficult to define unambiguously (see Brief and Aldag 1977), extrinsic outcomes follow or are contingent on work and are independent from the content of the work. Extrinsic outcomes are also generally viewed as depending on sources external to the immediate task-person situation. In contrast, intrinsic consequences or outcomes are very much dependent on the content of the work being performed and reflect the internal response of a worker to experiences during and following the completion of a set of tasks (Brief and Aldag 1977).

An intrinsic focus allows a distinction between "good" and "bad" work. Jewish writers distinguished between occupations that were or were not suitable. Similarly, residents of monastic communities debated the relative virtues of spiritual versus nonspiritual work. In the modern era, behavioral scientists have placed great emphasis on defining and understanding the nature and consequences of "good" work (e.g., Warr 1987). These efforts have typically focused on the nature of the work performed and the organization of tasks (e.g., Hackman and Oldham 1980). Nord, Brief, Atieh, and Doherty's (1988, 1990) distinction between extrinsic and intrinsic focus parallels, to some extent, the definition of work and employment.

The Four Cells of the Typology

The dimensions outlined by Nord, Brief, Atieh, and Doherty (1988) offer four principal cells of work values. The extrinsic-nonsecular nexus is most typified by the Protestant work ethic, which emphasized salvation of the soul as the ultimate reward of earthly labor. "Unlike money, status or other extrinsic outcomes, which are reaped in this world, salvation is non-secular" (Nord et al. 1988). In contrast, the secular, extrinsic outcomes focus on money and other material rewards. As noted by Nord et al. (1988), modern economic theories focus primarily on the material rewards for work (e.g., wages) and generally ignore the specifics of how they should be spent. From the perspective of organized labor, union leaders have most frequently concentrated their efforts on the secular, extrinsic aspects of the employment relationship (e.g., wages, hours, benefits, and safety; Barling, Fullagar, and Kelloway 1992). Within the discipline of organizational behavior, the importance of extrinsic concerns is demonstrated in the extensive volume of literature examining both motivational and instrumental values of financial compensation (see Rynes and Gerhart 2000). It is important to note that secular, extrinsic outcomes can extend beyond individual outcomes and encompass advancing a revolutionary cause in support of the welfare of the larger society (e.g., Maoist China and the Cuban Revolution).

An intrinsic focus on work from a nonsecular or religious perspective tends to emphasize work as part of the process of developing the human spirit. The early years of the monastic movement were typified by the use of work as a means of preparing people to more effectively communicate with God. In the teachings of the Hindu religion, work is viewed as a process of purifying one's spirit with the ultimate purpose of transmigrating to Nirvana (Nord, Brief, Atieh, and Doherty 1988). In many respects, the intrinsic value of work from a religious or nonsecular perspective is part of the process to an extrinsic achievement (i.e., salvation or perfection).

The fourth and final categorization from the Nord, Brief, Atieh, and Doherty (1988) framework is the value of work from the perspective of secular, intrinsic outcomes. Like secular, extrinsic outcomes, secular examinations of intrinsic outcomes can be both collective (social) and individualistic (personal development). Nord et al. (1990) suggested that Marxist theory draws heavily on the notion of work (labor) being a form of individual self-expression. From the perspective of Marx, work is not only a means to an end but an end in itself (Nord et al. 1990). Marx viewed work from a collective perspective as a means through which people could relate to each other and help satisfy the needs of others. In the Marxian perspective, the outcome of work was valued, but the content of work was also important in terms of its impact on the development of the individual. As discussed later in this chapter, the intrinsic value of work is a topic that has long been of interest to researchers with a human relations or organizational behavior orientation to the study of work. Unlike the Marxist perspective, the behavioral (i.e., psychological) perspective has tended to focus sharply on intrinsic outcomes at the individual rather than the societal level. From an overly simplistic perspective, intrinsically focused behavioral research has tended to focus on the aspects of work that are closely associated with the nature of the job-related tasks being performed by individuals.

The Development of Work Values

The work values framework presented by Nord, Brief, Atieh, and Doherty (1988, 1990) presents values as a given or a societal norm with little consideration of how such values develop. Indeed, taken at face value, the Nord et al. typology does not allow for individual differences in work values, suggesting, if only implicitly, that a particular combination of values is dominant in a given society at a given time. In contrast to this static mode, developmental theorists have suggested that economic understanding and work values are acquired through a process of socialization that begins in childhood (Berti and Bombi 1988; Jahoda 1979) and carries into the adult years (for a review see Kelloway and Harvey 1999).

There is certainly evidence that children acquire knowledge about economic relationships in a value-laden fashion. For example, there are data suggesting that children progressively acquire understandings about wage relations and the relations between wages and type of work (e.g., Emler and Dickinson 1985). These understandings are conditioned by the children's own socioeconomic status in such a way that children may have strikingly different understandings of occupations (Dickinson and Emler 1992) and occupational aspirations. Gottfredson (1981) describes vocational aspiration as a developmental process of circumscription and compromise. In this view, children increasingly become aware of what occupations are appropriate for their gender and socioeconomic status. Within these boundaries, individual interests, abilities, and other personal characteristics determine the choice of occupation.

Thus, the available data uniformly suggest that concepts of work and employment relations are well developed in childhood. As Dickinson and Emler (1992:28) conclude:

[B]y the time young people enter the labour market they are equipped with the argumentative terms of employment relations. They are already discussing the cash value of jobs in terms of skill, responsibility, effort, and qualifications, and therefore prepared for a particular framework for debating and negotiating a definition of a fair day's pay.

Most researchers and theorists have framed this developmental sequence within a model of economic socialization in which children acquire knowledge of work and employment through vicarious learning. Bandura (1977:39) suggested that "much social learning occurs on the basis of casual or directed observation of behavior as it is performed by others in everyday situations." Although Dickinson and Emler (1992) identify five agents of economic socialization (i.e., language, family, mass media, peers, and schools), most of the research has focused on the role of parental socialization. Furnham (1987, 1990), for example, suggested that parents communicate their values, beliefs, and attitudes in the way they discuss their job, perform activities at home, and discuss their achievements. Several studies provide empirical support for the suggestion that parental socialization is an important factor in shaping individual work beliefs and work attitudes (e.g., Barling, Kelloway, and Bremermann 1991; Kelloway and Newton 1996; Kelloway and Watts 1994; Piotrkowski and Stark 1987).

Thus, there are sufficient data to support three central conclusions about how children learn about work. First, children acquire substantial information about work, working, and the nature of employment relationships long before they enter the workforce. Although the stereotype of young people as naive newcomers to the workplace is well established, the available evidence suggests that young people enter the workforce with a sophisticated understanding of work and employment. Second, this information is acquired through a process of economic socialization in which parents play a large but not an exclusive role. As a result, children's learning about work is not value neutral, it is conditioned by socioeconomic factors as well as children's observations of their parents' employment experiences. Finally, although this last conclusion remains more tentative than the preceding two, there is evidence that preemployment learning about work continues to exert an effect on individual attitudes and behaviors long after individuals enter the workforce and acquire more direct experience with the nature of work and employment (Kelloway and Harvey 1999).

Summary

It is clear that economic motives play a role in individual decisions regarding employment. It is equally clear, however, that economic motives play a more circumscribed role in employment than is generally believed. Economic motives are only one of the many reasons why individuals choose to accept or stay in employment (Pfeffer 1998b). Moreover, it is clear that money itself is imbued with a host of other meanings (status, security, etc.) that are only tangentially related to the economic function (Furnham and Argyle 1998).

We agree with Polanyi's (2001:75) observation that "the postulate that anything that is bought and sold must have been produced for sale is emphatically untrue." Economic motives do not provide an explanation of work and provide a limited explanation of employment. Individuals work outside of the context of employment, and some forms of work may be most appropriately seen as discretionary behavior within the context of employment. Kelloway and Barling (2000), for example, argued that knowledge work is principally defined as a discretionary behavior.

The framework outlined by Nord, Brief, Atieh, and Doherty (1988) allows for a much broader array of values than simple economic return. However, the Nord et al. (1988) framework presents work values at a societal or group level and, to some extent, as mutually exclusive taxonomic categories. We suggest that a more empirically sound view would be to allow for individual differences in the importance or valences assigned to work values and to view the work values described by Nord et al. (1988) as constituting a profile that differs among individuals.

Thus, individuals work and enter into various employment relationships for both secular and nonsecular outcomes associated with both the nature and the context of the task. The individual valences associated with these outcomes are derived through a lifelong process of socialization. It is possible for individuals to hold multiple, and conflicting, work values, and it is in the interplay of these values that individual motivations to work and to engage in employment are formed. Moreover, unlike models of economic man (Kaufman 1999), there is no implicit assumption that individuals attempt to maximize any of these outcomes.

The instrumental answer to the question of why people work really has more to do with employment than with work. That is, the focus of work values research has been on the meaning of employment and, more specifically, on what people want from their jobs (O'Brien 1992). Although it is not always clear that theorists are making a distinction between work and employment (Nord, Brief, Atieh, and Doherty 1988), the focus of work values research has been almost exclusively on paid employment as an instrumental activity. However, another body of literature has focused directly on the more proximal predictors or motivators of work behavior. Theories of work motivation have taken a different approach to the question of why people work, focusing on the task rather than employment, and it is to this literature that we now turn.

Work Motivation

Motivation is classically defined in behavioral theory as "a set of energetic forces that originate both within, as well as beyond, an individual's being to initiate work-related behavior, and to determine its form, direction, intensity and duration" (Pinder 1984:71). Although currently one of the most researched topics in organizational psychology and organizational behavior (Cooper and Robertson 1986; O'Reilly 1991), the study of work motivation started slowly, with the majority of research attention occurring in the middle to the last half of the 20th century (Latham and Budworth, in press).

For most of the early part of the 20th century, Smith's formulation of economic man was seen as a sufficient account of motivation. In keeping with the dominant scientific models of the day, the emphasis of researchers was solely on behavior, with no credibility accorded the notion that consciousness (e.g., cognition, affect) plays a causal role in behavior. Only that which is directly observable was seen as a suitable focus for scientific inquiry (e.g., see Watson 1913). Scientific management (Taylor 1911) was based on the premise that an individual worked for money and that providing wage increases was a sufficient motivator to increase productivity.

Through the period 1925 to 1950, there was growing recognition of consciousness as a motivating force and a move away from viewing all behavior in the context of simple stimulus–response mechanisms (Latham and Budworth, in press). The work of Mayo (1933) and the well-known Hawthorne studies (Roethlisberger and Dickson 1939) focused attention on nonmonetary factors such as social relations and work characteristics. In a broader arena, there was growing recognition of attitudes and motives in both organizational (e.g., Viteles 1932) and general (e.g., Thurstone 1929) psychology.

Arguably, the seminal theory of work motivation was Maslow's (1943) well-known hierarchy of needs theory, in which five sets of needs (i.e., physiological, safety, love, esteem, and self-actualization) were postulated and held to exist in a hierarchy governed by a principle of prepotency.

Although influential, neither Maslow's formulation nor Alderfer's (1972) re-formulation of the theory garnered consistent empirical support. Maslow's theory was one of the first to shift the focus of theorists to nonmonetary motivators and, by extension, to the conditions of work and employment.

Bolstered by the work of Mayo and his colleagues (e.g., Mayo 1933), Maslow's (1943) theory provided a foundation for the human relations movement, which continued and expanded the focus on nonmonetary motivations in the workplace. Dictums such as "The happy worker is a productive worker" summarized much of this work, which focused on satisfying individual needs, wants, and desires as a means of motivation. Job satisfaction (i.e., "how people feel about their jobs," Spector 1997) emerged as a major focus of inquiry and research by McGregor (1960) and Herzberg (1966). Herzberg, Mausner, and Snyderman (1959) focused attention on the intrinsic aspects of work that were held to be the causes of both job satisfaction and job performance.

Herzberg's focus on the intrinsic aspects of work led to the formulation of job characteristics theory (Hackman and Oldham 1976, 1980). This model posits that when three psychological states are fulfilled by the job (i.e., feelings of personal responsibility, the experience of meaningfulness, and knowledge of the results of one's performance), improved performance and satisfaction ensue. In this view, motivation is a result of the provision of intrinsic job features. Hackman and Oldham identified five intrinsic work characteristics, or *core job dimensions* in their terminology, which can lead to the three psychological states. First, providing both *task* and *scheduling autonomy* within the job can heighten the worker's feeling of personal responsibility. Second, a combination of *skill variety*, *task identity*, and *task significance* can enhance the experience that one's job is meaningful. Third, receiving *feedback* from the job itself or from one's supervisors or peers can provide knowledge of the results of one's own performance. Hackman and Oldham's propositions about the effects of intrinsic core job characteristics on workers' performance and satisfaction have consistently been replicated (Parker 2002), and there is considerable evidence supporting the validity of the model (e.g., see Fried and Ferris 1987; Loher, Noe, Moeller, and Fitzgerald 1985).

Despite the success of the job characteristics theory, the notion of a positive relationship between job satisfaction and performance (e.g., Brayfield and Crockett 1955; Vroom 1964) and the propositions of Herzberg's two-factor theory of work motivation (Biesheuvel 1975; for a review see Pinder 1984) did not garner unequivocal support, and the theory is now largely considered to be defunct.

Contemporary theories of motivation have tended to emphasize the role of cognitions and intentionality rather than needs or affective states such as job satisfaction. Expectancy theory (Vroom 1964), for example, suggests that motivation is a product of two cognitions: the importance assigned to outcomes (i.e., valences) and the perception that effort will lead to obtaining these outcomes. While there is some empirical support for these propositions, the expectancy model as a whole is conceptually problematic (Latham and Budworth, in press) and not strongly supported by the data. Despite these weaknesses, expectancy theory moved beyond stimulus-response or need-driven explanations to focus on work-related behavior as intentional.

Arguably the most successful motivation theory to date is goal-setting theory as explicated by Locke (1968; Locke and Latham 1990). Pinder (1984) claimed that goal setting is the single theory that has garnered the most empirical support and demonstrated the most validity. Goal-setting theory again emphasizes the intentionality of human behavior and is based on three central propositions: (a) Specific goals lead to higher performance than do vague or abstract goals; (b) assuming goal commitment, harder goals lead to higher performance than do easier goals; and (c) monetary incentives, feedback, and participation serve to build commitment to goals but do not affect performance directly (Locke 1968). Proponents of goal-setting theory note that goals underlie most contemporary theories of motivation (Locke 1968), and there is a great deal of empirical support for the propositions that constitute goal-setting theory (Locke and Latham 1990).

Goals are also emphasized in Bandura's (1977) formulation of social learning, later called social cognitive theory. Bandura suggested that individuals interact with their environment and that behavior is acquired through vicarious learning, symbolic learning, and self-regulation. Similar to expectancy theory, social cognitive theory posits that two cognitions, outcome expectancies and self-efficacy, play a role in self-regulation. Like goal-setting theory, the propositions of social cognitive theory have received considerable empirical support (for a review see Latham and Budworth, in press).

Summary

Motivation theorists have attempted to answer the question of why people work by positing constructs such as needs (e.g., Maslow 1943) or by focusing on characteristics of the work environment (e.g., Herzberg, Mausner, and Snyderman 1959; Hackman and Oldham 1980). More recently, motivation has been understood in terms of cognition, with goals (Locke and Latham 1990) and beliefs (e.g., self-efficacy; Bandura 1977) as its source. Essentially, the suggestion is that individuals engage in tasks (i.e., work) and enter into employment relationships that are consistent with their goals and self-perceptions.

Although there is a great deal of empirical support for the propositions of goal setting, relatively little attention has been paid to the origin of the goals. Locke and Henne (1986) provided a link between goal setting and work values by hypothesizing that goals mediate between values and behavior. Individuals formulate and become committed to goals as a result of their values. In turn, goals lead to behavior. Roberson (1990) provides a similar model linking work meanings to behavior through the intervening states of goals and intentions. The process thus described is analogous to the model of reasoned actions (Fishbein and Ajzen 1975), which suggests that the most proximal predictor of behavior is behavioral intent and, in turn, intent is the result of attitudes (i.e., evaluative judgments).

A theory of work motivation is deficient to the extent that it is static and does not allow for change in the initiating state. With regard to work values, O'Brien (1992:59) observes that "people become what they do." Consistent with the propositions of social learning theory, the suggestion is that individuals interact with their environment and come to value that which is obtainable and devalue that which is unobtainable. Thus, individuals in routine, repetitive work that offers none of the intrinsic features associated with good work (e.g., see Hackman and Oldham 1980) may come to value the only rewards that are obtainable: salary increases or work hour decreases. In this sense, economic socialization does not end when an individual enters the workforce. Rather, individual motivations and values continue to change as a result of experience (O'Brien 1992).

Conclusion

Schumaker (1979:2–3) began his consideration of work with this observation:

> Considering the centrality of work in human life, one might have expected that every textbook on economics, sociology, politics and related subjects would present a theory of work as one of the indispensable foundation stones for all further expositions. . . . However the truth of the matter is that we look in vain for presentations of theories of work in these textbooks.

We extend this observation to suggest that theories of work and theories of employment may, in fact, be quite different. Moreover, we suggest that the process of theory development has been specifically impeded by the failure to distinguish between the questions of "why people work" and "why people are employed."

One implication of this perspective is the need to examine work in various employment contexts and work that occurs in non-employment relations. Studies of the social or irregular economy (Ferman 1990) as well as examinations of work in retirement (Higginbottom, Barling, and Kelloway 1994) and unemployment (Grant and Barling 1994) lead to an answer to the question of why people work that is not tied to contemporary understandings of employment relations. We suggest that such an approach is necessary given the dramatic changes that have already occurred in our understanding of what constitutes employment relations. The growth of contingent employment and dramatic changes in industrial relations (Hartley and Stephenson 1992) have posed a challenge to our understanding of work and employment.

In our view, behavioral scientists are as of yet poorly equipped to deal with a restructuring of employment relations. By ignoring work in the social or irregular economy (Ferman 1990) in favor of an exclusive focus on paid employment, behavioral theorists have risked constructing and disseminating a truncated body of literature regarding the nature and effects of work and employment. Theories grounded in traditional employment contexts may be of little utility if these contexts are rapidly changing.

As noted by Block (2001), Polanyi's (2001) attack on the notion of freely regulated markets begins with his suggestion that markets are embedded in a societal context. Therefore, markets are subordinate to politics, religion, and social relations. Analogously, our answer to the question "Why do people work?" begins with the observation that both work and employment are embedded in a social context that attaches values to these activities and creates individual expectations for achievement and success.

Acknowledgments

Preparation of this chapter was supported by grants from the Social Sciences and Humanities Research Council of Canada and from the Nova Scotia Health Research Foundation.

References

Alderfer, Chris P. 1972. *Existence, Relatedness and Growth: Human Needs in Organizational Settings.* New York: Free Press.

Allegretti, Joseph G. 2000. *Loving Your Job, Finding Your Passion: Work and the Spiritual Life.* New York: Paulist Press.

Applebaum, Herbert A. 1984. *Work in Market and Industrial Societies.* Albany, NY: SUNY Press.

———. 1992. *The Concept of Work: Ancient, Medieval and Modern.* Albany, NY: SUNY Press.

Arendt, Hannah. 1959. *The Human Condition.* Garden City, NJ: Doubleday.

Bandura, Albert. 1977. *Social Learning Theory.* Englewood Cliffs, NJ: Prentice-Hall.

Barling, Julian, Clive Fullagar, and E. Kevin Kelloway. 1992. *The Union and Its Members: A Psychological Approach.* New York: Oxford University Press.

Barling, Julian, E. Kevin Kelloway, and Eric H. Bremermann. 1991. "Pre-employment Predictors of Union Attitudes: The Role of Family Socialization and Work Beliefs." *Journal of Applied Psychology,* Vol. 76, pp. 725–31.

Beard, Kathy M., and Jeffrey R. Edwards. 1995. "Employees at Risk: Contingent Work and the Psychological Experience of Contingent Workers." In Cary L. Cooper and Denise M. Rousseau, eds., *Trends in Organizational Behavior,* Vol. 2, Chichester, UK: Wiley, pp. 109–26.

Berti, Anna E., and Anna S. Bombi. 1988. *The Child's Construction of Economics.* New York: Cambridge University Press.

Biesheuvel, Simon. 1975. "One More Time, How Do We Motivate the Herzberg Theory?" *Psychologia Africana,* Vol. 16, pp. 33–44.

Block, Fred. 2001. Introduction. In Karl Polanyi, *The Great Transformation,* New York: Vacation Publishing.

Brayfield, Arthur H., and Walter H. Crockett. 1955. "Employee Attitudes and Employee Performance." *Psychological Bulletin,* Vol. 52, pp. 396–424.

Bridges, William. 1994. *Job Shift: How to Prosper in a Workplace without Jobs.* Reading, MA: Addison-Wesley.

Brief, Arthur P., and Ramon J. Aldag. 1977. "The Intrinsic–Extrinsic Dichotomy: Toward Conceptual Clarity." *Academy of Management Review,* Vol. 2, pp. 496–500.

———. 1989. "The Economic Functions of Work." In K. M. Rowland and G. R. Ferris, eds., *Research in Personnel and Human Resources Management,* Vol. 7, Greenwich, CT: JAI Press, pp. 1–23.

Brief, Arthur P., and Walter R. Nord. 1990. *Meanings of Occupational Work: A Collection of Essays.* Lexington, MA: Lexington Books.

Briskin, Allan. 1996. *The Stirring of Soul in the Workplace.* San Francisco: Jossey-Bass.

Burnett, John. 1994. *Idle Hands: The Experience of Unemployment, 1790–1990.* New York: Routledge.

Cappelli, Peter. 1999. *The New Deal at Work.* Boston: Harvard Business School Press.

Cooper, Cary L., and Ivan Robertson. 1986. Editorial foreword. In Cary L. Cooper and Ivan Robertson, eds., *International Review of Industrial and Organizational Psychology,* Chichester, UK: Wiley.

Dickinson, Julie, and Nicholas Emler. 1992. "Developing Conceptions of Work." In Jean F. Hartley and Geoffrey M. Stephenson, eds., *Employment Relations: The Psychology of Influence and Control at Work,* Cambridge, MA: Blackwell, pp. 19–44.

Donkin, Richard. 2001. *Blood, Sweat and Tears: The Evolution of Work.* New York: Texere.

Ehrenreich, Barbara. 2001. *Nickel and Dimed: On Not Getting By in America.* New York: Metropolitan Books.

Emler, Nicholas, and Dickinson, Julie. 1985. "Children's Representation of Economic Inequalities: The Effects of Social Class." *British Journal of Developmental Psychology,* Vol. 3, 191–98.

Farago, Anna. 2002. *The Patron Saint of Business Management.* Toronto, ON: Insomniac Press.

Feather, Norman T. 1990. *The Psychological Impact of Unemployment.* New York: Springer-Verlag.

Ferman, Louis A. 1990. "Participation in the Irregular Economy." In Kai Erickson and Steven P. Vallas, eds., *The Nature of Work: Sociological Perspectives,* New Haven, CT: Yale University Press, pp. 119–40.

Fishbein, Martin, and Icek Ajzen. 1975. *Belief, Attitude, Intention and Behavior: An Introduction to Theory and Research.* Reading, MA: Addison-Wesley.

Fox, Matthew. 1994. *The Reinvention of Work: New Vision of Livelihood for Our Time.* New York: HarperCollins.

Freidson, Edward. 1990. "Labors of Love in Theory and Practice." In Kai Erickson and Steven P. Vallas, eds., *The Nature of Work: Sociological Perspectives,* New Haven, CT: Yale University Press, pp. 149–61.

Fried, Yitzchak, and Gerald R. Ferris. 1987. "The Validity of the Job Characteristics Model: A Review and Meta-analysis." *Personnel Psychology,* Vol. 40, pp. 287–322.

Furnham, Adrian. 1987. "Predicting Protestant Work Ethic Beliefs." *European Journal of Personality,* Vol. 1, pp. 93–106.

———. 1990. *The Protestant Work Ethic: The Psychology of Work-Related Beliefs and Behaviors.* New York: Routledge.

Furnham, Adrian, and Michael Argyle. 1998. *The Psychology of Money.* London: Routledge.

Gallagher, Daniel G. 2002. "Contingent Work Contracts: Practice and Theory." In Cary Cooper and Ronald Burke, eds., *The New World of Work,* Oxford: Blackwell, pp. 311–27.

Gallagher, Daniel G., and Judi McLean Parks. 2001. "I Pledge Thee My Troth . . . Contingently: Commitment and the Contingent Work Relationship." *Human Resource Management Review,* Vol. 11, pp. 181–208.

Garson, Barbara. 1994. *All the Livelong Day.* New York: Penguin Books.

Geogheghan, Arthur. T. 1945. *The Attitude toward Labor in Early Christianity and Ancient Culture.* Washington, DC: The Catholic University of America Press.

Gottfredson, Linda S. 1981. "Circumscription and Compromise: A Developmental Theory of Occupational Aspirations." *Journal of Counseling Psychology,* Vol. 28, pp. 545–79.

Grant, Sally, and Julian Barling. 1994. "Linking Unemployment Experiences and Marital Functioning." In Gwendolyn P. Keita and Joseph R. Hurrell, eds., *Job*

Stress in a Changing Workforce: Investigating Gender, Diversity and Family, Washington, DC: American Psychological Association, pp. 311–27.

Hackman, J. Richard, and Greg R. Oldham. 1976. "Motivation through the Design of Work: Test of a Theory." *Organizational Behavior and Human Performance,* Vol. 16, pp. 250–79.

———. 1980. *Work Redesign.* Reading, MA: Addison-Wesley.

Handy, Charles. 1984. *The Future of Work.* London: Blackwell.

Harrell, Thomas W. 1949. *Industrial Psychology.* Oxford: Rinehart.

Hartley, Jean F., and Geoffrey M. Stephenson. 1992. "Introduction: The Psychology of Employment Relations." In Jean E. Hartley and Geoffrey M. Stephenson, eds., *Employment Relations,* London: Blackwell.

Herzberg, Frederick. 1966. "One More Time: How Do You Motivate Employees?" *Harvard Business Review,* Vol. 46, pp. 53–62.

Herzberg, Frederick, Bernard Mausner, and Barbara B. Snyderman. 1959. *The Motivation to Work.* New York: Wiley.

Higginbottom, Susan F., Julian Barling, and E. Kevin Kelloway. 1994. "Linking Retirement and Marital Satisfaction: A Mediational Model." *Psychology and Aging,* Vol. 8, pp. 508–16.

Jahoda, Marie. 1979. "The Construction of Economic Reality by Some Glaswegian Children." *European Journal of Social Psychology,* Vol. 9, pp. 115–27.

———. 1982. *Employment and Unemployment: A Social-Psychological Analysis.* Cambridge: Cambridge University Press.

Kaufman, Bruce E. 1999. "Models of Man in Economic Research." *Industrial and Labor Relations Review,* Vol. 43, pp. 72–88.

Kelloway, E. Kevin, and Julian Barling. 2000. "Knowledge Work as Organizational Behaviour." *International Journal of Management Reviews,* Vol. 2, pp. 287–304.

Kelloway, E. Kevin, and Steve Harvey. 1999. "Learning to Work." In Julian Barling and E. Kevin Kelloway, eds., *Young Workers: Varieties of Experience,* Washington, DC: APA Books.

Kelloway, E. Kevin, and Tricia Newton. 1996. "Family Socialization of Union Attitudes: The Role of Parental Union and Work Experiences." *Canadian Journal of Behavioral Science,* Vol. 28, pp. 113–20.

Kelloway, E. Kevin, and Laura Watts. 1994. "Pre-employment Predictors of Union Attitudes: Replication and Extension." *Journal of Applied Psychology,* Vol. 79, pp. 631–34.

Latham, Gary P., and Helen-Marie Budworth. In press. "The Study of Work Motivation in the 20th Century." In L. Koppes, ed., *The History of Industrial and Organizational Psychology,* Hillsdale, NJ: Laurence Erlbaum.

Lea, Stephen E. G., Roger M. Tarpy, and Paul Webley. 1987. *The Individual in the Economy: A Survey of Economic Psychology.* New York: Cambridge University Press.

Locke, Edwin A. 1968. "Toward a Theory of Task Motivation and Incentives." *Organizational Behavior and Human Decision Processes,* Vol. 3, pp. 157–89.

Locke, Edwin A., and Douglas Henne. 1986. "Work Motivation Theories." In Cary L. Cooper and Ivan Robertson, eds., *International Review of Industrial and Organizational Psychology,* New York: Wiley, pp. 1–36.

Locke, Edwin A., and Gary P. Latham. 1990. *A Theory of Goal Setting and Task Performance.* Englewood Cliffs, NJ: Prentice-Hall.

Loher, Brian T., Raymond A. Noe, Nancy L. Moeller, and Michael P. Fitzgerald. 1985. "A Meta-analysis of the Relation of Job Characteristics to Job Satisfaction." *Journal of Applied Psychology*, Vol. 70, pp. 280–89.

Maslow, Abraham H. 1943. "A Theory of Human Motivation." *Psychological Review*, Vol. 50, pp. 370–96.

Mayo, Elton. 1933. *The Human Problems of Industrialized Civilization*. Chicago: Scott, Foresman.

McGregor, Douglas M. 1960. *The Human Side of the Enterprise*. New York: McGraw-Hill.

Morse, N. C., and R. S. Weiss. 1955. "The Function and Meaning of Work and the Job." *American Sociological Review*, Vol. 20, pp. 191–98.

Nash, Laura, Scotty McLennan, and Ken Blanchard. 2001. *Church on Sunday, Work on Monday: The Challenge of Fusing Christian Values with Business Life*. San Francisco: Jossey-Bass.

Neff, Walter S. 1977. *Work and Human Behavior*, 2nd ed. Chicago: Aldine.

Nord, Walter R., Arthur Brief, Jennifer Atieh, and Elizabeth Doherty. 1988. "Work Values and the Conduct of Organizational Behavior." In Barry M. Staw and Lawrence L. Cummings, eds., *Research in Organizational Behavior*, Vol. 9, Greenwich, CT: JAI Press, pp. 1–42.

———. 1990. "Studying Meanings of Work: The Case of Work Values." In Arthur P. Brief and Walter R. Nord, eds., *Meanings of Occupational Work: A Collection of Essays*. Lexington, MA: Lexington Books.

O'Brien, Gordon E. 1992. "Changing Meanings of Work." In Jean E. Hartley and Geoffrey M. Stephenson, eds., *Employment Relations*, London: Blackwell.

O'Reilly, Charles A. 1991. "Organizational Behavior: Where We've Been, Where We're Going." *Annual Review of Psychology*, Vol. 42, pp. 427–58.

Pahl, Raymond E. 1988. *On Work: Historical, Comparative, and Theoretical Approaches*. Oxford: Basil-Blackwell.

Parker, Sharon K. 2002. "Designing Jobs to Enhance Well-Being and Performance." In Peter B. Warr, ed., *Psychology at Work*, 5th ed., London: Penguin Books, pp. 276–99.

Pfeffer, Jeffrey. 1998a. *The Human Equation: Building Profits by Putting People First*. Boston: Harvard Business School Press.

———. 1998b. Six Dangerous Myths about Pay. *Harvard Business Review*, May–June, 108–20.

Pfeffer, Jeffrey, and James N. Baron. 1988. "Taking the Workers Back Out: Recent Trends in the Structures of Employment." In Barry M. Staw and Lawrence L. Cummings, eds., *Research in Organizational Behavior*, Vol. 10, pp. 257–303.

Pinder, Craig. 1984. *Work Motivation: Theory, Issues, and Applications*. New York: Prentice-Hall.

Piotrkowski, Chaya S., and Elizabeth Stark. 1987. "Children and Adolescents Look at Their Parents' Jobs." In John H. Lewko, ed., *How Children and Adolescents View the World of Work*, San Francisco: Jossey-Bass, pp. 3–19.

Polanyi, Karl. 2001. *The Great Transformation: The Political and Economic Origins of Our Time*. New York: Vacation Publishing.

Richmond, Lewis. 2000. *Work as a Spiritual Practice*. New York: Broadway Books.

Rifkin, Jeremy. 1995. *The End of Work*. New York: Putnam's.

Roberson, Loriann. 1990. "Functions of Work Meaning in Organizations: Work, Meanings and Work Motivation." In Arthur P. Brief and Walter R. Nord, eds.,

Meanings of Occupational Work: A Collection of Essays, Lexington, MA: Lexington Books, pp. 107–34.

Roethlisberger, Fritz J., and William J. Dickson. 1939. *Management and the Worker.* Cambridge: Cambridge University Press.

Rousseau, Denise M. 1989. "Psychological and Implied Contracts in Organizations." *Employee Responsibilities and Rights Journal,* Vol. 2, pp. 121–39.

Rynes, Sara, and Barry Gerhart. 2000. *Compensation in Organizations: Current Research and Practice.* New York: Jossey-Bass.

Schumaker, Ernst Frederich. 1979. *Good Work.* New York: Harper and Row.

Shafritz, Jay M., and J. Steven Ott. 1996. *Classics of Organizational Theory,* 4th ed. Albany, NY: Wadsworth.

Smith, Adam. [1776] 1976. *The Wealth of Nations.* Edited by Edward Cannan. Chicago: University of Chicago Press.

Sohn-Rethel, Alfred. 1978. *Intellectual and Manual Labor.* London: Macmillan.

Spector, Paul. 1997. *Job Satisfaction.* Thousand Oaks, CA: SAGE Publications.

Stagner, Ross. 1950. "Psychological Aspects of Industrial Conflict II: Motivation." *Personnel Psychology,* Vol. 3, pp. 1–15.

Taylor, Frederick W. 1911. *The Principles of Scientific Management.* New York: Harper.

Thierry, Henk. 1992. "Pay and Pay Systems." In Jean E. Hartley and Geoffrey M. Stephenson, eds., *Employment Relations,* London: Blackwell.

Thomas, Keith. 1999. *The Oxford Book of Work.* Oxford: Oxford University Press.

Thurstone, L. L. 1929. "Theory of Attitude Measurement." *Psychological Review,* Vol. 36, pp. 222–41.

Tilgher, Adriano. 1930. *Work: What It Has Meant through the Ages.* New York: Harcourt, Brace.

Viteles, Morris S. 1932. *Industrial Psychology.* New York: Norton.

Vroom, Victor. 1964. *Work Motivation.* New York: Wiley.

Warr, Peter B. 1987. *Work Employment and Mental Health.* Oxford: Oxford University Press.

Watson, John B. 1913. "Psychology as the Behaviorist Views It." *Psychological Review,* Vol. 19, pp. 212–40.

Weber, Max. 1952. *The Protestant Ethic and the Spirit of Capitalism.* New York: Scribner's.

Whyte, William Foote. 1948. *Human Relations in the Restaurant Industry.* New York: McGraw-Hill.

CHAPTER 5

Labor Process Theory, Work, and the Employment Relation

PAUL THOMPSON AND KIRSTY NEWSOME
University of Strathclyde

For some, labor process theory (LPT) died with Braverman and his followers, or at best with some of the major responses to his work from Richard Edwards, Friedman, Burawoy, and others. Though its influence peaked in the mid-1980s, LPT remains arguably the dominant approach to workplace studies in the United Kingdom and has significant influence in critical scholarship in Europe, Australia, and North America. Its major impact has been on the sociology of work, but in different contexts it has exerted influence on labor history, industrial relations, and organization theory. The strong position in the United Kingdom, and to a lesser extent in Northern Europe, can be partly explained by institutionalization through the annual International Labour Process Conference and its associated publishing programs.[1]

From the early critiques of human relations by Braverman (1974) to the contemporary commentaries on the limits of human resource management (HRM) discussed in this chapter, LPT has had an enduring influence on the way that work and employment relations are conceptualized and researched. This chapter uses the idea of "waves" of labor process theory and research to provide a narrative structure. The first wave consisted of Braverman's work and its supportive arguments, the second was the major studies that followed in its wake from the late 1970s to the late 1980s, the third was the largely defensive responses to new paradigm theories in the following decade, and the fourth refers to contemporary research that is attempting to open LPT to wider issues of political economy. Throughout this discussion, we argue that LPT makes a useful contribution to industrial relations theories in two ways. A substantial body of rich, qualitative studies provide key insights into observed behavior and practices at work. In addition, a conceptual framework helps set work and employment relations in a broader context, thus making a contribution to what we call the "connectivity problem."

Core Theory

In the mind of many casual observers, the first and second waves of LPT are notable for associating LPT with a deskilling thesis or an emphasis on Taylorism as a control system. This standard assumption is mistaken and confuses the arguments put forward by Braverman (1974) and some initial supportive research (e.g., Zimbalist 1979) with a much broader and more varied body of work (see Thompson 1989). That work, which matured in the 1980s, consisted primarily of two overlapping research programs. The first sought to understand changing patterns of labor utilization and production systems; the second produced rival historical and contemporary accounts of managerial control. Deskilling and Taylorism were seen merely as two prominent strategies within those processes.

Early labor process writings can be seen as part of a wider trend in critical materialist scholarship. While there were continuities with older industrial sociology such as Baldamus (1961) on the wage–effort bargain, LPT can initially be seen as part of the development of a new generation of Marxist writings on the capitalist division of labor that also included French and Italian theorists such as Gorz (1976). Anglo-American LPT, however, developed its own distinctive theoretical framework and research program. The first and most influential attempt to pull together the threads of LPT, by Knights and Willmott (1990), took place at the end of the 1980s' wave of scholarship. The opening three chapters of that volume, by Littler, Thompson, and Paul Edwards, all focused on the production of a core theoretical framework.

That core begins from the unique character of labor as a commodity—its indeterminacy—and thus "the conversion of labor power (the potential for work) into labor (actual work effort) under conditions which permit capital accumulation" (Littler 1990:48). Thompson (1990) identified four principles that flow from this:

1. Because the labor process generates a surplus and is a central part of human experience in acting on the world and reproducing the economy, the role of labor and the capital–labor relationship are privileged in analysis.

2. There is a logic of accumulation that compels capital to constantly revolutionize the production of goods and services. This arises from competition between capitalists and between capital and labor. This logic has no determinate effects on any specific feature of the labor

process (such as use of skills), but it does place constraints on the willingness and ability of capital to dispense with hierarchical relations, empower employees, and combine conception and execution.

3. Because market mechanisms alone cannot regulate the labor process, there is a control imperative as systems of management are utilized to reduce the indeterminacy gap. Again, this imperative specifies nothing about the nature or level of control or the efficacy of particular management strategies and practices, nor does it preclude the influence of control mechanisms that originate from outside the workplace.

4. Given the dynamics of exploitation and control, the social relations between capital and labor in the workplace are of "structured antagonism" (P. Edwards 1990). At the same time, capital, in order to constantly revolutionize the work process, must seek some level of creativity and cooperation from labor. The result is a continuum of possible situationally driven and overlapping worker responses—from resistance to accommodation, compliance, and consent.

Such conceptions of a core theory have been attacked by HRM theorists as a structuralist straightjacket that explains managerial behavior within capital's requirement for control over labor (Storey 1985); by Marxists for setting aside the laws of capitalism, such as the labor theory of value (Spencer 2000); and by poststructuralists for neglecting issues of subjectivity and identity (O'Doherty and Willmott 2001). While many of these differences are simply outcomes of contending theoretical assumptions, to some degree criticisms of under- and overdetermination neglect the primary purpose of the core theory. The core theory does not, or at least has not, sought to explain or predict determinate relations between particular conditions and outcomes such as the use of a specific control strategy or degree of shared interest. Instead, it has tried to account for the variations and complexity of workplace relations and to identify key trends across sectors, companies, and nation-states, while setting out the systemic features of the capitalist labor process that shape and constrain those relations. The disciplines that study and the perspectives on the workplace are often strong on the former but neglect the latter. For example, in a recent overview, Frenkel (2003:135–37) argued that the contemporary workplace must be approached in terms of multiple embeddedness: the macrofields of globalization and new technology, the mesofield of transnational production networks, and the microfield of local institutions, cultures, and organization structures. This point is well made, but the distinctive perspective of LPT is that the capitalist labor process also has properties of structural embeddedness. The framework thus focuses primarily on the workplace level, while seeking to extend up to the causal powers manifest in mechanisms of capitalist social and market relations.[2]

The Relevance to Industrial Relations

The particular potential attraction of LPT for studying industrial relations and the dynamics of the employment relationship lies in its ability to locate traditional conceptions of conflict in the effort bargain and the frontier of control within a broader and potentially more coherent analytical framework. As Paul Edwards (1990:126) observed, the structured antagonism embedded in the capitalist labor process does not impose a direct logic on behavior: "it generates pressures which have to be interpreted and acted on by employers and workers." On a broader scale, the systemic qualities of capitalism are not experienced in the same way across societies as a result of the diversity of nation-states, sectors, and firms. Analysis has to be empirically sensitive to the interaction among structural, national, and other institutional dynamics (Smith and Thompson 1998).

The ultimate purpose of theory is to provide a robust framework for a research program. This section examines the strengths and some limits of classic, "second-wave" labor process research. While it is widely acknowledged that LPT had a major impact on industrial sociology, we argue that three actual or potentially significant contributions to industrial relations can also be identified.

Connectivity

First, the capacity of LPT to enhance connectivity across conceptual and empirical territories helped expand the scope of industrial relations as the discipline rethought its character and boundaries in the 1980s. This is evidenced by scholars working within a Marxist tradition, such as Richard Hyman. In later editions of his classic work *Strikes*, he recommended an analysis of the labor process as a means of understanding the broad pattern of workplace relations and the contradictory relations of conflict and cooperation between capital and labor at work (Hyman 1989:184–85). In another paper, "Theory and Industrial Relations," Hyman, while preferring the term "critical political economy," repeated the central argument of LPT that job regulation and the rules of the employment relationship are best approached "if we understand how labor power is transformed into productive labor, and the social and economic forces that structure that transformation" (1994:171). Paul Edwards (1992), the writer who provides the strongest link between LPT and industrial relations, also referred to the ability of a political economy approach to make links between workplace and national modes of labor regulation. There is also a sense in which LPT encouraged industrial relations to connect "downward" from the traditional mesolevel of collective actors and institutions. This is discussed in the next section.

Informal Industrial Relations

The identification of formal, collective resistance to deskilling and Taylorism by trade unions at the local level provided an explicit means of linking second-wave LPT and industrial relations (Pulignano 2001). However, a second, more extensive impact flowed from the direct emphasis on the dynamics of control, consent, and resistance at the point of production. This strengthens those tendencies in the discipline that have long sought to reach beneath institutional, formal patterns and to discover and explore hidden or informal realms of industrial relations and workplace conflict. While LPT has no a priori preference for particular methodologies, its strength has been in qualitative case studies and workplace-level ethnography.[3] In the British context, LPT built on the work of the 1970s' generation of radical industrial sociology and industrial relations writers such as Hugh Beynon (1975), Theo Nichols (Nichols and Beynon 1977), and Peter Armstrong (Nichols and Armstrong 1976). Extended case studies of Ford and Chemco combined an emphasis on the negative effects and limited changes to the organization of work with the practical and ideological problems of trade union organization.

A New View of Class Struggle

LPT provided a post-Marxist, materialist account of conflicts between capital and labor that moved beyond some of the constraints of existing debates on class struggle and industrial relations (Elger 2001:4). Braverman, as is well known, avoided a discussion of worker organization and ideology in relation to the changes in the labor process he so meticulously set out. Yet elsewhere (Braverman 1976), he made abundantly clear that he held to the traditional Marxist assumption that "objective" changes in workplace and society will lead to corresponding forms of class consciousness and struggle. In contrast, the work of many second-wave writers led them to try to disentangle LPT from Marxism or, more precisely, to disentangle those elements that pertain to the relations between production and political economy from the complete baggage of assumptions about society and social transformation. The central argument was that the dynamics of capital and labor as actors in the workplace cannot be assumed to be continuous with capital and labor as societal actors: "it cannot be empirically demonstrated that there is an automatic relationship between the labor process, class formation and social transformation as envisaged in the Marxist schema" (Thompson 1990:113). Elger (2001:5–6) argued that Thompson's theoretical analysis, alongside that of Paul Edwards (1986, 1990), furnished the analytical tools to differentiate structured antagonism in the labor process from the teleological assumptions within Marxism that workplace conflict must escalate toward the overthrow of capitalism. This differentiation is necessarily underpinned by a belief that workplace relations have a relative autonomy from wider social structures and processes. While this differentiation was used primarily to open up a space between LPT and orthodox Marxism, it is also fair to observe that it marks a difference from some other perspectives on industrial relations that emphasize the determinate or at least primary influences of societal institutions and norms on workplace behavior.

The Second-Wave Research Program

As indicated earlier, radical social science in the United Kingdom and the United States had a welcome orientation toward uncovering the informal dimensions of workplace relations. This orientation involved exploring the problematic boundaries between worker action in the labor process and trade unionism. As Beynon memorably put it in the classic empirical study of this period, *Working for Ford*, "Trade unionism is about work and sometimes the lads just don't want to work. All talk of procedures and negotiations tend to break down here" (1975:140). Even where workers were found to be less militant, as in the Chemco studies, every effort was made to identify the covert and sometimes individualistic ways that labor gets by and gets back at management (Nichols and Armstrong 1976). Nevertheless, among the limitations of such approaches was a tendency to search for class consciousness and, seldom finding it, to construct elaborate explanations for its non- or limited existence. In effect, "workers were treated as 'apprentice revolutionaries' whose behavior and attitudes are evaluated against an a-priori and unrealistic model of social agency and change" (Ackroyd and Thompson 1999:46).

Second-wave labor process writing did, of course, evince similarities with existing critical research. Certainly there was a determined effort, contra Braverman, to put resistance back in, but more as a driver of changes in capitalism than a demonstration of how it might be overthrown (Friedman 1977:48). Resistance was held as having a different context and object: a regime of managerial controls over the labor process, narrower than society-wide class struggle but broader than the simple wage–effort bargain.

Elaboration of this dialectic of control and resistance became a central feature of LPT: "the core of their research programme consists of a series of historically informed empirical studies focused on managerial control strategies and practices in work organisations" (Reed 1992:155). These studies (Friedman 1977; R. Edwards 1979; Littler 1982) are well known, and their details need not be repeated here. In one sense they shared a similar scope of analysis, seeking to make connections among workplace, industrial relations, the state, and broader social structures, though the dominant focus was on struggle at the micro level. Beyond conditions of the sale of labor power, detailed attention was paid to the myriad of job controls and wage–effort bargains, whether individual and informal or collective and organized.

The best-known empirical illustrations of what is referred to as the control-resistance paradigm were provided by Richard Edwards (1979) and Friedman (1977). Edwards seeks to restore the ongoing dialectic (neglected by Braverman) as a driver of the unfolding logic of the accumulation process. In an ambitious analysis (Edwards 1979), he represented this through the elaboration of sequential but overlapping regimes of simple, technical, and bureaucratic control. Each regime aims to close the indeterminacy gap in particular socioeconomic conditions. Those regimes in turn offer new constraints and possibilities for capital and labor, though ultimately their effectiveness will diminish as contradictions outweigh benefits, and capital will be compelled to search for new ways to achieve profitable production. One U.K. critic of Edwards accused him of providing a passive and noninteractive model of industrial relations (Penn 1982). This is unfair, though it is true that Edwards's dialectic is constructed at a fairly general level, with labor as an initially reactive agent.

Friedman's (1977) model is not sequential, though it is also historical in character. Moving from 19th century weaving and hosiery trades to the more familiar territory of the 20th century U.K. motor industry, his essential goal was to outline the conditions under which management develops strategies of direct control and responsible autonomy. Labor is not reactive, given that management choices are conditioned by the need to come to terms with worker organization in different labor markets. While the empirical story lacked the elegance of Richard Edwards's (1979) account, it achieved a more successful integration of the dynamics of the labor process, markets, and industrial relations. In the modern case studies, Friedman (1977) outlined how motor industry management oscillated between the two main strategic options, but he was sensitive to both the microlevel changes in managerial behavior and the range of individual and collective actions of employees. Localized job controls and informal organization expressed through powerful shop steward structures were central to negotiating "mutuality" of influence in work. Such influence was under continued attack by employers' attempts to extend direct control through new work measurement schemes, redundancies, and ending traditional bargaining agreements. Friedman's (1977) account of these struggles consciously tried to move away from traditional leftist dichotomies between trade union and socialist politics.

A concern for developing a more complex and localized politics of production also marked the work of Burawoy (1979, 1985). However, in these studies he shifted the focus to the production of consent. Consent is manufactured less through societal ideology and false consciousness and more within a relatively autonomous set of production relations. In particular, the emphasis was on what traditional industrial sociology had called "making out." Burawoy argued that participation in labor process "games" has the unintended effect of concealing the exploitative social relations of capitalist production and redistributes conflict from vertical to lateral (intra-employee) disputes. As Mahnkopf (1986:41) observed, contrary to the "contested terrain" thesis, Burawoy's analysis "can offer a plausible explanation for the failure of resistance by groups of workers." Such arguments are designed to break with the idea that politics is always about the state and challenge some views within industrial relations that the subject is only interesting when labor acquires power and uses it (Crouch, quoted in Clark 1995:595). These arguments are also less narrowly based around the effort bargain than they sound. Burawoy's reworking of Gramscian notions of hegemony involves notions of production politics that treats factory regimes also as "internal states" characterized by their own labor markets and forms of citizenship. Burawoy therefore prefigured later perspectives that saw the emergence of new and eventually dominant normative bases of control, though these were located firmly in material practices rather than discourses.

One can and should criticize some of the flaws and incompleteness of Burawoy's arguments (see Thompson 1989:165–72), but the overall outcome was positive. LPT had moved from a control and resistance model to a control, resistance, *and* consent model. An example of some of the benefits of this growing sophistication was seen in the writings of a new generation of feminist industrial sociologists (Pollert 1981; Westwood 1984). Ethnographic methods not only allowed a close observation of the conditions and informal practices of female wage labor, but the very marginalization of the concerns of women workers by the local and national trade union apparatus stimulated a focus on the dual sources of resistance and consent in gender-based modes of control and shop floor cultures.

Perhaps the most comprehensive account of a control, resistance, and consent perspective was developed by Paul Edwards in two books, an empirically based study written with Scullion (1982) and a much broader theoretical and historically grounded contribution (Edwards 1986). The latter confirmed the point already observed that labor process theory, though remaining materialist, was breaking with its narrowly Marxist origins. Though both works engaged in the arguments discussed earlier in the chapter about what underpins and differentiates class, factory, and other forms of "sectional" consciousness, Edwards commented, "Neither is workplace struggle to be equated with class struggle. Indeed a basic argument running through this study is that conflicts in work relations have no necessary connotations for wider class conflict" (1986:7). Like other writers he was keen to move away from a control *versus* resistance model to one that recognizes a variety of forms of conflict and accommodation.

In the earlier set of case studies, Paul Edwards and Scullion (1982) integrated analysis of a wide range of behaviors in the effort bargain within particular regimes of control. Detailed case studies showed how workers adapt their actions, such as absence, labor turnover, the use of sanctions, and sabotage, to particular modes of control over work or payment. Conversely, they illustrated how management develops policies and practices in areas such as the provision of overtime as a means of transacting with powerful shop floor controls. These case studies combined to illustrate how "matters at the point of production" are indicative not just of battles over the frontier of control but also of "how workers are persuaded to release their labour power" (Edwards and Scullion 1982:151).

Within this analysis both the formal and informal dynamics of conflict are presented. Indeed, for Edwards and Scullion (1982), conventional measures of trade union strength and density per se are at best imperfect indicators of an institutional apparatus; it is the ability of workers to resist management and to attain their own ends in battles over the frontier of control that is of utmost importance. As we indicated earlier, Paul Edwards (1990) also referred to the dynamics of workplace regulation as having a "relative autonomy" in the sense that forces external to the labor process are simultaneously mediated by internal forces within it. The implication is that similar external situations can produce different internal labor process outcomes because of the distinctiveness and peculiarities of particular points of production.

The Limits of Second-Wave Research

Second-wave research demonstrated numerous strengths and a distinctive competence in analyzing workplace-level patterns of control, resistance, conflict, and accommodation. Though some of the best-known studies were criticized for a tendency toward monocausal explanation—the "panacea fallacy"—that capital always seeks and finds a particular solution to its control problems (Littler and Salaman 1982), this was not true of the later and more detailed case studies such as those by Paul Edwards and Scullion (1982) and Thompson and Bannon (1985). Nevertheless, before we move on to later waves of research, it is worth pausing to note a number of limitations to this body of work.

First, in some studies the different forms of conflict still tend to be seen in reactive terms as responses to the exertion of managerial control rather than as having more complex internal and external drivers. In addition, employee action and organization are still largely judged against a set of criteria of which collective action and organization are the goal and norm. As Ackroyd and Thompson (1999:50) observed,

> The differences between events such as absence or strikes is cast in terms of the degree of formal organization that is needed to develop them and make them effective instruments of class action. Informal practices such as fiddling or sabotage, lacking any formal organisation, are taken to be ineffective surrogates for striking and other acts which have formal organization as their basis.

Second, while the concept of the relative autonomy of the labor process opened space to see distinctive workplace dynamics, it has its downside. When the relativity becomes the dominant focus, it creates the potential, if unintended, legitimation of a narrow frame of analysis.

A great strength of LPT is its capacity to connect the workplace to a broader political economy. Without that, the research program can disappear into microlevel case studies of control and skill strategies whose causal chain ends at the factory gate. Even Burawoy's considerable insights into the process of manufacturing consent are constrained by the underconceptualization of the broader bases of normative integration, including its industrial relations dimension (Mahnkopf 1986).

With hindsight we can also observe that second-wave research was located primarily inside national economies that had at that stage limited exposure to intensified global competition. This is related to a third weakness. The template for a national economy was too often taken to be the United States. As Thompson and Smith (1998) demonstrated, *Labor and Monopoly Capital* (Braverman 1974) appeared when the United States had yet to face the challenge from Japan and when its institutions, such as the multidivisional firm, and labor–management practices were considered the most modern available. References to other countries and economies in the book were thin on the ground. Even then it was unwise to speak of the capitalist labor process as a single experience—today it would be impossible. This lack of a comparative analysis was also picked up on by critics of Richard Edwards (Penn 1982) and is particularly problematic in relation to the traditional, though limited, strengths of cross-national studies by industrial relations scholars. Labor process debates did increasingly try to deal with wider political dynamics and an analysis of the state (Burawoy 1985; Thompson 1989). However, they largely failed to capture the complexities of relations between capital, labor, and the state within the international division of labor. We return to this question later in the chapter.

Rival Paradigms: LPT under Fire

As a reaction to some of the preceding debates, labor process theory and research continued to add complexity and contingency, with a focus on variations in management control and skill formation strategies and practices, and more sophisticated typologies of conflict and consent. Such reactions, while generating useful empirical work, took LPT further away from connections to a bigger picture. This was doubly unfortunate because by the late 1980s its previous hegemony, at least in the sociology of work, came under sustained attack from rival paradigms. Each posed a different challenge, which we shall briefly outline before examining the response of labor process theory and research.

Paradigm Breakers

The mid-1980s saw the emergence of paradigm-break theories such as post-Fordism and flexible specialization (Piore and Sabel 1984; Lash and Urry 1987). Through an emphasis on new strategic contingencies that required a break with traditional corporate structures, Taylorist work organization, and adversarial industrial relations, these new theories shared substantially the same assumptions as those within the business and management literature. What marked these approaches was an unshakable optimism with respect to trends in work and employment. While the causal chain begins "out there" in markets and technologies, the argument moves inexorably down the design chain to flexible production, high skills, and high-trust industrial relations. More recently the new economy baton has been passed to proponents of the knowledge economy (Despres and Hiltrop 1995). Details of the plot (knowledge as driver of change) and some of the characters (expert labor, independent subcontractors) change, but the optimistic message about a move from command and control to collaborative high-trust, high-commitment work relations remains the same.

While such perspectives have worked at the macro level of social theory, influential mesolevel approaches have pushed a similar message. The theory of lean production was promoted by an MIT team through the best-selling *The Machine That Changed the World* (Womack, Jones, and Roos 1990). The tone was still relentlessly optimistic: employees working smarter not harder in multiskilled teams operating with expanded responsibilities and powers. The post-Fordist factory of the future, according to Kenney and Florida (1993), would require unions to break from the old reactionary Fordist paradigm if they wished to be partners in the new "innovation mediated production."

Paradigm-break arguments had an unfortunate tendency to mix description, prescription, and prediction. That was less true of mesolevel perspectives compatible with such frameworks. For example, writers within an emergent progressive HRM framework were more careful to present mutual-gains industrial relations as a strategic choice for employers and unions (Kochan, Katz, and McKersie 1986). Nevertheless, the future path for successful work and employment relations was unmistakable. Such arguments were later added to the largely U.S.-based high-performance work systems (HPWS) literature (Huselid 1995; Lawler, Mohrman, and Ledford 1995). They emphasized the interlocking elements of the management of the modern firm: teamwork and employee involvement reinforced by enhanced investment in selection, training, and skill formation, as well as mutual-gains industrial relations. While macro- and middle-level paradigm-break arguments posed a challenge to radical industrial relations perspectives with their orientation to collectivism and divergent interests, the emphasis in LP research on Taylorism and deskilling and on control and resistance was also brought into question. The dominant view of control was challenged from another direction.

The Cultural Turn

In the 1990s the influence of postmodernism peaked in most of the social sciences. What is relevant for our purposes is the belief in what became known as the cultural turn: the argument that the reproduction of everyday life and the basis of domination had shifted from the material to the symbolic (Lash and Urry 1993). For LPT this was experienced as both an external and internal critique. With reference to the latter, key participants in the debate began to draw on Foucauldian notions of power and identity to understand how (post)modern individuals are constituted by and subjugated to the discourses and disciplines of the modern corporation (Knights and Willmott 1989). At one level such arguments can be seen as a radical version of mainstream arguments in the business and management literature that culture and the management of commitment have displaced control and bureaucracy (see in particular Willmott 1993). The outcome—that individuals "buy into" the system—is held in common, but the explanation is sought in processes of seduction (by corporate values), surveillance, and self-discipline.

While Braverman is dismissed for neglect of worker agency, Burawoy's emphasis on the way that workers participate in the production of consent is regarded as not so much wrong as incomplete. What postmodernists see as missing is an analysis of identity. An individual's sense of self and existential insecurity about that self are the basis of human existence. The individualizing tendencies of capitalist work and employment relations and the intrusion of corporate cultures on personal identity accentuate those insecurities and undermine the individual's search for a stable and secure identity (O'Doherty and Willmott 2001).

Empirical support for these propositions is not very strong. Some of the more prominent support comes from a small number of Foucault-influenced case studies on work organization and new management practices (Sewell and Wilkinson 1992; Barker 1993; Sewell 1998). These are summarized by Pulignano (2001:13–14):

[T]his stream of literature claims the presence of systems of surveillance aiming at socialising individuals at the workplace. Individuals therefore become embedded in disciplinary mechanisms of either "peer pressure" within teamwork as a form of mutual control . . . or visual and electronic tests, which are used to identify faults easily traced back to workers on the line.

Surveillance thus replaces control as the central concept and, as with the broader arguments on the modern corporation, collective resistance, even of an informal kind, is seen as marginalized or eliminated.

Such perspectives have had a much more limited impact on debates in industrial relations given the focus on the individual rather than the collective, on identities rather than interests, and the complete lack of attention to the institutional underpinnings of the employment relationship. While it is inappropriate to spend too long on the arguments, as we shall see in the next section, there are links, albeit of an indirect kind.

Responses and Reactions: On the Defensive

We can see paradigm-break and postmodern challenges to LPT as part of a wider belief that the "forward march of labor" had been halted. At the same time, parallel arguments were reshaping the territory of traditional industrial relations. A combination of labor market and organizational restructuring, plus changes in the mode of state regulation, was seen as producing significant obstacles to traditional union functions of interest aggregation and solidaristic action. Taken together with changes inside organizations to individualize the employment relationship, this led to talk of a fracturing of collectivism (Bacon and Storey 1994).

Given the hype and superficiality of much of this transformation agenda, some radical industrial relations theorists were cautious about the extent and character of changes in the basic mechanisms of representation and bargaining or of managerial ideology and action (MacInnes 1987; Kelly 1990). While skepticism was understandable, the debate on both sides also revealed some of the limitations of existing frameworks. As Ackroyd and Thompson (1999:146–47) commented:

> First, the decline of trade unions has too often been taken to be synonymous with disappearance of workplace resistance and recalcitrance. Second, the decline of traditional forms of male, full-time manufacturing labour is taken as equivalent to the marginalization of all labour. Third, the challenge to historically dominant forms of collectivism is substituted for the end of collectivism as such.

Mainstream industrial relations was particularly vulnerable to paradigm-break claims, given its orientation to procedural and institutional forms and practices. When combined with an overreliance on large data sets and quantitative survey materials rather than in-depth or longitudinal field-work, the discipline was underequipped to respond to aspects of these changes, although, as we indicated earlier, this is not universally true. Where attention was paid to informal effort bargaining and the contested management of the employment relationship, the best traditions of industrial relations overlapped with those of industrial sociology (Brown and Wright 1994). Such themes are strongly present in the next wave of LPT.

Third-Wave Research Programs: The Dark Side of Flexibility

In the 1990s a new, third wave of labor process research fought a necessary, if somewhat defensive, battle to analyze the continuities and constraints associated with lean production and other new management practices: "Labour process theorists have been in the forefront of analyzing the rapid changes in technology, management strategies, and production techniques that have occurred under the term Japanisation or 'lean production'" (Pulignano 2001:2). As we indicated earlier, while lean production was not a macrolevel social theory in its own right, the concept was the driving force of workplace restructuring, an umbrella term that embraces a paraphernalia of workplace change and innovation (Elger 1996). More optimistic accounts allude to the introduction of teamwork, greater workplace flexibility and more conceptual tasks and responsibilities in the work process, and a new mutual-gains industrial relations framework.

In contrast, a wealth of qualitative research emerged illustrating the dark side of these lean production regimes. These accounts, heavily reliant on the control-resistance framework for their theoretical basis, reviewed the opportunities these new workplace regimes present to actively extend labor control. For example, Graham's (1995) account of life on the line at Subaru–Isuzu unpacked the all-encompassing dimensions of managerial control under the new system, advancing the notion of a pervasive "invisible iron cage" of control over individual workers (p. 98). A further argument was that work under lean production, far from providing a replacement to the mind-numbing stress of mass production, systematically intensifies work by specifically and comprehensively removing any obstacles to the extraction of effort. This evidence highlighted that, as a result, authority and real power move upward to management, while increased accountability and intensified work are forced downward to lower levels (Parker and Slaughter 1995; Rinehart, Huxley, and Robertson

1997; Bradley, Erickson, Stephenson, and Williams 2000). Thus, workers not only are expected to involve themselves fully in continuous improvement but also should expect that their contribution will be policed more closely (Geary 1995).

Additional accounts have attempted to broaden this analysis to embrace the implications for the formation of interests. The argument is that under lean production regimes, management actively attempts to secure worker identification with broader organizational norms. While this has, to an extent, been a perennial purpose of managers going back at least to the human relations movement, this ideological dimension is internal to work relations. Task-centered participation provides the conditions under which the burden of competitiveness can be experienced directly (Geary 1995; Garrahan and Stewart 1992). MacDuffie (1995), among others, alludes to managerial attempts under lean production to dilute trade-union-sponsored forms of workplace collectives and further constrain workers' ability to resist. Indeed, these critical perspectives have highlighted attempts to deny workers access to the machinery of collective regulation and effectively bypass, if not marginalize, workplace trade union organization (Danford 1997, 1998; Stewart 1996; Bradley, Erickson, Stephenson, and Williams 2000).

The value of this research agenda is that it provides an indispensable antidote to optimistic claims of workplace transformation, which remain stubbornly persistent in much of the managerially oriented literature. Moreover, by restoring emphasis on the experience of employees (Ackers, Smith, and Smith 1996), labor process analysis is able to explore the implications of restructuring for collective forms of workplace regulation, creating useful connections to the territory of industrial relations. While research such as that of "life on the line" by Delbridge (1998) highlights the capacity for capital to secure "superexploitation" under lean production, it also demonstrates that workers continue to adopt an array of resistive responses to this extension of control.

However, much of the research activity in the 1990s remained locked within a particular workplace and point-of-production focus. Indeed, the ability to locate and make connections between labor process change and wider changes at the level of political economy remained somewhat elusive.

Theoretical Innovation: Remapping Labor Agency

This third-wave research program had significant theoretical consequences. It challenged the accuracy of claims to a fundamental shift in the locus of control. It accepted that the normative sphere had been an expanding area of managerial practice, without endorsing the view that these controls replaced or even marginalized the more traditional mechanisms of bureaucratic rationalization, work intensification, and aspects of scientific management (Warhurst and Thompson 1998). In challenging the claim that new management practices in the "cultural" sphere have been effective, LPT restored the traditional differentiation between what can be found in discourse and practice. In contrast to the postmodernist view that subjectivity of labor is no longer a significant source of resistance, a substantial body of workplace research has identified that employees remain knowledgeable about management intentions and outcomes and retain the resources to resist, misbehave, or disengage (e.g., McKinlay and Taylor 1996; Thompson and Findlay 1999). Part of this argument involved reasserting the significance of work and employment relations as the primary terrain in which structured antagonism and divergent interests are reproduced, rather than merely one site in which more general processes of identity formation are located.

All these arguments flowed from and were compatible with the core theory outlined earlier but added little to the conceptual armory of LPT. That was provided largely by Ackroyd and Thompson's (1999) work on organizational misbehavior. Initially this was associated with a much-quoted critique of the previously identified overlapping views of HRM and postmodern writers, who emphasized the hegemony of new forms of cultural control and electronic surveillance (Thompson and Ackroyd 1995).

However, the larger study involved a more systematic and distinctive mapping of worker action and agency, a project that involved "not only recovery but re-conceptualisation," based on "four distinct loci of struggle, over working time, working effort, the product of work and work identities" (Elger 2001:8). Each dimension of misbehavior is described as a form of *appropriation* underpinned by group self-organization around a variety of interests and identities. The term *misbehavior* is used ironically to draw attention to what is missed and misunderstood by orthodox accounts that assume conformity of behavior as the norm and to signify counterproductive behavior—anything you do at work that you are not supposed to do.

The framework draws on traditions in industrial relations, sociology, and anthropology (Collinson and Ackroyd, in press) but constitutes a conceptual innovation for LPT and beyond in two ways. First, it moves beyond the control and resistance model. Referring to the term *appropriation,*

Fleming commented that "rather than resistance being conceived as a negative reaction to power the authors instead frame misbehaviour as an active set of practices that attempt to recover a degree of autonomy at work" (2001:190–91). Clearly, this argument extends the view that the workplace has a degree of relative autonomy within which struggles over divergent interests and identities take place. Second, it seeks to resolve some of the disputes about subjectivity through an explicit focus on identity: "Interests and identities are not opposites. They reciprocally and discursively form one another" (Ackroyd and Thompson 1999:55). Fleming, who is sympathetic to a Foucauldian perspective, went on to praise the inclusion of identity in the multidimensional framework because "a whole new realm of workplace practice is rendered visible as modalities of resistance that were ignored in the past" (2001:191). This analysis of identity includes extensive treatment of the increase in sexual misbehavior as a complex set of workplace conflicts and of workplace humor as a form of cultural subversion.

In their concluding chapter, Ackroyd and Thompson (1999) spelled out explicitly that they accepted the labor process analysis based on a structured antagonism between capital and labor, with any other connection between workplace conflicts and wider social changes as analytically distinct and politically contingent.

> Our essential purpose has been to take this kind of argument and ratchet it down one notch further. In other words, whereas a second generation of labour process writers developed a concept of worker resistance that was to be treated as a phenomenon in its own right rather than a conceptual and practical derivation of class struggle, we are asking readers to accept that there is another realm of workplace behaviour that should not be understood merely as a form of or step to what has become identified with the term resistance. (Ackroyd and Thompson 1999:165)

It is argued that while formal, collective struggles are by no means redundant, individual or group-based informal action has grown in relative weight, often connected to new identity-based issues. Enhanced managerial efforts to mobilize employee emotions, commitment, and personality through corporate culture and customer care programs meet worker identities and interests on a new, more contested terrain. Contemporary research from a labor process perspective is putting flesh on that argument, best represented by Taylor and Bain's (2003) graphic account of how call center workers are using humor as a tool of both informal and formal resistance.

This shift of emphasis has led some labor process writers at the Marxist end of the spectrum to express doubts over the value of such innovations. While sharing postmodern claims of seduced and subordinated subjectivity as the grounds of critique, Martinez and Stewart (1997) and Stewart (2002) argued that Ackroyd and Thompson (Thompson and Ackroyd 1995; Ackroyd and Thompson 1999) accepted too much of the decline-of-collectivism thesis. In the first instance the problem is said to be a result of a degree of methodological individualism that reduces conflict to a struggle for individual autonomy within organizations *sui generis* rather than capitalist work and employment relations in particular, an orientation reflected in a preference for the term *employee* rather than *labor.*

The gap between these positions is less than it seems. Ackroyd and Thompson (1999:162–65) did not see localized and broader forms of collective action and organization as mutually exclusive, nor did they hold that conditions for the latter have disappeared. Other theorists within a Marxist tradition accept that such an elaboration of the full range of employee misbehavior and resistance is part of the defense of collective labor capacities and a bulwark against arguments that infer high levels of employee consent and cooperation from low levels of strike activity (Kelly, in press).

The tension concerns not so much what misbehavior is as what it isn't—organized and conscious collective action by labor as a wider class agent. If such action remains possible, it is true that neither Ackroyd and Thompson nor their critics have adequately theorized how we might move from one to the other (Elger 2001). To that extent, third-wave labor process debates and research have continued to take place on a smaller stage than in earlier periods. The next and final section discusses what potential exists for broadening the scope of analysis.

Opening Out the Analysis: A Fourth Wave?

Labor process theory and research are beginning to expand the analysis and restore some of the lost or diminished connections to the bigger picture in a number of ways.

Global Political Economy, Work, and Employment Relations

One of the ways in which LPT analysis is being widened is by examining the major trends in work and employment and the strategies pursued by firms and nation-states in an increasingly globalized economy. Part of the critique of paradigm-break theories is a rejection of the idea that there are or should be universal production systems, whether in the form of flexible specialization or lean production. This picks up on the earlier-noted need to break from the assumptions in first-wave LPT that the United States is the capitalist exemplar *par excellence*. However, while it is useful to introduce political considerations such as the influence of national institutional settlements on employment relations, it is not enough. Indeed, it would reproduce some of the weaknesses of traditional cross-national sociological and industrial relations literature.

As Thompson and Smith (1998) have argued, there is a need to re-conceptualize the new rules of the global political economy, mapping the levels and influences on work organization and politics. That means, in particular, having to disentangle the various levels of influence offered by the international trends and forces of global capitalism. These include the distinct institutional patterning of work within a given country, the borrowing and diffusion of new "best practices," and the specificities of workplace-level historical and local contingencies (Smith and Meiksins 1995). An important stream of research within the labor process framework seeks to further this agenda. Its most important expression has been in the work of Elger and Smith (1994, 1998; Smith, in press) on patterns of Japanization of production globally and more specifically in the United Kingdom.

Within this framework for capturing the nuances of labor process change in today's workplace and political economy, it is recognized that there may be a difference in the degree and character of embeddedness between work and employment relations. Employment relations are still likely to have a predominantly national or regional institutional imprint, while work is more likely to be influenced by globally perceived best practices and diffusion through production and service chains. As a result of the dynamics of convergence and divergence, there are now distinctive patterns of workplace practices across and within countries:

> With the spread of more decentralized and informal labor-man-agement interactions, the vocabulary of industrial relations, developed to understand the traditional formal institutions of labor relations, should correspondingly change. There is a clear need for new theory to analyze the implications of the shifts underway in the process of labor-management interaction. (Katz, in press)

The tradition in LPT of asserting the relative autonomy of the labor process can thus continue but in a new and more complex context.

Reconnecting the Big Picture: Disconnected Capitalism and High-Performance Work Systems

There has also been a second form of restoring a stronger emphasis on political economy. Pulling together a variety of critical contributions, Thompson (2003) recently examined the nature and limits of high-performance work systems (HPWS) as a means of overcoming some of the traditional barriers to employee innovation and commitment and resolving issues of mutual gains and divergent interests. As we saw earlier, HPWS can be conceived as a junior partner in paradigm-break perspectives. A new bargain within progressive and integrated human resource systems at the workplace level is envisaged (Appelbaum, Bailey, Berg, and Kalleberg 2001). In return for greater discretionary effort in the work process, employers will invest in human capital and in trust- and social-adhesion-building measures in the employment relationship. In higher-performance workplaces, unions may have little option but to move away from adversarial attitudes and defense of work rules toward an embrace of partnership and comanagement of change (Bélanger, Lapointe, and Lévesque 2002).

LPT does not, or at least should not, have any problem with this bargain in principle or with the idea of mutual gains in particular circumstances. The structured antagonism between capital and labor can produce accommodation as well as resistance. Nevertheless, the extent of shared interests is not simply a variable chosen by employers or unions but is shaped by a variety of endogenous and exogenous conditions. In current conditions, the HPWS bargain has proved to be hugely unstable, marked by a fundamental tension between growing contingency and insecurity in the employment relationship and the qualitative intensification of labor.

Discretionary effort is being requested from employees, including taking over responsibility for career development when many employers are making less investment in training and skill development and are unable to deliver any degree of job security (Cappelli 1995; Beynon, Grimshaw, Rubery, and Ward 2002). This is accurately described by Wilkinson and Ladipo (2002) as a collectivization of effort and decollectivization of risk. In a welcome development, survey research exploring the insecurity thesis across a wide variety of sectors has moved beyond issues of labor market flexibility toward an examination of the rising incidence of work intensification, stress, and declining employee control over pace and flow of work (Heery and Salmon 2000; Green 2001; Burchell, Ladipo, and Wilkinson 2002). This is supported by parallel cross-national case studies of HPWS that indicate fundamental tensions manifested in transfer of risk and insecurity as labor bears the cost of structural adjustment (Murray, Belanger, Giles, and Lapointe 2002). Interestingly, this frequently applies just as much to core workers and firms that develop track records of high performance (Konzelmann and Forrant 2003).

Clearly these trends have multiple causes, but LPT is trying to explain a shift in the dynamics of capital accumulation instead of relying primarily on the constraints of the control imperative and the persistence of managerial hierarchy. Using broader evidence, it points to the dominance of financial circuits of capital and the impact of capital markets driven through systematic rationalization by the pursuit of shareholder value (Lazonick and O'Sullivan 2000; Froud, Johal, and Williams 2002) and profitability from the whole value chain (Altmann and Deiß 1998). Successive waves of downsizing and delayering as firms seek ways of cutting costs to improve financial performance create circumstances that Konzelmann and Forrant (2003) called creative work in destructive markets. By analyzing large longitudinal data sets, Littler and Innes (2003) were able to show that there is a strong association between dominant patterns of downsizing and "deskilling"; the loss of key skills from the profile of the labor force was described as a process of "deknowledging" the firm.

HPWS advocates sometimes note the difficulties of employers in creating and sustaining new workplace bargains, but their predominant workplace focus and lack of attention to the dynamics of capitalist political economy mean that it is underexplored and inadequately explained. In other words, such limitations can be located in the inadequate conceptualization by HRM of the systemic context within which the development of coherent, integrated bundles of practices are envisaged. To summarize, LPT is not merely making a critique of the limits of HPWS but trying to connect workplace practices to a changing "big picture," labeled *disconnected capitalism* by Thompson (2003), because the domains of work relations, employment policy, and governance increasingly operate according to contradictory dynamics. Of course, there is not a single picture or trend that is generalizable equally across all sectors or countries, and the state at the national or regional level still has a significant role in setting the terms of competition. Nevertheless, trends in product and capital markets *are* making the world a smaller place, and the extent of institutional distinctiveness is diminishing.

(Re)Mobilizing Labor

Something that has been largely left out of this picture is the role of labor, not so much at the level of local resistance, as we have demonstrated, but as a broader agency. Yet survey and case study evidence has convincingly demonstrated that conditions of broken bargains and divergent interests exist in the "new workplace." This can be seen in decreasing commitment to work and to current employers and decreasing satisfaction with job security (Cappelli, Bassi, Katz, Knoke, Osterman, and Useem 1997; Heery and Salmon 2000:14–16). In such circumstances, calculative compliance is a much more likely feature of employee behavior than are commitment and discretionary effort.

In addition, a further wave of case study research drawing on a labor process perspective has begun to explore more systematically the wider industrial relations situation and the prospects for union renewal (Stewart and Wass 1998; Danford, Richardson, and Upchurch 2003). Reviewing the impact of HPWS within the aerospace industry, Danford, Richardson, and Upchurch (2003:572) outlined how functional flexibility, cellular working, and business improvement initiatives were supported by a move toward workplace partnership, which, in conditions of intensified competition and downsizing, had the potential to erode the social base of independent union representation.

What this suggests is that regardless of how desirable a partnership approach from unions may be, employers are frequently unable to deliver the conditions that would make it viable. This may seem like a gloomy prognosis, but such studies also suggest greater union resilience and capacity for collective action than are often acknowledged (Danford, Richardson, and Upchurch 2003).

However, there is still a conceptual gap between the general model of control, resistance, consent, and accommodation and understandings in fourth-wave LPT of the micromobilization context. In this respect, it is helpful that Danford, Richardson, and Upchurch (2003) drew on Kelly's (1998) reworking of mobilization theory, which provided a useful starting point for filling that gap. This framework sought to locate the propensity for worker collectivism by analyzing "the processes by which workers acquire a collective definition of their interests in response to employer-generated injustice" (Kelly 1998:1). The particular formulations involved, for example, the key roles assigned to injustice, attribution, and identity within a context of Marxist long-wave theory, are less important than the preference for intermediate concepts that break with the mode of radical analysis in which interests and expected outcomes are attributed to labor. The failure of those interests and outcomes to appear then becomes the locus of explanation. The emphasis should be on the conditions—organization, opportunity, leadership, and so on—and political economic contexts in which labor interests and power resources are mobilized.

Conclusion

The core theoretical principles of LPT combine analysis of the structural constraints and imperatives that derive from the capitalist labor process with analysis of the situational scope in which managerial and employee actors shape relevant outcomes. A workplace orientation, often based on qualitative case studies, allows LPT to explore the informal dynamics of the control and effort bargain while locating those social relations within a broader political economy. The findings therefore strengthen those strands of industrial relations theory and research that focus on similar themes. LPT has an added potential attraction for radical industrial relations in that it has developed a post-Marxist account of conflicting interests and manufactured consent at work that differentiates between capital and labor as workplace and societal actors.

LPT's core conceptual framework and attention to the dynamics of workplace relations mean that the research programs of LPT have demonstrated considerable resilience in the face of theoretical and empirical challenges (Jaros 2003). In particular, it has proven well equipped to counter the overly optimistic and frequently unrepresentative claims of paradigm-break and HRM accounts of economy and workplace. Looking beneath the formal, institutional level, LPT has helped to refute "end of collectivism" arguments by demonstrating the persistence of old and existence of new forms of resistance and misbehavior. For example, by treating union power as an indication of workers' ability to mobilize collective resources in pursuit of an acceptable degree of control and autonomy at work, new research breaks down "what has become a false dualism between industrial relations and the labor process" (Danford, in press). Bolstered by an expanded scope of analysis and methodologies that add to the traditional case study orientation, LPT can make a strong contribution both to the understanding of work and employment trends and to the new forms of labor politics that are generated from them.

Notes

[1] Eighteen volumes of papers around key themes have been published from the conference since 1985. The current series is *Critical Perspectives on Work and Organization* (London: Palgrave).

[2] Of course, there are noncapitalist labor processes, for example, in the public sector and under state socialism. LPT has examined such circumstances, though with a recognition of the need for additional theoretical resources such as radical Weberianism (see Thompson and McHugh 2002:365–73; Smith and Thompson 1992).

[3] For an excellent U.S. study that pulls together and highlights the methodological distinctiveness of much of this evidence, see Hodson (2001).

References

Ackers, Pete, Chris Smith, and Paul Smith. 1996. "Against All Odds? British Trade Unions in the New Workplace." In Pete Ackers, Chris Smith, and Paul Smith, eds., *The New Workplace and Trade Unionism,* London: Routledge, pp. 1–41.

Ackroyd, Stephen, and Paul Thompson. 1999. *Organizational Misbehaviour.* London: Sage.

Altmann, Norbert, and Manfred Deiß. 1998. "Productivity by Systemic Rationalization: Good Work, Bad Work, No Work?" *Economic and Industrial Democracy,* Vol. 19, no. 1, pp. 137–60.

Appelbaum, Eileen, Tom Bailey, Peter Berg, and Arne L. Kalleberg. 2001. *Manufacturing Advantage: Why High Performance Work Systems Pay Off.* Ithaca, NY: Economic Policy Institute and ILR Press.

Bacon, Nick, and John Storey. 1994. "Individualism and Collectivism and the Changing Role of Trade Unions." *Proceedings of the Twelfth Annual Labour Process Conference* (Aston University, Aston, UK, April 1994).

Baldamus, William. 1961. *Efficiency and Effort: An Analysis of Industrial Administration.* London: Tavistock.

Barker, James R. 1993. "Tightening the Iron Cage: Concertive Control in Self-Managing Teams." *Administrative Science Quarterly,* Vol. 38, no. 3, pp. 408–37.

Bélanger, Paul R., Paul-Andre Lapointe, and Christian B. Lévesque. 2002. "Workplace Innovation and the Role of Institutions." In Gregor Murray, Jacques Belanger, Anthony Giles, and Paul A. Lapointe, eds., *Work and Employment Relations in the High-Performance Workplace.* London: Continuum.

Beynon, Hugh. 1975. *Working for Ford.* Wakefield, UK: E.P. Publishing.

Beynon, Hugh, Damian Grimshaw, Jill Rubery, and Kevin Ward. 2002. *Managing Employment Change.* Oxford: Oxford University Press.

Bradley, Harriet, Mark Erickson, Carol Stephenson, and Steve Williams. 2000. *Myths at Work.* Cambridge, UK: Polity Press and Blackwell.

Braverman, Harry. 1974. *Labor and Monopoly Capital.* New York: Monthly Review Press.

———. 1976. "Two Comments." *Monthly Review,* Vol. 28, no. 3, pp. 119–24.

Brown, William, and Mike Wright. 1994. "The Empirical Tradition in Workplace Bargaining Research." *British Journal of Industrial Relations,* Vol. 32, no. 3, pp. 153–65.

Burawoy, Michael. 1979. *Manufacturing Consent: Changes in the Labor Process under Monopoly Capitalism.* Chicago: Chicago University Press.

———. 1985. *The Politics of Production.* London: Verso.

Burchell, Brendan J., David Ladipo, and Frank Wilkinson, eds. 2002. *Job Insecurity and Work Intensification.* London: Routledge.

Cappelli, Peter. 1995. "Rethinking Employment." *British Journal of Industrial Relations,* Vol. 33, no. 4, pp. 563–602.

Cappelli, Peter, Laurie Bassi, Harry Katz, David Knoke, Paul Osterman, and Michael Useem. 1997. *Change at Work.* New York: Oxford University Press.

Clark, John. 1995. "Is There a Future for Industrial Relations? A Review Article." *Work, Employment and Society,* Vol. 9, no. 3, pp. 593–605.

Collinson, David, and Stephen Ackroyd. In press. "Resistance, Misbehaviour and Dissent." In Stephen Ackroyd, Rosemary Batt, Paul Thompson, and Pamela Tolbert, eds., *The Oxford Handbook of Work and Organization,* Oxford: Oxford University Press.

Danford, Andy. 1997. "The New Industrial Relations and Class Struggle in the 1990s." *Capital and Class,* no. 61, pp. 107–41.

———. 1998. *Japanese Management Techniques and British Workers.* London: Mansell.

———. In press. "New Union Strategies and Forms of Work Organization in UK Manufacturing." In Bill Harley, Jeff Hyman, and Paul Thompson, eds., *Participation and Democracy at Work: Essays in Honour of Harvie Ramsay,* London: Palgrave.

Danford, Andy, Mike Richardson, and Martin Upchurch. 2003. *New Unions, New Workplaces: A Study of Union Resilience in the Restructured Workplace.* London, Routledge.

Delbridge, Rick. 1998. *Life on the Line in Contemporary Manufacturing.* Oxford: Oxford University Press.

Despres, Charles, and Jean-Marie Hiltrop. 1995. "Human Resource Management in the Knowledge Age: Current Practice and Perspectives on the Future." *Employee Relations,* Vol. 17, no. 1, pp. 9–23.

Edwards, Paul K. 1986. *Conflict at Work: A Materialist Analysis of Workplace Relations.* Oxford: Blackwell.

———. 1990. "Understanding Conflict in the Labour Process: The Logic and Autonomy of Struggle." In David Knights and Hugh Willmott, eds., *Labour Process Theory,* London: Macmillan, pp. 125–53.

———. 1992. "Industrial Conflict: Themes and Issues in Recent Research." *British Journal of Industrial Relations,* Vol. 30, pp. 361–404.

Edwards, Paul K., and Hugh Scullion. 1982. *The Social Organization of Industrial Conflict: Control and Resistance in the Workplace.* Oxford: Blackwell.

Edwards, Richard. 1979. *Contested Terrain: The Transformation of the Workplace in the Twentieth Century.* London: Heinemann.

Elger, Tony. 1996. *Manufacturing Myths or Miracles: Work Reorganisation in British Manufacturing since 1979.* Warwick Labour Studies Working Paper 11. Coventry: Centre for Comparative Labour Studies, University of Warwick.

———. 2001. "Critical Materialist Analyses of Work and Employment: A Third Way?" Paper presented at the international workshop "Between Sociology of Work and Organisation Studies: The State of the Debate in Italy and in the United Kingdom" (Bologna, 16–17 November 2001).

Elger, Tony, and Chris Smith, eds. 1994. *Global Japanization? The Transnational Transformation of the Labour Process.* London: Routledge.

————. 1998. "Exit, Voice and 'Mandate': Management Strategies and Labor Practices of Japanese Firms in Britain." *British Journal of Industrial Relations,* Vol. 36, no. 2, pp. 185–208.

Fleming, Peter. 2001. "Beyond the Panopticon?" *Ephemera,* Vol. 1, no. 2, pp. 190–94.

Frenkel, Stephen. 2003. "The Embedded Character of Workplace Relations." *Work and Occupations,* Vol. 30, no. 2, pp. 135–53.

Friedman, Andy. 1977. *Industry and Labour: Class Struggle at Work Monopoly Capitalism.* London: Macmillan.

Froud, Julie, Sukhdev Johal, and Karel Williams. 2002. "Financialisation and the Coupon Pool." *Capital and Class,* no. 78, pp. 119–51.

Garrahan, Phil, and Paul Stewart. 1992. *The Nissan Enigma: Flexibility at Work in a Local Economy.* London: Mansell.

Geary, John. 1995. "Work Practices: The Structure of Work." In Paul Edwards, ed., *Industrial Relations: Theory and Practice in Britain,* Oxford: Blackwell, pp. 368–96.

Gorz, Andre. 1976. *The Division of Labour: The Labour Process and Class Struggle in Modern Capitalism.* Brighton, UK: Harvester.

Graham, Laurie. 1995. *On the Line at Subaru-Isuzu: The Japanese Model and the American Worker.* Ithaca, NY: ILR Press.

Green, Francis. 2001. "It's Been a Hard Day's Night: The Concentration and Intensification of Work in Late Twentieth Century Britain." *British Journal of Industrial Relations,* Vol. 39, no. 1, pp. 53–80.

Heery, Edmund, and John Salmon, eds. 2000. *The Insecure Workforce.* London: Routledge.

Hodson, Randy. 2001. *Dignity at Work.* Cambridge: Cambridge University Press.

Huselid, Mark. 1995. "The Impact of Human Resource Management Practices on Turnover, Production and Corporate Financial Performance." *Academy of Management Journal,* Vol. 38, no. 2, pp. 635–72.

Hyman, Richard. 1989. *Strikes,* 4th ed. London: Macmillan.

————. 1994. "Theory and Industrial Relations." *British Journal of Industrial Relations,* Vol. 32, no. 2, pp. 165–79.

Jaros, Stephen. 2003. "Marxian and Postmodernist vs Labour Process Theories of Workplace Behaviour and Politics: Further Critiques of Competing Paradigms." *Proceedings of the 21st International Labour Process Conference* (Bristol, UK, April 2003).

Katz, H. In press. "Industrial Relations and Work." In Stephen Ackroyd, Rosemary Batt, Paul Thompson, and Pamela Tolbert, eds., *The Oxford Handbook of Work and Organization,* Oxford: Oxford University Press.

Kelly, John. 1990. "British Trade Unionism 1979–89: Change, Continuity and Contradictions." *Work, Employment and Society,* special issue, pp. 29–65.

Kelly, John. 1998. *Rethinking Industrial Relations: Mobilization, Collectivism and Long Waves.* London: Routledge.

————. In press. "Labour Movements and Mobilization." In Stephen Ackroyd, Rosemary Batt, Paul Thompson, and Pamela Tolbert, eds., *The Oxford Handbook of Work and Organization,* Oxford: Oxford University Press.

Kenney, Martin, and Richard Florida. 1993. *Beyond Mass Production: The Japanese System and Its Transfer to the U.S.* Oxford: Oxford University Press.

Knights, David, and Hugh Willmott. 1989. "Power and Subjectivity at Work: From Degradation to Subjugation in Social Relations." *Sociology,* Vol. 23, no. 4, pp. 535–58.

————, eds. 1990. *Labor Process Theory.* London: Macmillan.

Kochan, Thomas A., Harry Katz, and Robert McKersie. 1986. *The Transformation of American Industrial Relations.* New York: Basic Books.

Konzelmann, Suzanne, and Robert Forrant. 2003. "Creative Work in Destructive Markets." In Brendan Burchell, Stephen Deakin, Jonathan Michie, and Jill Rubery, eds., *Systems of Production: Markets, Organization and Performance,* London: Routledge, pp. 128–58.

Lash, Scott, and John Urry. 1987. *The End of Organized Capitalism.* Cambridge, UK: Polity Press.

Lash, Scott, and John Urry. 1993. *Economies of Signs and Space.* London: Sage.

Lawler, Edward, Allan Mohrman, and Gerald Ledford. 1995. *Creating High Performance Organizations.* San Francisco: Jossey-Bass.

Lazonick, William, and Mary O'Sullivan. 2000. "Maximising Shareholder Value: A New Ideology for Corporate Governance." *Economy and Society,* Vol. 29, no. 1, pp. 13–35.

Littler, Craig R. 1982. *The Development of the Labor Process in Capitalist Societies: A Comparative Analysis of Work Organisation in Britain, the USA and Japan.* London: Heinemann.

————. 1990. "The Labour Process Debate: A Theoretical Review." In David Knights and Hugh Willmott, eds., *Labor Process Theory,* London: Macmillan, pp. 46–94.

Littler, Craig R., and Peter Innes. 2003. "Downsizing and Deknowledging the Firm." *Work, Employment and Society,* Vol. 17, no. 1, pp. 73–100.

Littler, Craig R., and Graeme Salaman. 1982. "Bravermania and Beyond: Recent Theories of the Labour Process." *Sociology,* Vol. 16, no. 2, pp. 251–69.

MacDuffie, John P. 1995. "Workers' Roles in Lean Production: The Implications for Worker Representation." In Steve Babson, ed., *Lean Work: Empowerment and Exploitation in the Global Auto Industry,* Detroit: Wayne State University Press, pp. 54–70.

MacInnes, John. 1987. *Thatcherism at Work.* Milton Keynes, UK: Open University Press.

Mahnkopf, Birgit. 1986. "Hegemony and Consent: Patterns of Regulation in Internal Company Social Relations and Their Legitimation Effect." *Berkeley Journal of Sociology,* Vol. 31, pp. 35–52.

Martinez, Lucio M., and Paul Stewart. 1997. "The Paradox of Contemporary Labour Process Theory: The Rediscovery of Labour and the Decline of Collectivism." *Capital and Class,* no. 62, pp. 49–77.

McKinlay, Alan, and Phil Taylor. 1996. "Power, Surveillance and Resistance: Inside the 'Factory of the Future.'" In Pete Ackers, Chris Smith, and Paul Smith, eds., *The New Workplace and Trade Unionism,* London: Routledge, pp. 279–300.

Murray, Gregor, Jacques Belanger, Anthony Giles, and Paul A. Lapointe, eds. 2002. *Work and Employment Relations in the High-Performance Workplace.* London: Continuum.

Nichols, Theo, and Pete Armstrong. 1976. *Workers Divided.* Glasgow: Fontana.

Nichols, Theo, and Hugh Beynon. 1977. *Living with Capitalism.* London: Routledge and Kegan.

O'Doherty, Damian, and Hugh Willmott. 2001. "Debating Labour Process Theory: The Issue of Subjectivity and the Relevance of Poststructuralism." *Sociology,* Vol. 35, no. 2, pp. 457–76.

Parker, Mike, and Jane Slaughter. 1995. "Unions and Management by Stress." In Steve Babson, ed., *Lean Work: Empowerment and Exploitation in the Global Auto Industry*, Detroit: Wayne State University Press, pp. 41–54.

Penn, Roger. 1982. "'The Contested Terrain': A Critique of R.C. Edwards' Theory of Working-Class Fractions and Politics." In David Dunkerely and Graeme Salaman, eds., *The International Handbook of Organization Studies, 1981*, London: RKP, pp. 183–94.

Piore, Michael, and Charles J. Sabel. 1984. *The Second Industrial Divide: Possibilities for Prosperity*. New York: Basic Books.

Pollert, Anna. 1981. *Girls, Wives, Factory Lives*. London: Macmillan.

Pulignano, Valeria. 2001. "Understanding British Trends in the Sociology of Work: Some Reflections from an Italian Perspective." Paper presented at the international workshop "Between Sociology of Work and Organisation Studies: The State of the Debate in Italy and in the United Kingdom" (Bologna, 16–17 November 2001).

Reed, Michael. 1992. *The Sociology of Organisations*. London: Harvester.

Rinehart, James, Chris Huxley, and David Robertson. 1997. *Just Another Car Factory? Lean Production and Its Discontents*. New York: ILR Press.

Sewell, Graham. 1998. "The Discipline of Teams: The Control of Team-Based Industrial Work through Electronic and Peer Surveillance." *Administrative Science Quarterly*, Vol. 43, pp. 406–69.

Sewell, Graham, and Barry Wilkinson. 1992. "'Someone to Watch Over Me': Surveillance, Discipline and the JIT Labour Process." *Sociology*, Vol. 26, no. 2, pp. 271–89.

Smith, Chris. In press. "Beyond Convergence and Divergence: Organisations in a Complex Country Context." In Stephen Ackroyd, Rosemary Batt, Paul Thompson, and Pamela Tolbert, eds., *The Oxford Handbook of Work and Organization*, Oxford: Oxford University Press.

Smith, Chris, and Pete Meiksins. 1995. "System, Society and Dominance in Cross-National Organizational Analysis." *Work, Employment and Society*, Vol. 9, no. 2, pp. 241–67.

Smith, Chris, and Paul Thompson. 1992. *Labour in Transition: The Labour Process in Eastern Europe and China*. London: Routledge.

———. 1998. "Re-evaluating the Labor Process Debate." *Economic and Industrial Democracy*, Vol. 19, no. 4, pp. 551–78.

Spencer, David. 2000. "Braverman and the Contribution of Labour Process Analysis to the Critique of Capitalist Production—Twenty-Five Years On." *Work, Employment and Society*, Vol. 14, no. 2, pp. 223–43.

Stewart, Paul. 1996. "Beyond Japan, Beyond Consensus? From Japanese Management to Lean Production." In Paul Stewart, ed., *Beyond Japanese Management: The End of Modern Times*, London: Frank Cass, pp. 1–20.

———. 2002. "The Problem of the Collective Worker in the Sociology of Work in the UK." *Sociologia del Lavoro*, Vol. 86–87, pp. 145–64.

Stewart, Paul, and Victoria Wass. 1998. "From 'Embrace and Change' to 'Engage and Change': Trade Union Renewal and the New Management Strategies in the UK Automotive Industry." *New Technology, Work and Employment*, Vol. 13, no. 2, pp. 77–93.

Storey, John. 1985. "The Means of Management Control." *Sociology*, Vol. 19, no. 2, pp. 193–211.

Taylor, Phil, and Peter Bain. 2003. "Subterranean Worksick Blues: Humour as Subversion in Two Call Centres." *Organization Studies*, Vol. 24, no. 9, pp. 1487–509.

Thompson, Paul. 1989. *The Nature of Work*, 2nd ed. London: Macmillan.

———. 1990. "Crawling from the Wreckage: The Labour Process and the Politics of Production." In David Knights and Hugh Willmott, eds., *Labour Process Theory*, London: Macmillan, pp. 95–124.

———. 2003. "Disconnected Capitalism: Or Why Employers Can't Keep Their Side of the Bargain." *Work, Employment and Society*, Vol. 17, no. 2, pp. 359–78.

Thompson, Paul, and Stephen Ackroyd. 1995. "All Quiet on the Workplace Front? A Critique of Recent Trends in British Industrial Sociology." *Sociology*, Vol. 29, no. 4, pp. 1–19.

Thompson, Paul, and Eddie Bannon. 1985. *Working the System: The Shop Floor and New Technology*. London: Pluto Press.

Thompson, Paul, and Patricia Findlay. 1999. "Changing the People: Social Engineering in the Contemporary Workplace." In Laurence Ray and Andrew Sayer, eds., *Culture and Economy after the Cultural Turn*, London: Sage, pp. 162–88.

Thompson, Paul, and David McHugh. 2002. *Work Organisations*, 3rd ed. Basingstoke, UK: Palgrave.

Thompson, Paul, and Chris Smith. 1998. "Beyond the Capitalist Labour Process: Workplace Change, the State and Globalisation." *Critical Sociology*, Vol. 24, no. 3, pp. 193–215.

Warhurst, Chris, and Paul Thompson. 1998. "Hands, Hearts and Minds: Changing Work and Workers at the End of the Century." In Paul Thompson and Chris Warhurst, eds., *Workplaces of the Future*, London: Macmillan, pp. 1–24.

Westwood, Sally. 1984. *All Day Every Day: Factory and Family in the Making of Women's Lives*. London: Pluto Press.

Wilkinson, Frank, and David Lapido. 2002. "What Can Governments Do?" In Brendan J. Burchell, David Ladipo, and Frank Wilkinson, eds., *Job Insecurity and Work Intensification*, London: Routledge, pp. 172–84.

Willmott, Hugh. 1993. "Strength Is Ignorance; Slavery Is Freedom: Managing Culture in Modern Organizations." *Journal of Management Studies*, Vol. 30, no. 4, pp. 515–52.

Womack, James, Daniel T. Jones, and Daniel Roos. 1990. *The Machine That Changed the World*. New York: Rawson Associates.

Zimbalist, Andrew, ed. 1979. *Case Studies on the Labor Process*. New York: Monthly Review Press.

Chapter 6

Theories of the Employment Relationship: Choosing between Norms and Contracts

Michael L. Wachter
University of Pennsylvania

The employment relationship is the construct at the heart of any industrial relations system. Most workers are employed inside firms, and their dealings with their employer are thus partially outside the protections offered by whatever competitive forces operate in the labor market. This appears to leave nonunion workers without much protection against unfair outcomes and unfair dealings to the extent that the firm has an unequal bargaining advantage. Although there are many commentators who believe that the system works badly, it can be argued that nonmarket mechanisms have evolved that provide substantial, if incomplete, protection to workers. In this paper I analyze labor market theories that address this issue, particularly how an employment relationship can work when it appears to be entirely one-sided and stacked in favor of the firm. In so doing, I analyze the choice of norms versus contracts as a method of forming agreements to guide the relationship and the extent to which these methods are either self-enforcing or require judicial enforcement.[1]

To address this question, it is necessary to analyze the three types of labor market relationships that are prevalent in the economy. The first is the labor service market, an external labor market in the sense that its activities take place outside the boundaries of an individual firm. Within this market are very different relationships in terms of their formality, spanning the subcontracting market at one extreme and the markets for personal services and for spot labor on the other extreme. The second type is the employment relationship inside the nonunion firm. This involves a firm and its employees, rather than two independent agents as in the prior case. The third type is the employment relationship inside the union firm, which is distinct from the prior case because of the substantial regulatory apparatus of the National Labor Relations Act (NLRA).[2]

The parties' relationships in each of these markets are markedly different from one another. In the labor service market, two independent parties reach an agreement to transact, that is, to provide labor services in return for a package of terms and conditions of employment. The terms and conditions reflect an agreement, and since the relationship is entirely voluntary, it is assumed to represent a joint profit-maximizing point for the parties. With respect to enforcement, these agreements are intended to be primarily self-enforcing. However, since the agreements are contracts in the legal definition of that term, state enforcement by courts provides the ultimate enforcement mechanism. The governance structure for the labor service market is thus contracting based.

In the employment relationship inside nonunion firms, the agreements are frequently determined by the firms rather than bargained over term by term by the parties. Although labor contracting in the external market sometimes features take-it-or-leave-it terms, the nonunion sector operates almost entirely on this basis.[3] As in the labor-contracting markets, the terms are intended to be self-enforcing. However, unlike the former case, the terms are essentially norms of behavior[4] and thus are enforced nonlegally. Since the norms are effectively determined by the firm, the governance structure of the nonunion employment relationship is hierarchical. There are a few exceptions where legal enforcement is available to enforce government-mandated terms, such as the rules governing employment discrimination, the funding of retirement plans, and occupational safety and health.[5]

In the union labor market, the parties bargain over the individual terms of the contract rather than having them be determined by the firm. Not only are the agreements legally enforceable contracts, but the relationship between the parties is also heavily regulated by statute in a manner quite different from the law of contracts. Of particular importance is that the relationship is not entirely voluntary. Workers have a right to unionize, and if they do, the firm must bargain with the union over the mandatory terms, including wages, hours, and other conditions of employment.

Why do these very distinct forms exist? This paper provides an answer to this question. I presuppose that the primary purpose of each of the alternative structures is to maximize the value of the wealth available to the parties. To be successful, each of the structures has to resolve the four key features of industrial organization theory: match-specific assets, asymmetric information, risk aversion, and transaction costs (Rock and Wachter 1996, 1999).[6] The central question then is: how do the terms of the employment relationship work to protect the parties' agreements with respect to the four characteristics? Are the terms of the agreement interpretable as maximizing the joint profit of the parties? Are the enforcement protections adequate?

Historical Antecedents to the Enforcement Issue

Historically, labor market analysis addressed the bargaining process, albeit indirectly, when it inquired whether the treatment of workers by firms was "fair" by some metric. Typically, such inquiries have discussed the difficulties of reaching fair results given the disproportionate bargaining power available to firms and the potential for the arbitrary use of that power.[7]

Numerous reasons have been offered for workers' not receiving their just deserts. In discussing this question, the important distinction is between firms and markets. Some commentators bemoan the outcomes of competitive markets that generate wages and working conditions below what those commentators believe to be fair. But I take this line of inquiry to be limited, given the many positive attributes associated with competitive outcomes. Moreover, policy cannot improve on those outcomes.

A more useful approach is to criticize labor market outcomes as being noncompetitive, which many commentators have historically done. This criticism was best captured by classical monopsony theory; monopsony would generate equilibrium market wages that are below competitive levels. In classical monopsony markets, individual firms exercise market power and can set the wage below the value of the worker to the firm (Boal and Ransom 1997). If this is the problem, the optimal solution is to make the market more competitive. Antitrust enforcement policies that make markets more competitive, rather than monopsonistic, improve outcomes and result in higher wages and employment.

Unions are another solution to classical monopsony. Unions raise wages above the level that firms would voluntarily pay on their own accord. If labor markets are monopsonistic, union-inspired wage increases move the labor market closer to a competitive equilibrium and increase employment. Historically, when classical monopsony theory was more popular, unions were viewed as a procompetitive market force (Kaufman 2002; Wachter 2003). It is difficult to maintain this position today.

Current models of monopsony recognize that the source of the upward-sloping supply curve is labor market friction such as costs associated with recruiting and retaining workers. In these models, it makes no sense to think of the monopsony wage as being "too low" because of market power, and there is no reason to assume that a higher wage results in an efficiency gain (Manning 2003). Consequently, union-inspired wage increases do not represent a countervailing power that improves the functioning of the labor market.

The most important line of inquiry, which is at the heart of the debate over labor market outcomes, is to focus on the problems that occur at the level of the firm, not the market. At the firm level, a failure to achieve just desserts can potentially arise because of the very nature of the corporate form. The corporate form creates and enforces an organizational structure of centralized management. The corporate directors or the executive officers they designate wield hierarchical governance powers. By design, management calls the shots in the sense of organizing economic activity inside the firm. In the nonunion firm, centralized management allows the firm to dictate the terms and conditions of employment and to create an enforcement mechanism that resolves intrafirm disputes in an approved manner (Rock and Wachter 2001).

It is typically this one-sided hierarchical structure that is criticized when commentators discuss issues of unequal bargaining power, arbitrary authority, and hierarchical governance. Inside the firm, workers may not be adequately protected by competitive forces acting at the market level. First, employees are asked to make commitments to their jobs, which makes them relatively immobile. Second, workers are likely to have less information than the employer about labor market conditions, including the value of the worker to the firm and prevailing conditions elsewhere in the labor market. Finally, employers can exercise their power in ways that take advantage of workers' lack of bargaining power. While some workers receive the optimal market wage, others may not.

The primary policy mechanism for dealing with hierarchy inside firms has been labor unions and the collective bargaining mechanism that they provide and champion. Unions bring intrafirm power sharing so that both the terms of the labor agreement and the enforcement mechanism are a result of collective bargaining, which reduces the hierarchical power of management over labor matters. By writing enforceable collective bargaining contracts, unions can prevent employers from exercising their power arbitrarily, harming individual workers. By using their rights to collect information related to the collective bargaining process, unions can equalize the information available to workers.

In analyzing these three forms, I will make use of the labor-contracting literature.[8] This literature is efficiency oriented, asking whether stylized employment practices can be interpreted as a way of dealing with market problems such as the arbitrary use of power, informational asymmetries, relative risk aversion, and the need to make match-specific investments. More generally, it asks whether the observable stylized features of labor market relationships are interpretable as the parties' resolution of these market problems in a joint profit-maximizing manner. In this literature, issues of fairness and unequal bargaining power are recast into different terms with more precise meanings, namely, opportunistic behavior and asymmetric information.

To date, the labor-contracting literature has paid little attention to the enforcement question. Specifically, enforcement issues are viewed as unimportant because the stylized labor-contracting arrangements are largely self-enforcing. To the extent that third parties assist in enforcement, it is through reputational effects on other firms or workers. Judicial enforcement, although mentioned, plays no interesting role. In this paper I pay particular attention to the enforcement question.

The Four Factors of the Labor-Contracting Relationship

In this section I rely on the labor-contracting literature to examine how the parties attempt to resolve problems arising from their need to make investments in their relationship (i.e., match investments), their differences in risk aversion, asymmetric information, and transaction costs.[9]

The first of the factors is investments in the relationship, that is, match-specific investments. Investments in the match provide the basic rationale for long-term attachments between a firm and an employee or between a contractor and a subcontractor. Effectively, the employees or subcontractors become more valuable in their current job than they would be if hired anew in a different job. The original explanation for this job-specific value was that such employees had job-specific training, whether formal or learning by doing, so that their increased productivity was a result of knowing more about how to perform the job. But in ongoing relationships, much more is involved in making established workers more valuable than new workers. For example, when circumstances change, an understanding of how the parties have responded to unanticipated events can lead to a greater ability to resolve these difficulties. Many other examples of the intuitive capital that workers attain with tenure can be given. It is best to refer to the broader scope of knowledge and understanding as *match investment* rather than the traditional term *job-specific training*.

The difficulty that arises when match investments are present is the holdup problem. Workers are worth more in their current job than they are in the external labor market. The gap between an employee's value on the current job and the employee's value in the external labor market creates a quasi rent that is subject to *ex post* expropriation by one party. Either party could threaten to terminate the relationship if not given a larger share of the profits. Since match-specific investments create value for both firms and workers, there is an efficiency gain if the parties can make the appropriate level of investment without fear of opportunistic behavior by the other party.

The general solution is for both parties to invest in the match so they incur sunk costs. Once sunk costs are incurred, both parties lose if the ongoing relationship is terminated. The result is that neither party can credibly threaten to opportunistically terminate the relationship, since doing so would result in a loss to the threatening party. Joint investments are thus a self-enforcing agreement.

The second of the four factors is asymmetric information. Asymmetric information exists when it is relatively more costly for one of the parties to observe or monitor the quantity of inputs or outputs, the state of technology, or product market. In order to maximize the parties' joint profits, the information needs to be used by the parties so that they can adjust to whatever conditions actually exist. The difficulty is that since the disadvantaged party cannot verify the informed party's claim, the informed party can misstate the actual information to put itself in the best position possible. That is, the informationally advantaged party can use the power opportunistically to improve its return, even if it means decreasing the size of the joint surplus available to both parties.

This creates a dilemma. Efficiency requires that the party with the correct information be given the right to collect the information and to use it on behalf of the parties' joint interests. But how can the disadvantaged party be protected from the misuse of the information advantage? The general solution is to restrict the channels through which the informationally advantaged party can use the information. While the advantaged party can use and profit from its information, it cannot do so in a manner that harms the uninformed party.

Are such mechanisms available? The answer is generally yes, although the mechanisms may not be perfectly self-enforcing. As an example of such an arrangement, when product market conditions are known to one party (say, the firm) but not to the other (say, the worker), the agreement allows the firm to alter the amount of labor it purchases but not the wage rate. For the mechanism to be self-enforcing, the firm cannot reduce the wage rate. If the firm were able to reduce the wage rate, it could falsely claim that product demand had decreased and hence that it needed to reduce wages to reduce labor costs. However, since demand had not declined, the firm could maintain employment and output levels. Profits would increase because the cost of labor would be lower as a consequence of the wage reduction. On the other hand, if the firm is forced to reduce employment or hours of work in response to a proclaimed downturn in demand, its output and thus its profits fall. This type of agreement is self-enforcing because the firm does not have an incentive to misstate market conditions, as this would result in a decrease rather than an increase in profits. Thus, the firm will not act opportunistically.

Risk aversion is the third of the four factors. Risk aversion arises when one of the parties, typically the worker, is more risk averse than the other. Efficient risk bearing thus requires that the workers' returns be smoothed so that their own income is affected only by their own performance and not by exogenous (to them) fluctuations in the revenue and profits of the firm. Although problems of risk aversion are partially resolved by smoothing income, there is no perfect solution because of the problem of moral hazard. Specifically, if the worker's return were entirely guaranteed, the worker could reduce work effort without fearing a reduction in income.

Solving the problem of risk aversion is made difficult by the presence of asymmetric information. Since a worker's behavior is imperfectly known to the firm, the firm cannot be certain when the worker is shirking or the external workplace environment is adverse. The resulting solution leaves the worker with a greater variance in income than would otherwise be desirable.[10]

The solution to risk aversion points out a problem with all the self-enforcing solutions, namely, that they are all second best in the limited sense that none would be adopted in a world where behaviors such as opportunism, asymmetric information, and moral hazard were not present. For example, absent information asymmetries, the firm facing a decline in labor demand might best maximize its own profits and the workers' utility by a reduction in both hours of work and the wage rate. Forcing the firm to make the entire adjustment through a reduction in demand is thus second best. However, second-best solutions are not necessarily market failures that give rise to policy improvements. Information asymmetries, potential opportunism, and moral hazard are real economic costs just like any other economic cost, such as workers' insistence on being paid to work. Consequently, the self-enforcing arrangements worked out by the parties are arguably first best, given the restricted set of solutions available to them.

Transaction costs are the costs associated with negotiating, writing, and enforcing contracts. High transaction costs occur when the parties interact frequently, when the interactions are connected rather than independent events, and when the environment over which the parties interact evolves over time. These conditions are all present in an ongoing relationship. The greater the number of contingencies that affect the relationship over time, the greater is the cost of contracting. High transaction costs pose a threat to the potential surplus that the relationship can generate.

The contracting problem is exacerbated when the value at stake in each individual contingency is low. When the transaction is a low-value event, the benefit of contracting to protect the transaction is low, and hence even moderate contracting costs are detrimental to joint surplus. Transaction costs are also higher the more match assets and asymmetric information there are in the relationship. Match investments and asymmetric information give rise to the potential for opportunistic behavior, and regulating this behavior requires a more detailed and hence costly contract.

Overall, the main problem created by the high transaction costs of contracting is that they can reduce or erase the joint surplus available from creating and maintaining the ongoing employment relationship. It is the presence of transaction costs that make the enforcement issue complex. If match investments, asymmetric information, and risk aversion are present but transaction costs are low, the parties can write a complete contract. This means that every possible future state of the world is known and addressed by the contract or that the parties can fully allow recontracting when the environment changes. When a contract is complete, disputes are easily resolved, since the courts can enforce the terms of the contract.

When transaction costs are high, the parties face a discrete choice. Writing contracts to address all potential circumstances becomes costly. If the costs are high enough, the parties may decide on an alternative mechanism for protecting the potential surplus from the relationship. Each of the three institutional structures discussed is best suited for a very different transaction-cost setting. Consequently, as I argue later, when the parties decide on how to handle transaction costs, they are effectively choosing an institutional structure, and since each of these structures carries its own enforcement mechanism, the parties are also choosing among alternative enforcement mechanisms.

The Choice of Using Markets or Firms

From the perspective of enforcement issues, the choice among alternative organizational structures is critical. In this section, I analyze the threshold organizational decision: whether to conduct the transaction inside the firm or outside the firm. To understand the striking differences between the enforcement mechanisms protecting intrafirm and extrafirm transactions, it is worth looking briefly at the existing theory of the firm.

Two Prevailing Models

There are two prevailing models of the firm: the property rights theory and the transaction cost theory. Although the theories were developed separately, they are highly complementary and, indeed, for our purposes can be viewed as a single theory. The property rights approach focuses on the role of physical and intangible capital and posits that the core of the firm is best defined by the physical and intangible capital over which the firm has residual control rights. The transaction cost approach focuses more on human capital and the optimal degree of vertical integration, that is, which labor suppliers should be brought inside the firm and into the employment relationships and which should be left outside the boundaries of the firm. In their respective domains, these approaches share critical assumptions and develop complementary insights.

The critical insights shared by the two models are the need to regulate residual control rights and the impossibility of doing so by contract. Even in a relationship where the parties have contracted over a number of predictable and verifiable contingencies, there will inevitably be contingencies over which the parties cannot contract or have not contracted. Particularly in an ongoing relationship, in which the environment evolves over time, this residual class of contingencies can become large and can include many of the central problems facing the relationship. By its very nature, the residual class of contingencies contains those contingencies that make contracts very expensive to write. Consequently, any existing contract is necessarily incomplete (Holmstrom 1999).

How then, are disputes resolved when they involve residual contingencies over which the parties have not contracted? The answer is that one of the parties will bargain and effectively purchase the rights of residual control. The party that purchases the residual control rights will then use its own mechanism for resolving problems involving contested residual contingencies.

Property Rights Theory

Let us first look at the problem of the ownership of residual control rights over physical (tangible) and intangible capital. The conclusion of the property rights theory is that a firm is defined by the physical and intangible capital over which it has residual control rights. Alternatively stated, at the core of the firm are these residual control rights.

Take the case of the development and production of a network switch by the hypothetical company NetSwitch. Numerous tasks need to be accomplished before the product can be marketed. For example, machinery has to be built to produce the switch, and if the switch is an intermediate product, it has to be integrated into other equipment. Although NetSwitch may be able to do all the tasks, it is likely that some tasks, including the two just mentioned, will be left to other firms. More specifically, few firms are fully integrated from the supplier of intermediate goods through the distribution system to final consumers. In dealing with the various cooperating firms, some rights of control are necessarily contracted away. For example, when NetSwitch deals with the equipment seller, it may agree on specifications for the equipment and give the equipment maker some "control" rights, such as the decision of how best to build the machine that produces the switch. This major transaction is typically protected by contract. Similarly, NetSwitch may contract with the distributor or end user of its product. Here again, certain control rights would be transferred to the distributor or end user.

With several firms involved, ambiguities can arise as unanticipated contingencies occur. If a contingency is unanticipated, it cannot be contracted for in advance. Who gets to decide what happens in this circumstance? Alternatively stated, who has the control rights to resolve the unanticipated contingent-state problems? This is the core problem that the property rights model addresses. The solution proposed by the model is that one of the parties must buy the residual control rights. The party that owns the residual control rights then gets to decide the outcome when a dispute arises within the range of contingencies where the contract is incomplete (Hart and Moore 1990).

The "owner" of the residual control rights is best described as the owner of the asset. The term *owner* usually refers to the individual or entity that gets to "call the shots." The owner is thus the person or entity that has the right to direct the use of the asset as long as that use does not infringe on those rights that have previously been contracted away. The core of the firm is thus the assets over which the firm has residual control rights. Indeed, at the core of each of the firms in the network switch example, whether the supplier of production machinery, the end user, or NetSwitch, are the assets over which each of the firms has residual control rights.

If a dispute arises between parties having contractual rights to an asset, the dispute can be referred to the courts for resolution. The threshold issue for the court to determine is whether the dispute is over matters that are covered by the contract. If the matter is covered by the contract, the court resolves the dispute by applying the terms of the contract. However, if the dispute involves residual control rights that are not covered by the contract, the owner of the residual control rights decides the dispute by fiat, that is, by exercising the power that comes with ownership.

In my example, we can assume that NetSwitch will purchase the residual control rights because it has the most at stake and the best overview of the switch's potential. At the core of NetSwitch are thus the residual control rights over the creation, production, and sale of the switch.

Transaction Cost Theory

The transaction cost theory is similar to the property rights theory in that it focuses on residual control rights in a world of incomplete contracting. The difference is that the transaction cost theory deals with labor rather than capital inputs. With this basic difference, the theory is otherwise remarkably similar.

NetSwitch will want to use labor inputs on its owned capital. The problem posed by organizing the human capital is similar to that involving the physical and intangible capital. Some labor services can be contracted for. But here again, not all contingencies can be anticipated and described in a contingent-state contract. Residual issues will inevitably arise. Consequently, whereas the firm will contract for some labor services, other labor services will be brought inside the firm.

The manner in which the parties cope with inevitable contractual incompleteness provides the basis for a positive theory of the employment relationship inside firms, and it frames differences from the labor service and collective bargaining modes.[11]

The theory posits that the determination of which relationships are brought inside the firm depends on the transaction costs involved in the relationship. When transaction costs are low, the parties can write contingent-state contracts to protect the integrity of their transactions. Transactions can thus be left in the market, with the market providing the parties with unequaled high-powered incentives for joint profit-maximizing behavior. In addition, the parties can rely on market information to estimate asset values and opportunity costs. With information symmetrically available to the parties, the potential for opportunism is reduced, and the reliability of third-party enforcement, should that prove necessary, is increased (Williamson 1996).

Transaction costs are high in the employment relationship due to a full range of factors such as large numbers of match-specific assets and the high degree of information asymmetry (Williamson, Wachter, and Harris 1975). When transaction costs are high and contract governance is too expensive, the relationships are brought inside the firm, where they are governed by the intrafirm hierarchical governance structure. From the perspective of transaction cost theories, the decision to bring relationships within the firm is the decision to opt for the intrafirm governance structure over market governance.

Central to the transaction cost approach is the use of hierarchical organizational structure to direct the overall activity of the various components, including employees, brought inside the firm. The hierarchy directs activity using self-enforcing rules and standards. It is this apparatus that replaces market and legal contracts as the organizational mechanism for transacting (Williamson 1996).

Transaction cost theories have played a larger role in labor economics and industrial relations than property rights theories, presumably because of the focus on labor as the central actor. However, incorporating property rights theory resolves important problems that are present when the transaction cost model is considered alone. For example, placing control over access to specialized nonhuman capital at the center of the theory of the firm resolves a weakness of the transaction cost theory. Since employees cannot constrain their basic right of job mobility, at least to any meaningful extent, human capital cannot be at the core of the firm providing its defining feature.

What prevents specifically skilled employees from holding up the firm? The property rights answer is that employees follow the orders of the asset owner because the owner can deny continued access to the assets in which the employee has made investments or can grant access to even more valuable assets if the employee is a loyal and productive agent. Because the value of the specific human capital is tied to particular and transferable nonhuman capital, the nonhuman capital within the firm serves as the glue for the specific human capital (Holmstrom 1999; Rajan and Zingales 2001).

The property rights theory also clears up another ambiguity present in the discussion of asset specificity. The parties who jointly make asset-specific investments do not jointly own the assets. One party buys the asset in the sense of buying the residual rights of control not otherwise ceded to others by contract. The owner can then direct its use. Consequently, in our hypothetical network switch example, when the specialized supplier remains independent, she is the owner of the assets that create the semi-finished goods, but NetSwitch owns the residual rights of control when it purchases her assets. Similarly, employees do not jointly own the assets in which they and the firm make specific investments. Common ownership is inferior to sole ownership because of the efficiency gain when the party that prizes the residual control rights most highly gets to purchase those rights. If employees want to become residual claimants, they have to tie their compensation to the profits or free cash flow that the firm's nonhuman assets can generate. Employees do not regularly become the suppliers of capital because of risk aversion and the nondiversification that follows when an individual has her human and nonhuman capital assets in the same firm.

Enforcing the Arrangements of Market Players and Employment Relationship Players

In this section, I focus directly on the impact of contracting in the three different types of organizational structures: the contracting model and the employment relationship in the nonunion firm and the union firm. In so doing, I show that the four industrial factors—match-specific investments, asymmetric information, risk aversion, and transaction costs—largely explain the choice of contracting mechanism. I also relate these models to the theory of the firm and the distinction it draws between extrafirm, or market, transactions and intrafirm transactions. I address the normative question: If the prototypical labor market problem is unequal bargaining power and the unilateral and arbitrary use of power, how are these difficulties controlled in the various theories? Ultimately, what is the enforcement mechanism, and how does it work?

Contract Governance in the Labor Service Market

The labor-contracting model applies to transactions between firms and between workers and firms in the external labor market. It is the market type that has been extensively modeled by economists since it contains few institutional features and no embedded theory of the firm. Labor market transactions take place outside the firm, and the environment is one where transaction costs are low compared with alternative organizational structures. The governance structure is contract based, and the final authority for resolving disputes is the judicial system rather than a firm's hierarchy.

The firm and the worker (or another firm) set out to resolve one or more of the typical problems involving match investments, risk aversion, asymmetric information, and transaction costs. Their agreement is codified in either an explicit or implicit agreement. As Hart (1995) pointed out, this is essentially the principal–agent relationship, which assumes that the actors can write a complete contract that includes appropriate penalties should anyone deviate from the contract terms.

The contract between the parties, although enforceable in court should that be necessary, is intended to be largely or entirely self-enforcing. This recognizes the central goal of deterring opportunistic behavior while recognizing that enforcement costs can be large. Much of the contracting research, in fact, focuses on the types of arrangements that have strong self-enforcing characteristics, and it is assumed that the parties consciously choose labor contracts that have this property.

If the self-enforcing features of contracts are strong enough to deter all opportunistic behavior, any remaining enforcement issues are trivial. In this world, the role of third-party enforcement is uninteresting, whether it involves private third parties or the courts. Indeed, in much of the economics literature, legal enforcement is rarely explicitly mentioned.

However, in a complex world, self-enforcing features rarely fully protect the vulnerable party. In this case, third-party enforcement enters the picture. Third-party enforcement includes the role of private actors, such as other firms and potential workers. Reputational effects are generally seen as the first line of protection should self-enforcement mechanisms fail. Contracts that are enforced by this method are not perfectly self-enforcing because of their reliance on third parties.

Firms or employers are deterred from acting opportunistically because their bad play would eventually be discovered by the labor market and they would suffer reputational losses greater than their potential opportunistic gains. The opportunistically acting employer would then be forced to pay higher wages in order to induce new workers to join the firm and thus would have higher labor costs. Also, other firms might be less willing to act as customers or suppliers of the firm because of concerns that its bad treatment of its own employees makes the firm less generally trustworthy.

But what if judicial enforcement is required? At this point the labor-contracting literature goes silent. However, if the contract is complete, as is typically assumed, the legal solution remains trivial. Take the simplest case, when one party decides not to live up to the terms of the agreement. If nonperformance, whether intentional or inadvertent, were to occur, the court's role would be to read the contract and enforce the agreed-upon penalty. Given the law's response, this situation rarely triggers legal intervention because the nonperforming party will simply pay the penalty required by the contract and avoid the additional costs of a lawsuit.

The judicial enforcement issue becomes more interesting when the contract between the parties is incomplete. This is also typically the boundary where the field of law and economics interfaces with standard economics. There is extensive literature dealing with the two primary questions that frequently arise. First, what legal rules should be adopted to deal with partially incomplete contracts resulting from unintentional gaps in the contract? Second, how should the courts respond when contracts are largely incomplete so that there is more gap than content?

The first of these questions has largely been resolved. It is now generally accepted that the normatively appropriate legal response to partially incomplete contracts is to assist the parties in their profit-maximizing goals while protecting any otherwise unprotected societal interests. This goal is accomplished by adopting the legal rule that is efficient with respect to the problem at hand. The general assessment of contract law is that, as a positive matter, it largely acts in accordance with the normative goal of maximizing the surplus available to the contracting parties. For example, contract law acts as a set of default terms that the parties can adopt by leaving the terms unspecified or that they can overwrite with a term of their choosing (in circumstances where externalities are not present). The result is to provide a standard-form contract that can be adopted so as to minimize the transaction costs of contracting or to allow the parties to adopt whatever terms satisfy their particular profit- or surplus-maximizing goals. Consequently, when the parties omit terms, the courts fill the gaps with the default terms of contract law.

In addition, there is widespread agreement that when a contract is inadvertently incomplete, the court should and, in fact, does fill the gap by adopting the term that the parties themselves would have written had they appreciated the contingency. This is an important conclusion of the legal contract literature: the courts play the role that the labor-contracting literature would want them to play when contracts are inadvertently incomplete. Since the gaps are filled by terms that the parties themselves would have chosen had they known of the gap, the resulting contract still works in a manner that maximizes the surplus available to the parties. Consequently, even though the labor-contracting literature generally ignores enforcement issues, the omission is not a problem because it works entirely in the spirit of the underlying literature.

For these reasons the labor-contracting literature does a good job of describing the theory and practice of the external markets for labor services. More generally, it both describes and predicts what law and economics scholars call relational contracts, which are pervasive not only in labor service markets but in many commercial markets where the agents are in a continuing, long-term relationship.

Less attention has been paid to the second question: how to address agreements that are primarily incomplete. What should be done when the parties intentionally leave wide gaps in their agreement? The position consistent with this paper is that the courts' response should be to treat the existing contract as complete and to treat issues that arise in the gaps as not covered by the contract.[12]

A simple example illustrates the point. Suppose a builder hires a self-employed laborer to work for him for one week. The laborer meets all the criteria to qualify as self-employed. The two agree to the laborer's hourly wage, the hours to be worked, and the right of the laborer to exit the relationship at will. After a few initial jobs are performed, the builder assigns the laborer to a task that she refuses to perform. The builder responds by withholding all pay.

The laborer grieves in court, claiming that the builder breached their contract by assigning her to the task and asks to be compensated for the time worked. Since the contract is entirely incomplete with respect to work assignment, the court has no guidance as to how to fill the gap. Typically, in such circumstances, the court will treat the contract as complete as to its few terms, ruling that the work assignment is outside of the contract. Since the assignment issue was not contracted for, it cannot be breached. However, the court will enforce the contract as to its hourly pay term, allowing the laborer to recover for hours worked.

More generally, contract law fully protects the interests of parties to the extent that they can do the foundational work of constructing a contract that accomplishes their goals. It is not protective otherwise. Except in the very rare situations where the courts apply defenses such as unconscionability, duress, or coercion, the mission of the law of contracts is to enforce the terms of contracts. From the perspective of labor relations, which often sees workers as a vulnerable class in their dealings with corporations, the law of contracts does very little to equilibrate the power of the parties. This is one of the arguments used in the labor relations literature to defend the statutory protection accorded unions by the NLRA.

A final relevant issue regarding the contract law of labor services is that contract case filings and litigations are actually quite rare.[13] This in part supports the ability of self-enforcing mechanisms and private reputational effects to protect parties from opportunistic behavior. The finding is also consistent with the idea that judicial enforcement is important as a deterrence. Critically, however, deterrence appears to be sufficient so that the litigation costs are typically avoided.

Litigation is expensive and wastes resources. In this sense, contract law works best if it works at the deterrence stage. Moreover, when they cannot be resolved by the parties themselves, disputes are often handled by alternative dispute resolution methods, including arbitrators familiar with the parties' relationship. Although evidence about the frequency with which cases are litigated in this venue is sparse, the anecdotal evidence suggests that usage is infrequent.

Norm Governance in the Employment Relationship of the Nonunion Firm

In the employment relationship in the nonunion firm, the parties rely on norms to guide their behavior, with the firm's hierarchical governing structure serving as the ultimate authority for resolving disputes. The problems to be solved by the parties to the nonunion employment relationship are similar to those found in the labor-contracting market, namely, match investments, asymmetric information, risk aversion, and transaction costs. In much of the theoretical literature, the models do not distinguish the labor-contracting sector from the nonunion employment relationship. Since the parties are dealing with the same types of problems, the inference is that the substantive features of the arrangements are similar. Moreover, both sectors are assumed to be affected by reputational effects that dissuade firms from dealing opportunistically.

There is, however, a critical difference between the contracting mechanism of the nonunion employment relationship and that of the external labor market contract. Hierarchy rather than contracts is used to develop the terms and conditions of employment and to dictate the norms of behavior that will be rewarded or penalized. Should a dispute arise, the firm dictates its resolution. Even though the norms of behavior appear to be like contract terms, the courts make no attempt to enforce what appear to be the parties' agreed-upon terms.

Take, for example, the paradigmatic problem when a firm discharges a worker and the worker believes that the discharge is without cause. Should the employee take the case to court, as she sometimes does, the courts generally apply the employment-at-will doctrine. Employment at will stands for the principle that an employer can fire an employee for good reason, bad reason, or no reason at all (Ehrenberg 1989). If taken literally, this rule seems to promote opportunism.

The employment-at-will rule also appears to contradict the assertion that the courts protect the interests of the parties. Remember that contract theory predicts and the facts suggest that the courts will fill contract gaps using the term that the parties themselves would have chosen. Moreover, courts will often enforce the parties' own practices even if they are not codified in the contract. Note that although employers seem to have enormous arbitrary discretion under employment at will, relatively few seem to make use of it. Instead, human resource management preaches that firms should follow the self-enforcing norm of discharging employees only for cause and also claims that firms generally do adopt this loftier standard of behavior. Consequently, although one might expect the courts to adopt the discharge-only-for-cause principle since it is the term generally being practiced, the courts adhere to the employment-at-will rule. The courts' paradoxical passive role in these intrafirm disputes is explained by two factors: how the courts treat agreements marked by largely incomplete contracts and the distinction between governance inside the firm and governance in external market relationships (Rock and Wachter 1996).

If the parties to the employment relationship were to provide numerous contract terms, the court could play the active role of filling in the gaps or applying the parties' own norms. Errors would not likely be large, because of the guidance provided by the numerous existing terms about how the parties wished to handle similar disputes. In the employment relationship, however, the reverse is true. The gaps are large, and there are fewer relevant existing terms. Here the probability of judicial error is great, largely because the courts are too uninformed to make educated guesses. And judicial error raises the costs of the parties' relationship rather than lowering them.

In the presence of large gaps, the helpful court points out that the dispute is not a contract dispute because there is no contract and hence the court lacks jurisdiction. The role of the courts in such situations is analogous to their role when they are asked to resolve a dispute when the contract is largely incomplete. As noted earlier, in this circumstance the court narrowly draws the four corners of the contract to include only those terms that clearly meet the conditions required for contract formation. All other issues are assumed to be outside the contract and hence not accessible to judicial enforcement. In other words, the courts acknowledge and respect the boundaries of the firm. Inside the firm, hierarchy is used to resolve disputes, not the courts. So interpreted, the employment-at-will doctrine is a statement that the court lacks jurisdiction.

If the employer can exercise arbitrary power based on a hierarchical decision-making process, how is the sanctity of employment agreements protected? Unequal bargaining power would surely appear to prevail in this environment. But can or do firms exercise such arbitrary power? The theory of the firm proves especially useful in providing an answer here. The answer has two elements.

The first element explains why the hierarchical structure is needed. Although hierarchical governance and centralized management can create unequal bargaining power, they also create much of the joint surplus available to society. For centralized management to be effective, it cannot be subject to the ultimate jurisdiction of the courts to resolve private matters. Otherwise, judicial enforcement would undermine the legitimacy of centralized management and open numerous disputes to judicial second-guessing. Once the parties have chosen the organizational form, the courts respect the choice and acknowledge that the firm's boundary is a judicial boundary. But what then controls the acknowledged unequal bargaining power?

The second element is that while the intrafirm governance is hierarchical, it has self-enforcing features that exceed even those available in external market relationships. All of the controls available to external market participants are at work within the firm, with the exception of judicial enforcement. These include the strong self-enforcing features of the norms and the reputational effects exerted by third parties. But what offsets the availability of judicial redress?

The exceptional feature of the employment relationship is that it is an intensively repeat-play market. It is this feature that provides workers with considerable bargaining power. It is now well known that informal norm governance works best in repeat-play situations where the very high frequency of the interactions provides an aggrieved party the opportunities needed to sanction and thus deter bad play (Ellickson 1991).

The reason is that self-help methods are much stronger in such situations. This is particularly true where, as in the employment relationship, high-frequency interactions involve information asymmetries where the employees' day-to-day activities are imperfectly monitored. In this situation, a firm that engages in bad play by not following the norms can be sanctioned by the employees. In the repeat-play, low-monitoring context, the employees can engage in techniques running from work slowdowns to outright sabotage. In this situation it is the firm that lacks bargaining power, since the remedy—increased monitoring—can be prohibitively expensive for the same reason that contract writing is prohibitively expensive (Rock and Wachter 1996).

Whether the norms of the nonunion sector provide a workable resolution to the problems of the employment relation is an empirical question. At least at this point in time, it appears that the system does work, given the rise in the percentage of workers in this sector. Certainly, important questions have been raised at times about some aspects of this relationship, particularly where asymmetric information makes it difficult for employees to determine whether the employer is actively opportunistic. Examples are the statutory interventions to regulate employment discrimination, pension plans, and occupational safety and health. In these cases, as was true in the earlier cases of regulation of work hours, child labor, and minimum wages, the regulations have carved out specific areas for judicial enforcement while leaving the bulk of the employment relationship unregulated and the firm's hierarchical governance mechanism outside the purview of judicial review (Bennett and Taylor 2002).

If exclusions for government regulation prove to be an acceptable policy response to major norm failures when they emerge, the nonunion sector can benefit from a bifurcated enforcement mechanism that allows for very inexpensive nonunion contracting mechanisms in all but those identifiable areas where management opportunism is most likely to occur.

Statutory and Contract Enforcement of Union Employment Relationships

The major exception to the rule of employment at will for resolving intrafirm employment disputes is the union sector of the U.S. economy. The bargaining mechanism in the union sector operates in a manner that can be partially predicted by the labor-contracting literature. The employer and employees reach an agreement that covers wages and other terms and conditions of the relationship. The provisions of the collective bargaining agreement (CBA) are enforceable under contract law. Like many ongoing commercial contracts, the parties resolve disputes by appealing to third-party arbitrators rather than relying directly on the courts. The arbitrators apply the usual standards of contract law to the dispute at hand by interpreting the evidence and the parties' conduct in the context of the agreement.[14]

With respect to the substantive terms of the employment relationship, there are important similarities and differences between the union sector and the two alternative structures. For example, there is evidence that some of the adjustment patterns followed by union firms are similar to those followed by nonunion firms and by parties in the labor-contracting market. These include upward-sloping age–earning profiles, filling many slots through internal promotions, and wages that are relatively inflexible with respect to downward adjustments during periods of economic slack (Rock and Wachter 1996).

On the other hand, there is general agreement that union workers are paid considerably more than comparably skilled nonunion workers doing comparable work. Although the union wage premium may have declined over the past decade, it is still material.[15] On a normative basis, the substantive terms of the CBA are thus more favorable to employees than are the outcomes in the nonunion sector and the external market for labor services.

The greatest distinctions among these three forms, however, involve the element of power sharing and the manner in which disputes are resolved. While the labor-contracting sector uses contract law and the nonunion sector uses hierarchy as their enforcement mechanisms, the union sector uses the elaborate superstructure of the NLRA that promotes power sharing. The result is that, whereas the formation of an external labor market contract is entirely voluntary and thus inferentially maximizes joint profits, the collective bargaining contract has numerous mandatory features.

Under the NLRA, once the workers have chosen to be represented by a union, the firm commits an unfair labor practice if it declines to bargain with the union in good faith over the terms and conditions of employment. While the firm retains its hierarchical structure to unilaterally implement changes unrelated to the employment relationship, it is constrained during the bargaining process from unilaterally implementing changes that do affect the employment relationship. In this sense the firm loses some of its residual control rights, which, as described earlier, allow it to call the shots. Moreover, if the parties cannot reach an agreement, they can use the economic weapons of strikes and lockouts against each other.

Consequently, although collective bargaining contracts may maximize joint profit, there are no legal or market forces making this so (Wachter and Cohen 1988). This is a very important distinction. The claim that contract law is efficient assumes that the parties voluntarily enter into their relationship and bargain for terms in an atmosphere where the threat of coercion or duress is absent and where there are few mandatory terms. The bargaining structure in the union sector is very different from this; hence, it would be surprising for the resulting CBA to have the welfare aspects of the unconstrained commercial contract.

An apparent negative upshot of the power sharing is that numerous disputes arise and make the relationship highly litigious. The parties frequently litigate even minor disputes involving the contract rights of individual workers or of management. In addition, the parties frequently litigate "unfair labor practices," that is, allegations that either management or the union has violated the other's statutory rights. Such statutory-based litigation is, of course, entirely absent in labor service contracts in the external labor market. Moreover, while the CBA itself is enforced under contract law, the rights established by the NLRA are enforceable under the act, with the National Labor Relations Board serving as the court of record. The high costs of the current collective bargaining system are without dispute (Gould 1993; Weiler 1990).

The differences in the cost of the enforcement mechanisms are even greater when we compare union collective bargaining with the nonunion employment relationship. Remember that the difference between the labor-contracting sector and the nonunion employment relationship is that the latter operates without the backdrop of a judicial or third-party enforcement mechanism and all its associated deterrence of opportunistic behavior. This makes the nonunion enforcement mechanism even less costly than the labor-contracting mechanism. Consequently, the cost difference in the enforcement mechanisms between the intrafirm union and nonunion sectors is particularly large.

Costly contracting and enforcement are thus major problems facing the union sector. Can enforcement be conducted so as to support the joint interests of the parties, or is it inherently costly and adversarial? The theory of the firm and contract theory suggest a pessimistic assessment.

First, the activities performed inside firms are those for which residual control issues are prevalent, and residual control rights involve precisely those events that are not easily predicted before the fact and therefore cannot easily be incorporated into contracts. Second, contract theory predicts that contracts work best when the contracting terms are largely self-enforcing and when the threat of litigation is sufficient to deter remaining possibilities of opportunism. Finally, there are no proposals for making it less adversarial.

So why does the union sector engage in explicit contracting, and why are litigation costs so high? There are two answers: either unions use their power to achieve noncompetitive wages and benefits, or management cannot be trusted and acts opportunistically. To an extent, however, the issues may dovetail into one explanation.

The fact that unions can and do achieve noncompetitive benefits for their members is one of the most widely supported economic regularities in labor market research. If unions achieve these gains, the use of explicit contracting takes on a special role: it codifies and makes legally enforceable the noncompetitive returns. This special role is magnified by the fact that the relationship is not entirely voluntary. A firm cannot refuse to bargain with a union that has been certified to represent its workforce. In this context, it is likely that the unhappy party will do whatever it can to escape from the unfavorable terms that it views as being forced on it.

The sources of the union pay premium, the wage and benefit clauses, are themselves low-cost items that generate little in the way of litigation. The payment of wages and to an extent the payment of benefits can be observed and verified by the parties. It is the contingencies prompted by the wage and benefit clauses that introduce litigation and increase transaction costs. Specifically, if the workers are being paid more than comparable nonunion workers would be paid, the firm can be expected to engage in tactics to substitute nonunion for union labor wherever possible or to change work rules or assignments to make the wage and benefit premium less onerous. Given the potential scope of management activities to evade the premium, protecting against these contingencies is a major undertaking. The result is a host of contract clauses dealing with work assignment, discharge, relocation, subcontracting, and work rules in general.[16]

This then is the contracting problem faced by the union sector. If management will search for methods to lower labor costs, then the contract has to be elaborate enough to foreclose as many of these as can be anticipated before they occur. This generates two well-known contracting problems. First, management has asymmetric information about the cost and benefits of proposed initiatives, and its information cannot be easily observed or verified by the union. Second, the union is attempting to foresee future management initiatives that are very difficult to predict with any accuracy. These initiatives, after all, are the very residual steps that management itself believes it cannot contract over because of the difficulty of identifying them beforehand. The upshot is that the union must cast a wide contracting net that constrains management behavior over a substantial range.

Expansive contracting provisions to restrict the use of information by the informed party render the union employment relationship less flexible, since many avenues of adjustment normally open to managers cannot be used. Such restrictions include preventing management from taking initiatives whose primary goal is to reduce the union's noncompetitive advantage. But since there is no way of verifying motive, restrictive contract terms also prevent many changes that would maximize joint profit. Indeed, because of the union's difficulty in verifying information asymmetrically known to the firm, even measures that would increase the profits of both sides may be foreclosed. This, for example, supports the widely cited claim that nonunion automakers can pay union wages and benefits and still have lower unit labor costs. More generally, the result of this inflexibility is to raise unit labor costs without generating direct benefits to either the firm or the union (except for the indirect benefit of protecting the noncompetitive results).

The second explanation for the contract morass is that management cannot be trusted and acts opportunistically. The high litigation costs are caused by the need to constrain opportunism. In the context of the union sector, the commentators who follow this line focus on the claim that managers are anti-union in the sense of attempting to keep or make their plant or company nonunion. Specifically, the pointed attacks on management's actions in the union literature involve the fact that management has never accepted unionization as the appropriate organizational structure for dealing with its employees (Weiler 1990).

On this claim itself there is little disagreement. Even promanagement commentators agree that most nonunion firms attempt to remain nonunion and that, in some cases, firms with unionized operations attempt to become nonunion. In addition, there is broad agreement that both sides have historically used practices that have been found to be unfair labor practices under the NLRA. Whether management's position is driven more by the noncompetitive agreements achieved by labor unions or by their unwillingness to share power with unions is a topic that is beyond the scope of this paper.

The two stories—that unions achieve noncompetitive results and that management cannot be trusted—are thus just two elements of the same story. If unions achieve noncompetitive results that place the firm at a competitive disadvantage in its product markets or that reduce shareholders' returns below some anticipated level, then management can be expected to use whatever mechanisms are available to it to escape from that noncompetitive position. The result is the high litigation costs and adversarial context in which the parties often operate.

Given the disadvantages of unusually high contracting and enforcement costs, what advantages are offered by the union form? There are two situations where collective bargaining offers the preferred organizational structure. The first is when society wants to promote noncompetitive results in the labor market, which was arguably the case at the time of the passage of the NLRA (Wachter 2003; Kaufman 2002).[17] The second case is when management cannot be trusted, even absent a union wage premium. Here *untrustworthy* means that nonunion managers use the hierarchical power inherent in the nonunion form to force noncompetitive terms and conditions of employment on imperfectly mobile workers who have made match investments and who may suffer from informational disadvantages that keep them in the dark as to actual conditions or opportunities.

Conclusion

In this paper I have argued that when economic actors in the labor market choose a method for organizing the provision of labor services, their choice is determined by the parties' specific costs associated with the four problems of match-specific investments, asymmetric information, risk aversion, and transaction costs. The costs relate to both labor and capital. The boundaries of the firm, that is, the choice between using markets or hierarchy, are determined not only by the costs associated with organizing labor services in these two different organizational forms but also by the need to control the costs associated with residual rights of control over physical and intangible assets.

The external labor-contracting market, the nonunion employment relationship, and the collective bargaining structure of the union sector are each likely to be cost efficient under some economic circumstances. Economic actors are more likely to choose the external contracting model to guide their interests when the transaction costs of contracting are low. This is likely to occur when the parties do not need to interact continuously, there are relatively few match investments, and the critical information relevant to the transaction is available to both parties. When this structure is available and markets are competitive, the parties' interests are well protected. Not only can they rely on the power of self-enforcing contract terms and reputational effects, but should these fall, they can rely on judicial enforcement as well. The problems of inequality of bargaining power and the exercise of arbitrary hierarchical powers are less problematic in this environment because the parties are using competitive markets rather than hierarchy to guide their activity.

Different enforcement issues arise when the activities are brought inside the firm. At least in the nonunion firm, judicial enforcement is absent, so the parties are left to the binding powers of the self-governing norms that they follow, augmented by third-party reputational effects that occur when firms or workers can be labeled as bad players. Why should workers be willing to abjure the protections of market contracting and work inside firms? The theory of the firm provides the answer.

For capital to create value, individual firms must have residual control rights over their key physical and intangible capital. The result is hierarchical governance whereby the executive officers get to call the shots on behalf of the shareholders, who receive the residual income generated by the owned assets. For hierarchical governance to work, the executive officers have to be able to manage the business and affairs of the corporation. Even in corporation law, the courts give managers great discretion in conducting the business and affairs of the corporation. Although the shareholders get to vote for the directors in their role of residual claimants, they exercise almost no other control rights normally associated with ownership. The reason is to protect the integrity of hierarchical governance and its ability to maximize shareholders' value.

These same concerns devolve into the nonunion employment relationship as well. Hierarchical governance means that the managers get to decide about employment issues with little second-guessing by courts. Workers are willing to relinquish the protections of the external labor market because of the increased wages available to those who are given access to valuable nonhuman capital. In the high-transaction-cost, continuous-interaction setting of the employment relationship, match-specific investments are frequent, and asymmetric information problems are endemic.

For the firm to be successful, it has to decide on the capital stock over which it needs to have residual control. In the nonunion sector, the firm also decides on the norms and specific standards of the employment relationship. Both the firm and its workers have much at stake in making their relationship work. The success of the nonunion sector of the economy suggests that the system must be working, at least tolerably and perhaps much better than that. There is still inequality of bargaining power, which is inherent in the system. But it is at least arguable that the norm-based governance system, policed by the ability of either party to penalize bad play in the transaction-intensive relationship, works reasonably well (Rock and Wachter 2001).

But a hierarchical, norm-based system may not always work. Although the firm has the appropriate incentives to treat workers fairly, the managers may not act this way because of either individual managers' idiosyncratic behavior or firm policy. When this occurs, workers can seek the heightened protections of the NLRA, whereby the contract formation process itself is protected by contract law and the union certification and collective bargaining processes have distinct statutory protections.

Alternatively, government labor market regulation—narrowly targeted to resolve specific intrafirm problem areas such as employment discrimination, pension regulation, and occupational safety and health—can reduce the attractiveness of unions. By carving out problem areas and resolving them while leaving hierarchical governance in place, policy has made the nonunion form much more successful than it otherwise would likely have been (Bennett and Taylor 2002).

The collective bargaining system was originally envisioned to serve the needs of a wide spectrum of workers, not just those dissatisfied with the nonunion sector. Collective bargaining was viewed as a good in itself. However, if collective bargaining is a good, it is an expensive one. The theory of the firm teaches that the hierarchical, norm-based system that eschews contracts and legal enforcement is the low-cost contracting and enforcement mechanism to be used inside firms. The nonunion system has many cost advantages over the union system as long as management opportunism can be adequately controlled by self-enforcing mechanisms combined with reputational effects. If this nonunion system works—in the sense that workers feel adequately protected by it against firm opportunism—then the union alternative is likely to be at a material disadvantage.

Acknowledgments

I am grateful to Bruce Kaufman for many useful suggestions, to Bonnie Clause and Sarah Sisti for research assistance, and to William Draper for library assistance.

Notes

[1] A term of an agreement is self-enforcing if none of the parties to the agreement would find it profitable to use the discretion available to them to redistribute profits to themselves. Agreements that self-enforce thus do not require or benefit from either judicial enforcement or even from private, third-party effects such as reputational effects.

[2] Throughout this article, I refer to the National Labor Relations Act as the regulatory mechanism for protecting unionized workers. Of course, other federal and state laws are also involved in regulating the collective bargaining mechanism (e.g., the Railway Labor Act).

[3] The fact that one party may dictate contract terms to another does not imply that the terms are unfair. The contract terms may entirely or partially reflect competitive market pressures, and the lack of bargaining over the terms may merely reflect the parties' desires to reduce contracting costs (Posner 2003).

[4] See Rock and Wachter (1996). For my purposes, a useful definition of norms is "rules or standards enforced solely by private (i.e., nonstate) actors." The term describes what the parties actually do and is not intended to have any normative content. See, for example, Ellickson (1991).

[5] In addition, the employer and individual employees sometimes write enforceable contracts governing major one-time events such as starting pay, severance pay, or restrictions on competing with the company should the employee quit.

[6] An asset is match specific if an alternative user can redeploy it only with substantial sacrifice of productive value. An asset is general when there exists a ready secondary market so that the asset can be sold at approximately the firm's current use value. Asymmetric information exists when it is relatively more costly for one of the parties to observe or monitor the quantity of inputs or outputs, the state of technology, or the product market. Risk aversion exists when an individual views risk as bad and is willing to take a lower return or benefit in order to reduce the risk that she faces. Transaction costs refer to the costs of organizing the activities of the inputs and outputs.

[7] Some argue that the efficiency argument is circular. If markets are competitive and workers have choices and can contract freely, then reasonably efficient outcomes will result from the freedom of contract. The problem, according to these commentators, is that workers cannot contract freely, have limited information and limited choices because they are weak in comparison with the firm, and cannot protect themselves. If one assumes this to be true, the collective bargaining apparatus of the union employment relationship would be favored over the nonunion employment relationship (Atleson 1983; Gould 1993; and Weiler 1990).

[8] The economics literature on self-enforcing labor market contracts is extensive. See, for example, Carmichael (1989), Lazear (2000), and Gibbons (1998).

[9] This section draws from Wachter and Wright (1990) and Rock and Wachter (1996, 1999).

[10] This is the efficiency wage problem, whereby increases in wages above competitive levels are actually profit enhancing because they lower monitoring costs by more than the wages increase costs (Ackerlof and Yellen 1986).

[11] The transaction cost theory of the firm was first introduced by Coase (1937) and was developed to its current state by Williamson (1975) and others working in that tradition. For a discussion of its implications for labor market contracting, see Rock and Wachter (1996).

[12] According to Schwartz (1992), the courts in general do respond in this fashion.

[13] Moreover, this is true for contract law overall. See Galanter (2001).

[14] The range of the collective bargaining agreement is also predicted by contracting theory. Wages, nonwage benefits, hours, and other terms and conditions of employment are covered. Moreover, contracts almost never materially limit the employer's ability to direct the firm through capital expenditure decisions or other nonlabor issues.

[15] There is considerable evidence that unions succeed in achieving a wage and benefit premium, that is, wages and benefits above those paid to comparable workers in the nonunion sector. See, for example, Hirsch and Addison (1986), Kaufman (in press), and Linneman and Wachter (1986). Although there is a claim that unions raise productivity and that the premium is paid out of noncompetitive profits, there is little evidence to support this claim.

[16] It is difficult to empirically verify the effects of contract restrictions on the flexibility of managers to adjust to changing circumstances. This reflects the difficulties of modeling the specific effects of particular contract restrictions. However, there is considerable evidence on the effects of unions on firm profitability. See, for example, Ruback and Zimmerman (1984) and Hirsch (1997).

[17] During the 1930s, the industrial public policy goal was "stabilizing business" or avoiding "excessive competition," which was understood to mean restricting competition. In this context, unions were viewed as a positive force: a countervailing power to that exercised by corporations (Wachter 2003).

References

Ackerlof, George A., and Janet L. Yellen. 1986. *Efficiency Wage Models of the Labor Market*. New York: Cambridge University Press.

Atleson, James B. 1983. *Values and Assumptions in American Labor Law*. Amherst: University of Massachusetts Press.

Bennett, James T., and Jason E. Taylor. 2002. "Labor Unions: Victims of Their Own Political Success." In James T. Bennett and Bruce E. Kaufman, eds., *The Future of Private Sector Unionism in the United States*, New York: Sharpe.

Boal, William M., and Michael Ransom. 1997. "Monopsony in the Labor Market." *Journal of Economic Literature*, Vol. 35, no. 1 (March), pp. 86–112.

Carmichael, H. Lorne. 1989. "Self-Enforcing Contracts, Shirking and Life Cycle Incentives." *Journal of Economic Perspectives*, Vol. 3, no. 4 (Fall), pp. 65–84.

Coase, Ronald. 1937. "The Nature of the Firm." *Economica,* New Series, Vol. 4, no. 16 (November), pp. 386–405.

Ehrenberg, Ronald. 1989. "Workers' Rights: Rethinking Protective Labor Legislation." In Lee Bawden and Felicity Skidmore, eds., *Rethinking Employment Policy*, Washington, DC: Urban Institute Press.

Ellickson, Robert C. 1991. *Order without Law: How Neighbors Settle Disputes*. Cambridge, MA: Harvard University Press.

Galanter, Marc. 2001. "Contract in Court; or Almost Everything You May or May
    Not Want to Know about Contract Litigation." *Wisconsin Law Review*, Vol.
    2001, no. 3, pp. 577–627.
Gibbons, Robert. 1998. "Incentives in Organization." *Journal of Economic Perspec-
    tives*, Vol. 12, no. 4 (Fall), pp. 115–32.
Gould, William B., IV. 1993. *Agenda for Reform: The Future of Employment Rela-
    tionships and the Law*. Cambridge, MA: MIT Press.
Hart, Oliver. 1995. *Firms, Contracts, and Financial Structure*. Oxford: Clarendon
    Press; New York: Oxford University Press.
Hart, Oliver, and John Moore. 1990. "Property Rights and the Nature of the Firm."
    Journal of Political Economy, Vol. 98, no. 6 (December), pp. 1119–58.
Hirsch, Barry T. 1997. "Unionization and Economic Performance: Evidence on Pro-
    ductivity, Profits, Investment, and Growth." In Fazil Mihlar, ed., *Unions and
    Right-to-Work Laws: The Global Evidence of Their Impact on Employment*,
    Vancouver: Fraser Institute, pp. 35–70.
Hirsch, Barry T., and John T. Addison. 1986. *The Economic Analysis of Unions: New
    Approaches and Evidence*. Boston: Allen and Unwin.
Holmstrom, Bengt. 1999. "The Firm as a Subeconomy." *Journal of Law, Economics,
    and Organization*, Vol. 15, no. 1 (April), pp. 74–102.
Kaufman, Bruce E. 2002. "The Future of Private Section Unionism: Did George
    Barnett Get It Right after All?" In James T. Bennett and Bruce E. Kaufman,
    eds., *The Future of Private Sector Unionism in the United States*, New York:
    Sharpe.
———. In press. "What Unions Do: Insights from Economic Theory." *Journal of
    Labor Research*.
Lazear, Edward P. 2000. "Performance Pay and Productivity." *American Economic
    Review*, Vol. 90, no. 5 (December), pp. 1346–61.
Linneman, Peter, and Michael L. Wachter. 1986. "Rising Union Premiums and De-
    clining Boundaries among Noncompeting Groups." *American Economic Review*,
    Vol. 76, no. 2 (May), pp. 103–8.
Manning, Alan. 2003. *Monopsony in Motion: Imperfect Competition in Labor Mar-
    kets*. Princeton, NJ: Princeton University Press.
Posner, Richard A. 2003. *Economic Analysis of Law*, 6th ed. New York: Aspen.
Rajan, Raghuram G., and Luigi Zingales. 2001. "The Firm as a Dedicated Hierarchy:
    A Theory of the Origin and Growth of Firms." *Quarterly Journal of Economics*,
    Vol. 116, no. 3 (August), pp. 805–51.
Rock, Edward B., and Michael L. Wachter. 1996. "The Enforceability of Norms and
    the Employment Relationship." *University of Pennsylvania Law Review*, Vol.
    144, no. 5 (May), pp. 1913–52.
———. 1999. "Tailored Claims and Governance: The Fit between Employees and
    Shareholders." In Margaret Blair and Mark J. Roe, eds., *Employees and Corpo-
    rate Governance*, Washington, DC: Brookings Institution, pp. 121–59.
———. 2001. "Islands of Conscious Power: Law, Norms, and the Self-Governing
    Corporation." *University of Pennsylvania Law Review*, Vol. 149, no. 6 (June),
    pp. 1619–700.
Ruback, Richard S., and Martin B. Zimmerman. 1984. "Unionization and Profitabil-
    ity: Evidence from the Capital Market." *Journal of Political Economy*, Vol. 92,
    no. 6 (December), pp. 1134–57.

Schwartz, Alan. 1992. "Relational Contracts in the Courts: An Analysis of Incomplete Agreements and Judicial Strategies." *Journal of Legal Studies,* Vol. 21, no. 2 (June), pp. 271–318.

Wachter, Michael L. 2003. "Judging Unions' Future Using a Historical Perspective: The Public Policy Choice between Competition and Unionization." *Journal of Labor Research,* Vol. 24, no. 2 (Spring), pp. 339–57.

Wachter, Michael L., and George M. Cohen. 1988. "The Law and Economics of Collective Bargaining: An Introduction and Application to the Problems of Subcontracting, Partial Closure, and Relocation." *University of Pennsylvania Law Review,* Vol. 136, no. 5 (May), pp. 1349–417.

Wachter, Michael L., and Randall D. Wright. 1990. "The Economics of Internal Labor Markets." *Industrial Relations,* Vol. 29, no. 2 (Spring), pp. 240–62.

Weiler, Paul C. 1990. *Governing the Workplace: The Future of Labor and Employment Law.* Cambridge, MA: Harvard University Press.

Williamson, Oliver E. 1975. *Markets and Hierarchies: Analysis and Antitrust Implications.* New York: Free Press.

———. 1996. *The Mechanics of Governance.* New York: Oxford University Press.

Williamson, Oliver E., Michael L. Wachter, and Jeffrey E. Harris. 1975. "Understanding the Employment Relation: The Analysis of Idiosyncratic Exchange." *Bell Journal of Economics,* Vol. 6, no. 1 (Spring), pp. 250–78.

CHAPTER 7

Why a Balance Is Best: The Pluralist Industrial Relations Paradigm of Balancing Competing Interests

JOHN W. BUDD
University of Minnesota

RAFAEL GOMEZ
London School of Economics

NOAH M. MELTZ
University of Toronto

The pluralist industrial relations paradigm analyzes work and the employment relationship from a theoretical perspective rooted in an inherent conflict of interest between employers and employees interacting in imperfect labor markets. The employment relationship is viewed as a bargaining problem between stakeholders with competing interests; employment outcomes depend on the varied elements of the environment that determine each stakeholder's bargaining power.[1] Modeling the employment relationship as a bargaining problem raises central questions about the distribution of resources and the rules governing interactions between employers and employees. As a result, corporations, labor unions, public policies, and dispute resolution procedures are important institutions (broadly defined) and research subjects in pluralist industrial relations. Moreover, individual employees, managers, owners, and union leaders are viewed as human agents rather than purely economic, rational agents. Behavioral elements of individual decision making—cognitive limitations, emotions, social or cultural norms and values, habits, intrinsic as well as extrinsic motivators, and concern for others, fairness, and justice—are therefore important.

The pluralist industrial relations school of thought traces back to Sidney and Beatrice Webb in England, John R. Commons (the father of U.S. industrial relations), and members of the Wisconsin school of institutional labor economists in the early 20th century. Its views were enshrined in the New Deal U.S. labor policies of the 1930s Great Depression era and cemented in practice by a generation of postwar scholar-arbitrators. This school of thought continues today as the mainstream industrial relations paradigm in North America.[2] With the postwar rise to dominance of the neoclassical paradigm in economics, however, industrial relations has been frequently criticized for allegedly being limited to atheoretical fact gathering and therefore not being a legitimate academic paradigm. Coase (1984:230) attacked the early institutional economics of Commons and others by claiming that "[w]ithout a theory they had nothing to pass on except a mass of descriptive material waiting for a theory, or a fire." Traditional industrial relations has also frequently been criticized for emphasizing facts over theory (Dunlop 1993). In reality, with the theoretical foundations of imperfect labor markets and human agents, employment outcomes do not have to be viewed as completely (and mechanically) determined by rational individuals and market forces; careful analysis of real-world institutions and practices is therefore a hallmark of industrial relations scholarship. But this scholarship stems from a specific theoretical perspective, not from the lack of theory.[3]

The pluralist industrial relations school of thought also often embraces a balancing paradigm. Commons (1919:43) focused on the need for "the equilibrium of capital and labor" rather than the domination of one or the other. Kochan (1980:21, emphasis in original) emphasized that "industrial relations theories, research, and policy prescriptions must be conscious of the relationships among the goals of workers, employers, and the larger society and seek ways of achieving a workable and equitable *balance* among these interests." Imbalances of income, from a pluralist perspective, can reduce economic growth by depressing consumer purchasing power and preventing investments in human and physical capital. Excessive corporate power that creates substandard wages and working conditions can burden society with welfare-reducing social costs. Behavioral elements of decision making imply that individual perceptions of balance or fairness can affect employee turnover, productivity, and other industrial relations outcomes. A central analytical tenet of the pluralist school, therefore, is that employment relations outcomes emerge and persist not because they are necessarily the most efficient—as would be the case under a neoclassical paradigm—but because they strike a balance between the competing interests of different individuals, stakeholders, and institutions.

Moreover, since individuals are viewed analytically as human rather than economic agents, industrial relations scholarship dating back to the early 20th century questions not only how employees behave but also what standards of treatment they deserve as human beings in a democratic society. With imperfect labor markets, the presence of powerful corporations or desperate competition among workers can result in substandard employment conditions. Thus, the analytical foundations of pluralist industrial relations also create a strong normative agenda: creating a balance between the competing interests in the employment relationship. Individual, organizational, and social outcomes beyond efficiency or productivity are therefore important dimensions of industrial relations scholarship. Launched by the inequality of the early 20th century employment relationship, these analytical tenets and normative issues continue to be very relevant for the employment relationship a century later.

The Central Interests of the Employment Relationship

The starting point for scholarship on the employment relationship is the objectives of this relationship (Budd 2004). In neoclassical economics, these objectives reduce to allocative efficiency. The invisible hand of competitive markets will guide self-interested individuals toward efficient outcomes in which aggregate welfare is maximized and scarce resources are used to their most productive ends. The key objective is therefore efficiency: companies want efficient production processes to maximize profits, consumers want efficient companies to maximize value, and employees want efficient employment opportunities to maximize their earnings and leisure. With rational individuals and competitive markets, there is no divergence between public and private interests: no groups have a power advantage over others, and market prices (including wages) fully reflect social value. Workers participate in the determination of their working conditions through entry into desirable jobs and out of undesirable ones (Troy 1999); outcomes are viewed as equitable or fair because each commodity—labor included—is rewarded with its economic value (McClelland 1990).

In contrast, a hallmark of the industrial relations perspective is that workers are not simply commodities (Kaufman 1993; Webb and Webb 1897). Workers are human beings with aspirations, feelings, emotions, needs, and rights; work provides more than extrinsic, monetary rewards by fulfilling important psychological and social needs. Moreover, if markets are not competitive, then prices do not accurately reflect social value (Slichter 1924; Stabile 1993). Thus, a realistic analysis of welfare requires explicit consideration of the nature of work and workers' lives.

The industrial relations paradigm therefore explicitly considers interests of the employment relationship that are not limited to (but include) efficiency.

The nature of work and workers' lives were graphically apparent to Commons and other early institutionalists through the labor problems of the early 20th century: excessive working hours, low wages, dangerous working conditions, and widespread worker insecurity as a result of business cycles, seasonal labor demand, accidents or disease, old age, and discriminatory or arbitrary firings (Kaufman 1993, 1997). According to government surveys around 1910, 85% of wage earners had a standard workweek of more than 54 hours, and among iron and steel industry workers, over 40% worked more than 72 hours per week, and about 20% worked more than 84 hours per week (Lauck and Sydenstricker 1917). The long hours were often for low pay in dangerous and unhealthy conditions. A March 1911 fire at the Triangle Shirtwaist Company in New York City killed 146 workers because of inadequate and locked fire exits. According to one estimate, industrial accidents resulted in 25,000 deaths, 25,000 permanent disability cases, and 2,000,000 temporary disability cases per year, which implies that during World War I, U.S. casualties were greater in the workplace than on the battlefield (Downey 1924).

The long hours at low pay in dangerous and unhealthy conditions were also marked by great insecurity. Many lived with a constant fear of unemployment. A government investigation of nearly 30,000 male workers in 1909 found that only 37% did not have any time lost from work over the course of a full year; half of the workers lost four or more months (Lauck and Sydenstricker 1917). Labor was frequently viewed as just another input in the production process, no different from machines or raw materials. In the drive system of the foreman's empire, workers were arbitrarily dismissed for any reason, no matter how abusive (Jacoby 1985; Lichtenstein 1989). With mass manufacturing methods emphasizing repetitive, narrowly defined tasks by individual workers to achieve high output, workers had no contact with the final product and had minimal control over the content of their job. Even Adam Smith ([1776] 1937:734) recognized that while this division of labor has efficiency advantages, there were other concerns since specialization renders workers "stupid and ignorant." Because of these conditions, the early institutionalists identified not only efficiency, but also equity and self-actualization as the key objectives of the employment relationship: "greater efficiency in production; greater equity in the distribution of economic rewards, the utilization of labor, and the administration of employment policies in the workplace; and greater individual happiness and opportunities for personal growth and development" (Kaufman 1993:13).

These basic objectives continue to be important in the contemporary industrial relations paradigm. Jack Barbash (1987, 1989) and Noah Meltz (1989) both rooted the field of industrial relations in the study of efficiency and equity. According to Barbash (1987:172), equity consists of "(1) having a say in the work, (2) due process in the handling of complaints, (3) fair treatment at work, (4) meaningful work, (5) fair compensation and secure employment." Both Barbash and Meltz further emphasized the multifaceted relationship between efficiency and equity; the need for equity stems from the need to protect human labor from the abuses of a pure efficiency regime and the need to treat human labor fairly in order to achieve superior efficiency. In other words, sometimes efficiency and equity clash; at other times they are complements. Thus, the central feature of the industrial relations paradigm is balancing the distinct, yet mutually dependent, interests of employers and employees: efficiency and equity (Meltz 1989).

Budd (2004) extended this thinking by distinguishing between equity and voice. Equity is fair employment standards for both material outcomes (such as wages and safety) and personal treatment (especially nondiscrimination). Voice is the ability to have meaningful input into decisions, including both industrial democracy and autonomy or control. The basis for the equity–voice distinction is the view that equity is instrumental and can be provided unilaterally by employers or government regulations, while voice is intrinsic and can be achieved only by worker participation. Thus, while equity and voice might often be mutually supporting, they can also be competing objectives of the employment relationship; industry-wide collective bargaining, for example, might be very effective at establishing equitable minimum wage standards, but at the expense of rank and file participation in decision making. In Budd's (2004) analysis, therefore, the central interests of the employment relationship are efficiency, equity, and voice.[4]

The Theory of Competing Interests

The fundamental *theoretical* assumptions of pluralist industrial relations are that (1) there is a conflict of interest in the employment relationship, (2) labor markets are not perfectly competitive, and (3) employees are human beings, not simply commodities or factors of production. These assumptions yield a theoretical perspective of the employment relationship significantly distinct from the other views of the employment relationship: neoclassical economics, human resource management, and critical industrial relations. Neoclassical economics is built around rational agents in competitive markets.[5] Conflict is not an important construct; buyers and sellers of labor or other commodities simply search for transactions that maximize their utility. Work is undertaken only to earn money to afford leisure and consumption. Competitive markets simultaneously maximize aggregate welfare and place checks on abuse (Friedman and Friedman 1980; Troy 1999).

In contrast, pluralist industrial relations, critical industrial relations, and human resource management reject the deterministic importance of competitive markets and rational economic agents but differ from each other in their view of employment relationship conflict (Budd 2004; Hills 1995; Kaufman 1993; Kochan 1998). Human resource management embraces a unitarist view of conflict in which employment policies and practices can align the interests of employees and employers (Fox 1974; Lewin 2001). At the other end of the spectrum, employment relations conflict in the critical or Marxist industrial relations paradigm is rooted in unequal power relations between classes throughout society (Giles and Murray 1997; Hyman 1975). In between these two views is the pluralist industrial relations perspective that the employment relationship is characterized by a variety of competing interests—higher wages versus lower labor costs, employment security versus flexibility, safe work pace versus high output—as well as shared interests—productive workers, profitable employers, a healthy economy; in other words, employment relationship conflict is pluralist (Clegg 1975; Fox 1974) or mixed-motive (Kochan 1998; Walton and McKersie 1965) and is certainly not pathological (Barbash 1984).

These contrasting views of employment relationship conflict are essential for understanding the theoretical paradigm of the pluralist industrial relations school. Institutions such as unions and laws plus processes for bargaining and dispute resolution are important objects of analysis in industrial relations, unlike the human resource management school, because they provide alternative means for mediating conflicts of interest (Adams 1995; Budd 2004; Walton and McKersie 1965; Weiler 1990). In contrast to critical industrial relations, research in pluralist industrial relations tends to view workplaces as influenced by the external environment (Dunlop 1993; Kochan, Katz, and McKersie 1986) rather than as embedded in a larger political economy of class-based conflict. In contrast to critical or Marxist industrial relations, class is not a crucial analytical concept in pluralist industrial relations.[6] And because pluralist industrial relations embraces mixed-motive conflict that includes shared labor–management goals, individual and organizational performance is also an important research topic (Appelbaum and Batt 1994; Kleiner, Block, Roomkin, and Salsburg 1987; Levine 1995).

The pluralist view of conflict is intimately related to a belief that labor markets are not perfectly competitive. Sidney and Beatrice Webb, John R. Commons, and other early institutionalists attributed the labor problem of the early 20th century to the superior power of large corporations over individual employees (Kaufman 1993, 1997). This superior power stemmed from market imperfections: isolated company towns, mobility costs and lack of family savings or other resources, segmented markets, and excess labor supply. From this theoretical perspective, laws and unions are viewed as mechanisms for leveling the playing field between employers and employees, thereby promoting the optimal operation of markets rather than interfering with it (as predicted by theories rooted in competitive markets). Common research questions in pluralist industrial relations therefore include how labor markets work (Kaufman 1988) and the effects of unions and laws on workers, firms, and the economy (Belman and Belzer 1997; Freeman and Medoff 1984; Slichter, Healy, and Livernash 1960).

In fact, the pluralist view that imperfect labor market structures should be the benchmark by which to judge policy interventions continues to have currency (Manning 2003). Card and Krueger's (1995) findings that the effects of minimum wage laws are not consistent with models of perfect competition reinforce the importance of modeling the labor market as a zone where a combination of costly job search, mobility restrictions, and informational asymmetries gives employers monopsony power. That is, labor markets can be imperfect even in situations where there is apparent labor market competition among employers to attract workers. And even in human capital theory—one of the bedrock theories of neoclassical labor economics—the employment relationship becomes a bargaining problem if there are informational asymmetries, such as employers' not being able to observe workers' investments in human capital and outsiders' not knowing a workers' current productivity (Chang and Wang 1996). Moreover, in these situations, private actions produce suboptimal training investments, so—consistent with the pluralist tradition—there is a need for institutional intervention.

The final theoretical element of the pluralist industrial relations paradigm is modeling individuals as human or behavioral agents rather than purely economic agents (Budd 2004; Kaufman 1988, 1999). In contrast to neoclassical economics, work is not viewed solely as a source of income. The interests of workers can therefore be complex: avoiding drudgery and other affronts to personal dignity (Barbash 1984; Hodson 2001), participating in decision making (Freeman and Rogers 1999), or the fulfillment of self-actualization (Kaufman 1993; Webb and Webb 1897). Decisions by workers and managers are not always made on a purely rational basis. Aggression and frustration might lead to strikes (Wheeler 1985), coercive comparisons might affect wage outcomes (Ross 1948), and complexity might create internal labor markets at odds with competitive forces (Doeringer and Piore 1971; Lester 1988). The recent growth in quasi-rational and experimental economics offers mainstream economic theory a way of modeling human actions that brings economic thought closer to the long-standing pluralist paradigm, but such modeling continues to be a hallmark of pluralist rather than neoclassical research on the employment relationship.[7]

In sum, the building blocks of the pluralist industrial relations paradigm yield a theory of competing interests: the employment relationship is modeled as a bargaining problem between stakeholders with competing and shared interests, such as cost discipline and PEEP (price, equity, effort, and power; Barbash 1984), efficiency and equity (Meltz 1989), or efficiency, equity, and voice (Budd 2004). The competing interests are not reconciled solely by market forces—which are often imperfect and often favor employers—but also by complex individual and collective interactions shaped by institutions, behavioral decision-making factors, customs, and values.[8] At the same time, the shared interests bind the stakeholders together, and the focal point of the pluralist industrial relations paradigm is resolving conflicts of interest to produce mutual gain (Barbash 1984; Budd 2004; Commons 1934; Kochan 1998; Meltz 1989).[9] This theoretical perspective of the employment relationship provides testable hypotheses regarding the determinants of employment outcomes.

The pluralist industrial relations conception of the employment relationship as a mixed-motive interaction between human agents in imperfect labor markets is a legitimate theory of the employment relationship. One can challenge the accuracy of the assumptions that underlie this theory, but the industrial relations paradigm cannot be dismissed as either atheoretical or entirely normative. Even among leading industrial relations scholars, however, these assumptions are typically labeled the *normative* foundations of industrial relations (e.g., Kochan 1998). The singular emphasis on the label *normative* should be amended: these assumptions reflect beliefs about how the employment relationship works as much as how it should work; they are no more normative than the neoclassical economics assumptions of rational economic agents and competitive markets. The pluralist industrial relations model is as much of a theory of the employment relationship as is the neoclassical economics model; it is not as easily reduced to mathematical modeling through tractable maximization problems, but it generates testable hypotheses about behavior, outcomes, and relationships between various quantities.

The Importance of Balancing Competing Interests

A central feature of this pluralist industrial relations paradigm is balancing competing interests in the employment relationship:

> If the democratic state is to attain its fullest and finest development, it is essential that the actual needs and desires of the human agents concerned should be the main considerations in determining the conditions of employment. . . . We see, therefore, that industrial administration is, in the democratic state, a more complicated matter than is naively imagined by the old-fashioned capitalist, demanding the "right to manage his own business in his own way." . . . In the interests of the community as a whole, no one of the interminable series of decisions can be allowed to run counter to the consensus of expert opinion representing the consumers on the one hand, the producers on the other, and the nation that is paramount over both. (Webb and Webb 1897:821–23)

The emphasis on balance is rooted in the theoretical assumptions of pluralist industrial relations, but there are also important normative implications associated with these theoretical assumptions. We first consider these normative implications and then describe the importance of the balancing paradigm for positive research on the employment relationship. By viewing workers as human rather than economic agents—and as people rather than commodities—normative questions are unavoidable: How should people be treated (Webb and Webb 1897)? What rights do they have in a democratic society (Derber 1970)? Who does the economic system serve (Slichter 1948)? As argued by Richard Ely (1900:72–73, emphases in original), "Among the most serious mistakes is to consider man simply as a *producer* of goods, one '*by whom*' are all things of interest to [economics], while the infinitely greater truth is that man is the one '*for whom*' they are all produced" and that "in making of man the best possible manufacturing machine they make him a very poor sort of a man."

As a result, it is common for industrial relations to assert that human beings are entitled to decent working and living conditions as well as democratic rights of participation in decision making (Budd 2004): the view that "the labor market is to be tempered by more humane considerations" than "a purely Darwinian view of unrestrained labor market competition" (Meltz 1989:111).[10] A true industrial democracy requires the protection of all interests in the employment relationship: owners, workers, consumers, and the public (Webb and Webb 1897). As people, workers are entitled to standards of work that respect inherent human dignity, such as a living wage (Bowie 1999; Ryan 1912) and autonomy or control (Bowie 1999; Hodson 2001). As people and as citizens in a democratic society, workers are entitled to have a voice in decisions that affect their work lives (Adams 1995; Budd 2004; Gross 1999; Lauck 1926). At the same time, the pluralist industrial relations paradigm fully respects capitalism and the business owners' need to make a profit.[11] Thus, striking a balance between the competing objectives of employers and employees is warranted.

The need for balancing competing interests can also be grounded in a human rights perspective (Budd 2004). Conflicts between efficiency, equity, and voice are conflicts between property rights and labor rights. Property rights have traditionally been viewed as the foundation of individual freedom and liberty, but in the employment relationship, property rights serve economic efficiency as much as liberty. Property rights in this context are therefore not inviolable, and the evolution of human rights thought has elevated second-generation economic and social rights to equal status with first-generation civil and political rights. Thus, the conflict between property rights and labor rights represents a conflict between competing human rights. As these human rights are equal, they must be balanced. The pluralist industrial relations paradigm focuses on balancing property rights with labor rights in order to balance efficiency, equity, and voice (Budd 2004).

The arguments for balance just discussed are normative arguments for how the employment relationship should work. But the industrial relations emphasis on balance should not be dismissed as a solely normative desire. The theoretical foundations of industrial relations also yield the key testable prediction that the employment relationship works best when competing interests are balanced. Note carefully that this is not a normative statement about how the employment relationship ought to work but an analytical claim about how the employment relationship actually works. In other words, pluralist theory implies not only that a lack of balance in the employment system creates suboptimal outcomes but that unbalanced outcomes are ultimately unstable and short-lived.

These analytical claims are illustrated in figure 1. Panel A summarizes the traditional neoclassical economics framework: perfect competition and individual freedoms create a balance between employers and employees (and all other market participants), which yield optimal economic outcomes that maximize efficiency and utility. Thus, a critical building block of neoclassical theory is competitive markets. In contrast, panel B sketches the pluralist industrial relations framework: equality between employers and employees promotes healthy rather than destructive competition and supports both freedom and optimal economic and social outcomes. A critical building block is not competitive markets but a balance between competing interests. As revealed by the differences in the direction of causality in figure 1, the neoclassical economics and industrial relations schools of thought favor different policy interventions: neoclassical economics—with causality running from competition to optimality—favors policies (typically the lack thereof) that promote competitive markets and unregulated economic exchange, whereas industrial relations—with causality running from balance to optimality—favors policies to promote equity and balance in the system.

FIGURE 1

The Role of Balance in the Neoclassical Economics and Industrial Relations Paradigms

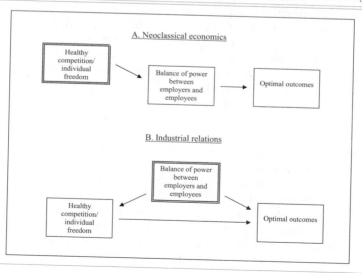

Given these different world views, it is not surprising that the old institutionalists sought not only to reduce market imperfections (such as unemployment and its negative effects through public works and unemployment insurance programs) but to equalize bargaining power between employers and employees through unionization (Kaufman 1997). At the workplace, shop committees and other systems of checks and balances were advocated to develop industrial goodwill and productivity (Commons 1919). Modern scholarship on high-performance work practices further emphasizes the importance of equitable treatment for maintaining efficiency in the workplace.[12] Barbash (1989:116–17) asserted, "Humans as distinguished from inanimate commodities require fairness, voice, security and work of consequence to make their maximum contributions to real efficiency," and Meltz (1989:110) argued, "An employer dedicated to the purest form of short-run profit maximization without any reference to the human element in the factors of production is likely to create a negative reaction that in the long run will impede the achievement of the desired efficiency."

In other words, apart from being good in a moral sense, equity and voice are also instrumentally important because their absence is a primary source of industrial tension. In pluralist industrial relations, the presence of imperfect markets and human (not purely economic) agents means that equity and voice are needed to generate perceptions of fairness among workers, which is required if workers are to voluntarily accept the conditions of the modern employment relationship. This occurs at every level of the employment relationship and also extends to the economy as a whole.[13] Individuals born without initial endowments of wealth and lacking access to the decision-making process involved in generating these outcomes are more likely to perceive the system as unfair. If there is no serious effort on the part of government, management, or labor to address these imbalances, then why should the disenfranchised respect the system in the first place? These questions are not new; indeed, the role of voice and fairness expectations in justifying the distribution of wealth has some interesting historical and biblical antecedents.[14] Pluralist industrial relations applies these analytical propositions to the micro and macro dimensions of the employment relationship (see the following sections) and hypothesizes that the employment system is most effective when competing interests are balanced.

Finally, consider the philosophical underpinning of the balancing paradigm, which literally extends back to the very foundations of Western thought. Here we see how both normative and positive implications of the balancing paradigm are intertwined. The Golden Mean—originally a mathematical relation—was argued by Aristotle to extend to the proper governance and conduct of societal and individual action. According to Aristotle, moderation between two extremes is the key to acting virtuously and to fulfilling the needs of a community. Aristotelian justice therefore includes a central industrial relations belief: might does not make right (Solomon 1992). Note carefully that these views include both the normative and positive implications of balance discussed earlier. Normatively, it is argued that individuals should act virtuously and should not favor might over right. Positively, it is argued that communities operate most effectively when individuals are virtuous and when might does not make right. As in the balancing of competing interests between human agents interacting in imperfect markets, the true virtue is a "golden mean" between extremes—normatively and analytically.

Balancing Competing Interests: The Micro Level

Many of the early institutionalists disputed not the analytical value of the neoclassical economics paradigm but rather its incomplete treatment of the employment relationship and the economy and its narrowness when applied to public policy (Yonay 1998). We share a similar perspective on other schools of thought on the employment relationship; Marxist analyses reveal the importance of embedded power relations, and the human resource management school contributes to our understanding of the determinants of organizational performance. By including aspects of markets, conflict, and human agents from the other schools, the pluralist industrial relations paradigm provides a unique theoretical framework for understanding the employment relationship through the linkages between efficiency, equity, and voice, which are absent in competing paradigms. This section describes two important examples at the micro level where the balancing paradigm adds analytical value: collective bargaining and high-performance work practices.[15]

Collective Bargaining: Market Impediment or Mediating Institution?

In the standard neoclassical economics model, competition among firms, workers, consumers, investors, and suppliers under ideal conditions yields optimal prices, output, wages, and consumption. The interests of the employment relationship are fulfilled by competition: allocative efficiency is achieved, equity is fulfilled because all factors of production are rewarded with their economic value (what McClelland 1990 calls "marginal productivity justice"), and employee voice is provided through entry and exit into desirable jobs and out of undesirable ones (Troy 1999). To those who believe that employers and employees are equals interacting in competitive markets and the legal arena, labor unions are monopolies that reduce economic welfare by impeding the operation of competitive markets and violating the liberties of individuals to freely enter into economic relationships (Epstein 1983; Friedman and Friedman 1980; Troy 1999). In the human resource management paradigm, unions are also viewed negatively as adversarial, outside organizations that add detrimental conflict and bureaucracy to the employment relationship (Mahoney and Watson 1993).

The industrial relations paradigm yields very different predictions. Dating back to the late 19th century, labor unions and collective bargaining have been central methods in industrial relations for balancing competing employment relationship objectives: "By the Method of Collective Bargaining, the foreman is prevented from taking advantage of the competition [between workers] to beat down the earnings of the other workmen" (Webb and Webb 1897:174). Since the pluralist paradigm assumes that labor markets are imperfect and the bargaining power of employers typically dominates that of individual workers, a natural solution to this imbalance is for workers to unionize and better match the power of employers. Dominant areas of industrial relations scholarship, therefore, include analyzing the effects of unions on wide-ranging outcomes and exploring what type of unionism is best suited to different environments.

Against the backdrop of a business unionism philosophy that dominated much of the U.S. labor movement and a scientific management approach that dominated much of U.S. business, unions pursued employee rights by winning seniority systems, grievance procedures, and predictable wage increases in the postwar period. The resulting system of job-control unionism consists of very detailed and legalistic union contracts, enforced by a quasi-judicial grievance procedure, that tie employee rights to very narrowly defined jobs while removing labor from decision making (Katz 1985; Kochan, Katz, and McKersie 1986). In the neoclassical economics paradigm, such work rules are viewed as distortionary restraints on the employment relationship that stem from the monopoly power of unions and that harm productivity and profits. In the industrial relations paradigm, work rules, seniority rights, and grievance arbitration are seen as balancing competing interests by bringing justice into the workplace while also largely maintaining management's right to manage and serving the mass manufacturing need for stability and predictability. Unions might therefore improve economic as well as social outcomes.

Consider also the frequently researched union wage premium. It is well documented that wages for unionized workers in the United States are approximately 15% higher than for similar nonunion workers (Lewis 1986). In neoclassical economics, this union wage premium is arguably the classic demonstration of the distortionary power of labor unions. In contrast, the National Labor Relations Act was enacted in 1935 explicitly to help unions raise wages because of the pluralist industrial relations model in which market imperfections create imbalances and suboptimal economic and social outcomes (Kaufman 1996). This contrast starkly reveals the differing analytical views of these two schools of thought on the employment relationship.

Similarly, while debates in the fields of economics and human resource management over the role of unions in the 21st century workplace focus narrowly on efficiency concerns, pluralist industrial relations scholars cast a wider net by analyzing the effects of new forms of unionism not only on organizational performance but also on workers and society (Budd 2004; Heckscher 1988; Turner, Katz, and Hurd 2001). Thus, the industrial relations paradigm produces a very different set of analytical predictions about labor unions and collective bargaining than other paradigms. Similar differences are apparent in the research on high-performance work practices.

High-Performance Work Practices: Win-Win or Work-Work?

By many accounts, the employment relationship, especially in North America, has been transformed since the 1970s (Appelbaum and Batt 1994; Cappelli 1999; Heckscher 1988; Kochan, Katz, and McKersie 1986; Osterman, Kochan, Locke, and Piore 2001; Piore and Sabel 1984). Competitive pressures have caused a breakdown in traditional forms of collective bargaining, a decline in union power, and the adoption of new practices and polices to manage labor. Some of these policies focus on slashing labor costs through concessions, decertifying unions, and adding more contingent workers; other practices attempt to enhance organizational performance through high-performance work practices such as flexible work arrangements, performance-based pay, employee participation, work teams, and job security. Arguably the most important research stream that has resulted from this sharp increase in the interest in high-performance work practices is analyzing the effects of these practices. By implication, this line of inquiry also addresses the more fundamental question of why these practices exist. The uniqueness and significance of the industrial relations paradigm are illustrated by the increased understanding of these issues that can result from integrating the analytical tenets of the balancing paradigm.[16]

In the neoclassical economics and human resource management paradigms, questions about the effects of high-performance work practices largely reduce to efficiency: Are firms that adopt such practices more profitable than those that do not? Do work teams produce higher-quality output than individuals in narrowly defined jobs? Are workers who are involved in production decisions more loyal and productive than those who are not? The literature often concludes that companies do well by doing good (Baker 1999): high-performance polices (if implemented jointly and not piecemeal) increase organizational performance (Batt 1999; Huselid 1995; Ichniowski, Shaw, and Prennushi 1997).[17] The effects on workers beyond efficiency-related issues are frequently ignored because in neoclassical economics, dissatisfied workers are free to quit, and in the human resource management paradigm, a unitarist employment relationship means that what's good for employers is good for employees.

The pluralist industrial relations paradigm reveals the narrowness of this research. By modeling the employment relationship as a set of competing interests, the effects of human resource policies on workers are of equal importance to the effects on organizational performance. It is employees who are directly affected by any modification in human resource practices, and so productivity and profitability cannot be the only benchmarks by which to judge the success of these practices. High-performance work practices that appear to create a win-win situation for workers and employers in a unitarist framework can be seen as "management by stress" in a pluralist framework: new tools for increasing the pace and effort of work while increasing the uncertainty of rewards and security (Parker and Slaughter 1995). Moreover, the competing-interests framework posits that there is not always a unity of interests between employees and employers, and this yields a critical prediction for the research on high-performance work practices: high-performance work practices that balance employer and employee interests will be more successful, while those that do not will be more likely to fail (Delaney and Godard 2001).

The pluralist industrial relations paradigm can also make a valuable contribution toward a more general understanding of how individual and organizational performance can be improved by such practices, since this paradigm incorporates what is of value to labor as well as management. If high-performance work practices enhance productivity and profits, it is ultimately because they are attuned to labor's as well as management's interests (Osterman 2000). In fact, pluralist industrial relations scholars frequently distinguish between two types of efficiency: allocative (or formal) and real (Barbash 1989; Meltz 1989). Allocative efficiency encompasses the technical procedures needed to maximize output given certain constraints. This view of efficiency treats labor simply as a commodity no different from other factors of production. The analytical treatment of labor in industrial relations, however, includes human elements of labor with interests distinct from those of employers, and therefore the rationalization of the workforce along formally efficient criteria can create problems of alienation, shirking, and low morale. Moreover, allocative efficiency can create a distributive tension between wages and profits (Barbash 1989).

Therefore, in order to enhance *real* efficiency, the industrial relations paradigm predicts that allocative efficiency needs to be tempered by workers' interests, such as equity and voice. In other words, workers are distinct from other organizational inputs because of their human requirements for fairness, voice, and job security as preconditions for making maximal contributions to real efficiency. In fact, while economists recognize that cooperative behavior among economic agents is needed when markets are incomplete or imperfectly competitive (Olson 1982, 2000), it is less well recognized that nonmarket institutions such as unions and works councils can foster long-term relationships between employers and employees. Once in place, these relationships limit the extent of pecuniary gain that one party can extract from the other. Ongoing relationships also produce repeated interactions among actors, which are conducive to the sharing of information and the development of trust. Trust in the employment relationship is not determined exogenously; it is formed and reinforced by being responsive to the other side's interests.

Industrial relations theory therefore predicts that the sole pursuit of allocative efficiency within organizations can create counterproductive forces that impair organizational performance. Anecdotally, this prediction is supported by countless examples, including well-publicized bankruptcies at Eastern Airlines and elsewhere that resulted from management's overzealous drive for wage and work rule concessions.[18] Wage structures that are felt to be inequitable create a lack of motivation and an unwillingness to adapt and cooperate with management (Akerlof and Yellen 1986). The moderate adoption of high-performance work practices increases employee satisfaction, esteem, and commitment, but extensive adoption reduces employee well-being because of higher levels of stress (Godard 2001).

Conversely, industrial relations theory predicts that human resources practices will improve organizational performance when workers' distinct interests are considered. In cross-national comparisons, Adams (1995) found that successful team-based and lean production systems require employees who are highly committed to improving the production process and that this commitment stems from job security and employee beliefs that the financial benefits of productivity improvements will be equitably shared. Gordon (1996) also concluded that token gestures are not sufficient to improve commitment and hence performance. Rather, three conditions are identified for successful cooperation: a real and perceived equitable sharing of productivity gains with workers, significant employment security (so that workers do not worry that production innovations will result in layoffs), and substantial institutional changes to build up employee voice and group involvement. In other words, organizational performance depends on equity and voice. Thus, the analytical framework of pluralist industrial relations differs from the economic approach in that nonpecuniary or intrinsic outcomes are an essential input in determining the efficiency of the employment relationship, and it differs from the human resource management paradigm in recognizing the interests of workers as distinct from those of employers.

Balancing Competing Interests: The Macro Level

The pluralist industrial relations paradigm also predicts that balance matters at a macro level: gross inequalities in society or the economy negatively affect outcomes. This prediction runs counter to the general tendency in economics to assume that there are macrolevel trade-offs between efficiency and equity, but it echoes the microlevel industrial relations claims that efficiency and equity are complementary goals, at least within some range (Barbash 1989; Meltz 1989).[19] The macrolevel examples discussed here are the role of balance in shaping the New Deal policy responses to the Great Depression and recent macroeconomic research on positive long-run associations between balanced (equitable) distributions of income and economic performance.

The Benefits of Balance in the Policy Realm:
The Example of the New Deal

In the United States, the intellectual beliefs of the pluralist industrial relations paradigm are clearly reflected in the New Deal public policies of the Roosevelt administration. The labor problems of the first decades of the 20th century—low wages, long hours, dangerous working conditions, and widespread unemployment and worker insecurity—were thought to stem from excess labor supply, minimal worker savings, few social safety nets, and various labor market imperfections that gave companies a significant advantage in bargaining power over individual employees (Kaufman 1997). Although the early institutionalists were concerned with the quality of workers' lives, this was not just a normative problem. Greater corporate power was believed to impose significant negative externalities on the economic and social system: impoverished individuals could not advance their education and become better workers and citizens, desperate families turned to crime, and labor disputes disrupted production. It was additionally believed that this inequality between labor and management depressed consumer purchasing power and prevented macroeconomic stabilization (Kaufman 1996). In short, these are analytical propositions that the economy would work better if there were greater balance between employers and employees.

The macrolevel New Deal policies of the 1930s sought to create a balance through public works programs to provide jobs, the encouragement of unionization, minimum wage and maximum hours legislation to prevent cutthroat competition, and social safety nets to cushion the economic and social harms of adverse events (Bernstein 1985; Kaufman 1996). The National Labor Relations Act (1935), therefore, protects workers' efforts at forming unions and engaging in collective bargaining to increase workers' purchasing power. The Fair Labor Standards Act (1938) created a national minimum wage, a mandatory overtime premium for covered workers for hours worked in excess of a weekly standard (now 40 hours), and restrictions on child labor. A social safety net was established by the Social Security Act (1935) through insurance for the unemployed, disabled, and elderly. These public policies reflect the intellectual (not just normative) tenets of pluralist industrial relations (Budd 2004): labor is more than a commodity; labor and management are not economic or legal equals (in other words, there is an imbalance of bargaining power); there is at least some conflict of interest that cannot be resolved by unitarist management policies, but this is pluralist employment relationship conflict, not class-based or societal conflict; and employee voice is important. As summarized by panel B of figure 1, these intellectual tenets imply that if these policies can create a greater balance between employers and employees, then healthy rather than destructive competition results and outcomes improve.

Balanced Distributions of Income and the Promotion of
Stability and Growth

The New Deal policies of the 1930s were set against a backdrop of economic and social instability: strikes, bread lines, Hoovervilles of homeless squatters, hunger marches, mass migration out of the Dust Bowl, and the like. Thus, the New Deal policies were intended not only to improve the workings of the labor market but also to promote social and political stability. This logic mirrors the global stability philosophy of the International Labour Organization (ILO) as enshrined in its preamble from 1919: "Universal and lasting peace can be established only if it is based upon social justice" and "conditions of labor exist involving such injustice hardship and privation to large numbers of people as to produce unrest so great that the peace and harmony of the world are imperilled."

This logic continues to be important in the 21st century, especially in light of the well-publicized globalization backlash. The widespread protests in Seattle against the World Trade Organization (WTO) in the fall of 1999 stemmed from perceived imbalances between corporations and other interests in the WTO's system of free trade. Creating a greater balance in the global trading system appears critical to the future of this system—a prescription that underlies the United Nation's Global Compact initiative and is embraced even by the business press (Magnusson 2003). In fact, the evidence is not just anecdotal in this regard; across a broad spectrum of countries, there appears to be a positive long-run association between balanced (equitable) distributions of income and economic performance (Alesina and Rodrik 1994; Persson and Tabellini 1994).[20]

Two major political–economic models have been advanced to explain the observed positive relation between income equality and economic growth: fiscal policy models based on public choice theory and models of political instability (see figure 2).[21] The argument of the fiscal policy theories is that income inequality induces large segments of the population to support redistributive policies (such as high taxes) that dampen growth-promoting activities, such as incentives for investments in physical and human capital (Alesina and Rodrik 1994; Persson and Tabellini 1994). The higher the inequality of wealth and income, the higher the rate of taxation and consequently the lower the growth rate. Countries that have low initial disparities in income are hypothesized to face fewer political pressures to redistribute, while in more unequal societies, publicly induced distortionary taxation and redistribution ultimately lower growth.

FIGURE 2

Political–Economic Channels Linking Income Inequality to Lower Growth

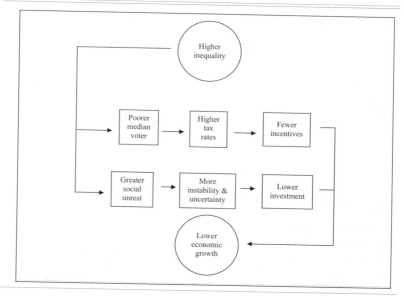

The second class of models is based on social and political discontent. In terms that are strikingly similar to long-standing pluralist industrial relations beliefs and to the ILO's preamble, inequality in these models is hypothesized to fuel sociopolitical instability, which can take on varied forms such as crime, riots, coups, strikes, and other forms of industrial conflict, which in turn reduce investment and therefore economic growth (Alesina and Perotti 1996).

But does a balancing paradigm have empirical support? Empirical evidence in favor of the second class of models would support the balancing paradigm because inequality likely reflects a lack of balance and hence instability in the employment relations system, which reduces macroeconomic performance. The evidence, as it happens, is more strongly in favor of the instability model than the high-tax fiscal policy model (Perotti 1994). Countries with more egalitarian pretax distributions of income tend to support higher levels of transfers—not lower, as predicted by the fiscal policy model—and higher growth rates (Benabou 2000). To wit, figure 3 presents a comparison of Gini ratios to tax revenue as a percentage of GDP among the 29 member states of the Organisation

FIGURE 3
Pretax Inequality and Tax Revenue, 1998 (29 OECD Countries)

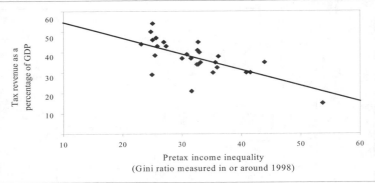

Sources: Authors' calculations from Deininger and Squire (1998) and OECD (N.D.).

for Economic Co-operation and Development (OECD). The slope of the regression line and associated correlation coefficient is negative (–0.68), indicating that countries with more pretax inequality also have lower tax-to-GDP ratios (less redistribution).[22]

There is, by way of contrast, stronger support for the social instability model. Cross-national regressions reveal a positive link between inequality and instability, as well as a negative relationship between instability and investment (Alesina and Perotti 1996). Increased inequality is therefore likely associated with reduced economic growth.[23] Note that these results are entirely consistent with the pluralist industrial relations paradigm and its hypothesis that balance is important not just for how the economy should work (a normative contention) but for how the economy does work (a positive contention). The continued currency of this paradigm is further reinforced in the literature on transition economies in which the persistence of inefficient state-owned enterprises (as in China) during privatization can be explained by their contributions, not to corporate efficiency, but to social stability and improved macroeconomic performance (Bai, Li, Tao, and Wang 2000).

Conclusions

The pluralist industrial relations paradigm models the employment relationship as an imperfectly competitive bargaining problem between stakeholders with competing interests. This framework has concrete theoretical implications for the operation of the employment relationship:

wages are not always equal to marginal productivity, unions can enhance organizational performance as well as social welfare, and fairness and emotions matter, to name just a few. In fact, this paradigm is very similar to the theory of institutional economics which, while outside the mainstream of the economics profession, is certainly a well-defined, viable school of thought.

Real-world empirical analysis is a central part of this pluralist industrial relations paradigm, but contrary to popular assertions, it is not just institutional description. Careful analysis of real-world institutions and practices is needed because employment relationship outcomes are not completely determined by purely rational economic agents operating in perfectly competitive markets (Manning 2003). Contemporary industrial relations scholarship requires real-world analysis because it is still largely driven by the belief that "knowledgeable tinkering can improve the functions of a generally satisfactory system" (Mangum and Philips 1988:18). The early institutionalists not only thought that they had an accurate explanation (i.e., theory) for the labor problem, they also wanted to design policies to solve it (Kaufman 1993).

Historical and contemporary pluralist calls for reform emphasize balancing competing employment relationship interests. This is partly a normative prescription based on respect for human dignity and democratic principles, but the emphasis on balance is also a theoretical proposition positing that balance matters for how the employment relationship works. To wit, poor labor–management relations are arguably responsible for at least part of the decline of the U.S. auto and steel industries, and defective Firestone tires (responsible for over 250 deaths) were significantly more likely to have been produced during two critical periods of labor–management conflict than during periods of relative labor calm (Krueger and Mas 2004). The analytical premise that balance matters is therefore rooted in the central theoretical assumptions of the pluralist industrial relations school. Contrary to popular belief, the emphasis on balance does not mean that the pluralist industrial relations paradigm is only a normative science. In fact, when the neoclassical economics paradigm is used to argue that labor markets should be unregulated, this is as much of a normative statement as any of the pluralist industrial relations arguments regarding balance.

Analytical research on, and normative support for, labor unions is another dominant part of industrial relations scholarship, but the viability of the pluralist industrial relations paradigm is not entirely dependent on the fortunes of organized labor. The fundamental precept of balancing competing interests in imperfect markets is embraced, for example, in other academic disciplines (such as business ethics), theories (such as stakeholder theory), and popular institutions (such as the Catholic Church and the United Nations). In the wake of the corporate and foreign exchange scandals of the early 21st century, a number of commentators advocate adding checks and balances to markets, corporations, and global economic institutions—this is a pluralist principle.[24] The push for fair trade and other initiatives to make sure that the benefits of economic markets are widely shared is intellectually consistent with the predictions of the pluralist industrial relations paradigm.[25]

Most importantly, perhaps, the pluralist industrial relations paradigm recognizes that the employment relationship is complex. In contrast to the models of the other major schools of thought—neoclassical economics, human resource management, or critical (Marxist) industrial relations—this relationship cannot be reduced to a single overriding principle. In short, the balancing paradigm tells us to be humbler than we normally prefer to be: the pursuit of a singular objective (only efficiency, or equity, or voice) and the reliance on a single mechanism (only markets or internal management) can be socially harmful. Workers, after all, are complex human agents with extrinsic and intrinsic expectations and rights.

To understand the workings of the employment relationship and to create policies and practices that promote broadly shared prosperity and long-lasting democratic freedoms, the pluralist paradigm argues that the employment relationship should be modeled as a complex bargaining problem between human agents operating in imperfect markets, one in which competing interests need to be balanced in order to ensure not only efficiency but also fulfillment of workers' rights. While rooted in the scholarship of Commons and the Webbs from 100 years ago, for which we are grateful, this pluralist industrial relations paradigm continues to be theoretically and normatively rich in the 21st century.

Dedication and Acknowledgments

This chapter is dedicated to the memory of Noah M. Meltz. Noah submitted the original proposal for this chapter and significantly shaped its structure and content. We are honored to have had the opportunity to complete his project. We are grateful to Bruce Kaufman for his thoughtful comments and to all those who participated in the industrial relations theory workshop, held at the International Industrial Relations Association meetings in Berlin in 2003.

Notes

[1] Modeling the employment relationship as a bargaining problem does not mean that pluralist industrial relations is concerned solely with explicit bargaining situations. Rather, this paradigm is concerned with the full range of employment-related issues, from macrolevel policy and labor movement issues to microlevel interactions between employees and supervisors. Modeling the employment relationship as a bargaining problem means that all of these issues are set against a backdrop of stakeholders with competing interests interacting in imperfect rather than competitive markets. This is consistent with Manning's (2003) emphasis on the indeterminacy of monopsonistic labor markets rather than the determinacy of competitive markets.

[2] In contrast, mainstream industrial relations in Great Britain has more of a critical or Marxist theoretical foundation.

[3] Or returning to the early institutionalists, when neoclassical economists "accuse institutionalists of having no theory, what they mean is that institutionalists had no theory *of the neoclassical type;* this is the only type of theory they recognize" (Yonay 1998:68, emphasis in original). Manning (2003) emphasized the need for empirical research because the unequivocal theoretical effects of public policies in the competitive model are uncertain when labor markets are imperfect.

[4] The use of equity and voice is consistent with Barbash's (1984:40) PEEP (price, equity, effort, and power), which includes "having a voice in the terms of employment" as well as a certain amount of autonomy and freedom. Osterman, Kochan, Locke, and Piore (2001:11–12) also identified efficiency and a number of worker goals as the central interests of the employment relationship: (1) work as a source of dignity, (2) a living wage, (3) diversity and equality of opportunity, (4) solidarity or social cohesion, and (5) voice and participation. These can be summarized as efficiency, equity, and voice.

[5] Mainstream economics now includes a significant amount of research rooted in constrained maximization by rational individuals that does not rely on the assumption of competitive markets, but we follow Kaufman (in press) and others in declining to label this mainstream research as neoclassical because such a broad definition of *neoclassical* renders it vacuous. Moreover, the neoclassical economic model taught in textbooks and used when most economists make policy recommendations includes competitive markets as a core principle (Manning 2003). For an example of a more expansive definition of *neoclassical,* see Boyer and Smith (2001).

[6] In other words, the pluralist view of employment relationship conflict is that it is limited to the workplace, and therefore competing interests can be balanced with appropriate workplace interventions such as labor unions. Marxist industrial relations sees employment relationship conflict as part of a larger class conflict such that workers' interests cannot be fulfilled without changing the power structure of classes, for example, by replacing capitalism with socialism. A business unionism focus on workplace-level collective bargaining is therefore viewed as incomplete at best.

[7] See Thaler (2000) for examples of economists who are now more interested modeling economic behavior as if individuals acted more like *Homo sapiens* than as *Homo economicus*. One of the winners of the 2002 Nobel Prize in economics was Daniel Kahneman, a founding figure of the movement challenging widely held beliefs about economic rationality.

[8] Institutional economics similarly rejects the neoclassical economics view of the primacy of the market; rather, the importance of institutions and their rules, cultures, histories, values, and norms for guiding economic and non-economic activity are emphasized (Tool 1993). While pluralist industrial relations and modern institutional economics share John R. Commons as a critical founding figure, there is unfortunately a lack of interaction between the two schools. Institutional economics is not to be confused with the "new institutional economics," in which market imperfections such as transaction costs and asymmetric information give rise to the importance of institutions (webs of rules) while maintaining the neoclassical economics emphasis on individual utility maximization and efficiency, and therefore a general skepticism of the benefits of government regulation (Dow 1997).

[9] Compare this to Kelly's (1998:132) critical perspective, in which the focal point of industrial relations is viewed as "injustice and the ways in which workers define and respond to it."

[10] In this respect, the pluralist view of competing interests shares much more in common with the forefathers of economic thought in the classical economics school than with their neoclassical progeny. Adam Smith—all too often viewed as the father of free-market conservatism—was quite skeptical of the alleged benefits accruing from the pure application of efficiency (higher profits) at the expense of greater equity (higher wages). Indeed, in *The Wealth of Nations* (Smith [1776] 1937) not only did Smith view merchants and manufacturers with deep suspicion, he also qualified his praise of the self-equilibrating economy with a darker vision of the dehumanizing potential of a profit-oriented society. Until recently, Smith's views would have run counter to the approach taken by many mainstream economists, but for over a century his views have run parallel to the approach of the pluralist school of thought and the theory that a balance of competing interests is the optimal outcome for a society over the long run.

[11] The difference between the pluralist industrial relations conception of earning profits and the neoclassical economics emphasis on *maximizing* profits is therefore much more than semantics. Earning rather than maximizing profits is also consistent with business ethics in the Aristotelian and Kantian traditions (Bowie 1999; Solomon 1992). In fact, the pluralist industrial relations balancing paradigm in general is consistent with these ethical perspectives (Budd 2004).

[12] Note that the pluralist tradition prefigured these new forms of workplace design by more than half a century (Kaufman 2001).

[13] In human resource management, see the large body of literature on distributive and procedural justice (Folger and Cropanzano 1998). For discussions of fairness in labor market outcomes, see Rees (1993) and Solow (1990).

[14] In an agricultural society, land is the primary source of wealth. The Bible relates that after the land of Israel was divided among the 12 tribes, in every Jubilee (50th) year, land was to be restored to the families within their tribes (Leviticus 25:8–55). Even if a person was forced by economic circumstances to sell his land and become a servant, the sale was only until the next Jubilee. Hertz (1968:533) observed, "In this way the original equal division of the land was restored. The permanent accumulation of land in the hands of a few was prevented, and those whom fault or misfortune had thrown into poverty were given a 'second chance.'"

[15] Kaufman (2004) argued that the early institutionalists sought a balance on three levels: in internal firm governance, external labor markets, and national policy making. In this section we consider institutional arrangements within the first two of these levels. In the following section we consider national policy making and social stability issues. Note that our examples are intended to be illustrative of the continued relevance of the balancing paradigm, not comprehensive.

[16] Another important research stream tries to explain the uneven diffusion of these practices across firms given the alleged benefits trumpeted by supporters. By focusing on market imperfections, unequal distribution of resources, and the importance of nonmarket institutions and behavior, the pluralist industrial relations paradigm can also help explain why not all firms adopt high-performance work practices.

[17] The productivity effects of these practices are not universal and also do not necessarily translate into improved corporate profitability (Cappelli and Neumark 2001).

[18] Roach (1996) argued that U.S. business leaders during the early and mid-1990s made profitability improvements through the unsustainable low-road approach of cost cutting.

[19] Okun (1975) is perhaps the classic discussion of the perceived fundamental trade-off between efficiency and equity, as reflected in the remark that "tradeoffs are the central study of the economist. 'You can't have your cake and eat it too' is a good candidate for the central theorem of economic analysis" (p. 1). Similar sentiments are echoed in economics textbooks: "policies designed to divide the proverbial economic pie more equally, inadvertently cause the size of the pie to shrink" (Baumol, Blinder, and Scarth 1991:124).

[20] For a discussion of microlevel problems of too much income inequality, see Krueger (2003).

[21] A third class of models to explain a negative relationship between income inequality and economic growth relies on imperfect credit markets: low-income individuals face borrowing constraints and are therefore limited in the investments in human and physical capital that they can make (Benabou 1994, 2000). In principle, this focus on imperfect markets is consistent with the pluralist industrial relations paradigm, though an industrial relations theory would focus on labor market imperfections.

[22] The failure of the fiscal policy model to account for the persistence of high-inequality and low-taxation regimes can be explained by the industrial relations paradigm: the absence of voice institutions that translate public demands into policy.

[23] Mobilization theory, in turn, provides a framework for predicting when perceived imbalance or injustice translates into collective action to redress this imbalance (Kelly 1998).

[24] See Kelly (2001), Korten (1999), Phillips (2002), Soros (2000), and Stiglitz (2002).

[25] There is a large body of literature on international trade with imperfect product markets (Grossman 1992), but industrial relations scholars should inject this research with analyses of globalization characterized by imperfect labor markets that favor employers.

References

Adams, Roy J. 1995. *Industrial Relations under Liberal Democracy: North America in Comparative Perspective*. Columbia: University of South Carolina Press.

Akerlof, George A., and Janet L. Yellen. 1986. *Efficiency Wage Models of the Labor Market*. Cambridge: Cambridge University Press.

Alesina, Alberto, and Roberto Perotti. 1996. "Income Distribution, Political Instability, and Investment." *European Economic Review*, Vol. 40, no. 6 (June), pp. 1203–28.

Alesina, Alberto, and Dani Rodrik. 1994. "Distributive Politics and Economic Growth." *Quarterly Journal of Economics*, Vol. 109, no. 2 (May), pp. 465–90.

Appelbaum, Eileen, and Rosemary Batt. 1994. *The New American Workplace: Transforming Work Systems in the United States*. Ithaca, NY: ILR Press.

Bai, Chong-En, David D. Li, Zhigang Tao, and Yijiang Wang. 2000. "A Multitask Theory of State Enterprise Reform." *Journal of Comparative Economics*, Vol. 28, no. 4 (December), pp. 716–38.

Baker, Ted. 1999. *Doing Well by Doing Good: The Bottom Line on Workplace Practices*. Washington, DC: Economic Policy Institute.

Barbash, Jack. 1984. *The Elements of Industrial Relations*. Madison: University of Wisconsin Press.

———. 1987. "Like Nature, Industrial Relations Abhors a Vacuum: The Case of the Union-Free Strategy." *Industrial Relations/Relations Industrielles*, Vol. 42, no. 1 (Winter), pp. 168–79.

———. 1989. "Equity as Function: Its Rise and Attrition." In Jack Barbash and Kate Barbash, eds., *Theories and Concepts in Comparative Industrial Relations*, Columbia: University of South Carolina Press, pp. 114–22.

Batt, Rosemary. 1999. "Work Organization, Technology, and Performance in Customer Service and Sales." *Industrial and Labor Relations Review*, Vol. 52, no. 4 (July), pp. 539–64.

Baumol, William J., Alan S. Blinder, and William Scarth. 1991. *Economics: Principles and Policy*. Toronto: Harcourt Brace Jovanovich.

Belman, Dale, and Michael H. Belzer. 1997. "The Regulation of Labor Markets: Balancing the Benefits and Costs of Competition." In Bruce E. Kaufman, ed., *Government Regulation of the Employment Relationship*, Madison, WI: Industrial Relations Research Association, pp. 179–219.

Benabou, Roland. 1994. "Human Capital, Inequality, and Growth: A Local Perspective." *European Economic Review*, Vol. 38, no. 4 (April), pp. 817–26.

———. 2000. "Unequal Societies: Income Distribution and the Social Contract." *American Economic Review*, Vol. 90, no. 1 (March), pp. 96–129.

Bernstein, Irving. 1985. *A Caring Society: The New Deal, the Worker, and the Great Depression*. Boston: Houghton Mifflin.

Bowie, Norman E. 1999. *Business Ethics: A Kantian Perspective*. Malden, MA: Blackwell.

Boyer, George R., and Robert S. Smith. 2001. "The Development of the Neoclassical Tradition in Labor Economics." *Industrial and Labor Relations Review*, Vol. 54, no. 2 (January), pp. 199–223.

Budd, John W. 2004. *Employment with a Human Face: Balancing Efficiency, Equity, and Voice*. Ithaca, NY: ILR Press.

Cappelli, Peter. 1999. *The New Deal at Work: Managing the Market-Driven Workforce.* Boston: Harvard Business School Press.

Cappelli, Peter, and David Neumark. 2001. "Do 'High-Performance' Work Practices Improve Establishment-Level Outcomes?" *Industrial and Labor Relations Review,* Vol. 54, no. 4 (July), pp. 737–75.

Card, David, and Alan B. Krueger. 1995. *Myth and Measurement: The New Economics of the Minimum Wage.* Princeton, NJ: Princeton University Press.

Chang, Chun, and Yijiang Wang. 1996. "Human Capital Investment under Asymmetric Information: The Pigovian Conjecture Revisited." *Journal of Labor Economics,* Vol. 14, no. 3 (July), pp. 505–19.

Clegg, H. A. 1975. "Pluralism in Industrial Relations." *British Journal of Industrial Relations,* Vol. 13, no. 3 (November), pp. 309–16.

Coase, R. H. 1984. "The New Institutional Economics." *Journal of Institutional and Theoretical Economics,* Vol. 140 (March), pp. 229–32.

Commons, John R. 1919. *Industrial Goodwill.* New York: McGraw-Hill.

———. 1934. *Institutional Economics: Its Place in Political Economy.* New York: Macmillan.

Deininger, Klaus, and Lyn Squire. 1998. "New Ways of Looking at Old Issues: Inequality and Growth." *Journal of Development Economics,* Vol. 57, no. 2 (December), pp. 259–87.

Delaney, John T., and John Godard. 2001. "An Industrial Relations Perspective on the High-Performance Paradigm." *Human Resource Management Review,* Vol. 11, no. 4 (Winter), pp. 395–429.

Derber, Milton. 1970. *The American Idea of Industrial Democracy, 1865–1965.* Urbana: University of Illinois Press.

Doeringer, Peter B., and Michael J. Piore. 1971. *Internal Labor Markets and Manpower Analysis.* Lexington, MA: Lexington Books.

Dow, Gregory K. 1997. "The New Institutional Economics and Employment Regulation." In Bruce E. Kaufman, ed., *Government Regulation of the Employment Relationship,* Madison, WI: Industrial Relations Research Association, pp. 57–90.

Downey, Ezekiel H. 1924. *Workmen's Compensation.* New York: Macmillan.

Dunlop, John T. 1993. *Industrial Relations Systems,* rev. ed. Boston: Harvard Business School Press.

Ely, Richard T. 1900. *Outlines of Economics.* New York: Macmillan.

Epstein, Richard A. 1983. "A Common Law for Labor Relations: A Critique of the New Deal Labor Legislation." *Yale Law Journal,* Vol. 92, no. 8 (July), pp. 1357–408.

Folger, Robert, and Russell Cropanzano. 1998. *Organizational Justice and Human Resource Management.* Thousand Oaks, CA: Sage.

Fox, Alan. 1974. *Beyond Contract: Work, Power and Trust Relations.* London: Farber and Farber.

Freeman, Richard B., and James L. Medoff. 1984. *What Do Unions Do?* New York: Basic Books.

Freeman, Richard B., and Joel Rogers. 1999. *What Workers Want.* Ithaca, NY: ILR Press.

Friedman, Milton, and Rose Friedman. 1980. *Free to Choose: A Personal Statement.* New York: Harcourt Brace Jovanovich.

Giles, Anthony, and Gregor Murray. 1997. "Industrial Relations Theory and Critical Political Economy." In Jack Barbash and Noah M. Meltz, eds., *Theorizing in Industrial Relations: Approaches and Applications,* Sydney: Australian Centre for Industrial Relations Research and Teaching, pp. 77–120.

Godard, John. 2001. "High Performance *and* the Transformation of Work? The Implications of Alternative Work Practices for the Experiences and Outcomes of Work." *Industrial and Labor Relations Review,* Vol. 54, no. 4 (July), pp. 776–805.

Gordon, David M. 1996. *Fat and Mean: The Corporate Squeeze of Working Americans and the Myth of Managerial "Downsizing."* New York: Free Press.

Gross, James A. 1999. "A Human Rights Perspective on U.S. Labor Relations Law: A Violation of the Freedom of Association." *Employee Rights and Employment Policy Journal,* Vol. 3, no. 1, pp. 65–103.

Grossman, Gene M., ed. 1992. *Imperfect Competition and International Trade.* Cambridge, MA: MIT Press.

Heckscher, Charles C. 1988. *The New Unionism: Employee Involvement in the Changing Corporation.* New York: Basic Books.

Hertz, J. H., ed. 1968. *Pentateuch and Haftorahs: Hebrew Text, English Translation and Commentary,* 2nd ed. London: Soncino Press.

Hills, Stephen M. 1995. *Employment Relations and the Social Sciences.* Columbia: University of South Carolina Press.

Hodson, Randy. 2001. *Dignity at Work.* Cambridge: Cambridge University Press.

Huselid, Mark A. 1995. "The Impact of Human Resource Management Practices on Turnover, Productivity, and Corporate Financial Performance." *Academy of Management Journal,* Vol. 38, no. 3 (June), pp. 635–72.

Hyman, Richard. 1975. *Industrial Relations: A Marxist Introduction.* London: Macmillan.

Ichniowski, Casey, Kathryn Shaw, and Giovanna Prennushi. 1997. "The Effects of Human Resources Management Practices on Productivity: A Study of Steel Finishing Lines." *American Economic Review,* Vol. 87, no. 3 (June), pp. 291–313.

Jacoby, Sanford M. 1985. *Employing Bureaucracy: Managers, Unions, and the Transformation of Work in American Industry, 1900–1945.* New York: Columbia University Press.

Katz, Harry C. 1985. *Shifting Gears: Changing Labor Relations in the U.S. Automobile Industry.* Cambridge, MA: MIT Press.

Kaufman, Bruce E., ed. 1988. *How Labor Markets Work: Reflections on Theory and Practice by John Dunlop, Clark Kerr, Richard Lester, and Lloyd Reynolds.* Lexington, MA: Lexington Books.

———. 1993. *The Origins and Evolution of the Field of Industrial Relations in the United States.* Ithaca, NY: ILR Press.

———. 1996. "Why the Wagner Act? Reestablishing Contact with Its Original Purpose." In David Lewin, Bruce E. Kaufman, and Donna Sockell, eds., *Advances in Industrial and Labor Relations,* Vol. 7, Greenwich, CT: JAI Press, pp. 15–68.

———. 1997. "Labor Markets and Employment Regulation: The View of the 'Old' Institutionalists." In Bruce E. Kaufman, ed., *Government Regulation of the Employment Relationship,* Madison, WI: Industrial Relations Research Association, pp. 11–55.

———. 1999. "Expanding the Behavioral Foundations of Labor Economics." *Industrial and Labor Relations Review,* Vol. 52, no. 3 (April), pp. 361–92.

———. 2001. "The Practice and Theory of Strategic HRM and Participative Management: Antecedents in Early Industrial Relations." *Human Resource Management Review*, Vol. 11, no. 4 (Winter), pp. 505–33.

———. 2004. *The Global Evolution of Industrial Relations: People, Ideas, and the IIRA*. Geneva: International Labor Organization.

———. In press. "The Institutional and Neoclassical Schools in Labor Economics." In Dell Champlin and Janet Knoedler, eds., *The Institutional Tradition in Labor Economics*, Armonk, NY: Sharpe.

Kelly, John E. 1998. *Rethinking Industrial Relations: Mobilization, Collectivism and Long Waves*. London: Routledge.

Kelly, Marjorie. 2001. *The Divine Right of Capital: Dethroning the Corporate Aristocracy*. San Francisco: Berrett-Koehler.

Kleiner, Morris M., Richard N. Block, Myron Roomkin, and Sidney W. Salsburg, eds. 1987. *Human Resources and Firm Performance*. Madison, WI: Industrial Relations Research Association.

Kochan, Thomas A. 1980. *Collective Bargaining and Industrial Relations: From Theory to Policy and Practice*. Homewood, IL: Irwin.

———. 1998. "What Is Distinctive about Industrial Relations Research?" In George Strauss and Keith Whitfield, eds., *Researching the World of Work: Strategies and Methods in Studying Industrial Relations*, Ithaca, NY: ILR Press, pp. 31–45.

Kochan, Thomas A., Harry C. Katz, and Robert B. McKersie. 1986. *The Transformation of American Industrial Relations*. New York: Basic Books.

Korten, David C. 1999. *The Post-corporate World: Life after Capitalism*. San Francisco: Berrett-Koehler.

Krueger, Alan B. 2003. "Inequality, Too Much of a Good Thing." In Benjamin M. Friedman, ed., *Inequality in America: What Role for Human Capital Policies?* Cambridge, MA: MIT Press, pp. 1–75.

Krueger, Alan B., and Alexandre Mas. 2004. "Strikes, Scabs and Tread Separations: Labor Strife and the Production of Defective Bridgestone/Firestone Tires." *Journal of Political Economy*, Vol. 112, no. 2 (April), pp. 253–89.

Lauck, W. Jett. 1926. *Political and Industrial Democracy, 1776–1926*. New York: Funk and Wagnalls.

Lauck, W. Jett, and Edgar Sydenstricker. 1917. *Conditions of Labor in American Industries: A Summarization of the Results of Recent Investigations*. New York: Funk and Wagnalls.

Lester, Richard A. 1988. "Wages, Benefits, and Company Employment Systems." In Bruce E. Kaufman, ed., *How Labor Markets Work: Reflections on Theory and Practice by John Dunlop, Clark Kerr, Richard Lester, and Lloyd Reynolds*, Lexington, MA: Lexington Books, pp. 89–115.

Levine, David I. 1995. *Reinventing the Workplace: How Business and Employees Can Both Win*. Washington, DC: Brookings Institution.

Lewin, David. 2001. "IR and HR Perspectives on Workplace Conflict: What Can Each Learn from the Other?" *Human Resource Management Review*, Vol. 11, no. 4 (Winter), pp. 453–85.

Lewis, H. Gregg. 1986. *Union Relative Wage Effects: A Survey*. Chicago: University of Chicago Press.

Lichtenstein, Nelson. 1989. "'The Man in the Middle': A Social History of Automobile Industry Foremen." In Nelson Lichtenstein and Stephen Meyer, eds., *On the Line: Essays in the History of Auto Work,* Urbana: University of Illinois Press, pp. 153–89.

Magnusson, Paul. 2003. "Trade Talks: Can Rich Nations Keep the Poor on Board?" *Business Week,* September 8, p. 56.

Mahoney, Thomas A., and Mary R. Watson. 1993. "Evolving Modes of Work Force Governance: An Evaluation." In Bruce E. Kaufman and Morris M. Kleiner, eds., *Employee Representation: Alternatives and Future Directions,* Madison, WI: Industrial Relations Research Association, 135–68.

Mangum, Garth, and Peter Philips, eds. 1988. *Three Worlds of Labor Economics.* Armonk, NY: Sharpe.

Manning, Alan. 2003. *Monopsony in Motion: Imperfect Competition in Labor Markets.* Princeton, NJ: Princeton University Press.

McClelland, Peter D. 1990. *The American Search for Justice.* Cambridge, MA: Basil Blackwell.

Meltz, Noah M. 1989. "Industrial Relations: Balancing Efficiency and Equity." In Jack Barbash and Kate Barbash, eds., *Theories and Concepts in Comparative Industrial Relations,* Columbia: University of South Carolina Press, pp. 109–13.

Okun, Arthur M. 1975. *Equality and Efficiency, the Big Tradeoff.* Washington, DC: Brookings Institution.

Olson, Mancur. 1982. *The Rise and Decline of Nations: Economic Growth, Stagflation, and Social Rigidities.* New Haven, CT: Yale University Press.

———. 2000. *Power and Prosperity: Outgrowing Communist and Capitalist Dictatorships.* New York: Basic Books.

Organisation for Economic Co-operation and Development. n.d. *Trends in Tax Burdens and Tax Structures.* Paris: Organisation for Economic Co-operation and Development. <http://www.oecd.org/document/8/0,2340,en_2649_37427_1907528_119656_1_1_37427,00.html> [November 18, 2003].

Osterman, Paul. 2000. "Work Reorganization in an Era of Restructuring: Trends in Diffusion and Effects on Employee Welfare." *Industrial and Labor Relations Review,* Vol. 53, no. 2 (January), pp. 179–96.

Osterman, Paul, Thomas Kochan, Richard Locke, and Michael J. Piore. 2001. *Working in America: A Blueprint for the New Labor Market.* Cambridge, MA: MIT Press.

Parker, Mike, and Jane Slaughter. 1995. "Unions and Management by Stress." In Steve Babson, ed., *Lean Work: Empowerment and Exploitation in the Global Auto Industry,* Detroit, MI: Wayne State University Press, chapter 2.

Perotti, Roberto. 1994. "Income Distribution and Investment." *European Economic Review,* Vol. 38, no. 3–4 (April), pp. 827–35.

Persson, Torsten, and Guido Tabellini. 1994. "Is Inequality Harmful for Growth?" *American Economic Review,* Vol. 84, no. 3 (June), pp. 600–622.

Phillips, Kevin. 2002. *Wealth and Democracy: A Political History of the American Rich.* New York: Broadway Books.

Piore, Michael J., and Charles F. Sabel. 1984. *The Second Industrial Divide: Possibilities for Prosperity.* New York: Basic Books.

Rees, Albert. 1993. "The Role of Fairness in Wage Determination." *Journal of Labor Economics,* Vol. 11, no. 1 (January), pp. 243–52.

Roach, Stephen S. 1996. "The Hollow Ring of the Productivity Revival." *Harvard Business Review,* Vol. 74, no. 6 (November–December), pp. 81–89.

Ross, Arthur M. 1948. *Trade Union Wage Policy.* Berkeley: University of California Press.

Ryan, John A. 1912. *A Living Wage: Its Ethical and Economic Aspects.* New York: Macmillan.

Slichter, Sumner H. 1924. "The Organization and Control of Economic Activity." In Rexford Guy Tugwell, ed., *The Trend of Economics,* New York: Knopf, pp. 301–55.

————. 1948. *The American Economy: Its Problems and Prospects.* New York: Knopf.

Slichter, Sumner H., James J. Healy, and E. Robert Livernash. 1960. *The Impact of Collective Bargaining on Management.* Washington, DC: Brookings Institution.

Smith, Adam. [1776] 1937. *An Inquiry into the Nature and Causes of the Wealth of Nations.* Edited by Edwin Cannan. New York: Modern Library.

Solomon, Robert C. 1992. *Ethics and Excellence: Cooperation and Integrity in Business.* New York: Oxford University Press.

Solow, Robert M. 1990. *The Labor Market as a Social Institution.* Cambridge, MA: Blackwell.

Soros, George. 2000. *Open Society: Reforming Global Capitalism.* New York: Public Affairs.

Stabile, Donald R. 1993. *Activist Unionism: The Institutional Economics of Solomon Barkin.* Armonk, NY: Sharpe.

Stiglitz, Joseph E. 2002. *Globalization and Its Discontents.* New York: Norton.

Thaler, Richard H. 2000. "From *Homo Economicus* to *Homo Sapiens.*" *Journal of Economic Perspectives,* Vol. 14, no. 1 (Winter), pp. 133–41.

Tool, Marc R., ed. 1993. *Institutional Economics: Theory, Method, Policy.* Boston: Kluwer.

Troy, Leo. 1999. *Beyond Unions and Collective Bargaining.* Armonk, NY: Sharpe.

Turner, Lowell, Harry C. Katz, and Richard W. Hurd, eds. 2001. *Rekindling the Movement: Labor's Quest for Relevance in the Twenty-First Century.* Ithaca, NY: ILR Press.

Walton, Richard E., and Robert B. McKersie. 1965. *A Behavioral Theory of Labor Negotiations.* New York: McGraw-Hill.

Webb, Sidney, and Beatrice Webb. 1897. *Industrial Democracy.* London: Longmans, Green.

Weiler, Paul. 1990. *Governing the Workplace: The Future of Labor and Employment Law.* Cambridge, MA: Harvard University Press.

Wheeler, Hoyt N. 1985. *Industrial Conflict: An Integrative Theory.* Columbia: University of South Carolina Press.

Yonay, Yuval P. 1998. *The Struggle over the Soul of Economics: Institutionalist and Neoclassical Economists in America between the Wars.* Princeton, NJ: Princeton University Press.

CHAPTER 8

The New Institutionalism, Capitalist Diversity, and Industrial Relations

JOHN GODARD
University of Manitoba

An institutional perspective was central to much early industrial relations (IR) research in North America. At its best, this perspective focused on the rules and norms underpinning economic activity, viewing the institutions of work and employment as embedded within, and largely inseparable from, broader social, economic, and political institutions (e.g., Perlman 1928; Commons 1924, 1934, 1961). Although this perspective did not provide much in the way of nomological theory, it did suggest a distinctive approach for analyzing and explaining work and employment relations (e.g., see Kaufman 2003).

This perspective was to gradually disappear from the field. During the 1960s and 1970s in particular, it came to be supplanted by a narrower focus on the institutions of collective bargaining. The field did undergo some broadening and reorientation in the 1980s and 1990s, with the emergence of a new paradigm focusing on changes in work and employment relations in both the union and nonunion sectors (e.g., Kochan, Katz, and McKersie 1986; Cappelli, Katz, Knoke, Osterman, and Useem 1997). But this paradigm does not adequately allow for the broader institutional environments of work and employment relations. Although its proponents have posited a central role for strategic choice and acknowledged the importance of institutions in accounting for how firms and nations have adapted to economic and technological developments, focus has ultimately been on the extent to which convergence has or has not occurred as a result of these developments. There has been little systematic explanation of what continues to be substantial variation within and across nations and the role of broader institutional environments in accounting for this variation.

This chapter establishes both the need and the basis for a "new institutionalist" IR, one that accounts for the broader institutional environments within which work and employment relations are embedded and their implications for the interests, orientations, and actions of the parties. To do this, I draw extensively on the new institutionalism in the social sciences, especially as it has developed over the past decade in comparative political economy and socioeconomics (e.g., Hall and Soskice 2001; Hollingsworth, Muller, and Hollingsworth 2002). The chapter's focus is on explaining cross-national variation in IR, because it is national-level institutional environments and traditions that primarily define IR systems. However, a central argument is that understanding how institutional environments shape work and employment relations is also critical to understanding the nature of these relations and variation therein within a particular nation.

I begin with an assessment of developments in the mainstream IR literature over the past two decades, arguing that there is need to place greater emphasis on the sources of diversity within and between capitalist economies and to develop a broader institutionalist perspective. I then discuss the essential components of the new institutionalism as they apply to IR. Next, I draw out some implications of this literature for the study of IR. Finally, I outline some essential characteristics of a new institutionalist IR, comparing this approach to that of mainstream IR. Throughout, I define industrial relations broadly to include all topics relevant to understanding work and employment relations.

Industrial Relations and Convergence Theory

At least since the 1950s, industrial relations scholars have tended to proceed as if IR represents, in the words of John Dunlop (1993:46), a separate "subsystem" of society. This has been especially so in the United States, where researchers have tended to study IR in isolation from broader institutions and hence to either disregard the implications of these institutions for work and employment or to take them largely for granted. The result has been a tendency to view market forces and technology as the main driving forces behind both changes to and variation in work and employment relations, with largely uniform effects across national IR systems.

This view was initially most reflected in Kerr, Dunlop, Harbison, and Myers (1960). For these authors, a pluralist industrial relations system similar to the one believed to characterize the United States would become increasingly widespread as other nations approached the same level of industrial (i.e., market and technological) development. However, over the past two decades, this version has given way to a somewhat more managerial version, one that argues that changes to markets and technology have created virtually universal pressures toward enhanced flexibility in both employment relations and the organization of work. Although this more recent version was initially developed outside of the field of IR (Piore and Sabel 1984; Kern and Schuman 1985), it has since come to be widely accepted within it and is most clearly reflected in what is referred to in Godard and Delaney (2000) as the "new paradigm" in IR. As with most social science paradigms, it varies somewhat depending on the author. I provide a stylized version that is intended to provide a fair approximation of the arguments and assumptions of what, for present purposes, can simply be referred to as the "new IR literature."

The New Industrial Relations Literature

The general argument of the new IR literature has been that labor and employment relations in developed nations have been undergoing a shift away from the bureaucratic, pluralistic industrialism predicted by Kerr, Dunlop, Harbison, and Myers (1960) and generally believed to characterize the United States in the postwar era, to the more flexible, postindustrialism anticipated by management theorists and futurists in the late 1960s (e.g., Woodward 1965; Bennis 1967; Toffler 1972). This new era is generally defined by

1. more flexible employment relations, including an increase in part-time, temporary, and contract workers and a decrease in job stability (see Cappelli 1999; Supiot 2001);

2. a weakening of labor unions and decentralization of collective bargaining (see Katz 1993; Supiot 2001), allowing greater flexibility in employer practices; and

3. the adoption of more flexible, high-performance forms of work organization and human resource management practice based on teamwork and directed at achieving high levels of employee involvement (Kochan, Katz, and McKersie 1986; Kochan and Osterman 1994).

These developments are in turn believed to require shifts in both state and labor union policies, away from the more adversarial, pluralist model toward a more cooperative, managerial one in which restrictions on employers are loosened, high-performance policies are encouraged, and unions adopt a new "partnership" or "mutual gains" role or face marginalization and decline.

The new IR is less deterministic and more conscious of the importance of institutions than the postwar convergence thesis. Although

Kerr, Dunlop, Harbison, and Myers (1960:221–39) were cautious to acknowledge diversity, attributing it to cultural and institutional traditions, their central argument was that such diversity would diminish over time, thus giving rise to uniformity. In contrast, the new IR literature suggests that strategic choices also play an important role and that both ideologies and institutions can serve as barriers to change (Kochan, Katz, and McKersie 1986). But it is still largely assumed that change is ultimately driven by economic and technological forces and that these forces tend to be immutable and largely invariant across nations.[1] Actors may respond to these forces in somewhat different ways depending on their ideologies,[2] and established institutions may filter the pressures associated with them. But while the nature and valence of change may vary, those changes that do occur tend to be broadly similar across all developed nations (Locke and Kochan 1995:365, 368).

Whither Convergence?

There seems little doubt that important changes have been taking place over the past few decades or that economic and technological developments have mattered. By pointing to and attempting to explain these changes and the developments associated with them, the new IR literature has made an important contribution. Yet despite some acknowledgment that cross-national variation remains and that institutions also matter (e.g., Locke 1995:22), the emphasis on change and convergence has tended to blind many IR scholars to what may be the real story of the past few decades: the persistence of widespread diversity. It is even possible that, despite common changes overall, variation in the nature and extent of change has actually increased the amount of diversity across developed nations (e.g., Traxler 2003:149; Thelen 2001; Kitschelt, Lange, Marks, and Stephens 1999; Iversen and Pontusson 2000). For example, union coverage now ranges from 15% in the United States, to 33% in Canada, to 65% in Germany, to over 90% in Sweden (Carley 2003). Moreover, although most nations have seen some decentralization in collective bargaining, northern European and Nordic nations continue to be characterized primarily by industry-level collective bargaining, in some cases (e.g., Sweden) with a high degree of coordination across industries (Golden, Wallerstein, and Lange 1999; Thelen 2001), and some nations (e.g., Spain, Italy, Ireland) have actually seen a centralization of bargaining (Baccaro 2003).

Continued and perhaps even increasing diversity also appears to be the case with regard to employment arrangements. For example, part-time work does appear to have become more pervasive (although not, it appears, in the United States). Yet within the developed world, it ranged from 5% in Finland, to 13% in the United States, to 34% in the Netherlands as of 2002 (Organisation for Economic Co-operation and Development [OECD] 2004). OECD data suggest that the prevalence of temporary work also varies extensively, from 4% in the United States, to 13% in Canada and Germany, to 32% in Spain (OECD 2004). Moreover, the rights and protections for those in such work appear to diverge considerably (Booth, Dolado, and Frank 2002:183; Nicoletti, Scarpetta, and Boylaud 2000). For example, temporary workers in Germany now have the right to wage and benefit levels that are equivalent to those of their full-time counterparts unless their collective agreement stipulates otherwise (European Foundation for the Improvement of Living and Working Conditions 2003). In the United States, many such workers are not even eligible for collective bargaining coverage under the law.

In addition, job stability continues to vary considerably. OECD data suggest that, as of 1998, the percentage of those in a specific firm for less than one year was only 8.3% in Japan, compared with 14.3% in Germany and 27.8% in the United States (Auer and Cazes 2000:382). Labor market supports also continue to vary widely, with the United States spending only 0.15% of GDP on active labor market programs as of 2001, compared with 1.20% in Germany and 1.57% in the Netherlands (OECD 2002).

A similar argument might be advanced with regard to the organization of work. Comparative data on this topic are difficult to obtain, but it appears that the extent to which new forms of work organization have been adopted varies considerably across nations. For example, a 1996 E.U. survey found that the percentage of employers reporting teams ranged from 10% in Spain, to 31% in Germany, to 56% in Sweden (EPOC Research Group 1997:65). It appears that the specific practices adopted, and the way in which they have been adopted, also vary extensively across nations (Katz and Darbishire 2000).

To be fair, the available data may suffer from a number of weaknesses and may not in any case be sufficient to permit any definitive conclusions. Yet to the extent that the trends identified in the IR literature do indeed reflect broader global developments, the implications of these developments and hence the nature and extent of change seem to have varied considerably across nations, and considerable diversity seems to remain. Neither the new IR literature nor IR theory in general provides much basis for explaining this variation and diversity. The assertion that it reflects varying rates of adaptation to global developments offers little in the way of theoretical explanation, especially because it appears that different nations have been adapting not just at different rates but also in different ways, depending on established institutions and traditions (Thelen 2001). Any argument that continuing diversity reflects IR institutions is also at best a partial one, in part because it fails to adequately address why these institutions continue to vary, and in part because it tends to be unduly narrow.

In addition, the extent to which the changes predicted by the new IR have taken place appears to vary considerably within as well as across nations. Thus, for example, although a majority of employers in the United States and Canada appear to have adopted some of the alternative work practices associated with the high-performance model, only a small minority appear to have fully adopted this model, and it appears that the approach underlying their adoption varies by firm or industry (Godard 2004a). Similar results likely pertain with regard to employment practices and collective bargaining. As Katz and Darbishire (2000) argued, diversity may have been increasing within as well as across nations. The new IR literature has not only failed to anticipate this variation, it has also been unable to adequately account for it (see Godard 2004a).

The shortcomings of the new IR ultimately reflect a failure to address how the broader institutional environment of work and employment relations shapes the interests and orientations of the parties, the power resources that they are able to draw upon, and the various pressures and constraints to which they are subject (see Godard and Delaney 2000; Delaney and Godard 2001). Particularly important may be the way in which the employment relation is constituted by law, the role of normative as well as legal rules and regulations, and the broader socioeconomic environment within which the parties interact, including firms' governance structures, interfirm relations, and, ultimately, state policies and traditions (Godard 2002).

The new IR literature has begun to pay some attention to these factors (see Godard 2004a). In particular, there has been a growing recognition that the nature and extent of changes to work organization have varied in accordance with national level differences. But systematic explanation of the nature and role of these differences and why they continue has been lacking. Part of the reason for these failings may have been an absence of an accessible body of literature on which IR scholars could draw to account for diversity. However, such a literature has been developing since at least the early 1990s. Referred to for present purposes as the "new institutionalism," it provides the basis for a broader and more institutionally informed approach to IR. In the following sections, I outline the essential characteristics of the new institutionalist literature and address its implications for the field of IR.

The New Institutionalism and Capitalist Diversity

For present purposes, the new institutionalism can be defined to include all contemporary literature addressing how rules (broadly defined) embodied in economic, social, and political institutions account for substantive questions of economy and society, with a particular focus on the *relations* between the economic, the social, and the political. However, this definition can be seen as somewhat provisional because it masks considerable variation within and across disciplines in both topic area and theoretical emphasis. For example, in economics the new institutionalism has tended to focus on the implications of laws and incentive structures for rational self-interested action (e.g., North 1990). In contrast, sociologists have tended to focus on the importance of normative rules and belief structures in shaping both how economic actors think and the constraints to which they are subject (e.g., Scott 1995). In political studies, there have been three strands of new institutionalism, one of which explores the implications of political structures for strategic behavior, following a rational-choice, game-theoretic perspective (Weingast 2002), another of which emphasizes the importance of norms and paradigms that guide policy formation and implementation (March and Olsen 1989), and yet another of which focuses on how long-term historical processes explain state structures, power relations, and ultimately public policies (Pierson and Skocpol 2002).

A distinctive literature has also emerged on business systems and varieties of capitalism. The former has focused on cross-national differences in the institutional environments of firms, including cultural conventions to which they are subject, state structures and policies, firms' governance systems, interfirm relations, and labor market institutions (e.g., Whitley 1996). The latter has gone a step further, arguing that there are complementarities between institutional arrangements, making it possible to identify different varieties of capitalism, each with its own logic (Hall and Soskice 2001). This work has in turn been augmented by a number of scholars in the area of comparative political economy, who have also concerned themselves more specifically with the role of labor institutions and cross-class alliances in accounting for variation in national economic policies and institutions associated with different business systems (Thelen 2002).

These differences suggest that there is in fact more than one "new institutionalist" literature and that what one finds depends on where one looks. However, while it may be possible to find inconsistencies across or even within topics and disciplines, these can be thought of as occurring within a nascent, broader paradigm united by a common focus on the importance of rules that undergird economic, social, and political arrangements forming the institutional environment within which parties act. This common focus means that these contributions tend to be complementary far more often than they are contradictory and that differences largely involve matters of emphasis (e.g., Hall and Taylor 1998; Thelen 2002).

Some of the contributions to the new institutionalist literature that are most relevant to the field of industrial relations include Wolfgang Streeck's (1992) work on the institutional conditions of the German system of diversified quality production; David Soskice's (1999) work on divergent production regimes and the role of labor market institutions within these regimes; Gosta Esping-Andersen's (1999) work on the social foundations of labor market behavior and institutions; Sanford Jacoby's (1991) work on the historical foundations of employer IR ideologies in the United Kingdom and the United States; Colin Crouch's (1993) analysis of European state traditions and IR; Ronald Dore's (1997, 2000a) sociological analysis of Japanese capitalism; Christel Lane's (1989, 1995) historically informed comparative analysis of IR in Germany, France, and Britain; and Kathleen Thelen's (1991, 2000, 2001) work on collective bargaining structures in Europe. But rather than specifically review these contributions, I outline the main components of the new institutionalist literature, drawing on these contributions where relevant.

The Importance of Rules

At the core of the new institutionalist literature is an emphasis on the importance of rules. Three types of rules can be identified: (1) formal rules, residing in legal regulations and established incentive structures; (2) informal rules, residing in taken-for-granted conventions, beliefs, knowledge, norms, and values; and (3) constitutive rules, residing in more fundamental and often taken-for-granted legal rights and political institutions that shape power relations in a society. Which form of rules receives emphasis depends on the version of new institutionalism one reads. But common to all versions is recognition that actors do not behave in an institutional vacuum but are instead part of a broader community of actors subject to (and constitutive of) rules and norms. These rules and norms and the institutional arrangements they embody do not just constrain and facilitate behavior, they also shape the power resources of actors and provide the cognitive and normative templates for interpretation and ultimately strategic interaction (Godard 2002; Scott 1995:43; Hall and Taylor 1996:939). Under the new institutionalism, the question is therefore not how actors seek to rationally achieve goals per se but rather why they have the goals they appear to have, the role of rules in shaping how one course of action comes to be viewed as more rational to the attainment of these goals than another, and how, indeed, what is rational comes to be defined. In IR, for example, the question would be not just how employers or unions pursue a particular course of action but also what identities or orientations underlie that course of action (e.g., Locke and Thelen 1995), what taken-for-granted rules and assumptions guide it, and what purpose it is expected to serve.

Economic Institutions and the Importance of Business Systems

The rules and norms that underpin action also embody a common set of understandings and expectations about the distribution and use of economic resources (e.g., property rights), the relations between actors, and the behavior of these actors. Thus, they are the basic building blocks of economic institutions as commonly understood. Those institutions most frequently identified in the new institutionalist literature primarily involve business system characteristics, for example, interfirm coordination mechanisms and trading relations (e.g., markets vs. networks), the predominant employer financing and control system (e.g., stock markets vs. banks), educational and training systems (disorganized vs. organized), employee representation systems (e.g., works councils), and collective bargaining structures (coordinated vs. uncoordinated; see Whitley 1996). Generally speaking, these characteristics are believed to have implications for the interests and orientations of employers, particularly the extent to which employers can be expected to develop a long-term stakeholder orientation and cooperative relations with employees and other stakeholders, or a short-term shareholder-value orientation and arms-length, competitive relations with employees and other stakeholders (e.g., Vitols 2001a; Gospel and Pendleton 2003:565–67). Thus, for example, these characteristics can have implications for employers' willingness to invest in human resources and to provide meaningful long-term job security, both of which have longer-term payoffs and hence are more likely to prevail within business systems that foster a longer-term orientation. They are also believed to have implications for employer participation in industry-level bargaining and vocational training systems (Gospel and Pendleton 2003). This can in turn be expected to have implications for the orientations and identities of unions and workers, particularly whether they adopt a cooperative, partnership orientation based on trust or an adversarial, competitive one based on distrust (Swenson 1989).

Institutional Complementarities and Varieties of Capitalism

The "varieties of capitalism" approach extends the business systems literature, arguing that it is possible to identify distinctive varieties of capitalism, each with its own institutional logic. This approach has been developed in a number of recent volumes (e.g., Berger and Dore 1996; Crouch and Streeck 1997; Kitschelt, Lange, Marks, and Stephens 1999; Iversen, Pontusson, and Soskice 2000; Yamamura and Streeck 2003), although it is now most closely associated with the work of Hall and Soskice, as developed in the introductory chapter to their 2001 edited volume, *Varieties of Capitalism: The Institutional Foundations of Comparative Advantage.*

Under this approach, authors typically distinguish between what are often referred to as *liberal market economies* and *coordinated market economies*. In liberal market economies, interfirm relations tend to be competitive, firms rely primarily on stock market financing, there is only limited vocational training, and unions and collective bargaining play a limited role in the representation of workers or determination of the terms and conditions of employment. In coordinated market economies, interfirm relations tend to be cooperative and long term, firms rely primarily on bank financing or cross-ownership, there is a high degree of vocational training, and unions and collective bargaining play a central role in the representation of workers and the determination of the terms and conditions of employment. The former is most exemplified by the United States, the latter by Germany and, to a lesser extent, Japan.

Under the Hall and Soskice (2001) formulation, these differences reflect different ways of resolving problems of economic coordination within national economies. Liberal market economies rely primarily on markets and hierarchies, while coordinated economies rely more on strategic interactions and networks. Neither of these solutions is necessarily superior to the other. Rather, the performance of an economy depends not on whether it adheres to any singular, universally superior logic but rather on how well it has succeeded in developing complementarities in accordance with its own logic (Hall and Soskice 2001; Hall and Gingerich 2001).[3]

For example, Hall and Soskice (2001:24) argue that strong unions and coordinated wage bargaining make it more efficient for German firms to cooperate in the German training system, because the standardization of pay renders them less vulnerable to "hold up" by their employees and the "poaching" of skilled workers by other firms. They also argue that, because firms in liberal market economies are under pressure to maximize short-term profitability, they require flexible employment arrangements that allow for short-term adjustments, giving rise to labor markets with lower job stability and employer training, which in turn result in a labor force with lower investments in specific skills yet higher investments in general skills (Hall and Soskice 2001:25, 30). In a similar vein, Wolfgang Streeck (1992, 1997) argues that high pay levels require German firms to specialize in high-quality production and that this has traditionally been sustained by a combination of interdependent factors, including a vocational training system that ensures high skill levels, industry-level bargaining that standardizes wages, regulated markets that encourage collaboration, and codetermination laws that enhance trust.

In addition, differences in institutional logic may have implications for the types of innovation and change that occur and for a nation's sources of comparative advantage (Soskice 1999; Hall and Soskice 2001). For example, coordinated market economies tend to sustain high levels of labor–management and interfirm trust and therefore tend to elicit levels of cooperation that support ongoing, incremental innovation and change. In contrast, institutions in liberal market economies tend to foster low levels of cooperation and trust but are more conducive to periodic, radical innovation and change because firms are subject to fewer restrictions and commitments (Hall and Soskice 2001:36–44). Thus, the way in which each type is likely to adapt to various economic and technological forces at a particular point in time is likely to be substantially different. Different logics may in this respect offer different comparative advantages, thus giving rise to cross-national patterns of specialization. For example, while radical innovation is conducive to success in fast-moving technology sectors, incremental innovation tends to be conducive to success in capital goods sectors such as machine tools and transport equipment, which require continuous improvement in quality and costs (Hall and Soskice 2001:39).

Social Institutions and Conventions

The varieties-of-capitalism literature—especially the Hall and Soskice (2001) formulation—has tended to focus on complementarities between economic institutions. However, many contributors have argued that social institutions and norms play an important role in underpinning economic institutions. For example, Esping-Andersen (e.g., 1999:45) has argued that different social policies and labor market institutions can be attributed in part to different family traditions and the values that underlie these traditions. Streeck (1997:39–40) has argued that German social norms emphasize quality over quantity, thus ensuring a market for high-quality products necessary to sustain the German system of diversified quality production, with its high-skill, high-quality employment relations. Dore (1997, 2000a, 2000b) has argued that the Japanese model is underpinned by a normative environment in which employees are viewed not as human "resources," but rather as members with corresponding rights and by a "productivist" culture that values long-term commitments and hence fosters long-term economic relationships based on trust and reputation.

The Role of the State

The new institutionalist literature also points to the implications of state policies and institutions for economic and social institutions, implications that go beyond legal constraints (Godard 2002; Lindberg and Campbell 1991). For example, Estevez-Abe, Iversen, and Soskice (2001) argue that social policies providing generous employment and unemployment protection provide safeguards for workers who develop high firm- or industry-specific skill levels, thus providing a further underpinning for the German high-quality production strategy, which requires such levels. Elsewhere (Godard 1997), I argue that state economic policies that create high unemployment lessen problems of labor cooperation by, in effect, coercing workers to cooperate (also see Jacoby 1999). Such conditions may in turn lessen the need for "high-commitment" policies, with the state effectively addressing problems of cooperation for the employer. Institutional analyses in sociology (Dobbin, Edelman, Meyer, Scott, and Swidler 1988; Dobbin, Edelman, Meyer, and Scott 1993; Edelman 1990) show how employment laws shape the normative as well as legal environments of employers, with implications for their human resource management practices.

States also play a critical role in shaping the broader institutional environments of work and employment. For example, both Vitols (2001b) and Doremus, Keller, Pauly, and Reich (1998:22–51) show how state policies have shaped financial markets and the principal–agent relation between managers and owners in the United States and in Germany and Japan, giving rise to the predominance of stock market control in the former and bank control in the latter. Wood (2001) argues that state policies protecting the regulation and coordination of economic activities on the supply side (e.g., training) are critical to the functioning of a coordinated market economy, while liberal market economies require policies that ensure competition and flexibility. Casper (2001) makes a similar argument with regard to the implications of contract law, arguing that German contract law is oriented more toward regulating contracts to ensure that they are fair and hence limiting price competition, while the U.S. approach is to enforce contracts as written, allowing the exploitation of power imbalances and hence promoting price competition. As the business system literature suggests, these differences may have important implications for whether employers can be expected to adopt a long-term, stakeholder orientation and hence for IR/HRM practices. Finally, states play a critical role in determining the rights and obligations of the parties to an employment relationship, in effect shaping the extent to which this relationship is constituted by law as one of subordination rather than of partnership, with potentially important implications for employer obligations and orientations (Armour, Deakin, and Konzelmann 2003) and for employee trust levels (see Godard 2002:268–73), as discussed more fully later in the chapter.

State Traditions, Structures, and Paradigms

The new institutionalist literature does not just address the implications of state policies; it also analyzes their foundations. In particular, new institutionalists point to the importance of state policy traditions and paradigms that limit the range of alternatives considered (see Hall 1993; Visser and Hemerijck 1997; Lehmbruch 2001). Although subject to continuous change and evolution, these traditions and paradigms tend to be path dependent, subject to major reevaluation primarily only in times of crisis (Hall 1984, 1993). Even at these times, the changes that occur are likely to reflect a shift that builds from the established paradigm if they are to achieve permanence over the long run. For example, in his study of European state traditions, Crouch (1993) found that the success of attempts by states to alter industrial relations institutions or to imitate those of other countries depends highly on established policies and traditions. In a similar vein, King and Rothstein (1993) concluded that Sweden was able to establish an active labor market policy in the 1950s because it was consistent with prior interventionist policies and hence enjoyed considerable institutional legitimacy, while a tradition of limited state intervention in the United Kingdom meant that similar efforts failed there.

New institutionalists also point to the importance of state structures. For example, the ways in which policies are formulated may vary considerably, depending on whether various interest groups are included in the policy formation process (e.g., unions under corporatism) and whether there is proportional representation, thereby requiring parliamentary coalitions in order to alter, for example, labor market institutions (e.g., King and Wood 1999; Wood 2001). In addition, states develop elaborate bureaucracies to execute existing policies, and these bureaucracies are characterized by rules and norms that militate against substantial change (March and Olsen 1989), although the extent to which this may be the case can vary considerably (e.g., French statism vs. British voluntarism). The effects of political forces may also be limited by institutions that decentralize or disperse the authority of the state (as in the United States) or insulate the exercise of state authority from political forces (e.g., the dispersion of power through arms-length institutions, such as labor boards). State structures may also shape political forces by providing resources or legitimacy to various constituencies; for example, corporatist institutions for the administration of state policy may enhance the power and legitimacy of labor (Swank 2002:1–8).

The importance of state paradigms and structures becomes apparent when analyzing U.S.–Canadian differences in labor law (also see Taras 1997). In Canada, a tradition of "Tory paternalism" and an emphasis on "peace and good government" partly explain a history of stronger regulation of industrial disputes (e.g., mandatory conciliation requirements) than in the United States, where a tradition of market liberalism and an emphasis on "life, liberty, and the pursuit of happiness" partly explain a history of limited regulation, in which the parties have been left to fight matters out on their own. These tendencies may have been enhanced by different political structures. For example, Bruce (1989) shows how the rise and institutionalization of a democratic socialist party (the CCF/NDP) in a highly federalized, multiparty parliamentary system with strong party discipline have made the passage of stronger labor laws more likely in Canada than in the United States, where similar conditions have not held.

The Politics of Economics: Alliances and Compromises

Differences in institutional arrangements can also reflect differences in the relations between labor and capital and the arrangements that best suit their interests (see Hall 1986; Thelen 2002). Although it is often assumed that the extent to which labor-friendly policies are adopted reflects the distribution of power resources within a political system, new institutionalists argue that such policies can also reflect alliances between employer and labor groups. For example, Swenson (1989) found that the system of centralized bargaining characteristic of Sweden until the early 1980s was not just a reflection of union power but also served the interests of large employers subject to international competition in low-wage industries. In turn, Swenson and Pontusson (2000) showed how labor–capital alliances shifted in the 1980s, resulting in the breakdown of centralized bargaining. Similarly, Thelen (2001) argued that the German system of coordinated, multi-industry bargaining helps to sustain Germany's coordinated market economy and thus serves employer as well as union interests. Mares (2001) demonstrated how employer interests with regard to social policies vary across and within nations, with important implications for social policy formation and ultimately labor market institutions.

History Really Matters

Institutional arrangements and the paradigms that underpin them tend to reflect economic, political, and social traditions that have become embedded in established rules, norms, and expectations. To an extent, these rules, norms, and expectations can be viewed as cultural. However, whereas cultural explanations (e.g., Hofstede 1980) can be ahistoric and overly general, institutional explanations tend to be grounded in (and hence explained by) historical processes and to be more institutionally specific. Thus, in addition to shaping the broader normative and cultural expectations to which the parties are subject, these rules, norms, and expectations help both to explain existing institutional arrangements and to constrain the range of feasible state policy options. For example, the roots of the German codetermination system can be traced to the establishment of works councils after the First World War and ultimately to major debates over industrial democracy emergent in the first half of the 19th century (Frege 2004). The roots of the Swedish system of social democracy, with its strong labor institutions, can be traced back even further, beginning with the abolishment of serfdom in the 14th century and the right of peasants to elect their own representatives in parliament beginning in the 15th century (Olsen 2002:112–13). The roots of U.S. liberalism, with its strong emphasis on property rights and its weak state and labor institutions, can be traced largely to the abundance of land during the early development of the United States, the conditions of the

American Revolution, and its founding religious values (e.g., see Hutton 2002:49–85).

With regard to unions, Jacoby (1991) showed how differences in the economic and social development of the United States and the United Kingdom created circumstances under which employers in the former were able to weaken skill levels and fight unions, while employers in the latter continued to rely on skilled workers and developed a higher tolerance for and willingness to work with unions. Thus, labor relations in the United States came to involve lower levels of trust and more adversarial union–management relations than in the United Kingdom, which was able to develop a tradition of voluntary union recognition. It may be argued that these different traditions underlie contemporary differences in labor law regimes (see Wood and Godard 1999).

Although the foundations of established institutions are to an extent evolutionary, developing in accordance with ongoing historical processes, they also typically reflect historic compromises at critical junctures in a nation's development. For example, Weiss (1993) showed how the Japanese employment system is in part a reflection of Japan's state-driven development in the 1880s and the policies associated with it, particularly as they pertained to the need to develop and retain skilled labor. Manow (2001:100–114) argued that the broader social market paradigm that supports the German system of IR can be traced to the welfare regime established to address working-class unrest during the late 19th century, again in an era of state-driven industrialization.[4] Finally, Lehmbruch (2001) argued that policies encouraging corporatist interest associations and cartels at this point in time, and a preference for "decentralized self-administration" in the implementation of state programs during this period, helped establish the basis for the "social partnership" model to emerge in Germany after World War II.

Some Implications of the New Institutionalism for Industrial Relations

In general, the new institutionalism suggests that it is not possible to understand labor and employment relations and changes therein without understanding their broader institutional environments, and that it is in turn not possible to understand these environments without understanding state policies and traditions and, ultimately, the economic, political, and social foundations of these policies and the institutions they support. Substantial changes can occur, and strategic choices and actions may make an important difference in the nature and processes of these changes, but to paraphrase Marx, "Man [sic] makes his own history, but he does not do so under institutional conditions of his own choosing." Understanding these conditions is critical not only for understanding what is taking place but also for understanding the extent to which various alternatives may or may not be possible. In other words, the new institutionalism has important implications not just for positive analyses of IR but also for prescriptive analyses addressing state policies, union strategies, and employer practices.

With regard to the new IR, this literature demonstrates that economic and technological developments do not impose an immutable logic on economic and IR systems, regardless of whether this logic is thought to be pluralist or more unitarist and managerial. Rather, the extent to which they matter, and the way in which they come to be reflected in IR practices, is largely a function of the institutional arrangements characteristic of this system. Thus, for example, the predominant response to the economic pressures and uncertainties of the past two decades has been substantial deregulation and weakening of organized labor in the United States, a response that appears to have been most dramatic in the 1980s. Yet in Germany it has been more gradual and has entailed "controlled decentralization" and "re-regulation," with labor unions continuing to play a critical role (Thelen 2001). These differences follow readily from the differences between liberal and coordinated market economies theorized under the varieties-of-capitalism approach, because where the competitiveness of the former is based on radical innovation and requires high levels of flexibility yet little cooperation with labor, the competitiveness of the latter is based on incremental innovation and requires lower levels of flexibility yet considerable peace and cooperation with labor. Thus, the differing adaptations of the United States and Germany to the pressures of the past two decades do not just reflect different institutional environments, they also reflect different institutional *requirements* and ultimately different employer interests (Thelen 2000, 2001).

The new institutionalism also suggests that the sorts of changes and adjustments that occur within a market economy may be more predictable and have greater historical continuity than has often been assumed or acknowledged by the new IR or by recent variants of transformation theory (e.g., Kuruvilla and Erickson 2002) and mobilization theory (Kelly 1998). For example, although recent variants of transformation and mobilization theory might have enabled one to predict the emergence of some form of "new deal" for unions and workers in the United States during the 1930s, they do not do a very good job of explaining the nature of this deal and, perhaps more important, its subsequent functioning and degeneration. The new institutionalism does, because it focuses on existing institutional arrangements and the economic, social, and political traditions in which they are embedded. Under this approach, state emphasis on the protection of property rights, market competition, and ultimately the promotion of individual economic gain (Hutton 2002), coupled with traditions of individualistic values, weak administrative law, and employer political power, meant that the New-Deal labor law model was unlikely to succeed, despite attempts to sell it as complementary to free markets through the discourse of "free" collective bargaining and macroeconomic gains (Kaufman 1996).

Under the new institutionalism, one must also understand national institutional traditions and norms in order to understand the rationale underlying (or at least used to justify) changes that take place in response to what appear as global developments. The question in this regard is not one of determining the most rational solution to a particular problem but rather one of understanding why the problem is defined as such in the first place and what values and priorities shape conceptions of the most rational course of action. Thus, for example, in a liberal market economy, unemployment has increasingly come to be viewed as a problem because it has negative implications for economic growth and ultimately for firm profits and stock market values. Yet for employers to lay off workers is viewed as legitimate as long as it is consistent with the maximization of shareholder value, and indeed, it is viewed as important for ensuring economic efficiency. In a coordinated market economy, unemployment may be defined as a problem because it is seen to aggravate problems of social exclusion and inequality and to place an increased burden on government spending, with implications for the state's ability to maintain social programs. For employers to lay off workers except as a last resort is viewed as illegitimate, because it is inconsistent with the role of firms as social institutions (Streeck 1997). Thus, we would expect layoffs to be much fewer and more restricted, and active labor policies much stronger, in coordinated than in liberal market economies, expectations that are borne out by the available data on job stability (Auer and Cazes 2000) and labor market protections (OECD 2002).

The new institutionalism may have particular relevance for understanding and theorizing cross-national variation in employer practices, particularly as they pertain to the high-performance paradigm. To an extent, such differences may be accounted for by differences in IR institutions. For example, Turner (1991) argued that German unions have had a greater ability than their U.S. counterparts to participate in work-place restructuring because of stronger shop floor rights. Locke and Thelen (1995) argued that workers and unions have been more willing to accept and participate in work reorganization because, unlike for their U.S. counterparts, employment security and union strength do not depend on narrow job definitions and rules related to job control. These explanations no doubt have merit, but the analysis in this paper suggests a more systemic explanation.

A new institutionalist explanation would be that the employment relation in liberal market economies is one of subordination, in which work-ers have few legal participation or codecision rights and employers remain largely unaccountable to employees. Firms in these economies are economic institutions managed primarily if not solely in terms of shareholder interests, and employees have little if any job security by law and little government support if needed. These circumstances thus create a problem of insecurity and distrust, which in turn makes it difficult and expensive to attempt to achieve the levels of commitment needed to sustain a high-involvement work system based on autonomous teams, the variant of the high-performance model advocated by its main proponents. These circumstances are also inimical to the kind of long-term employer commitments needed to overcome problems of distrust (Gospel and Pendleton 2003:568). This does not suggest that the approach promoted in the new IR literature is not adopted or that it necessarily fails. It does mean, however, that its adoption is likely to be relatively limited, that it tends to be more fragile where it is adopted, and that alternative forms of work organization based more on work intensification and coercion are more likely (Godard 2004a). In effect, the high-performance model, at least as advanced in the new IR, may not enjoy a very good fit with the institutional environment of a liberal market economy.

In a coordinated market economy, employees also find themselves in positions of subordination, yet they have participation and codecision rights that are often strong, and employers are partly accountable to them through representatives on supervisory boards. Firms are viewed as social institutions managed in accordance with the long-term interests of society, and employees have considerable job security by law and social assistance if needed. It is thus less expensive to attempt to achieve the levels of cooperation needed to sustain a high-involvement work system based on autonomous teams. Employers are also more likely to de-velop the kind of long-term employer commitments needed to develop and sustain trust, and workers can be confident in the ability of works councils to ensure that this trust is not violated (Streeck 1992:25; Hancke and Casper 1999:179). Thus, the high-performance model is more consistent with the institutional environment of a coordinated market economy, although paradoxically, there may be less need for it.[5]

Finally, although the new institutionalism is perhaps most obviously relevant to the development of comparative industrial relations theory, it is also relevant for studying variation within nations. The field of industrial relations has, at least in North America, been characterized by a tendency to take institutional environments for granted, especially where these environments appear to be invariant over time. Thus, for example, little attention has been paid to the underlying nature of the employment relation in liberal market economies and its implications for the interactions—in particular, trust problems—between employees and their employers. This has resulted in not only a tendency to overestimate the potential of the high-involvement variant of the high-performance model but also an inability to adequately explain variation in its adoption and success. Specifically, problems in achieving and maintaining high levels of trust and commitment mean that the costs of doing so can be high. Thus, the extent to which it makes sense to invest in the high-performance model may depend on the extent to which high commitment levels can make a difference to performance, which may depend (in part) on the relational power and attitudes of workers, which may in turn vary in accordance with factors such as technology, product characteristics, and organizational size (Godard 1998, 2004a). Yet in a coordinated market economy, such predictions may not hold because the structure of the employment relation does not create the same trust problems.

This difference may be even more important with regard to bargaining outcomes. In the United States, the institutional environment has traditionally meant that unions have adhered to a largely economistic, "business unionism" approach, and employers have both been hostile to unions and adopted a shareholder value orientation. This has made for a highly adversarial relation, in which economic power has come to play a central role. Yet in Germany the institutional environment has traditionally meant that both unions and employers have been more willing to act as social partners, and so the broader economic and social implications of various settlements have played a much greater role. This means that, while variation in bargaining power may provide the primary explanation for variation in collective agreements in the United States, it may not in Germany (Visser and Hemerijck 1997:63–80). Although one might argue that this simply reflects differences in bargaining structures, the new institutionalist approach suggests that it reflects broader institutional conditions and, indeed, that bargaining structures as well as outcomes essentially reflect this (e.g., Soskice 1990).

A New Institutionalist Industrial Relations?

The new institutionalist literature offers broad potential for refocusing and broadening IR, to bring it back into the mainstream of social science through increased emphasis on broad economic and social issues. It also seems clear that analyzing IR as one important component of a broader institutional configuration and locating it within a broader, more sociological understanding of history can enable scholars to move beyond the universalistic assumptions underlying much of the literature on work and employment practices.

The new institutionalist literature is not, however, without its limitations (e.g., Thelen 2002; Blyth 2003; Goodin 2003; Crouch 2003). Of particular relevance in the present context is a tendency for some authors—especially Hall and Soskice (2001) and a number of the contributors to their volume—to underestimate the importance of underlying labor–capital conflicts that are common across capitalist societies (Lane 1995:14). These conflicts may be seen to have a dualistic relationship with the institutional arrangements unique to a particular nation. On the one hand, they are important for explaining the development of institutional arrangements over time. On the other, established institutional arrangements are important for explaining how these conflicts are or are not manifest at a particular point in time, at the micro as well as the macro level. In the United States, for example, they are essentially addressed through a combination of market coercion and employer paternalism (Jacoby 1997), while in Germany they are addressed through a combination of representational rights and employer–employee partnerships.

A related problem has been a tendency of these authors to assume that economic systems, and more specifically states, inherently seek an economic equilibrium in which complementarities and hence economic performance outcomes are maximized.[6] Yet institutional arrangements have implications not just for economic performance but also for who benefits from that performance. Although all of the parties involved may have an interest in ensuring satisfactory economic performance and may use performance claims to justify their preferred arrangements, different interests are likely to be served by different arrangements or rules of the game (see Knight 1992; Boix 1998). Thus, the distribution of interests and power resources may play a critical role in accounting for how institutions come to be designed (Thelen 2002:387). Indeed, different arrangements have implications for how the parties define their interests, the power resources available to them in the pursuit of these interests, and the rules, norms, and strategies they follow in the course of doing so. This partly explains why different economies come over time to be characterized by distinctive institutional arrangements and yield different outcomes.

Finally, the issue of who benefits from particular institutional arrangements applies not just to economic outcomes but also to broader societal ones. Yet these outcomes have also been downplayed in much of the new institutionalist literature. The underlying agenda of much of this literature appears to be to establish that there are viable alternatives to neoliberalism, that these alternatives allow stronger social and labor market policies and more favorable societal outcomes, and that there thus continues to be substantial room for cross-national diversity. Yet, this argument has been underdeveloped and, indeed, increasingly overshadowed by a focus on the implications of institutions for economic performance (Blyth 2003:217). The ultimate question should not be how institutions explain economic performance but rather how they explain the extent to which various societal outcomes that one might associate with an advanced democracy (see Swift 2001) are satisfied. Economic performance may matter in this respect, but how and the extent to which this is the case is itself likely to vary depending on institutions, as may how and the extent to which some outcomes are achieved more successfully than others.

A new institutionalist IR would need to address these limitations. It would also require a more specific focus on IR issues, including those pertaining to workplace representation, the organization of work, employment practices, and, arguably in view of the emphasis of the new institutionalism, workplace norms. Thus, rather than simply replicating this literature, it would provide the basis for a distinctive variant of the new institutionalism, one that could be seen as part of a broader paradigm but which also contained a distinctive IR flavor and orientation. Its success would be judged in part on its own terms but also in part on its ability to contribute new insights to the new institutionalist literature and to the field of IR. In this regard, it would focus more on the political economy of IR, addressing how institutions shape and are shaped by the interests, orientations, resources, and ultimately actions of the parties and hence the politics as well as the economics of work and employment relations (see Godard 2004a). I next outline the essential characteristics of a new institutionalist IR and how it would differ from the mainstream IR literature.

First, IR scholars have tended to take the goals and orientations of the parties largely for granted. Assumptions are then made about the most rational form of behavior, whether it involves bargaining demands, adoption of new work practices, or choice of precarious employment practices. Under a new institutionalist perspective, these goals and orientations would be viewed as institutionally shaped and sustained, with implications for how the parties behave. Thus, for example, flexibility pressures have yielded very different responses from U.S. unions, with their historical focus on job control, than from Swedish unions, with their traditional solidaristic wage policies (Locke and Thelen 1995:337), and from German unions, with their traditional social partnership orientation.

Second, when IR scholars refer to institutions, they are typically referring only to institutions that shape or regulate the relationships between labor and management. A new institutionalist IR would address how broader economic institutions shape not only the labor–management relationship but also the power resources and orientations that the parties bring to this relationship. Thus, for example, the broader institutional environment in the United States gives rise to a short-term, shareholder-value orientation among employers and an insecure, low-trust, job-control orientation among workers and unions. In Germany, it gives rise to a longer-term, stakeholder orientation and a more secure, high-trust, partnership orientation among workers and their unions.

Third, although IR scholars have tended to recognize the importance of the state, they have generally restricted their attention to the implications of labor laws and policies, adopting a purely normative or at best pragmatic conception of policy formation. A new institutionalist IR would entail a broader conception of the role of the state, addressing its role in shaping the structure of the employment relation and business system characteristics as well as the economic conditions and regulations to which the parties are subject (see Godard 2002). It would also address the importance of state structures, traditions, and policy paradigms for explaining state labor and economic policies and the likelihood of various reforms to these policies. Thus, the U.S. tradition of a weak state with limited involvement in markets, coupled with a political system in which powerful employer interests are able to exert inordinate influence, has created circumstances that are hostile to effective labor law. The Swedish tradition of a strong state with substantial involvement in markets, coupled with a political system in which employers have had only limited influence, has created circumstances in which strong labor laws have been not only possible but taken for granted.

Fourth, IR scholars (with the noteworthy exception of Jacoby 1991, 1997) have tended to adopt a narrow conception of the importance of history, tending to focus on specific events over limited periods of time and to attribute these events to agency. The tendency has been to focus on single institutions and narrow topics. A new institutionalist IR would entail a broader, more sociological conception, focusing on broad developments and changes over long periods of time, tending to view them as part of an unfolding logic or process in which agency may matter, but only to a limited extent. A new institutionalist IR would also focus on the interrelations between multiple institutions and on broad topics (see Pierson and Skocpol 2002). Thus, for example, Canada's lack of a revolutionary break from Britain, its development by large fur-trading corporations and the state, and its early rule by a political-commercial- ecclesiastical elite help to account for an emphasis on peace and good government and hence stronger support for state involvement and administrative law than in the United States (see Olsen 2002:104–16; Taras 1997). Paradoxically, the New Deal model has thus fared better in Canada, as reflected in stronger labor laws and higher union density levels (Godard 2003a, 2004b, 2004c).

Fifth, while there has been a growing recognition of the importance of institutions, IR scholars have tended to focus on the importance of economic and technological developments for explaining change and variation. A new institutionalist IR would not ignore these developments but would more fully explore how institutional differences account for diversity in the way in which these developments have been addressed. For example, we would expect to observe a different variant of the high-performance model in the United States, where employers tend to have a short-term, shareholder orientation and employees have few stakeholder rights, than in Germany, where employers are more likely to have a long-term, stakeholder orientation and employees already have strong information-sharing, consultation, and codecision rights.

Sixth, IR scholars have tended to focus on the implications of IR structures and processes for employer, worker, and union outcomes. To the extent that broader outcomes have been considered, economic outcomes such as inflation and productivity growth have received primacy. A new institutionalist IR would focus more on societal outcomes. These would include the outcomes addressed by IR scholars but would ultimately entail a focus on the implications of work and employment institutions for principles normally associated with an advanced democratic society, such as dignity and freedom, fairness and equality, and representation and voice (Godard 2003b).

Finally, IR scholars have increasingly come to downplay the importance of power and conflict both in explaining the development of institutional arrangements relevant to IR and in accounting for the implications of these arrangements at a particular point in time. A new institutionalist IR would be grounded in an explicit understanding of underlying labor–capital conflicts and the role of institutions in shaping the nature and manifestation of these conflicts (Godard 1998, 2004a). In this latter regard, it would proceed from a theoretical realist perspective (Bhaskar 1975; Sayer 2002), one that recognized that although such conflicts may be largely unobservable at any particular point in time, they are important to understanding the structure and functioning of established arrangements in IR (see Godard 1993, 1994).

The Prospects for a New Institutionalist Industrial Relations

The development of a new institutionalist IR would be neither entirely new nor entirely foreign to IR as a field. Some of the work of the Wisconsin school—most notably Perlman's *A Theory of the Labor Movement* (1928)—proceeded from similar assumptions and indeed may have been an important precursor to the new institutionalism (Van de Ven 1993). Similarly, Dunlop's (1993) systems theory, with its identification of the "web of rules" as the core subject matter of IR, may be viewed as consistent with the new institutionalism. So may John R. Commons's (1934) emphasis on rules as the foundation of economies (see Kaufman 2003). In addition, there have been explicit attempts to address the importance of broader institutional environments in some of the comparative IR literature (e.g., Poole 1986). Thus, the development of a new institutionalist IR would serve more to extend than to break with the prior traditions of IR as a field of study. Indeed, it may be compatible with the research program (although not the assumptions) of the new IR, because it provides a basis for extending this program to study variation in employment practices and the outcomes associated with them.

Moreover, IR has figured prominently in the new institutionalist literature. This has been especially true with regard to labor movements—which are seen as playing a critical role in the historical development of economic, social, and political institutions—and collective bargaining, with important implications for the functioning of different production and political regimes (see Thelen 2002). A new institutionalist IR would thus bring much of this literature into the mainstream of the field.

It follows that the field of IR should be conducive to the development of a new institutionalism in the study of work and employment relations along the lines proposed in this chapter. Yet, like any alternative orientation, perspective, or paradigm, the variant of new institutionalism proposed in this chapter can be argued to suffer from a number of weaknesses. For example, one can argue that it underestimates the importance of economic and technological forces relative to their institutional counterparts, as reflected in current pressures to adopt market reforms in some coordinated marked economies (especially Germany and Japan); that it tends to be historically deterministic and hence does not sufficiently allow for agency (Hay and Wincott 1998); that it fails to incorporate the importance of either international regimes or differences in countries' locations within these regimes (see Haworth and Hughes 2003); and that it fails to address regional differences within nations (see Thompson, Rose, and Smith 2003). But these are matters for debate[7] and in any case largely involve differences in emphasis. The new institutionalism proposed here can be seen at minimum as establishing a basis for analyzing the institutional sources of variation in industrial relations and their implications for societal performance. The question is not whether all other sources of variation should be disregarded but rather the extent to which institutional explanations should be given primacy over these sources, either because they have greater explanatory power per se or because they are more interesting and relevant. Much may depend on what one is attempting to explain and what one considers interesting and relevant. Nonetheless, the underlying argument of this paper has been that increased focus on the broader institutional environment of work and employment relations may be critical to moving the field forward.

The main barriers to the development of a new institutionalist IR may be more institutional than theoretical. In particular, this development would require a major reorientation and, potentially, a realignment away from the field's traditional affiliation with economics and, more recently, industrial and organizational psychology, toward an affiliation with socioeconomics and comparative political economy. The extent to which such a realignment is possible and what its practical implications for the field might be are beyond the purpose of this paper.[8] However, in view of the field's current condition in North America, such realignment would likely do little harm and could even result in a rebirth of the field, a rebirth that would be largely consistent with the field's initial development.[9]

In reality, however, it is unlikely that a new institutionalism is likely to displace established approaches to IR, at least in the near future. One

reason is that these approaches have themselves become institutionalized, and it is unlikely that many of those wedded to them will be willing
or able to switch. Another is that although the new institutionalism has a
great deal to contribute to the field, its main contribution has to do with
broader issues of economy and society. It may have less to offer with
regard to many of the narrower, more focused topics that continue to
form an important part of the field (e.g., grievance arbitration). But it
could at minimum help to broaden the field's scope and relevance and,
ideally, frame ongoing research on narrower topics, encouraging greater
sensitivity toward broader institutional conditions and how they matter.

Conclusions

In this chapter, I have argued that the new IR has served to reorient
and broaden the field, to focus on changes in work and HRM practices
that have come to be associated with the pressures of globalization.
However, this literature has tended to underestimate the extent to
which diversity remains across and within capitalist economies, a problem that reflects the tendency of the field to isolate the study of work
and employment from the broader institutional environments and traditions within which they are embedded. The new institutionalist literature provides an ideal basis for addressing this problem. To this end, I
have proposed the development of a new institutionalist IR, one that
draws on but goes beyond this literature. This will ideally help to revital-
ize the field and restore its place within the social sciences.

Notes

[1] In confronting these forces, firms and nations are believed to face a choice
between a low-cost, low-commitment strategy and a high-quality, high-commitment
strategy, the latter of which is associated with more flexible, "high-performance"
practices and is widely advocated on the grounds that it yields advantages for
employers, employees, and unions (e.g., Kochan and Osterman 1994; Rubinstein and
Kochan 2001; Locke 1995). But there is really only one rational choice to make.

[2] Locke and Thelen (1995) provided a fascinating and valuable account of how
the "identities" of labor movements have shaped their responses to the developments
of the past few decades and the implications this has had for cross-national differences in restructuring. As Locke is associated with the new IR, this may be seen as
an exception to the argument in this section. However, even this analysis seems to
suggest that union identities serve mostly as irrational "sticking points" (p. 361) and
implies a longer-term convergence. It also does not address how broader institutional
environments shape the interests and strategies of either unions or employers or why
divergence may be rational.

[3] Frenkel and Kuruvilla (2002) refer to logics in their analysis of changing employment relations in Asian countries. Though similar in approach, they limit their conception to the logics adhered to by IR actors, not to any broader institutional logics of the sort envisaged under the varieties of capitalism approach.

[4] Specifically, rather than grant political rights, the state granted social rights in order to maintain social cohesion and economic cooperation, granting specific privileges to those groups whose cooperation was deemed most critical. These rights supported the evolution over time of cooperative, trust-based production regimes and the development of powerful mechanisms of economic coordination.

[5] Many of the employment practices associated with the high-performance model may be superfluous, either because they are already well established in some form through regulatory institutions and laws or because they address cooperation problems that are not of serious importance. There also may be important barriers to their adoption, thus requiring that the high-performance model be adopted incrementally over time rather than as a radical innovation. In Germany, for example, a strong vocational skill system militates against the cross-training and job switching needed for a full teamwork model (Streeck 1996). Thus, although the German system may be more conducive to high-performance practices, institutional differences mean that a very different version of the high-performance model may be required.

[6] To be fair, much of the earlier work of these authors is infused with an analysis of the roles of interests, power, and conflict (see especially Hall 1986), so this may reflect the focus of the Hall and Soskice (2001) volume on establishing the importance of complementarities and differing economic logics.

[7] Papers in a volume edited by Yamamura and Streeck (2003) address some of these possible limitations, especially the importance of broader economic and technological forces and differences in nations' locations within international regimes. In particular, see the papers by Gould and Krasner (2003) and by Katzenstein (2003).

[8] One particular problem has to do with the location of most IR scholars in business schools and the expectation that they can teach courses in organizational behavior and HRM. However, adoption of the approach suggested here could position them not only to infuse new life into these areas but also to teach courses in business and society and international business as well as IR.

[9] One particularly fruitful option would be for mainstream IR scholars to affiliate with the Society for the Advancement of Socio-Economics (SASE). This association already includes IR and HRM streams, but its primary distinction is its domination by new institutionalists from both economic sociology and political studies. Many of the authors cited in this paper are members. It could thus provide a fertile ground for development of a new institutionalist approach to IR. What makes it especially attractive is that it is truly international in its membership, with its annual meetings alternating between European and North American locations. Thus, it allows more comparative analysis than typically occurs in national IR meetings.

References

Armour, John, Simon Deakin, and Suzanne Konzelmann. 2003. "Shareholder Primacy and the Trajectory of UK Corporate Governance." *British Journal of Industrial Relations,* Vol. 41, no. 3, pp. 531–56.

Auer, Peter, and Sandrine Cazes. 2000. "The Resilience of the Long Term Employment Relationship." *International Labour Review,* Vol. 139, no. 4, pp. 379–408.

Baccaro, Lucio. 2003. "What Is Alive and What Is Dead in the Theory of Corporatism?" *British Journal of Industrial Relations,* Vol. 41, no. 4, pp. 683–706.

Bennis, Warren. 1967. "The Coming Death of Bureaucracy." *Management Review,* Vol. 56, pp. 19–24.

Berger, Suzanne, and Ronald Dore, eds. 1996. *National Diversity and Global Capitalism.* Ithaca, NY: Cornell University Press.

Bhaskar, Roy. 1975. *A Realist Theory of Science.* Leeds: Leeds Books.

Blyth, Mark. 2003. "Same As It Never Was: Temporality and Typology in the Varieties of Capitalism." *Comparative European Politics,* Vol. 1, no. 2, pp. 205–26.

Boix, Charles. 1998. *Political Parties, Growth, and Equality.* Cambridge: Cambridge University Press.

Booth, Alison, Juan Dolado, and Jeff Frank. 2002. "Symposium on Temporary Work." *Economic Journal,* Vol. 112, no. 480, pp. 181–89.

Bruce, Peter. 1989. "Political Parties and Labor Legislation in Canada and the U.S." *Industrial Relations,* Vol. 28, no. 2, pp. 115–41.

Cappelli, Peter. 1999. *The New Deal at Work.* Boston: Harvard Business School Press.

Cappelli, Peter, Harry Katz, David Knoke, Paul Osterman, and Michael Useem. 1997. *Change at Work.* New York: Oxford University Press.

Carley, Mark. 2003. "Collective Bargaining Coverage and Extension Procedures." *EIRO Observer,* no. 2/03, pp. 13–20.

Casper, Steven. 2001. "The Legal Framework for Corporate Governance: The Influence of Contract Law on Company Strategies in Germany and the United States." In Peter Hall and David Soskice, eds., *Varieties of Capitalism: The Institutional Foundations of Comparative Advantage,* Oxford: Oxford University Press, pp. 387–416.

Commons, John R. 1924. *Legal Foundations of Capitalism.* New York: Macmillan.

———. 1934. *Institutional Economics.* New York: Macmillan.

———. 1961. *Institutional Economics: Its Place in Political Economy.* Madison, WI: University of Wisconsin Press.

Crouch, Colin. 1993. *Industrial Relations and European State Traditions.* Oxford: Oxford University Press.

———. 2003. "Review of *Varieties of Capitalism.*" *British Journal of Industrial Relations,* Vol. 41, no. 2, pp. 359–61.

Crouch, Colin, and Wolfgang Streeck, eds. 1997. *Political Economy of Modern Capitalism.* London: Sage.

Delaney, John, and John Godard. 2001. "An IR Perspective on the High Performance Paradigm." *Human Resource Management Review,* Vol. 11, pp. 395–429.

Dobbin, Frank R., Lauren Edelman, John Meyer, and W. Richard Scott. 1993. "Equal Opportunity Law and the Construction of Internal Labor Markets." *American Journal of Sociology,* Vol. 99, pp. 396–427.

Dobbin, Frank R., Lauren Edelman, John Meyer, W. Richard Scott, and Ann Swidler. 1988. "The Expansion of Due Process in Organizations." In Lynn Zucker, ed., *Institutional Patterns and Organizations,* Cambridge, MA: Ballinger, pp. 71–100.

Dore, Ronald. 1997. "The Distinctiveness of Japan." In Colin Crouch and Wolfgang Streeck, eds., *Political Economy of Modern Capitalism,* London: Sage, pp. 19–32.

————. 2000a. *Stock Market Capitalism: Welfare Capitalism*. Oxford: Oxford University Press.

————. 2000b. "West Meets East: Will Japan Convert to Capitalism?" *Centre Piece: The Magazine of Economic Performance*, Vol. 3, no. 3, pp. 23–31.

Doremus, Paul N., William Keller, Louis Pauly, and Simon Reich. 1998. *The Myth of the Global Corporation*. Princeton, NJ: Princeton University Press.

Dunlop, John. 1993. *Industrial Relations Systems*, rev. ed. Boston: Harvard Business School Press.

Edelman, Lauren. 1990. "Legal Environments and Organizational Governance: The Expansion of Due Process in the American Workplace." *American Journal of Sociology*, Vol. 95, no. 6, pp. 1401–40.

EPOC Research Group. 1997. *New Forms of Work Organisation: Can Europe Realise Its Potential?* Dublin: European Foundation for the Improvement of Living and Working Conditions.

Esping-Andersen, Gosta. 1999. *Social Foundations of Postindustrial Economies*. Oxford: Oxford University Press.

Estevez-Abe, Margarita, Torben Iversen, and David Soskice. 2001. "Social Protection and Skill Formation: A Reinterpretation of the Welfare State." In Peter Hall and David Soskice, eds., *Varieties of Capitalism: The Institutional Foundations of Comparative Advantage*, Oxford: Oxford University Press, pp. 145–83.

European Foundation for the Improvement of Living and Working Conditions. [2003]. "Deal Reached on First National Cross-Sector Agreement for Temporary Agency Work." EIRO (European Industrial Relations Observatory On-Line). <http://www.eiro.eurofound.ie/2003/03/InBrief/DE0303202N.html.>

Frege, Carola. 2004. "The Discourse of Industrial Democracy: Germany and the United States." Paper presented at the Annual Meeting of the Industrial Relations Research Association (San Diego, CA, 3–5 January 2004).

Frenkel, Stephen, and Sarosh Kuruvilla. 2002. "Logics of Action, Globalization, and Changing Employment Relations in China, India, Malaysia, and the Philippines." *Industrial and Labor Relations Review*, Vol. 55, no. 3, pp. 387–412.

Godard, John. 1993. "IR Theory and Method: Modernist and Post-Modernist Alternatives." In Roy Adams and Noah Meltz, eds., *Industrial Relations Theory: Its Nature, Scope, and Pedagogy*, Metuchen, NJ: IMLR Press/Rutgers University and Scarecrow Press, pp. 283–306.

————. 1994. "Beyond Empiricism: Towards a Reconstruction of IR Theory and Research." In David Lewin and Donna Sockell, eds., *Advances in Industrial and Labor Relations*, Vol. 6, Greenwich, CT: JAI Press, pp. 1–35.

————. 1997. "Managerial Strategies, Labour and Employment Relations, and the State." *British Journal of Industrial Relations*, Vol. 35, no. 2, pp. 399–426.

————. 1998. "An Organizational Theory of Variation in the Management of Labor." In David Lewin and Bruce Kaufman, eds., *Advances in Industrial and Labor Relations*, Vol. 8, Greenwich, CT: JAI Press, pp. 25–66.

————. 2002. "Institutional Environments, Employer Practices, and States in Liberal Market Economies." *Industrial Relations*, Vol. 41, no. 2 (April), pp. 249–86.

————. 2003a. "Do Labor Laws Matter? The Density Decline and Convergence Thesis Revisited." *Industrial Relations*, Vol. 42, no. 3, pp. 458–92.

————. 2003b. "Labour Unions, Workplace Rights, and Canadian Public Policy." *Canadian Public Policy*, Vol. 29, no. 4, pp. 449–67.

————. 2004a. "A Critical Assessment of the High Performance Paradigm." *British Journal of Industrial Relations,* Vol. 42, no. 2, pp. 349–78.

————. 2004b. *Trade Union Recognition: Statutory Unfair Practice Regimes in the USA and Canada.* Employment Relations Research Series No. 29. London: Department of Trade and Industry, U.K. Government.

————. 2004c. "The U.S. and Canadian Labour Movements: Markets vs. States and Societies." In Geoffrey Wood and Mark Harcourt, eds., *Trade Unions and the Crisis of Democracy: Strategies and Perspectives,* Manchester: Manchester University Press, pp. 105–45.

Godard, John, and John Delaney. 2000. "Reflections on the High Performance Paradigm's Implications for IR as a Field." *Industrial and Labor Relations Review,* Vol. 53, no. 2, pp. 482–502.

Golden, Miriam, Michael Wallerstein, and Peter Lange. 1999. "Postwar Trade Union Organization and Industrial Relations in Twelve Countries." In Herbert Kitschelt, Peter Lange, Gary Marks, and John D. Stephens, eds., *Continuity and Change in Contemporary Capitalism,* Cambridge: Cambridge University Press, pp. 194–230.

Goodin, Robert E. 2003. "Choose Your Capitalism?" *Comparative European Politics,* Vol. 1, no. 2, pp. 203–14.

Gospel, Howard, and Andrew Pendleton. 2003. "Finance, Corporate Governance, and the Management of Labour." *British Journal of Industrial Relations,* Vol. 41, no. 3, pp. 557–82.

Gould, Erica, and Stephen D. Krasner. 2003. "Germany and Japan: Binding vs. Autonomy." In Kozo Yamamura and Wolfgang Streeck, *The End of Diversity? Prospects for German and Japanese Capitalism,* Ithaca, NY: Cornell University Press, pp. 51–88.

Hall, Peter. 1984. "Patterns of State Policy: An Organizational Approach." In S. Bornstein, D. Held, and J. Krieger, eds., *The State in Capitalist Europe,* London: Unwin Hyman.

————. 1986. *Governing the Economy: The Politics of State Intervention in Britain and France.* Cambridge: Polity Press.

————. 1993. "Policy Paradigms, Social Learning, and the State: The Case of Economic Policy Making in Britain." *Comparative Politics,* Vol. 25 (April), pp. 275–96.

Hall, Peter, and Daniel Gingerich. 2001. "Varieties of Capitalism and Institutional Complementarities in the Macroeconomy: An Empirical Analysis." Paper presented at the Annual Meeting of the American Political Science Association (San Francisco, CA, August 2001).

Hall, Peter, and David Soskice. 2001. "An Introduction to Varieties of Capitalism." In Peter Hall and David Soskice, eds., *Varieties of Capitalism: The Institutional Foundations of Comparative Advantage,* Oxford: Oxford University Press, pp. 1–68.

Hall, Peter, and Rosemary Taylor. 1996. "Political Science and the Three New Institutionalisms." *Political Studies,* Vol. 44, pp. 936–57.

————. 1998. "The Potential of Historical Institutionalism: A Response to Hay and Wincott." *Political Studies,* Vol. 46, pp. 898–902.

Hancke, Bob, and Steven Casper. 1999. "Reproducing Diversity: ISO 9000 and Work Organization in the French and German Car Industry." In Sigrid Clack, Glenn

Morgan, and Richard Whitely, eds., *National Capitalisms, Global Competition, and Economic Performance*, Amsterdam: John Benjamins, pp. 173–90.

Haworth, Nigel, and Stephen Hughes. 2003. "International Political Economy and Industrial Relations." *British Journal of Industrial Relations*, Vol. 41, no. 4, pp. 665–82.

Hay, Colin, and Daniel Wincott. 1998. "Structure, Agency, and Historical Institutionalism." *Political Studies*, Vol. 46, pp. 951–57.

Hofstede, Geert. 1980. *Culture's Consequences: International Differences in Work-Related Values*. Beverly Hills, CA: Sage.

Hollingsworth, J. Rogers, Karl H. Muller, and Ellen Jane Hollingsworth, eds. 2002. *Advancing Socio-economics: An Institutionalist Perspective*. Latham, MD: Bowman and Littlefield.

Hutton, Will. 2002. *The World We're In*. London: Little Brown.

Ichniowski, C., Thomas Kochan, David Levine, Craig Olson, and George Strauss. 1996. "What Works at Work." *Industrial Relations*, Vol. 35, no. 3, pp. 299–333.

Iversen, Torben, and Jonas Pontusson. 2000. "Comparative Political Economy: A Northern European Perspective." In Torben Iversen, Jonas Pontusson, and David Soskice, eds., *Unions, Employers, and Central Banks*, Cambridge: Cambridge University Press, pp. 1–37.

Iversen, Torben, Jonas Pontusson, and David Soskice, eds. 2000. *Unions, Employers, and Central Banks*. Cambridge: Cambridge University Press.

Jacoby, Sanford. 1991. "American Exceptionalism Revisited: The Importance of Management." In Sanford Jacoby, ed., *Masters to Managers*, New York: Columbia University Press, pp. 173–200.

———. 1997. *Modern Manners: Welfare Capitalism since the New Deal*. Princeton: Princeton University Press.

———. 1999. "Melting into Thin Air? Downsizing, Job Stability, and the Future of Work." *Chicago-Kent Law Review*, Vol. 75, pp. 1195–234.

Katz, Harry. 1993. "The Decentralization of Collective Bargaining: A Literature Review and Comparative Analysis." *Industrial and Labor Relations Review*, Vol. 47, no. 1, pp. 3–22.

Katz, Harry, and Owen Darbishire. 2000. *Converging Divergences: Worldwide Changes in Employment Systems*. Ithaca: Cornell University Press.

Katzenstein, Peter J. 2003. "Regional States: Japan and Asia, Germany and Europe." In Kozo Yamamura and Wolfgang Streeck, *The End of Diversity? Prospects for German and Japanese Capitalism*, Ithaca, NY: Cornell University Press, pp. 89–114.

Kaufman, Bruce. 1996. "Why the Wagner Act? Re-establishing Contact with Its Original Purpose." In David Lewin, Bruce Kaufman, and Donna Sockell, eds., *Advances in Industrial and Labor Relations*, Vol. 7, Greenwich, CT: JAI Press, pp. 15–68.

———. 2003. "The Organization of Economic Activity: Insights from the Institutional Theory of John R. Commons." *Journal of Economic Behavior and Organization*, Vol. 52, pp. 71–96.

Kelly, John. 1998. *Rethinking Industrial Relations*. London: Routledge/LSE.

Kern, H., and M. Schuman. 1985. *The End of the Division of Labor*. Munich: Beck.

Kerr, Clark, John Dunlop, Frederick Harbison, and Charles Myers. 1960. *Industrialism and Industrial Man*. New York: Oxford University Press.

King, Desmond, and Bo Rothstein. 1993. "Institutional Choices and Labor Market Policy." *Comparative Political Studies*, Vol. 26 (July), pp. 147–77.

King, Desmond, and Stewart Wood. 1999. "The Political Economy of Neoliberalism: Britain and the United States in the 1980s." In Herbert Kitschelt, Peter Lange, Gary Marks, and John D. Stephens, eds., *Continuity and Change in Contemporary Capitalism*, Cambridge: Cambridge University Press, pp. 371–97.

Kitschelt, Herbert, Peter Lange, Gary Marks, and John D. Stephens, eds. 1999. *Continuity and Change in Contemporary Capitalism*. Cambridge: Cambridge University Press.

Knight, J. 1992. *Institutions and Social Conflict*. Cambridge: Cambridge University Press.

Kochan, Thomas, Harry Katz, and Robert McKersie. 1986. *The Transformation of American Industrial Relations*. New York: Basic Books.

Kochan, Thomas, and Paul Osterman. 1994. *The Mutual Gains Enterprise*. Boston, MA: Harvard Business School Press.

Kuhn, Thomas. 1962. *The Structure of Scientific Revolutions*. Chicago: University of Chicago Press.

Kuruvilla, Sarosh, and Christopher Erickson. 2002. "Change and Transformation in Asian Industrial Relations." *Industrial Relations*, Vol. 41, no. 2, pp. 171–227.

Lakatos, I. 1978. "The Methodology of Scientific Research Paradigms." In J. Worrall and G. Currie, eds., *Philosophical Papers*, Cambridge: Cambridge University Press.

Lane, Christel. 1989. *Management and Labour in Europe: The Industrial Enterprise in Germany, Britain, and France*. Aldershot, UK: Edward Elgar.

———. 1995. *Industry and Society in Europe: Stability and Change in Britain, Germany, and France*. Aldershot, UK: Edward Elgar.

Lehmbruch, Gerhard. 2001. "The Institutional Embedding of Market Economies: The German 'Model' and Its Impact on Japan." In Wolfgang Streeck and Kozo Yamamura, eds., *The Origins of Nonliberal Capitalism: Germany and Japan in Comparison*, Ithaca, NY: Cornell University Press, pp. 39–93.

Lindberg, Leon, and John L. Campbell. 1991. "The State and the Organization of Economic Activity." In John L. Campbell, J. Rogers Hollingsworth, and Leon Lindberg, eds., *Governance of the American Economy*, Cambridge: Cambridge University Press, pp. 356–95.

Locke, Richard. 1995. "The Transformation of Industrial Relations? A Cross-National Review." In Kirsten Wever and Lowell Turner, eds., *The Comparative Political Economy of Industrial Relations*, Madison, WI: IRRA, pp. 9–32.

Locke, Richard, and Thomas Kochan. 1995. "Conclusion. The Transformation of Industrial Relations? A Cross-National Review of the Evidence." In Richard Locke, Thomas Kochan, and Michael Piore, eds., *Employment Relations in a Changing World Economy*, Cambridge, MA: MIT Press, pp. 359–84.

Locke, Richard, and Kathleen Thelen. 1995. "Apples and Oranges Revisited: Contextualized Comparisons and the Study of Comparative Labor Politics." *Politics and Society*, Vol. 23, no. 3, pp. 337–67.

Manow, Phillip. 2001. "Welfare State Building and Coordinated Capitalism in Japan and Germany." In Wolfgang Streeck and Kozo Yamamura, eds., *The Origins of Nonliberal Capitalism*, Ithaca, NY: Cornell University Press, pp. 94–120.

March, James, and Johan Olsen. 1989. *Rediscovering Institutions: The Organizational Basis of Politics.* New York: Free Press.

Mares, Isabela. 2001. "Firms and the Welfare State: When, Why, and How Does Social Policy Matter to Employers?" In Peter Hall and David Soskice, eds., *Varieties of Capitalism: The Institutional Foundations of Comparative Advantage,* Oxford: Oxford University Press, pp. 184–212.

Nicoletti, Giuseppe, Stephano Scarpetta, and Olivier Boylaud. 2000. "Summary Indicators of Product Market Regulation with an Extension to Employment Protection Legislation." Economics Dept. Working Paper No. 226. Paris: Organisation for Economic Co-operation and Development.

North, Douglass. 1990. *Institutions and Institutional Change.* Cambridge: Cambridge University Press.

Olsen, Gregg. 2002. *The Politics of the Welfare State: Canada, Sweden, and the United States.* Don Mills, ON: Oxford University Press.

Organisation for Economic Co-operation and Development. 2002. *OECD Employment Index, Statistical Abstract.* Paris: Organisation for Economic Co-operation and Development.

———. [2004]. "Labour Market Statistics—Data." *Corporate Data Environment.* <http://www1.oecd.org/scripts/cde/members/lfsdataauthenticate.asp> [2004].

Perlman, Selig. 1928. *A Theory of the Labor Movement.* New York: Augustus Kelley.

Pierson, Paul, and Theda Skocpol. 2002. "Historical Institutionalism in Contemporary Political Science." In Izra Katznelson and Helen Milner, eds., *Political Science: The State of the Discipline,* New York: Norton, pp. 693–721.

Piore, Michael, and Charles Sabel. 1984. *The Second Industrial Divide.* New York: Basic Books.

Poole, Michael. 1986. *Industrial Relations: Origins and Patterns of National Diversity.* London: Routledge and Kegan Paul.

Rubinstein, S., and T. Kochan. 2001. *Learning from Saturn.* Ithaca, NY: Cornell University Press.

Sayer, Andrew. 2002. *Realism and Social Science.* London: Sage.

Scott, W. Richard. 1995. *Institutions and Organizations.* Thousand Oaks, CA: Sage.

Soskice, David. 1990. "Wage Determination: The Changing Role of Institutions in Advanced Industrialized Countries." *Oxford Review of Economic Policy,* Vol. 6, no. 4, pp. 36–61.

———. 1999. "Divergent Production Regimes: Coordinated and Uncoordinated Market Economies in the 1980s and 1990s." In Herbert Kitschelt, Peter Lange, Gary Marks, and John D. Stephens, eds., *Continuity and Change in Contemporary Capitalism,* Cambridge: Cambridge University Press, pp. 101–34.

Streeck, Wolfgang. 1992. "Productive Constraints: On the Institutional Conditions of Diversified Quality Production." In Wolfgang Streeck, ed., *Social Institutions and Economic Performance,* London: Sage, pp. 1–40.

———. 1996. "Lean Production in the German Automobile Industry: A Test Case for Convergence Theory." In Suzanne Berger and Ronald Dore, eds., *National Diversity and Global Capitalism,* Ithaca, NY: Cornell University Press, pp. 138–70.

———. 1997. "German Capitalism. Does It Exist? Can It Survive?" In Colin Crouch and Wolfgang Streeck, eds., *Political Economy of Modern Capitalism,* London: Sage, pp. 33–54.

Supiot, Alain. 2001. *Beyond Employment: Changes in Work and the Future of Labour Laws in Europe.* Oxford: Oxford University Press.

Swank, Duane. 2002. *Global Capital, Political Institutions, and Policy Change in Developed Welfare States.* Cambridge: Cambridge University Press.

Swenson, Peter. 1989. *Fair Shares: Unions, Pay, and Politics in Sweden and West Germany.* Ithaca, NY: Cornell University Press.

Swenson, Peter, and Jonas Pontusson. 2000. "The Swedish Employer Offensive against Centralized Bargaining." In Torben Iversen, Jonas Pontusson, and David Soskice, eds., *Unions, Employers, and Central Banks,* Cambridge: Cambridge University Press, pp. 77–106.

Swift, Adam. 2001. *Political Philosophy.* London: Polity.

Taras, Daphne. 1997. "Collective Bargaining Regulation in Canada and the United States: Divergent Cultures, Divergent Outcomes." In Bruce Kaufman, ed., *Government Regulation of the Employment Relation,* Madison, WI: IRRA, pp. 295–342.

Thelen, Kathleen. 1991. *Union of Parts: Labour Politics in Postwar Germany.* Ithaca, NY: Cornell University Press.

———. 2000. "Why German Employers Cannot Bring Themselves to Dismantle the German Model." In Torben Iversen, Jonas Pontusson, and David Soskice, eds., *Unions, Employers, and Central Banks,* Cambridge: Cambridge University Press, pp. 138–72.

———. 2001. "Varieties of Labor Politics in the Developed Democracies." In Peter Hall and David Soskice, eds., *Varieties of Capitalism: The Institutional Foundations of Comparative Advantage,* Oxford: Oxford University Press, pp. 71–103.

———. 2002. "The Political Economy of Business and Labor in the Developed Democracies." In Izra Katznelson and Helen Milner, eds., *Political Science: the State of the Discipline,* New York: Norton, pp. 371–403.

Thompson, Mark, Joe Rose, and Anthony Smith, eds. 2003. *Beyond the National Divide? Regional Dimensions of Industrial Relations.* Montreal: McGill–Queen's Press.

Toffler, Alvin. 1972. *Future Shock.* New York: Bantam Books.

Traxler, Franz. 2003. "Bargaining, State Regulation, and the Trajectories of Industrial Relations." *European Journal of Industrial Relations,* Vol. 9, no. 2, pp. 141–62.

Turner, Lowell. 1991. *Democracy at Work. Changing World Markets and the Future of Labor Unions.* Ithaca, NY: Cornell University Press.

Van de Ven, Andrew. 1993. "The Institutional Theory of John R. Commons: A Review and Commentary." *Academy of Management Review,* Vol. 18, pp. 139–52.

Visser, Jelle, and Anton Hemerijck. 1997. *A Dutch Miracle: Job Growth, Welfare Reform, and Corporatism in the Netherlands.* Amsterdam: Amsterdam University Press.

Vitols, Sigurt. 2001a. "Varieties of Corporate Governance: Comparing Germany and the UK." In Peter Hall and David Soskice, eds., 2001. *Varieties of Capitalism: The Institutional Foundations of Comparative Advantage,* Oxford: Oxford University Press, pp. 337–60.

———. 2001b. "Welfare State Building and Coordinated Capitalism in Japan and Germany." In Wolfgang Streeck and Kozo Yamamura, eds., *The Origins of Nonliberal Capitalism: Germany and Japan in Comparison,* Ithaca, NY: Cornell University Press, pp. 171–99.

Weingast, Barry R. 2002. "Rational Choice Institutionalism." In Izra Katznelson and Helen Milner, eds., *Political Science: The State of the Discipline,* New York: Norton, pp. 660–92.

Weiss, Linda. 1993. "War, the State, and the Origins of the Japanese Employment System." *Politics and Society,* Vol. 21, no. 3, pp. 325–54.

Whitley, Richard. 1996. "The Social Construction of Economic Actors: Institutions and Types of Firm in Europe and Other Market Economies." In Richard Whitley and Peer Hull Kristensen, eds., *The Changing European Firm,* London: Routledge, pp. 39–66.

Wood, Stephen, and John Godard. 1999. "The Statutory Union Recognition Procedure in the Employment Relations Bill: A Comparative Analysis." *British Journal of Industrial Relations,* Vol. 37, no. 2 (March), pp. 203–45.

Wood, Stewart. 2001. "Business, Government, and Patterns of Labor Market Policy in Britain and the Federal Republic of Germany." In Peter Hall and David Soskice, eds., *Varieties of Capitalism: The Institutional Foundations of Comparative Advantage,* Oxford: Oxford University Press, pp. 247–74.

Woodward, Joanne. 1965. *Industrial Organisation: Theory and Practice.* London: Oxford University Press.

Yamamura, Kozo, and Wolfgang Streeck. 2003. *The End of Diversity? Prospects for German and Japanese Capitalism.* Ithaca, NY: Cornell University Press.

CHAPTER 9

Is Industrial Relations Theory Always Ethnocentric?

RICHARD HYMAN
London School of Economics

Let me begin with a preliminary explanation of the question that frames this chapter. To provide this it is necessary to begin, a little perversely, with some conclusions. These are drawn from my attempts to explore the relationship between theory and industrial relations over more than 30 years. This journey of exploration has led me to focus on problems of analysis and explanation that are usually neglected or marginalized in the industrial relations literature. Therefore, my principal purpose here is to illustrate why it is important to recognize the national embeddedness of our understandings of our field of study.

Conclusion 1: It Is Futile to Seek a Theory of Industrial Relations

"Facts have outrun ideas. Integrating theory has lagged far behind expanding experience" (Dunlop 1958:vi). Dunlop's eloquent appeal for greater theoretical coherence still resonates after almost half a century, but his project to construct a self-contained theory of industrial relations was flawed, for at least three reasons.

The first, which was the central concern of radical critics (including me) in the 1970s, was Dunlop's effort to interpret industrial relations through the systems theory of Talcott Parsons. His industrial relations system was a well-oiled machine, in which the different "actors" performed complementary roles, their pragmatic bias toward order and cooperation cemented by an "ideology" that treated conflict as pathological. Systems theory of this kind was fundamentally defective. It failed to appreciate that work and employment represent a field of tension, the intersection of contradictory social forces, where order and stability are always to some degree precarious. Typically, it also exaggerated the self-sustaining structural logic of the "system" while neglecting the importance of the experiences, aspirations, and initiatives of the human "actors" whose behavior represents and reproduces the reality of industrial relations.

Yet does this mean that an alternative theory of industrial relations is possible, one that avoids the deficiencies of Dunlop's model? My answer today would be no, for the second problem with Dunlop's effort was his assumption that a field of study that had evolved over the decades in an ad hoc fashion, responding to the pragmatic requirements of governments and managements rather than to any underlying intellectual rationale, could be given analytical coherence after the event. Consider the terms of reference of the Commission on Industrial Relations established by the U.S. Congress in 1912, the first occasion when the term *industrial relations* came into prominent public use:[1]

> The commission shall inquire into the general condition of labor in the principal industries of the United States including agriculture, and especially in those which are carried on in corporate forms; into existing relations between employers and employees; into the effect of industrial conditions on public welfare and into the rights and powers of the community to deal therewith; into the conditions of sanitation and safety of employees and the provisions for protecting the life, limb, and health of the employees; into the growth of associations of employers and of wage earners and the effect of such associations upon the relations between employers and employees; into the extent and results of methods of collective bargaining; into any methods which have been tried in any State or in foreign countries for maintaining mutually satisfactory relations between employees and employers; into methods for avoiding or adjusting labor disputes through peaceful and conciliatory mediation and negotiations; into the scope, methods, and resources of existing bureaus of labor and into possible ways of increasing their usefulness; into the question of smuggling or other illegal entry of Asiatics into the United States or its insular possessions, and of the methods by which such Asiatics have gained and are gaining such admission, and shall report to Congress as speedily as possible with such recommendations as said commission may think proper to prevent such smuggling and illegal entry. The commission shall seek to discover the underlying causes of dissatisfaction in the industrial situation and report its conclusions thereon.

The elements in this catalog, to which the not very meaningful label "industrial relations" was attached, reflected the practical concerns of public policy in a particular time and place, not the principles of any academic discipline. Yet a field of study that lacks an *analytical* basis for what it includes and excludes cannot belatedly be given theoretical underpinnings as a kind of intellectual sticking plaster (Hyman 1994:166).

This links to the third deficiency: the treatment of industrial relations as a largely self-contained sphere of social life. The premise of the idea of industrial relations theory is that the "industrial relations system" operates primarily in response to its endogenous laws of motion, its intrinsic principles and logic. In reality, such neat demarcations do not exist. We cannot understand work and employment unless we also have a theoretical understanding of the economy, of the law, of politics, of education, of the community, of gender relations. . . . Of course, few social analysts can aspire to theoretical insight that is both extensive and intensive; most of us are forced to specialize. But unless we are receptive to theories generated to explain other aspects of social life, our explanations of our own field of specialism will be inadequate.

Hence I conclude that while we certainly require theory *in* industrial relations, it is neither possible nor desirable to pursue a self-contained theory *of* industrial relations. To be persuasive, our theoretical efforts need to be founded in a different matrix.

Conclusion 2: We Need a Theory of Theory

What do we *mean* by a theory of/in industrial relations? It is ironic that most of those who have called for greater theoretical self-consciousness have not applied this principle to their own theoretical discussion. In the main, it is either taken for granted that we can recognize a theory when we see one, or else it is assumed that the only kind of theory is the hypothetico-deductive form.

Theory is not simple to define. The *Oxford English Dictionary* identifies seven distinct meanings; the most relevant for our purposes is the following:

> a scheme or system of ideas or statements held as an explanation or account of a group of facts or phenomena; a hypothesis that has been confirmed or established by observation or experiment, and is propounded or accepted as accounting for the known facts; a statement of what are held to be general laws, principles, or causes of something known or observed.

Here, we may note, some very different conceptions are conflated: bodies of ideas, hypotheses, general laws. Which of these do industrial relations writers have in mind when they speak of theory? This is frequently unclear. Wood, Wagner, Armstrong, Goodman, and Davis (1975) claimed that Dunlop presented the theoretical status of his systems model in three very different ways; similarly, Walker (1977) suggested that three different types or levels of theory should be distinguished for the purposes of industrial relations analysis. We may perhaps infer that what is meant by theory is itself a theoretical issue.

Most industrial relations writers who have explicitly addressed the theory of theory (e.g., Adams 1993) have assumed a linear relationship between facts and theory. In one direction, an accumulation of empirical information offers the basis for generalization. With sufficient established generalizations, "middle-range" theorizing becomes feasible; ultimately, it may be possible to construct "general theory." In the other direction, higher-level theory may be used to derive lower-level hypotheses, which in turn can be tested against empirical evidence. It is commonly insisted that theory construction is essentially an additive process, that theories are either true or false, and that a single empirical counterinstance is sufficient to falsify a theory.

These "commonsense" assumptions are implausible. It is unnecessary to endorse all Kuhn's (1962) analysis of scientific paradigms to recognize that the incrementalist model of theoretical innovation is misconceived. Even in the natural sciences, theory construction rests more on creative imagination than on the step-by-step elevation of generalizations: the theorist is architect, not bricklayer. Dunlop was absolutely correct to insist that an accumulation of facts does not add up to theoretical insight. In the reverse direction, a theory does not unproblematically generate a set of hypotheses, nor is empirical testing a straightforward matter.

Falsification, which since Popper has commonly been taken as the sine qua non of sound theory, is a slippery, deceptive notion. First, we have discretion in how we define and "operationalize" the relatively abstract concepts that constitute a theory, which can thus be redefined to fit awkward facts. Second, it is not only economists whose theories contain implicit *ceteris paribus* clauses; these can be elaborated to dismiss uncomfortable empirical evidence as irrelevant. Third, there are other criteria of theoretical merit than the elusive requirement of accuracy. Przeworski and Teune (1970) suggested three, which they term *generality, parsimony,* and *causality.* Generality concerns the range of situations covered (in other words, high generality entails few *ceteris paribus* exclusions). Parsimony is an issue of simplicity and succinctness: the more elaborate a theory, the more it resembles mere empirical description masquerading as generalization. In any effort of theorization, there is a necessary trade-off between accuracy, generality, and parsimony; if total accuracy is won at too high a price in terms of generality and parsimony, a theory is little use. Causality involves a different issue: merely to posit an empirical (e.g., statistical) association between phenomena is not in itself to present a theory. Theorization involves an effort at *explanation:* offering plausible reasons *why* specific phenomena are associated. For this reason, it is possible to question whether a simple model (such as Dunlop's specification of the industrial relations system in terms of actors and contexts) should be defined as a theory. What gave Dunlop's formulation theoretical content was his addition (to my mind, implausible) of Parsons's thesis of a "common value system" and a large measure of technical determinism. In other words, what he offered was not an "industrial relations theory" but an application to industrial relations of the theoretical assumptions prevalent in contemporary functionalist sociology and economic history.

Conclusion 3: Marx Is Necessary but Insufficient

The application of Marxist analysis to the study of industrial relations was once novel, challenging, and frequently shocking. Today, the influence of Marxist ideas on the understanding of work and employment is extensive, if not always recognized.

Perhaps the most crucial insight attributable to Marx is the importance of what he termed the "hidden abode" of production. The early writers in our field—the Webbs in Britain, Commons in the United States—indeed regarded an understanding of work itself as a necessary foundation for the study of rule making through labor legislation and collective bargaining. But too often, the attempt to establish industrial relations as a respectable, self-contained academic discipline involved a one-sided exploration of the "web of rules," their construction, and their application without systematic attention to the work that was being regulated. Above all else it has been Marxists who in recent years have exposed the inadequacy of such an approach. In any society, argued Marx, people's practical activity in securing their physical existence—producing food and shelter, caring for children, and so on—and the social relationships created through such activities shape the prevailing social institutions. If this proposition is accepted, it follows that we cannot understand industrial relations unless we understand production.

A key feature of Marx's analysis was his illumination of the ambiguous character of labor itself. Under capitalism the typical worker is an employee, performing work for an employer and receiving in return a wage or salary. At first sight, what is involved is an exchange (in the "labor market") between work and wages. Not so, insisted Marx. Rarely is a worker employed to perform a precise set of tasks that can be specified in detail in advance. Rather, what workers sell through the contract of employment is their *ability* to work—as Marx termed it, their "labor power"—thereby authorizing the employer to set them to work and to assume ownership of whatever they produce. The priority of the employer is to ensure that the value of what is produced generates a surplus (as large as possible) over the wages and salaries paid plus the other requirements of production. Employees, however, have different priorities. Employers therefore need an institutional apparatus to monitor, motivate, and if necessary coerce workers into producing such a surplus. Evidently, the institutions of industrial relations can usefully be understood as elements in this apparatus.

As I have often argued in the past (Hyman 1975, 1989), Marxist analysis offers an indispensable contribution to the understanding of industrial relations. Nevertheless, it is insufficient. Much of what Marx wrote involved a high level of generality and abstraction; it must be *interpreted* if we are to apply it to the concrete phenomena of industrial relations, particularly a century and a half after he was writing, when circumstances are in some respects very different. We may guess what Marx might have thought about contemporary theories and practices of human resource management (HRM), but we can do so only by extrapolation. This inevitably involves individual, idiosyncratic judgment.

What is also obvious today is that Marx paid at best limited attention to issues that are now regarded as of considerable importance in the world of work. One such issue is gender. Marx pointed out (drawing on the experience of the British textile industry) that employers often used women workers as a form of cheap labor, but his analysis of the role of gender in labor market dynamics was undeveloped. Even less adequate was his attention to the relationship between the sexual division of labor in employment and in the household. In recent years, feminist analysis has filled many of these gaps; some would regard this analysis as complementary to Marxism, but it is not in itself Marxist. Similarly, the role of ethnic differences and divisions at work and in the labor market was considered only peripherally by Marx but is today widely recognized as an important element of industrial relations.

A different kind of limitation is the role of ideas, beliefs, social norms, and indeed language in shaping industrial relations. To a large extent, Marx downplayed such considerations; in his analysis, "ideology" was largely derivative of material forces. Today, even many Marxists would qualify this assumption. Employers, workers, union representatives all operate on the basis of a repertoire of perceptions and assumptions that help shape their course of action. As sociologists have long insisted, we all possess "vocabularies of motive" that legitimize certain goals and forms of behavior and exclude others from serious consideration. Thus, my third conclusion is that any adequate understanding of industrial relations has to encompass such "ideological" dynamics.

Conclusion 4: The Object of Inquiry Varies Cross-Nationally

The more we focus on concrete realities, the clearer it becomes that while endeavoring to generalize, we must be sensitive to difference. If "institutions matter," as is commonly argued by those who study industrial relations, then we have to take account of those national differences in institutions that overlie any commonalities deriving from the general "laws" of production. Take one simple indicator: in 2001, in the countries of the European Union, over 70% of working-age women were in employment in Denmark and Sweden, but only 40% in Greece, Italy, and Spain (European Commission 2002). We can make sense of such large differences only through a sophisticated appreciation of the interconnections among economic structure, cultural norms, and public policy. Or again, union density is under 10% in France but over 80% in Sweden. Can we assume that trade unionism *means* the same thing in the two countries or that either can be adequately understood through theories developed in Britain or the United States at a time when unionization was around 40%? Or to take a more subtle difference, whereas in English we speak of employers and employees, in the countries of northern Europe the equivalent terms translate literally as "work givers" and "work takers." Does this terminology influence attitudes and behavior, leading to distinctive industrial relations outcomes? Or when continental Europeans refer to organizations of workers and employers as "social partners," how far does this imply a basically consensual understanding of industrial relations?

At a different level of analysis, we can note that there is a rapidly expanding literature on "varieties of capitalism" (e.g., Albert 1993; Crouch and Streeck 1997; Dore 2000; Hall and Soskice 2001; Hollingsworth and Boyer 1997). At its core is the argument that markets do not exist in a social vacuum: they are social institutions that are in turn "embedded" in the broader framework of each society (Granovetter 1985). Because no two societies are identical, it follows that market economies are differentiated: for many purposes it is more appropriate to speak of capitalisms in the plural rather than the singular.

Not only are systems of production, and the rules of employment with which they are associated, socially embedded, so are the ways in which those involved *think* about industrial relations (or whether they use the term at all). In fact, the English label that most of us take for granted does not easily translate into other languages, and the alternative ways in which processes and institutions of employment regulation are defined almost certainly affect approaches to analysis. At the same time, the ways in which intellectual life is socially organized, the demarcations between disciplines, and the relationship between academic work and public policy also vary substantially cross-nationally. We industrial relations scholars cannot assume that we have exact counterparts in other countries.

This fourth conclusion informs most of the remainder of my chapter, though I will return briefly to the other three.

The National Embeddedness of Conceptions of Industrial Relations: An Introduction to a Difficult Problem

Industrial relations systems became consolidated in the past century on a national basis. Each acquired unique characteristics, reflecting nationally distinctive economic structures, political traditions, and social practices. As we understand the term today, industrial relations is an invention of the era of the nation-state. This much is obvious to any intelligent student of comparative industrial relations; what is less obvious, perhaps, is that ways of conceptualizing industrial relations—or, indeed, whether the concept itself is regarded as coherent—likewise vary cross-nationally.

At the heart of the study of industrial relations is a complex interaction between theory and practice. The term itself, as we have seen, is an Anglo-Saxon invention, denoting at one and the same time an area of socioeconomic activity and the scholarly analysis thereof. The pioneers of this field of scholarship (the Webbs, Commons) were embedded in the world of public policy. Yet the pragmatic foundations of academic industrial relations ensured that intellectual perspectives were shaped by the nationally specific definitions of the key problems of the employment relationship. And when the reach of our subject extended beyond the English-speaking countries—even if the label *industrial relations* was often not attached—additional differentiation resulted from nationally distinctive intellectual traditions and modes of academic division of labor. In particular, there are obvious cross-national differences in the extent to which industrial relations constitutes a freestanding, multidisciplinary field of scholarship or is rather divided into a series of subdisciplines such as law, economics, sociology, and so on.

Industrial relations scholars speak different languages. In the banal sense, rather few English or American writers in the field (and they were its originators) have much fluency in other languages and are *au courant* with other literatures. But national specificities also shape the ways in which we conceptualize industrial relations. It has long been commonly accepted that there are different, and incompatible, understandings of what we are about when we talk industrial relations. The idea of a taxonomy of models, ideologies, perspectives, or frames of reference has long been embraced in order to give some coherence to the multiplicity of modes of understanding (or misunderstanding). Twenty years ago, Adams (1983:509, 526) wrote that "when viewing the empirical world members of the different schools neither look at nor see precisely the same things. The schools address different problems and they assess experience against different normative standards. . . . Industrial relations is not an internally self-consistent field of study. It is instead a confederacy of competing paradigms."

Why does the popularity of different paradigms vary with time and place? Part of the answer, as we have seen, is that national and linguistic differences shape the ways in which industrial relations is understood and analyzed (and, indeed, whether the idea of industrial relations is recognized as coherent in the first place). It is interesting that Dunlop, toward the end of his classic text, wrote that "it may seem a little surprising, but the different interests of academic experts seem to be largely a reflection of their type of industrial-relations system" (1958:329). (Perhaps only an American would find it surprising that the rest of the world does not always think American.) This *aperçu* may be understood in the light of the specific determinism of the "industrialism" project of which Dunlop was a coauthor (Kerr, Dunlop, Harbison, and Myers 1960): both the realities of a national industrial relations system and the perspectives of its academics were shaped by the orientation of its specific "industrializing elite." This is altogether too simplistic, at least for any "old" society. In Europe at least, national intellectual traditions and academic structures owe much to medieval inheritances, while the realities of industrial relations are to a large degree shaped by precapitalist "state traditions" (Crouch 1993), by the legitimating ideologies and rhetoric associated with the construction of the modern nation-state (Marks and McAdam 1996), and by subsequent class compromises, themselves in part reflecting the strength, articulation, and strategic priorities of labor movements.

As Cox (1977:127–28) has noted, different contexts (and different inter-ests, indeed) engender different modes of rationality.[2]

Does this imply that every nation has its own industrial relations the-ory (or complex of competing paradigms)? To a degree, perhaps; I have previously attempted to explore some of these differentiations (Hyman 1989, 1994, 1995; see also da Costa 1996; Milner 1994), and I pursue this issue again in the latter part of this chapter. But first let us simplify, by considering a heuristic dichotomy that ignores most nationally dis-tinctive features of approaches to industrial relations but captures, I believe, a vital confrontation: between Anglo-Saxon individualism and the collectivist presuppositions of the "European social model." This antinomy matches the familiar attempts to simplify the analysis of "alter-native capitalisms," today an accepted element in economic sociology; while markets (including labor markets) are socially embedded in ways that vary from country to country, nevertheless it makes sense to con-trast ideal types. As Albert (1993) has argued, one can plausibly identify a sharp contrast between "Anglo-American" and "Rhineland" models of capitalism. Is it not likely that these different models of capitalism favor distinctive modes of conceptualization of social relations and, in interac-tion with nationally specific theoretical and disciplinary traditions, shape the ways in which the terrain of industrial relations is perceived and interpreted? This is my concern here.

Anglo-Saxon Individualism

"There is no such thing as society," notoriously proclaimed a former British prime minister, an assertion that in much of Europe would be taken as evidence of insanity. Thatcher expressed the manic logic of social relations subordinated to market transactions: what Polanyi (1944) termed a "market society," poisoned by the predominance of values exalting individual freedom of contract and the self-interested pursuit of maximum economic returns within competitive markets. As Marx fa-mously described it, in such an environment the "fetishism of commodi-ties" dominates social relations.

Piore (1996:608) commented similarly that "in the United States there is a distinct tendency to consider society as a collection of individu-als." Elsewhere (1995:7, 24), he wrote that "we take the individual as the basic building block of socioeconomic systems. . . . We as a society are committed to individualism. We try to understand society as an aggregate of its individual members and the economy as a collection of individual producers and consumers. . . . We find it difficult to think of society as anything more than a collection of individuals and reject social theories predicated on the idea that human beings understand themselves only as part of cohesive social groups." This conception of social relations both reflects and reinforces a particular type of economic (dis)order. It also has a powerful impact on Anglo-Saxon academic perspectives.[3]

There are five features of Anglo-Saxon individualism that I consider of particular importance for industrial relations. The first links closely to the traditional British legal system, with its emphasis on freedom of contract (and the associated doctrine of restraint of trade) and its difficulties in admitting the idea of collective actors (except, interestingly, for the capitalist corporation; judges have had few problems in treating this as a sort of large-scale individual). In the academic world, the counterpart is rational-choice theory, which views social relations through the prism of *homo economicus*. To quote Piore again, "most rational choice theorists are American, and the theory's career within the social sciences seems to reinforce the idea that there is something peculiar about the American experience that makes it particularly plausible and appealing in this country" (1995:99). A classic example is Olson's (1965) endeavor to answer the question: why should a rational individual act collectively? If one starts from that question, as subsequent critics have noted, no plausible answer is possible. The logic of free riding and prisoners' dilemmas is that trade unionism cannot exist. Olson pointed to the provision of selective incentives, or else coercion, as an explanation for rationally chosen union membership, but neither could apply without preexisting collective organization; hence, the problem of explaining collectivism is merely deferred (Kelly 1998:chap. 5; Udéhn 1993). Since Anglo-Saxonism prefers facts to theory, so long as many workers *did* join trade unions, the logical impossibility of such behavior could be safely ignored. Once union membership declined, however, rational-choice theory could demonstrate that this was inevitable. Here it is perhaps worth adding, by way of qualification, that rational-choice approaches to industrial relations (e.g., Crouch 1982) have some limited plausibility where unions are defined primarily as economic actors, as is the case (though not unambiguously) with American "business unionism." Britain provides the closest European analog.

A second Anglo-Saxon characteristic is "voluntarism": the notion that employment regulation should be in large measure unconstrained by the "external" imposition of norms by legislation or other modes of state intervention. It must be noted that this assumption is actually in sharp contrast to that of the founders of industrial relations: the Webbs (1897) regarded the "method of legal enactment" as the ideal culmination of the historical evolution of employment regulation; Commons (1924) stressed the role of the state in constructing a capitalist market economy. But the Webbs misread the bias of the key industrial relations actors; in Britain, voluntarism is (or was until very recently) a deeply embedded tradition, shared by unions, employers, and governments alike (Hyman 2001b). In the United States, the restricted will and capacity of governments to intervene in the structuring of the labor market have similarly helped shape industrial relations as a sphere of relative autonomy. Such was the background to the emergence and consolidation of academic industrial relations as a field of analysis largely detached from the broader agenda of social science. The separation of "industrial relations" from "politics" also had the consequence that power has been difficult for industrial relations scholars to conceptualize (notoriously so in the case of Dunlop). In failing to problematize the dynamics of power, whether at the macro or the micro level, industrial relations writers in the Anglo-Saxon world typically "take existing power relations and forms of organisation of production as given" (Cox 1977:114).

A third characteristic of industrial relations analysis, once it achieved academic respectability as a freestanding sphere of intellectual endeavor, has been an exclusive, or at least predominant, focus on the company or workplace as its terrain. This links to a rather narrow conception of the employment relationship. While some Anglo-Saxon definitions of industrial relations claim to address "all aspects of people at work," in practice, the concern has normally been with the institutionalized relationships between employers and workers' representatives (Hyman 1982). In a context where collective bargaining is overwhelmingly centered on the individual company, this has made industrial relations primarily a microlevel field of study.

Fourth, Anglo-Saxon industrial relations scholarship, in the main, displays little or no concern with the tensions and contradictions between market dynamics and social protection and citizenship. The term *social wage*, which most Europeans take for granted, is virtually meaningless in English. Hence industrial relations is defined simply as the framework for reconciling conflicting pressures in employment, while "social policy" is a separate field addressed by completely different scholars.

A fifth aspect often evident in Anglo-Saxon industrial relations is parochialism and ethnocentrism. Britain is an island, as are Australia and New Zealand; the United States is continental in scope and largely self-sufficient. Those in large or self-contained countries have limited impetus to look outside their borders (or to achieve fluency in foreign languages). Hence scholarship in industrial relations (and in general) can readily become self-referential and take local experience as a universal norm. In countries with close neighbors, this less commonly occurs. In the time it takes to fly from New York to Chicago, a Parisian can reach 20 different European capitals. Lisbon is much closer to Oslo than Miami to San Francisco, but a journey will cross seven national frontiers. Any educated European is inevitably cosmopolitan.

These features combine to shape the responses of Anglo-Saxon industrial relations to current challenges: growing managerial unilateralism, declining union membership, the withdrawal or weakening of the limited preexisting statutory supports for collective bargaining, the fashionable discourse of "human resource management," the rise of surrogate systems of "industrial relations" without collective representation. The Anglo-Saxon debate has in the last decade or more centered around the issue of the end of (collective) industrial relations. The idea of crisis is all-pervasive.

What I have described as Anglo-Saxon industrial relations is neither monolithic nor all-encompassing. There are indeed discordant voices and vocal minorities, for example, the call for a refocusing of industrial relations as critical political economy (Giles and Murray 1989, 1996), Kelly's (1998) application of mobilization theory to trade unionism, or much more pervasively, the critical adoption of feminist perspectives. Yet these have made only a limited impact on Anglo-Saxon industrial relations orthodoxy, and in the main, alternative conceptions of the world of work have been developed *outside* the bounds of industrial relations as academically incorporated or conventionally understood.

The "European Social Model"

"The 'employment relationship,' although acknowledged as being at the heart of industrial relations study, is not in itself adequate to describe the processes at work in different European countries" (Milner 1994:28). One might take this argument a stage further: what in English has a clear and specific meaning, the employment relationship, becomes much more diffuse and wider-ranging in continental Europe. Consider the term *rapport salarial,* at first sight a literal equivalent. This concept, a central reference for the French *régulation* school (e.g., Boyer 1980), implies a relationship not merely between employers and employees but implicating other actors, in particular the state; not merely an economic exchange but a complex of rights, responsibilities, and obligations that guarantee workers a recognized status (Supiot 2001); and even in economic terms, the framework not only for a wage–work bargain but also for the definition of a range of other social entitlements.

This far broader understanding of the employment relationship is a feature of "Rhineland capitalism." In this formation, which Albert (1993) counterposed to Anglo-American economic liberalism, the sway of the market is substantially bounded. In distinct ways in different countries, the commodity status of labor is severely circumscribed; the freedom of contract, much more generally, is subject to legal and other constraints; and the conditions of employment, and of employees outside work, are recognized as of social and political concern. To adopt the distinction of Polanyi (1944), the countries of western Europe are market economies but not fully market societies. Markets represent vehicles for the organization of economic activity but are not assigned overriding political priority, and a market logic does not overwhelm social identity or political initiative. (Whether globalization and European economic integration are changing all this is another, and a crucially important, question.)

For the practice and the analysis of industrial relations, there are several important corollaries, which contrast sharply with the Anglo-Saxon framework. (Here too, it must be stressed, an ideal type inevitably oversimplifies; for a discussion of some of the ambiguities of the European social model, see Ebbinghaus [1999].)

First, collectivism is regarded as normal. Marx argued that "the individual is the social being," that individuals do not exist and cannot be understood except in terms of the network of social relations that define and sustain them; Durkheim argued that contracts are possible only on the basis of a prior structure of noncontractual social regulation. Interestingly, the most self-assertive individuals are typically supported by dense collective resources (Harrison 1991). In western Europe, mainstream parties of the right as well as the left have traditionally accepted that individuals are embedded in society and that social regulation is the prerequisite of individual welfare. The notion of solidarity can be used without embarrassment across the political spectrum. As Negt (2001:7) put it, "[S]olidarity entails that those who fall outside the bounds of power and prosperity—the unemployed, the homeless, the poor—that all these strata, groups and individuals are included in the scope of social welfare." Accordingly, analysts of trade unionism rarely consider the question of why individuals should organize collectively, or if they do, the main issue, in the terminology of Offe and Wiesenthal (1985), is not "willingness to pay" but "willingness to act," the ways in which union members and supporters can be mobilized or can mobilize themselves.

Second, Anglo-Saxon voluntarism has little resonance in most of continental Europe. It is true that in some countries, in particular in northern Europe, there is a powerful principle that the state should know its place (the catholic doctrine of subsidiarity, embraced as a key principle within the European Union, is also relevant here). Yet universally, the labor market is seen to be socially constructed and delimited: it is taken for granted that the state is, directly or indirectly, implicated in employment relationships. In most countries, law and collective bargaining are treated as complementary rather than contradictory (Supiot 2001:95–98). This perspective is equally influential for industrial relations actors and policy makers and for academic analysts: all recognize that industrial relations practice is to an important degree politically constructed.

Third, there is little sense of the company or workplace as a segregated society (though again, this may be changing in the face of internationalization). Employer solidarity and multiemployer collective bargaining contrast with the far greater decentralization in Anglo-Saxon countries. Trade unions, though in some cases strongly rooted in the workplace, have a much broader social identity, and their role often extends to detailed engagement in the formulation of public welfare and labor market policy and the administration of social benefits. (In some countries, such as France and perhaps also Italy, this may be more significant than their role as collective bargainers.) It may be symptomatic that in most European countries, and within the European Commission, the ministries responsible for industrial relations have titles such as Labor and Social Affairs. We may also note that elusive element of Eurospeak, *espace social*, usually translated as the "social dimension" but also meaning the sphere of industrial relations.

Fourth, conflict is rarely regarded as pathological. Economic dynamics generate conflicts that are more manageable when overtly expressed and collectively represented. The language of "social partners," so puzzling to most Anglo-Saxons, seems to reflect a consciousness of the precariousness of social order and the potential for economic antagonisms to explode into destructive civil warfare (the fate of much of Europe in the first half of the 20th century). Conflict management is regarded as an art that requires stable collective organization; in this sense, social partnership is virtually equivalent to the English concept of joint regulation, though it implies a higher level and a significantly broader agenda.

Again, referring back to the second point, the "partnership" involved may be with the state as third actor, even (or perhaps especially) where unions and employers' organizations display more conflict than cooperation in their interrelationship.

Finally, as hinted earlier, it is difficult for continental Europeans to be ethnocentric. Most European countries are too small to be confining. The rise of the European Union has reinforced sensitivities to diverse cross-national experience. The sources of cross-national diversity and the possibilities of convergence are both intellectual and practical issues. This has become even more a point of reference with the enlargement of the European Union to include many of the countries east of the old iron curtain.

We can add the facts that continental Europe has a far stronger theoretical tradition in academic life than have the Anglo-Saxon countries and that disciplinary identities are often more encompassing. This has inhibited the emergence of a distinctive cross-disciplinary field of "industrial relations" but has also meant that studies of the world of work have been less shallowly pragmatic and more reflective than has often been the case in the Anglo-Saxon context (Hyman 1995). Far more commonly than in Anglo-Saxon countries, concern is directed toward what Cox (1971:142) has called "broad structural changes."

All these factors entail that current challenges to established forms of employment regulation have stimulated very different responses from those in Anglo-Saxon countries. Rather than conceding the end of collectivism and abdicating to the employer all possibility of regulation, the central question in current European debate is how to reinstitutionalize the employment relationship at a societal level (Supiot 2001:52). It is notable that the idea that HRM may constitute an alternative to collective regulation of employment has barely arisen in most continental European countries, either among policy makers or in the field of academic analysis. The collectivist paradigm survives largely intact.

Adding Complexity: Varieties of Industrial Relations within Europe

After the presentation of a simple dichotomy between Anglo-American and continental European approaches to industrial relations, let me add a little necessary complexity. I shall illustrate very briefly, with a few examples, how national distinctiveness has made the current concerns of industrial relations scholarship in key respects noncommensurable.

As I argued earlier, in Britain and the United States the focal concern of modern industrial relations scholarship has been the practice and institutions of collective bargaining or, as Flanders (1970) put it (given his dissatisfaction with the very concept of collective bargaining inherited from the Webbs), of job regulation. Predominantly, attention has concentrated on relationships between trade unions and individual employers and in particular the dynamics of conflict and its containment; in both countries, collective organization and action among employers have long been relatively peripheral. Though Dunlop identified the state as the third actor in industrial relations, its role was barely theorized. We might note that while the Webbs, in their *Industrial Democracy* (1897), viewed the extension of legal enactment as the inevitable and desirable future for industrial relations—a theme developed some four decades later by Milne-Bailey in his remarkable study *Trade Unions and the State* (1934)—their perspectives were soon discarded: Kahn-Freund (1954) in Britain and Kerr and his collaborators (Kerr 1964; Kerr, Dunlop, Harbison, and Myers 1960) in the United States insisted that a detachment between political actors and job regulation was the hallmark of a "mature" industrial relations system. When, beginning in the 1960s in Britain at least, the state became more centrally involved, it was political scientists with their theories of corporatism rather than industrial relations specialists who did the most to make sense of the new trends.

If industrial relations is defined in terms of an autonomous sphere of job regulation through collective bargaining between trade unions and individual employers, it is not surprising that the subject was thrown into disarray by the rapid decline of trade union membership and in the coverage of collective bargaining. The vacuum was filled, of course, as Kaufman (1993) charted, by the advance of HRM as both managerial and academic practice. The paths in Britain and the United States have, however, diverged. In Britain the collapse of collective industrial relations has been less radical than in the United States, and the advance of HRM more superficial. More recently, indeed, in Britain there have been elements of a collective re-regulation of employment relations, primarily driven by the "social" legislation of the European Union. In key respects the practice of industrial relations in Britain has become partially Europeanized, giving a new vitality but also a new focus to industrial relations scholarship. (We may note, in passing, how the vocabulary of social partnership has become embedded in British discourse—though the institutional foundations and the diverse and contradictory meanings of the term in continental Europe are rarely appreciated.)

In most of western Europe the realities, and the intellectual mindsets, have been very different from those in Anglo-Saxonia. As noted earlier, the collective organization of economic interests, the social regulation of market transactions, and the systematic presence of the state in either the foreground or the background of these processes have been taken for granted in the practical and analytical conduct of industrial relations. This is, of course, one reason why the very concept of industrial relations translates so uncomfortably into continental languages and is in many countries avoided altogether. (Interestingly, the German Industrial Relations Association calls itself precisely that in English.)

I prepared some of this chapter while in Germany, so let me refer to a lead headline published while I was writing. It appeared in the *Frankfurter Rundschau* (a paper not given to sensationalism), which informed the reader that the opposition Christian Democrats (CDU) had launched an assault on free collective bargaining. I use this English term as translation for *Tarifautonomie*, but note how context transforms meaning. The core CDU proposal was that, in the case of severe economic difficulties in a company, management and works council should be entitled to negotiate an agreement that undercuts the terms of the sectoral collective agreement, whether or not the national union and employers' association agree. My purpose here is not to comment on the merits or otherwise of the proposal, but simply to remark that few Anglo-Saxon industrial relations scholars unfamiliar with the background would perceive it as an attack on free collective bargaining. This characterization becomes comprehensible only if we appreciate the historical evolution of a delicate, legally enshrined balance between trade unions and works councils, the exclusive right of the former (at least in theory) to undertake collective bargaining with employers, and the widespread perception that the primacy of multiemployer over single-employer regulation is the foundation stone of the whole industrial relations edifice. Beyond this, only the "external" union has the right to strike, while works councils are bound by a peace obligation; hence, the notional balance of forces underlying "free collective bargaining" would be absent within the proposed arrangement (Girndt 2003).

In many respects, the whole history of industrial relations scholarship in Germany has involved a debate over the nature, dynamics, and internal contradictions of *Tarifautonomie*. The philosophy underlying the concept can be traced back to the writings of Sinzheimer (1916) almost a century ago. Recognizably modern industrial relations scholarship centered on a debate around the character of the so-called dual system of industrial relations, with radicals in the 1960s and 1970s insisting that the legally mandated division of labor between works councils cooperating with management inside the company and trade unions undertaking collective bargaining outside (and enjoying a right to strike) fatally weakened labor. By the 1980s, however, it was generally accepted that the concept of a dual system was a misnomer, that the two sets of institutions were deeply interdependent, and that in hard times the legal rights of the councils were a major protection for trade union organization at the company level. In the past decade the discussion has been dominated by two questions. First, would the institutional arrangements formally established in the *neue Bundesländer* in 1990 really function as they did in the west, and if not, would their failure in the east have damaging feedback effects for Germany as a whole? Second, is the recent process of "organized decentralization," which has involved a controlled devolution of some bargaining functions to the workplace, simply the fine-tuning of a system that retains its essential integrity, or does it undermine the whole structure? Only from such a perspective can current disputes over free collective bargaining, German-style, be understood.

Italy provides a very different example of the impact of historical and institutional context on industrial relations thinking. It is impossible to make sense of most Italian literature in our field without appreciating three key features of this context. The first is the omnipresence of a state that for most of the past half century has been weak in political legitimacy, and of legal norms in part inherited from the fascist past but radically reshaped with the *statuto dei lavoratori* of 1970. The second is the bias to political engagement among the other key actors of industrial relations. The third is that efforts to establish some form of free collective bargaining have been halting and uncertain so that scholars have long complained of the weak institutionalization of the system.

Though industrial relations scholarship has been strongly rooted in the subdiscipline of labor law, in many respects its key insights have been drawn from political sociology, for the crucial underlying issue has been the adaptation of a balance of forces and the management of potentially explosive conflict between powerful actors. In the 1970s the focal puzzle was how the strongest communist party in the western world, and the main trade union confederation that was to some extent its satellite, lent stability and legitimation to a system of governance with a severe democratic deficit. The concept of political exchange *(scambio politico),* offered by Pizzorno (1978) as the key to understanding this paradox, soon became common currency in the comparative literature on trade unions and politics, but it is questionable how far Pizzorno's meaning can be understood outside its Italian context.

Another term widely adopted in the comparative literature is Regini's (1991) concept of *microcorporatism*. Detached from the Italian context, it is often used to mean little more than "social partnership" in the company and workplace. However, the concept was developed to explain another distinctively Italian puzzle. The clash between a militant and assertive workplace trade unionism, emboldened by the victories of the late 1960s and early 1970s, and a management that had concluded that it must recapture control in order to survive exploded in the traumatic Fiat conflict of 1980. For most commentators, this was the prelude to a systematic assault on workplace union power across Italian industry. What occurred, however, was a largely consensual reconstruction of company-level systems of employee representation, organizational restructuring, and workplace decision making. In ways analogous to the explanations of state-level (neo)corporatism a decade earlier, the theory of microcorporatism identified the continuing power resources of workplace trade unionism (not least because of the rights conferred by the *statuto*) as a factor inhibiting a large-scale management offensive but also stressed how a productivist tradition (dating back at least to Gramsci) made workplace militants receptive to the offer of involvement in company-level joint regulation.

To offer another instance, for much of the 1980s and 1990s there was in Italy a process of negotiated reform of industrial relations (and of the welfare system, which is itself inseparable from industrial relations), of peak-level agreements between unions and employers (typically brokered by government) that in many cases resulted in "bargained legislation." A key element in the process was a relaxation of the web of state regulation with a reciprocal extension of the scope of collective bargaining. A by-product was that the definite if at times precarious narrowing of the political divisions between union confederations was reflected in a convergence in intellectual perspectives among academics whose partisan allegiances have always been intense. Whether the "normalization" of the practice and the theory of industrial relations will survive the Berlusconi era remains to be seen; as I write, the issue has just provoked a massive general strike by all three main union confederations.

Let me end by considering the case of France. If much Italian scholarship sees the starting point for the modern industrial relations system as the "hot autumn" of 1969, the rarely spoken French question is: Whatever happened to 1968? The mass explosion of social, industrial, and political protest was the wasted opportunity of the French labor movement, and indeed, Boltanski and Chiapello (1999) titled one of their key chapters "1968: Crise et renouveau du capitalisme." Elsewhere (Hyman 2001a), I have charted how the rise, decline, and occasional reassertion of collective conflict are matched by the shifting interest in collective labor relations in the pages of *Sociologie du travail* (the closest French equivalent to an industrial relations journal). The vacuum of collective industrial relations as conventionally understood elsewhere (Rojot [1989] is one of the few to dispute the notion of French exceptionalism) is in turn reflected in the bewildering fragmentation of approaches to this field (or nonfield) of study.

Three broad questions seem to dominate the scholarly agenda, however, and the answers are driven by intellectual-ideological divisions that are difficult for any outsider to chart. First, how do we make sense of French trade unionism, a movement almost without members (at least in the private sector) yet with seemingly considerable political influence (or at least veto power)? Do numbers matter? (Labbé [1996] is one of the few to seek detailed data.) Do unions present, however opaquely, a progressive alternative to resurgent French (and international) capital, or are they reactionary defenders of vested interests (a polarization of viewpoints sharply displayed in the aftermath of the mass strikes of 1995 and no doubt soon to follow the confrontations in 2003)?

Second, how do we comprehend the complex interconnections between work and welfare and the role of unions in mediating the links between them? I have already mentioned that the French *école de regulation* has given us the concept of *rapport salarial*, essentially untranslatable but clearly identifying the "social wage" as a fusion of income from the employer and entitlements from the state. If the idea of the social wage is taken for granted in continental Europe though barely comprehensible in English, France is indeed exceptional in the degree to which trade unions have colonized the system and draw status and resources from this colonization (and hence are threatened organizationally by projects for "reform").

Third, what accounts for the seeming quiescence of private sector employees, despite a Tayloristic work regime and the virtual absence of independent collective voice? Is the main explanation to be sought at the societal level in the hegemony of an ideology of modernizing capitalism or at the company level in the success of French managements (perhaps the most systematic European practitioners of American-style HRM) in persuading employees that insecurity and stress are expressions of the beneficial qualities of the employment contract? In different ways, Boltanski and Chiapello (1999), Coutrot (1998), and Dejours (1998) all offer powerful interpretations of this paradox.

I should add that those critical of the current balance of power in work and employment rarely see the labor movement as an agency of change, as so often the task is one for the state. This can be seen, for example, in Supiot's (2001) call for a new *statut professionnel* (another untranslatable term, though note that the French render industrial relations as *relations professionnelles*): labor law should recognize the growth of types of work that fall outside the definitions of the traditional employment contract, social security should adapt to the declining fixity of the individual job, and both should recognize that two sexes are in the workforce. While the problems that Supiot addressed were general across Europe, the form of the solution was in many respects distinctively French, perhaps one reason why his report to the European Commission seems to have disappeared without trace.

I have given a small number of illustrations of the ways in which nationally specific institutional configurations and modes of analysis shape the focus, and the mind-set, of industrial relations scholarship. With more space it would be possible to multiply these instances several-fold. This might well lead us to ask: Can students of industrial relations communicate cross-nationally? My answer is: perhaps, but only if we first appreciate that in more than one way we do not speak the same language. As Adams (1995:58) commented, "[T]o a large extent to this point in history, Europe and North America have been studied as two solitudes in industrial relations. . . . If we are to understand each other one must no longer treat the other as exotica."

Learning from Each Other?

Let me end, diffidently, by suggesting some of the strengths in continental European approaches to our subject that could enrich Anglo-American industrial relations scholarship. First, Europeans do not regard industrial relations as a distinct discipline. This is a negative with important positive consequences, for in my view the Anglo-Saxon tendency to claim distinct disciplinary status for industrial relations has had damaging outcomes, detaching analysis from broader social science traditions, trivializing its conceptual apparatus, and privileging pragmatism over theoretical imagination.

Across continental Europe, the study of work and employment is located not in distinctive departments of industrial relations (nor, in general, of management) but in the broader social sciences: sociology, economics, law, and so on. If in the past this encouraged a certain fragmentation of research and analysis, my impression is that this is far less serious a problem than a couple of decades ago: labor economists, industrial sociologists, and labor lawyers have discovered how to speak to each other and have become sensitive to each other's problematics.

In all cases, a strong theoretical grounding is taken for granted. The theory may be drawn from the "classics" of Marx, Weber, and Durkheim or from more recent innovators but in any event entails a focus on big questions. This means that the first conclusion with which I began this contribution is embraced: the theories that are addressed to the world of work cannot be described as theories *of* industrial relations and are not intended as such. As a corollary, the themes of generality, parsimony, and causality that were discussed earlier pervade analysis. Typically, continental writers on employment regulation are *self-consciously* theoretical; the attempt is at one and the same time to illuminate the dynamics of industrial relations and to clarify the nature of theory itself. My second conclusion is taken for granted.

This has additional implications. When the (bilingual) German journal *Industrielle Beziehungen* was launched, its editors (1994:6) insisted on the need to link "the micro perspectives of employees and firms" to "the meso perspective of associations and intermediary actors" and "the macro perspective of state and society." Such emphasis on the interdependence of different *levels* of analysis is far more common, it seems to me, in continental approaches to employment regulation than in either Britain or North America. Conceptually and methodologically, too, it seems to me that there would be far broader agreement in continental Europe than in Anglo-Saxonia with the declaration of Miguélez and Prieto (1991:xxii) that "wage-labour relations have to be approached through three complementary analytical perspectives: the structure of relations of production (i.e. capitalist market relations), the actors in these relations and the practices of these actors. . . . Structures, actors and practices form part of the same reality: or better, they *are* the same reality."

A final lesson I would draw from continental Europe is the importance of *comparative* research and analysis. Cross-national comparison obliges the researcher to relativize perspectives on institutions and practices that are commonly taken for granted, and one of the tasks of scholarship is surely to make the strange familiar and the familiar strange. The broader the range of comparative reference, the more strongly grounded are our generalizations and the more encompassing our causal inferences. As suggested earlier, it is difficult for European scholars to remain parochial, particularly those from small countries with minority languages who wish to engage an international (which de facto tends to mean English-speaking) audience. The familiarity of our continental European counterparts with Anglo-American trends and literatures can be humbling when few of us can reciprocate. Note, however, that the academic point of reference for European students of employment is not necessarily that of industrial relations or HRM but commonly that of sociologists or political scientists who have brought to the study of employment regulation the theoretical concerns of their home disciplines.[4]

My modest proposal is therefore that those of us in the English-speaking world of industrial relations should learn greater ambition from our European colleagues. Theory should be embraced not as an opportunist pretext to legitimize an otherwise incoherent catalog of empirical and practical concerns but as a guide to intellectually significant research questions and as a framework for understanding and explanation. And a comparative perspective should be cultivated not as an optional extra but as a necessary basis for adequate understanding of our own national experience.

To conclude with a question of both theoretical and practical importance, is there a potential reconciliation between Anglo-Saxon individualism and the European social model? Possibly. As I often say, some of my best friends are individuals. The key issue is how to connect individualism and collectivism. This is in part a question of policy and practice: Is it possible to maintain a collectively defined framework for employment within which individual choices can be made, choices that are relatively unforced? In many respects, European industrial relations policy debates are grappling with this question. But the question is also partly theoretical, and this brings me back to my third conclusion. Marx himself (like all classic social thinkers) insisted that it was false to counterpose the individual to society. Individuals derive their identity, and in a sense their very existence, from the social relationships in which they are implicated; societies acquire their characteristics and their stability (or at times instability) from the ideas and actions of the individuals who compose them. Marx famously insisted that "people make their own history, but they do not make it just as they choose." Most prominent among the constraints on effective freedom to choose was capitalism itself, a system in which the "laws" of market transactions, in reality themselves the outcome of a multiplicity of social and political decisions, acquired an impersonal coercive force. What the varieties-of-capitalism literature tells us is that this coercive force in reality remains bounded, even in countries where the virtues of unfettered markets are an almost unquestioned point of faith, but the bounds differ markedly in nature and extent from country to country. In many respects, industrial relations is constituted by the contradictory interconnections between markets and other forms of social regulation as they impinge on work and employment; hence the realities of industrial relations differ cross-nationally. So to return to my starting point, of course we need theories to make sense of both similarities and differences across countries, but these will necessarily be drawn from the wider spectrum of social understanding. Hence they will not be theories *of* industrial relations but applications of more encompassing theoretical insight.

Acknowledgments

Elements of this chapter were presented at the IIRA European conference in Oslo in June 2001, the SASE conference in Aix-en-Provence in June 2003, and the IIRA world congress in Berlin in September 2003. I am grateful to participants for their comments.

Notes

[1] Morris (1987) has identified a few earlier, but marginal, uses of the term.

[2] Frege (2003), in an essay that I saw only as I was putting the finishing touches to this chapter, has argued very similarly in contrasting German and Anglo-American approaches to industrial relations.

[3] I should, no doubt, define what I mean by "Anglo-Saxon" and examine whether the label has analytical coherence. I use the term as more or less equivalent to "predominantly English-speaking." This is justifiable, I think, in that the term *industrial relations* is an English-language invention with limited resonance in countries where English is not the main language. However, my main focus is on Britain and the United States. Approaches to industrial relations in Canada bear important influences of the French connection via Québec; in Australia and New Zealand, the strong role of the state in shaping their industrial relations systems has significantly affected scholarly perspectives (Lansbury and Michelson 2003).

[4] It is particularly notable that the most prominent writing on European industrial relations in the United States is by such scholars. See, for example, the study of European trade unionism edited by Martin and Ross (1999).

References

Adams, Roy J. 1983. "Competing Paradigms in Industrial Relations." *Relations industrielles,* Vol. 38, no. 3, pp. 508–29.
———. 1993. "Theory Construction and Assessment: A Checklist." In Roy J. Adams and Noah M. Meltz, eds., *Industrial Relations Theory: Its Nature, Scope and Pedagogy,* Metuchen, NJ: Scarecrow, pp. 333–51.

————. 1995. "Industrial Relations in Europe and North America: Some Contemporary Themes." *European Journal of Industrial Relations,* Vol. 1, no. 1, pp. 47–62.

Albert, Michel. 1993. *Capitalism against Capitalism.* London: Whurr.

Boltanski, Luc, and Ève Chiapello. 1999. *Le nouvel esprit du capitalisme.* Paris: Gallimard.

Boyer, Robert. 1980. "Rapport salarial et analyse en termes de régulation: Une mise en rapport avec les théories de la segmentation du marché du travail." *Économie appliquée,* Vol. 2, pp. 491–509.

Commons, John. R. 1924. *Legal Foundations of Capitalism.* New York: Macmillan.

Coutrot, Thomas. 1998. *L'entreprise néo-libérale, nouvel utopie capitaliste?* Paris: Découverte.

Cox, Robert. W. 1971. "Approaches to a Futurology of Industrial Relations." *IILS Bulletin,* Vol. 8, pp. 139–64.

————. 1977. "Pour une étude prospective des relations de production." *Sociologie du travail,* Vol. 2/77, pp. 113–37.

Crouch, Colin. 1982. *Trade Unions: The Logic of Collective Action.* London: Fontana.

————. 1993. *Industrial Relations and European State Traditions.* Oxford: Clarendon.

Crouch, C., and Wolfgang Streeck, eds. 1997. *The Political Economy of Modern Capitalism: Mapping Convergence and Diversity.* London: Sage.

da Costa, Isabel. 1996. "L'étude des relations industrielles: Passé, présent, avenir." In Gregor Murray, Marie-Laure Morin, and I. da Costa, eds., *L'état des relations professionnelles,* Quebec: Presses de l'Université Laval.

Dejours, Christophe. 1998. *Soffrance en France: La banalisation de l'injustice sociale.* Paris: Seuil.

Dore, Ronald. 2000. *Stock-Market Capitalism, Welfare Capitalism: Japan and Germany versus the Anglo-Saxons.* Oxford: Oxford University Press.

Dunlop, John T. 1958. *Industrial Relations Systems.* New York: Holt.

Ebbinghaus, Bernhard. 1999. "Does a European Social Model Exist and Can It Survive?" In G. Huemer, M. Mesch, and F. Traxler, eds., *The Role of Employer Associations and Labour Unions in the EMU,* Aldershot, UK: Ashgate, pp. 1–26.

European Commission. 2002. *Employment in Europe 2002.* Luxembourg: Office of Official Publications.

Flanders, Allan. 1970. "Collective Bargaining: A Theoretical Analysis." In Allan Flanders, *Management and Unions,* London: Faber, pp. 213–40.

Frege, Carola M. 2003. "Industrial Relations in Continental Europe." In Peter Ackers and Adrian Wilkinson, eds., *Understanding Work and Employment: Industrial Relations in Transition,* Oxford: Oxford University Press, pp. 242–62.

Giles, Anthony, and Gregor Murray. 1989. "Industrial Relations Theory and Critical Political Economy: Why There Is No 'State of the Art.'" Paper presented to the IIRA Study Group on Industrial Relations Theory (Brussels).

————. 1996. "Trajectoires et paradigmes dans l'étude des relations industrielles en Amérique du Nord." In Gregor Murray, Marie-Laure Morin, and I. da Costa, eds., *L'état des relations professionnelles,* Quebec: Presses de l'Université Laval.

Girndt, Cornelia. 2003. "Abstimmungen über Arbeitsplätze." *Mitbestimmung,* Vol. 10/2003, pp. 48–51.

Granovetter, Mark. 1985. "Economic Action and Social Structure: The Problem of Embeddedness." *American Journal of Sociology,* Vol. 91, pp. 481–510.

Hall, Peter A., and David Soskice, eds. 2001. *Varieties of Capitalism: The Institutional Foundations of Comparative Advantage.* Oxford: Oxford University Press.

Harrison, Royden. 1991. "The Individual and Industrial Relations." *Industrial Tutor,* Vol. 5, no. 3, pp. 72–78.

Hollingsworth, J. Rogers, and Robert Boyer, eds. 1997. *Contemporary Capitalism: The Embeddedness of Institutions.* Cambridge: Cambridge University Press.

Hyman, Richard. 1975. *Industrial Relations: A Marxist Introduction.* London: Macmillan.

———. 1982. "Review of *Collective Bargaining and Industrial Relations.*" *Industrial Relations,* Vol. 21, pp. 100–113.

———. 1989. *The Political Economy of Industrial Relations: Theory and Practice in a Cold Climate.* London: Macmillan.

———. 1994. "Theory and Industrial Relations." *British Journal of Industrial Relations,* Vol. 32, no. 2, pp. 165–80.

———. 1995. "Industrial Relations in Europe: Theory and Practice." *European Journal of Industrial Relations,* Vol. 1, no. 1, pp. 17–46.

———. 2001a. "A la recherche de la mobilisation perdue." In A. Pouchet, ed., *Sociologies du travail: 40 ans après,* Paris: Elsevier.

———. 2001b. *Understanding European Trade Unionism: Between Market, Class and Society.* London: Sage.

Industrielle Beziehungen. 1994. Editorial. *Industrielle Beziehungen: Zeitschrift für Arbeit, Organisation und Management,* Vol. 1, no. 1, pp. 5–12.

Kahn-Freund, Otto. 1954. "Legal Framework." In A. Flanders and H. A. Clegg, eds., *The System of Industrial Relations in Great Britain,* Oxford: Blackwell, pp. 42–127.

Kaufman, Bruce E. 1993. *The Origins and Development of the Field of Industrial Relations in the United States.* Ithaca, NY: Cornell University Press.

Kelly, John. 1998. *Rethinking Industrial Relations: Mobilisation, Collectivism and Long Waves.* London: Routledge.

Kerr, Clark. 1964. *Labor and Management in Industrial Society.* New York: Doubleday.

Kerr, C., John T. Dunlop, Frederick H. Harbison, and Charles A. Myers. 1960. *Industrialism and Industrial Man.* London: Heinemann.

Kuhn, Thomas. 1962. *The Structure of Scientific Revolutions.* Chicago: University of Chicago Press.

Labbé, Dominique. 1996. *Syndicats et syndiqués en France depuis 1945.* Paris: L'Harmattan.

Lansbury, Russell, and Grant Michelson. 2003. "Industrial Relations in Australia." In P. Ackers and A. Wilkinson, eds., *Understanding Work and Employment: Industrial Relations in Transition,* Oxford: Oxford University Press.

Marks, Gary, and Doug McAdam. 1996. "Social Movements and the Changing Structure of Political Opportunity in the European Union." In G. Marks, Fritz W. Scharpf, Philippe C. Schmitter, and Wolfgang Streeck, eds., *Governance in the European Union,* London: Sage.

Martin, Andrew, and George Ross, eds. 1999. *The Brave New World of European Labour: European Trade Unions at the Millennium.* New York: Berghahn.

Miguélez, Fausto, and Carlos Prieto, eds. 1991. *Las relaciones laborales en España.* Madrid: Siglo XXI.

Milne-Bailey, Walter. 1934. *Trade Unions and the State.* London: Allen and Unwin.

Milner, Susan. 1994. "Comparative Industrial Relations: Towards New Paradigms?" *Journal of Area Studies*, Vol. 5, pp. 19–33.

Morris, Richard. 1987. "The Early Uses of the Industrial Relations Concept." *Journal of Industrial Relations*, Vol. 29, pp. 532–38.

Negt, Oskar. 2001. "Solidarität und das Problem eines beschädigten Gemeinwesens." *Gewerkschaftliche Monatshefte*, Vol. 1/2001, pp. 1–7.

Offe, Claus, and Helmut Wiesenthal. 1985. "Two Logics of Collective Action." In C. Offe, *Disorganized Capitalism*, Cambridge: Polity.

Olson, Mancur. 1965. *The Logic of Collective Action*. Cambridge, MA: Harvard University Press.

Piore, Michael. 1995. *Beyond Individualism*. Cambridge, MA: Harvard University Press.

———. 1996. "Au-delà des relations industrielles." In Gregor Murray, Marie-Laure Morin, and I. da Costa, eds., *L'état des relations professionnelles*, Quebec: Presses de l'Université Laval.

Pizzorno, Alessandro. 1978. "Political Exchange and Collective Identity." In C. Crouch and A. Pizzorno, eds., *The Resurgence of Class Conflict in Western Europe since 1968*, London: Macmillan.

Polanyi, Karl. 1944. *The Great Transformation: The Political and Economic Origins of Our Times*. New York: Farrar and Rinehart.

Przeworski, Adam, and Henry Teune. 1970. *The Logic of Comparative Social Inquiry*. New York: Wiley.

Regini, Marino. 1991. *Confini mobili*. Bologna: Il Mulino.

Rojot, Jacques. 1989. "The Myth of French Exceptionalism." In J. Barbash and K. Barbash, eds., *Theories and Concepts in Comparative Industrial Relations*, Columbia: University of South Carolina Press, pp. 76–88.

Sinzheimer, Hugo. 1916. *Ein Arbeitstarifgesetz*. Munich: Duncker and Humblot.

Supiot, Alain. 2001. *Beyond Employment: Changes in Work and the Future of Labour Law in Europe*. Oxford: Oxford University Press.

Udéhn, Lars. 1993. "Twenty-Five Years with *The Logic of Collective Action*." *Acta Sociologica*, Vol. 36, pp. 239–61.

Walker, Kenneth F. 1977. "Towards Useful Theorising about Industrial Relations." *British Journal of Industrial Relations*, Vol. 15, pp. 307–16.

Webb, Sidney, and Beatrice Webb. 1897. *Industrial Democracy*. London: Longmans.

Wood, S., A. Wagner, E. G. A. Armstrong, J. B. F. Goodman, and J. E. Davis. 1975. "The 'Industrial Relations System' Concept as a Basis for Theory in Industrial Relations." *British Journal of Industrial Relations*, Vol. 13, pp. 291–308.

Chapter 10

International Comparative Employment Relations Theory: Developing the Political Economy Perspective

Roderick Martin
University of Southampton

Greg J. Bamber
Griffith University

There is an emerging consensus amid scholars that employment relations systems result from interaction among international, national, sector, and enterprise-level influences. In their comparative essay on the transformation of industrial relations, Locke and Kochan (1995:365) viewed company employment relations strategies as "emanating from international pressures that are common to all the advanced industrial nations," but filtered through different institutional arrangements, so that "the valence of particular issues and changes in practices are quite varied in the different national contexts." Similarly, Katz and Darbishire (2000:8) "highlight the many similarities that now appear in the variation emerging in employment relations across countries," while recognizing the need to show how national employment relations institutions shape the pressures toward convergence. Both conclusions are cautious, even equivocal. For theoretical advance, this emerging consensus needs to be given a sharper focus, and the theoretical issues made more explicit.

This contribution seeks to provide a framework for a more focused assessment of the respective roles of international and national influences on employment relations. "How can we best characterize and explain the key features of national employment relations systems?" is therefore the central *problematique* considered in the paper. We focus on the macro level, on national employment relations systems, not on the enterprise level. In doing so we depart from the emerging convention of enterprise-level research associated with a strategic choice perspective. This focus on national-level employment relations systems is justified for several reasons. Macroeconomic policy making, labor markets, unions, and mechanisms for determining pay and conditions of employment continue to operate primarily at the national level (and textbooks continue to be written primarily in national terms, e.g., Gardner and Palmer 1997; Edwards 2003; Katz and Kochan 2003). There remain important national differences in employment legislation, for example, regarding industrial action or the role of unions. In collective bargaining specifically, there remain major differences even among countries within the European Union, where the Social Charter reserves the major employment relations issues, including collective bargaining, for national regulation, under the principle of subsidiarity. There are also significant national cultural differences with direct implications for employment relations, for example, in the degree of acceptance of power distance and employee attitudes toward management authority (Hofstede 1980; Isaac 2003; Black, forthcoming). Also, enterprise-level international comparative management research indicates significant differences among multinational corporations (MNCs) in employment relations practices according to country of origin, with European, Japanese, and U.S. MNCs, for example, typically adopting different practices (Ferner 1994, 1997; Ferner and Quintanilla 1998; Belanger, Berggren, Bjorkman, and Kohler 1999; Walsh 2001). In short, employment relations remains more subject to national differences, both in institutional arrangements and in culture, than other areas of business activity. It is therefore appropriate that comparative employment relations theory should focus on the national level, reflecting the historical and contemporary significance of national legislation, institutions, and cultures.

We understand by *employment relations systems* the institutions, values, practices, and outcomes of employers' and employees' actions insofar as they relate to the terms and conditions of employment (including the effort–reward bargain). There is a wide range of alternative characterizations of such systems. Some characterizations focus on the relation between systems of employment relations and the broader social and economic systems, as in Crouch's (1993) work or the varieties-of-capitalism literature (also Kitschelt, Lange, Marks, and Stephens 1999; Whitley 1999; Hall and Soskice 2001). In Whitley's (1999:40) analysis, for example, the key elements are the scope of market relationships, the degree of interdependence between employers and employees, and the level of employee discretion and involvement. Other characterizations, especially by scholars trained in the classic industrial relations tradition in Britain, concentrate on the specific employment relations features themselves, such as the role of legal enactment and collective bargaining, the level of organizational cohesion among employers or employees, and the degree of centralization in collective bargaining arrangements (Flanders 1970; Bain and Clegg 1974). This narrower focus is evident, for example, in Katz and Darbishire's (2000:2) work, where they refer to systems of employment relations "governing such matters as the rights of workers, unions and managers; the nature of work practices; and the structures and mechanisms of union representation."

In this paper we focus on four aspects of employment relations systems that incorporate the concerns of both the "external" and the "internal" traditions. We concentrate on four touchstones that represent key features of national employment relations systems, using these to help us evaluate international comparative employment relations theories.

The first touchstone is the role of the state in employment relations. How far do the state and the broader national regulatory regime determine the structures, policies, processes, and outcomes of employment relations? The national regulatory regime is seen as fundamental to the form of an employment relations system and to the economic and political system of which it is a part in much comparative research, as in Whitley's (1999) business systems approach or in Crouch's (1993) study of European state traditions.

The second touchstone is the degree of enterprise-level management autonomy in employment relations. How free is enterprise-level management to develop employment relations according to its own perceptions of the enterprise's strategic requirements? Employers may or may not be constrained by legislation, by government action, by other employers, by union power, or by public expectations.

The third touchstone relates to union organization, especially the density of union membership, the extent to which unions focus on economic issues, and the relationship between unions and political parties. While some union movements are class conscious and seek to politicize their members and to mobilize social movements, such as the *Confederazione Generale Italiana del Lavoro* (CGIL, General Italian Confederation of Labor) in Italy, others are more "businesslike" and relatively apolitical, such as, historically, the American Federation of Labor–Congress of Industrial Organizations (AFL-CIO) in the United States (R. M. Martin 1989).

The fourth touchstone is the pattern and role of collective bargaining in determining the terms and conditions of employment. The pattern includes the level of centralization or decentralization in collective bargaining. The role of collective bargaining reflects the extent to which collective determination rather than individual determination prevails.

These four issues have been treated in different ways in the main schools of comparative employment relations theory. In the first part of the paper we examine how the four issues have been addressed in three major approaches to comparative employment relations theory, the systems, strategic choice, and Marxist political economy approaches. The three approaches have been chosen to represent the major traditions in comparative industrial relations theory. We have chosen specifically to focus on the sociological and historical rather than the economic traditions of research for reasons of space, not because we do not recognize the importance of the economic dimension (Baron and Kreps 1999). To avoid an extended historical literature survey, the paper concentrates on a small number of key contributions. The first, systems approach, is classically represented by Dunlop's (1958) book *Industrial Relations Systems,* with the "late industrialization" approach adopted by Dore (1973) as an important evolutionary variant. The second approach, strategic choice, was developed from the systems approach and is represented by Kochan and colleagues in the United States (Kochan, Katz, and McKersie 1986; Kochan and Katz 1988) and Purcell in Britain (1989; also Purcell and Ahlstrand 1994). The third approach, Marxist political economy, is represented by the work of Hyman (1975, 1989, 2001) and Kelly (1998).

The different schools have been influential in the discipline at different times and in different countries. In the English-speaking world, systems theory was developed in the 1950s and has continued to provide a framework for international comparative work, at the very least providing a convenient checklist for comparative research (Walker 1967). Evolutionary theory was developed in the 1960s and, after a decline in the late 1970s and 1980s, revived in the 1990s. Strategic choice theory was developed in the 1980s and has become a dominant approach in the English-speaking world through providing the framework for much human resource management (HRM) research. Marxist models were especially important in the 1970s and, after marked decline in the 1980s, were revived in the late 1990s. Marxist theories of comparative employment relations were stimulated in the 1970s by high levels of industrial conflict in Europe in the late 1960s and early 1970s, the apparent success of militant unionism, and widespread interest in Marxism among social scientists generally, even in the United States. Braverman's influential *Labor and Monopoly Capital* was published in 1973 (see also Crouch and Pizzorno 1978). The revival of interest in the late 1990s was in a more academic, reflective context, with a more flexible, less militant, less dogmatic approach—more agency, less structure. In continental Europe, Marxist traditions remained strong throughout in Germany, France, and Italy.

In the following section we show how the three perspectives have addressed the four issues used as touchstones.

International Comparative Employment Relations from Three Theoretical Perspectives

The Role of the State

The industrial relations system, in Dunlop's (1958:7) analysis, comprises "certain actors, certain contexts, an ideology which binds the industrial relations system together, and a body of rules created to govern the actors at the place of work and work community." The treatment of the role of the state is limited. In Dunlop's version of systems theory, the state provides rules for the operation of the system, and changes in the balance of power in society are seen as changing the employment relations system. But there is little analysis of the role of politics and power in how the rules are actually created and how outcomes in the system are determined by other systems. The legal system provides a framework within which unions, employers, and their organizations conduct the processes governing employment relations, "the full range of rule making governing the workplace [which is] central to our industrial relations system" (Dunlop 1958:5). This relatively unquestioning treatment of the regulatory regime reflects the historical circumstances in which Dunlop was working. The Taft-Hartley Act of 1947 provided a legal framework acceptable to most employers and unions: the employers' "right to manage" was securely established, underpinned by "responsible" business unionism (Harris 1982). The period when Dunlop was writing was one of political consensus, economic expansion, and a relatively integrated society (apart from the strains over racial segregation and international cold war tensions). Management and labor had reached accommodation on a rule-governed system. This Dunlopian system "worked well in the post World War 2 years [in the United States] because it provided stability while also satisfying other basic economic and organizational needs of labor and management" (Kochan, Katz, and McKersie 1986:45).

Evolutionary systems theory was an extension of Dunlop's initial theory. In this extension the role of the state was also seen as being limited, although given greater prominence in analyses of Asian than of U.S. or U.K. systems. In the strong evolutionary approach developed by Kerr and his colleagues (1962:267), the industrialization process drives the development of employment relations systems toward convergence: "[industrialization] is the great transformation—successful, all embracing, irreversible." Different types of industrializing elites adopted different approaches to industrialization. However, middle-class industrializing elites achieved greatest success. Their approach involved a complex division of labor, with multiple occupational interests, and flexible means of reaching decisions, as in U.S. capitalism. This necessarily involved decentralization. Winning consent required the development of pluralist means of interest representation. Such developments were difficult to reconcile with a powerful role for the state.

The role of the state was given greater prominence in research into Asian employment relations, such as analyses of Japan (Dore 1973, 2000; Kuwahara 2004), than in research into U.S. or U.K. employment relations. Although the driving force for employment relations strategies was enterprise management, such strategies occurred within a framework of positive government industrial policy directed toward national economic development in Japan as, to an even greater extent, in South Korea (Park and Leggett 2004) and Singapore (Leggett 2003). Industrializing elites, drawn from political and economic leadership groups, molded the employment relations system according to their perceptions of the requirements of national economic development.

The interaction between elite state industrializing strategies and employment relations is evident in Sil's (2002) historical study of non-Western late-industrializing societies, Japan and Russia. Sil (2002:94) showed how elite strategies responded to the requirements of industrialization, resulting in tensions between elites and lower-status employees: "The pressures of catch-up industrialisation under the influence of external referents of success, the premium placed on preserving stable employment patterns and social order, and the absence of individualism [combined] to produce organizational dynamics that are not reflected in Western scientific management; but these changes and opportunities still leave considerable room for variation, shaped in part by the influence of distinctive historical inheritances and in part by the choices of actors in new institutions." Elites are more responsive to Western referents (including employment relations practices) than lower-status employees, who tend to be more committed to traditional cultures (and to job security). Although the industrializing elites operate through state as well as private sector institutions, and thus the analysis allocates a greater role to the state than in the strong evolutionary theory, the driving force remains the requirements of the industrialization process. International, national, sector, and enterprise-level influences interact with one another in the pursuit of industrialization.

In view of its focus on enterprise-level business strategy, it is not surprising that the strategic choice perspective has devoted little attention to the role of the state. The focus of strategic choice research on employment relations on the enterprise level is clearly expressed in Boxall and Purcell's (2003) *Strategy and Human Resource Management,* where the close link between HRM and business strategies is explored in detail. Even the issue of social legitimacy is treated primarily as an enterprise-level issue. The implications of this conceptual focus on the enterprise were reinforced by political and economic changes in the 1980s and 1990s, which relaxed the state's constraints on management's freedom to maneuver, for example in Australia, Britain, New Zealand, the United States, and elsewhere. However, neglecting the role of the state is misleading, even in the restricted strategic choice approach, since the increase in management power and consequent changes to employment relations were themselves a reflection of changes in state policies, at least in part.

In the United States the deregulatory policies adopted by successive administrations, Democrat as well as Republican, undermined the commitment to collective bargaining originally based on the New Deal legislation of the 1930s, resulting in a "representation gap" (Towers 1997). In Britain, the post-1997 New Labour government continued most of the industrial relations policies that had been initiated by the earlier Thatcher governments, although key details were reformed to facilitate—though not to encourage—union recognition. In Australia, Labor governments began to reduce the central role of unions before 1996, a process subsequently accelerated by conservative coalition governments. Elsewhere, the role of the state is more evident, as in the European Union, where the regulatory regime has sponsored social partnership. The state created enabling conditions for changes in employment relations systems to occur, in part in response to pressures from actors within the industrial relations system. The state's actions were thus fundamental to changes in enterprise-level management's capacity to undertake employment relations initiatives.

The state receives more attention in Marxist analyses than in systems or strategic choice approaches within the framework of comprehensive analyses of capitalist dynamics. The link between the state and employment relations, and the subordination of state relations to class relations, is evident (Gall 2003). As Hyman (1989:134) put it, "the emergent institutional linkages and tensions between employers, unions and the various agencies of state power must be located concretely within the dynamics and contradictions of capitalist production in its current conjuncture." The politics of the workplace are linked to state politics and the electoral process. The key function of the state is "to secure the often contradictory objectives of accumulation and legitimation" (Hyman 1989:217). Securing these objectives may lead the state to intervene in employment relations to support workers' interests when forced by workplace bargaining power and workers' electoral organization. However, the function of supporting capitalist accumulation takes priority over the function of legitimation, and the state's role is ultimately subordinate to class interests.

The Scope of Management Autonomy

In systems theory there is a high degree of autonomy for enterprise-level managers to conduct their employment relations. Using North American concepts and based on U.S. empirical research, the systems model is one of independent employers bargaining directly with union representatives within an agreed legal framework. Employers surrender little autonomy when they join collective organizations. Conceptions of company-level managerial prerogative and interfirm competition limit the scope for coordinated action amongst employers, although the degree of coordination differs between sectors. Coordination in collective bargaining is achieved through pattern bargaining, which is structured as much by unions as by employers. Union bargaining power constrains employer autonomy on only a relatively small range of issues, for example, the application of seniority rules.

Different versions of evolutionary theory provide different answers to the question of the degree of employer autonomy. The convergence and industrialization form of evolutionary theory (e.g., Kerr, Dunlop, Harbison, and Myers 1962) focuses on employers at the enterprise level, not the national or industry level. Enterprise management is the prime mover in employment relations. Management responds to external environmental changes (in technology, markets, cultural preferences), as in systems theory, in an overrationalistic manner (Mintzberg and Waters 1985). But whereas systems theory reflects a steady-state equilibrium—or at least the search for it—evolutionary theory is more dynamic. Enterprise management conducts employment relations according to its conceptions of the requirements of corporate strategy, itself molded by the requirements of industrializing elites. Less deterministic versions of evolutionary theory (e.g., Dore 1973) laid greater stress on national elite strategies and the institutional and cultural constraints on enterprise management freedom to maneuver than supporters of the industrialization thesis.

In the strategic choice perspective the enterprise is the primary unit of analysis, with management seen as having a high degree of autonomy: "It was management that initiated the new non-union personnel practices at the workplace and accelerated their expansion through strategic investment decisions. When management adjusted to economic pressures by broadening its activities to the workplace and strategic levels, it benefited from a significant power advantage and operated as the driving force in introducing change in industrial relations" (Kochan, Katz, and McKersie 1986:237). HRM—more broadly defined than non-union policies—involved a close association between human resource (HR) strategy and corporate strategy and provided the core of this firm-centric approach. In the strategic choice approach, the role of multiemployer bargaining is limited because enterprises wish to maximize the scope for achieving their own strategic priorities and responding to their own specific market circumstances. Increased competition, especially increased international competition, reduced the likelihood that enterprises would wish to use multiemployer industry-level collective bargaining as a means of eliminating wage costs as a way to secure competitive advantage. At the international level there are no employers' organizations that play a direct role in collective bargaining.

In Marxist frameworks the analysis of management autonomy is ambivalent. On the one hand the assumption is of management power and autonomy, with management interests prevailing (to simplify): "Under capitalist employment relations, management are the predominant though by no means the exclusive agents in the determination of employee relations" (Blyton and Turnbull 1998:101). On the other hand, the degree of autonomy available to management is limited, with competition forcing management to seek the most efficient means to maximize the extraction of surplus value. From this perspective, employment relations are determined ultimately by the competitive processes and structures of the capitalist political economy, not by the strategic choices of enterprise managers.

The Role of Union Organization

In systems theory the analysis of the role of unions is one-dimensional. Unions are conceived as unitary organizations, with agreed objectives, namely, the negotiation of the best possible terms and conditions of employment within the framework of agreed-on workplace rules. Union officials appear to be professional guardians of the rules, especially seniority rules. Within this framework the major strategic issue is seen as the trade-off between wages and job security, usually conceptualized within a labor market framework. Unions are regarded primarily as economic organizations, with limited institutional political ambitions, although individual union leaders often have extensive political connections with Democratic Party politicians.

The role of unions in the evolutionary forms of systems theory was secondary, responsive primarily to management strategies and to social, economic, and political contexts. Although personally politically sympathetic to trade unionism, neither Kerr nor Dore saw unions as the driving force for changes in employment relations systems. For example, Dore saw a major role of unionism in institutionalizing the management of labor following a period of high level of industrial conflict in Japan in the early 1950s, as earlier in the United States. Evolutionary theorists, as systems theorists, generally saw unions in economic terms, with little attention paid to their role as means for political mobilization.

Writers within the strategic choice paradigm generally see unions as having only a very limited role. The strategic choices facing unions have played a less prominent role than those facing enterprises, although some limited discussion of the former can be found in Katz and Kochan (2003). In strategic choice theory the enterprise-level linkage between business strategy and human resources strategy contributed to shifting the focus away from traditional concerns with employment relations themselves as a system or with the political and representational role of employees' organizations. The justification for union organization became contributing to efficiency and effectiveness at the enterprise level, not interest representation. Whereas employment relations research in the 1970s neglected management, especially in the United Kingdom, the 1990s focus on strategic choice and HRM tended to induce researchers to neglect unions. The assumptions of unity of interests embedded in strategic management thinking were visible in employment relations research, though the unitarist assumptions of "sophisticated modern" HRM strategies are no less contrary to the pluralist bases of late 20th century employment relations research than the unitarist assumptions of traditional paternalism.

Using the concepts of strategic choice, it is possible to construct a strategic choice approach to union activities. In this view, unions are engaged in competition for employee interest representation rights, with each other and with other forms of interest representation (e.g., works councils and other forms of employees' representative committees). In considering ways of increasing (or maintaining) market share, unions can follow strategies comparable to those followed by enterprises seeking to secure competitive advantage in product markets. Hence unions may follow price-based product or service differentiation, or withdrawal strategies. Union strategies will depend upon their external context (including employers' strategies, government policies, markets for products and labor, and the competitive strategies of other unions) and the extent to which union internal arrangements allow union leaders freedom to act strategically; union members may have a constraining influence—for instance, through elections, ballots, and conference procedures—on the ability of union leaders to follow specific strategies (R. Martin, Undy, and Gennard 1999).

In Marxist analyses, unions play a crucial role. Unions are political as well as economic organizations, a means of collective worker mobilization. Hence Kelly's (1998) mobilization theory (derived from Tilly 1978) provides a sophisticated analysis of union development. Mobilization theory identifies structural and subjective factors (interests, identification, opportunity) together with action categories (mobilization and organization). It provides a dialectical analysis of the interactions between employers and employees. It focuses on power and responses to the differential distribution of power as the central dynamic of employment relations. It recognizes the importance of political, social, and economic factors in the development of collective action. However, the framework provides only a limited basis for comparative employment relations. First, it focuses on only one aspect of employment relations, the collective mobilization of employees; little is said about the role of employers or the state. Second, it focuses on the areas in which the interests of employers and employees conflict, without analyzing the areas in which their interests coincide (R. Martin 1999).

The Scope of Collective Bargaining

In systems theories the primary mechanism for determining rules at the workplace was collective bargaining, and in practice, much research equated employment relations with collective bargaining. Collective bargaining provided mechanisms for regulating and institutionalizing potential industrial conflict, as well as for allocating the economic surplus.

Collective bargaining was the primary mechanism for managing employment relations in the classic evolutionary literature, as in Kerr, Dunlop, Harbison, and Myers (1962). The level at which bargaining primarily occurred—national, industrial sector, enterprise, or establishment—differed between countries, with complex multitiered systems in many countries. In the United States, as in Japan, bargaining occurred primarily at the enterprise level, while there was a greater role for the regional (*lander*) level employers' associations in Germany. Although the Japanese annual spring offensive (*shunto*) involved coordination between union organizations, the major elements were determined at the enterprise level. The internal focus of Japanese bargaining is evident in Dore's (1973) study of Hitachi in the early 1970s, as well as in more recent work (Ishikawa and Shiraishi 2001). Changes in technology, product markets, and the political context increased management's power and widened management's scope for choice in employment relations from 1980 onward.

In the strategic choice perspective, employment relations are determined either by unilateral management decision making or by collective bargaining. In the United States and Britain, managers' strong ideological commitment to a broad definition of managerial prerogatives undermined collective bargaining, although elsewhere, especially in Europe, there was less ideological opposition to collective bargaining (Poole, Mansfield, and Mendes 2001). The survival of collective bargaining thus depends upon government action, the legal framework, and the unions' ability to maintain their institutional strength, itself partly dependent upon product and labor market conditions in their recruitment territories. The decline of collective bargaining has been documented by writers in the strategic choice tradition in the United States and Britain. Thus, Kochan, Katz, and McKersie (1986) analyzed the collapse of the New Deal settlement that underpinned collective bargaining in the United States in the 1980s. In Britain, the 1998 Workplace Employment Relations Survey showed a significant contraction in the proportion of workplaces covered by collective bargaining as well as a narrowing of the range of issues covered by collective bargaining: "collective bargaining coverage has fallen steadily since 1984" (Millward, Bryson, and Forth 2000:160). In emphasizing the role of management initiative and the marginalization of union power, those using a strategic choice perspective have underscored the decline of collective bargaining. In place of supporting collective bargaining, U.S. labor policy has been increasingly concerned with the substantive rights of individual employees, but the level of substantive rights has been set low. A similar trend is evident in Britain, where the post-1979 Conservative governments weakened the power and limited the roles of unions. The post-1997 New Labour governments have been concerned to establish individual entitlements, including a minimum wage, rather than to provide legislative support for unions and the collective bargaining process per se (though New Labour has also legislated on union recognition).

Marxist assessments have varied as to the functions of collective bargaining. Some Marxists have opposed union involvement in institutionalized collective bargaining, as in their view it merely leads to compromise, class collaboration, and the preservation of capitalism (Bamber and Sheldon 2004). Among some Marxists, collective bargaining has become merely an aspect of the arena for class struggle, of limited independent significance. Others have accorded more legitimacy to collective bargaining, as they have seen it deliver tangible benefits to unions—by reinforcing unions' role as permanent organizations—as well as to union members (Wilczynski 1983). Kelly (1998), for example, saw collective bargaining as a means of enhancing collective mobilization, with political consequences, as well as an economic means of improving the terms and conditions of employment.

This section of the paper has focused on different theoretical perspectives applied to the four touchstones identified: the role of the state, the degree of enterprise-level management autonomy, the interpretation of unionism, and the significance of collective bargaining. We have discussed three major perspectives: systems theory and its first cousin, evolutionary theory; strategic choice; and Marxist political economy. The approaches outlined are conditioned by the intellectual traditions of the countries within which they were developed and the recent and current political issues facing capital and labor there. The strategic choice perspective became the dominant approach to international comparative research in English-speaking countries by the early 21st century. This approach involves only a limited role for the state and a focus on the enterprise, including a strong role for strategic HR directors, with economically oriented (in the limited sectors in which it exists) business unionism and decentralized bargaining structures. This model is both prescriptive, the basis for a "sophisticated modern" employment relations system, and descriptive of leading U.S. multinationals. Alongside this dominant model there are smaller groups adopting evolutionary and Marxist approaches. The strategic choice model can lead to overemphasis upon employment relations as an aspect of "the efficient management of HR" and to neglect of the democratic and representational role of collective organization as well as its mobilizing role. It can also lead to an "under-politicized" view of employment relations, in which the role of the state is neglected. In this regard, many of those working in the English-speaking world have neglected the continental European tradition of research in comparative employment relations, with its clear focus on the role of government. As Frege (2003:256) argued, "the future of the entire industrial relations discipline might well lie in the rediscovery and promotion of the continental European tradition of industrial relations as a socio-political process." A similar emphasis on the role of the state is evident in the work of Traxler, Blaschke, and Kittel (2001). The following section seeks to develop an integrated approach drawing from all three traditions.

An Integrated Political Economy Approach

The three approaches to employment relations discussed in the first section were developed between the 1950s and the early 1990s. Therefore, they do not fully take into account trends in the international political economy in the 1990s that have significant implications for employment relations. Three trends are especially relevant.

The first trend is the intensification of international competition manifested as globalization, especially in manufactured goods (international competition in most services remains less intense; Giles 2000). This was intensified further with China's growth as a major industrial competitor, increasingly displacing Japan and earlier "tiger" economies. Textiles initially provided China's leading edge into world markets, followed by a wide range of basic manufactured goods (Moore 2002). India is another "awakening giant," competing successfully with developed and newly industrializing economies, for instance, in providing call centers and information technology services. The economic ascent of China, India, and other developing economies has at least two implications for employment relations theory. Directly, their rise draws attention to a wider range of political and economic models of employment relations. Indirectly, their impact on the product markets for manufacturing and to a lesser extent for services in other economies undermines the viability of other systems.

The second trend is the spread of "deregulation" policies. Deregulation impacts directly and indirectly on employment relations. Directly, governments (e.g., the Thatcher U.K. government) have initiated moves to deregulate aspects of labor markets, and many such policies have had significant implications for employment relations (although many deregulatory policies have legitimized re-regulatory practices rather than promoted fundamental deregulation). Deregulation of product markets has fewer direct implications, but nevertheless can still have profound effects for employment relations, as in telecommunications and aviation

(Katz 1997; Calder 2003). In both sectors, deregulation has led to increased competition between traditional, bureaucratic organizations and new, more agile competitors. The new competitors were less bureaucratic and more flexible; followed HRM strategies involving more individualized employment relations policies, leaner and more flexible work organization, and lower pay levels; and were unionized to a much lesser extent than their older competitors.

The third trend is the collapse of communism. The collapse had three direct consequences for employment relations. First, in post-socialist economies it led to new systems of employment relations that combined new institutional forms with remnants of socialist culture and practice. Second, the collapse of communist internationalism weakened support for left-wing unionism, especially in the developing world. Moreover, third, the collapse of socialism boosted the confidence of capitalist ideologists, particularly liberal ideologists in the United States and the United Kingdom, with the impending "end of history" reinforcing neoliberalism and the anticollectivist and deregulatory policies mentioned earlier.

From the political economy perspective advocated in this paper, the focus of analysis is the distribution of power within the enterprise and in the larger society, a form of pluralist political economy that does not reduce employment relations to merely an aspect of class struggle. The integrated political economy perspective links systems of production, the role of government, the broader social and economic environment, and employment relations institutions at the enterprise, industry, national, and international levels. The approach advocated is similar to Wilkinson's "production systems" approach (Burchell, Deakin, Michie, and Rubery 2003). The perspective is generally applicable but is especially useful for exploring employment relations in newly industrializing economies, such as China, India, and South Korea, and in transitional former socialist economies in Eastern Europe, where the role of the state is more obviously important than in many developed market economies. The approach draws upon a non-Marxist (as well as Marxist) political economy tradition, involving a close analysis of the interaction between interests and institutions (Smith and Meiskins 1995; Pontusson and Swenson 1996; Murray, Lévesque, and Vallée 2000; Wailes 2000). Interests and institutions are influenced, in different ways and to different degrees, by national modes of integration into the international political economy (Wailes and Lansbury 2003).

Viewing employment relations as a sociopolitical process makes it feasible for international comparative employment relations research to reflect the full variety of employment relations systems. This variety is broader than the range of countries traditionally covered by comparative research. Although most comparative researchers have accommodated the Japanese system, few include the full range of Asian and European systems. For example, literature on the Chinese employment relations system is currently emerging (e.g., Zhu and Warner 2000), while within Europe it is necessary to incorporate the former socialist state systems (Ferner and Hyman 1998). To widen the range of systems covered by an adequate comparative model, a different approach is required, building on the strengths of the schools we have discussed. It should link employment relations to the wider political, economic, and social environments. It should be dynamic, incorporating endogenous and exogenous change. It should be capable of handling the diversity of international, national, and subnational institutions. It should recognize the plurality of interests, the duality of cooperation and conflict within the enterprise, and the dialectic between interests and institutions. The focus should include the bargaining power of participants in employment relations and the factors that influence the exercise of such power, inside and outside the enterprise.

The integrated political economy approach we are proposing moves beyond the debates on convergence and divergence (Van Ruysseveldt 1995; Budhwar and Debrah 2001). The approach focuses on the interaction between interests and institutions in the context of changes in the international political economy. Similar international developments may have different effects on employment relations, depending upon the mode of integration of the national economy into the international system. Hence the effects of globalization are likely to be different in a country heavily dependent upon exports, such as Sweden, from those in a large country with a large domestic market, such as the United States, and employment relations will be influenced accordingly (Bamber, Lansbury, and Wailes 2004:chap. 12). In the former, the pressures of international competition may require a dual system, with a "sophisticated modern" HRM strategy in the internationally oriented export sectors, while the domestically insulated service sector may retain more traditional structures. In the latter, employment relations may be expected to remain a more coherent system. In Central and Eastern Europe, the changes since 1989 have resulted in highly segmented employment relations systems, with limited spillover between segments.

Using such an approach, let us reconsider the four issues we identified as central pillars of employment relations.

The Role of the State

The political economy approach stresses the important role of the state and of political action. The role of the state was central even during the period of dominance of the classical systems model of the industrial relations system, since the Eisenhower political consensus provided the necessary enabling conditions for the relatively smooth functioning of the post–New Deal collective bargaining system. The role of the state retains its significance for all varieties of political economy. The vital role of the state in socialist and ex-socialist economies is evident. The Chinese Communist Party's decision to adopt a more reformist and open approach in 1978 was fundamental for subsequent developments, while political events have been crucial for former socialist states in Central and Eastern Europe. In developed market economies too, the role of the state is fundamental, at both the macro and the micro levels. The state plays the major role in perpetuating national business systems, which provide the context for employment relations. As Whitley (2002:xviii) argued, core national institutions, primarily the state, structure "the environment of economic actors so that distinctive economic logics become established that are associated with particular kinds of production systems. These latter consist of mutually interdependent combinations of production techniques, products and market types, forms of the division of labour at the workplace, authority structures and reward systems." Property relations are fundamental to employment relations and remain matters of national legislation.

At the micro level, labor legislation continues to proliferate, both for collective and for individual employment relations actors. Recognizing the importance of national regulatory regimes, the E.U.'s Social Charter reserved major issues of employment for national regulation, under the principle of subsidiarity. In short, at the macro level the state provides the framework for employment relations by providing the legal structure of property relations and thus structuring national business systems. The state also provides the legal and institutional arrangements whereby employment relations processes are conducted. The nature of such arrangements has significant influence on the outcomes of employment relations processes in most work situations. This influence is, of course, usually more direct in the case of public sector employers.

The linking role of the state in national business systems is evident in research in the continental European tradition. For example, coordinated market systems such as Germany's involve a close linkage between enterprises, the educational system, sector-level arrangements for industrial training, the employment relations system, and public policy (Wever 1995; Hall and Soskice 2001). Similarly, although the sector-level arrangements of the classic Swedish model weakened in the 1990s, the social contract survived (Hammarström, Huzzard, and Nilsson 2004). The European Union remains committed to tripartism and social partnership—involving the state, unions, and employers' organizations in joint decision making over the issues covered by the Social Charter—and has fostered the growth of tripartite institutions in the former socialist states of Central and Eastern Europe. (However, the impact of tripartite decisions upon business has been the source of much controversy, with employers, especially in Britain, accusing the European Union of reducing flexibility and undermining European competitiveness and unionists in Central and Eastern Europe regarding tripartite institutions as largely symbolic [R. Martin and Cristescu-Martin 2002:178–79].) Detailed national labor codes continue to seek to regulate employment relations even at enterprise level in some parts of Central and Eastern Europe.

The Scope of Management Autonomy

A major theme of recent employment relations research, especially from a strategic choice perspective, has been the increased scope of management autonomy. A key argument has been that traditional industrial relations is being displaced by HRM, often with an individualistic orientation. Researchers with a descriptive approach and especially those with a prescriptive one have emphasized the integration between HRM and business strategy, with differences in HRM strategies linked to differences in business strategy, typically analyzed using Porter's (1980, 1985) generic competitive advantage models. Strategies for employment relations are seen as third-order functional strategies, derived from corporate strategy, first order; structural approach, second-order (Purcell 1989). The descriptive literature has documented the decline of collective bargaining and the enhancement of managerial autonomy through HRM, while the prescriptive literature has outlined the employment relations policies and structures appropriate for the achievement of business objectives, as articulated in the Harvard manifesto on HRM, *Managing Human Assets* (Beer, Spector, Lawrence, Mills, and Walton 1984; also Dowling, Welch, and Schuller 1999).

Applying a political economy approach suggests that the descriptive literature exaggerates the degree of management autonomy. Management autonomy is constrained by state action and by the modus operandi of the national business system. It is also constrained by the structure of international competition within competitive product markets and on occasion by the bargaining power of employee organizations, especially in the public sector. Using an integrated political economy approach, we view managers as pursuing strategies shaped and constrained by the enterprise's political, economic, and social environments at international, national, industrial sector, and enterprise levels. There is no a priori assumption about the strength or the location of the constraints. A strategic choice perspective emphasizing increased management autonomy may be oversimplified, for at least four reasons. First, enterprise strategies are founded upon structures of property relations, themselves determined by state structures. There are major differences between systems in which property rights are invested unequivocally in private individuals and those in which property rights are invested in corporate bodies or the state, especially over ways in which economic surplus is distributed. Second, management initiative is constrained by the structure of international competition. Third, there are differences in national business systems and in the range of acceptable ways of conducting employment relations, the templates of acceptability, making some strategic choices more likely than others (Scott 1995). Fourth, public sector employment relations are usually bound more tightly by political considerations, including state traditions and public expectations.

The Role of Union Organization

Employment relations systems evidently differ in the extent and type of union organization. Among earlier writers, for example, Lange, Ross, and Vannicelli (1982) and Gourevitch and his colleagues (1984) followed a political economy approach in their analyses of union strategies in Western Europe in which they linked union strategies to economic crisis and showed divergent responses (also Goldthorpe 1984). They identified four broad approaches in their ideal-typical analysis of union responses to economic crisis. The first was a maximalist response, associated with some French Left unions, involving a refusal to cooperate in the management of the crisis at enterprise, sector, or national level. The second was an interventionist response, involving unions in a cooperative incremental approach, as in Italy. The third strategy was a defensive particularistic strategy, with union power used to obstruct changes, as by some British unions. The fourth strategy was a corporatist one, in which unions collaborated with the state and employers in income policies and broader economic and social programs. Swedish and, to some extent, German unions followed this approach, especially during periods of Social Democratic government. Lange, Ross, and Vannicelli (1982) distinguished between union movements according to four characteristics: market strength, political influence, interunion relations, and expectations. Such approaches are valuable, for they link organizational strategies to the national political and economic environments.

More recent empirical research has documented the decline in union membership, bargaining power, and institutional strength. The decline has been especially marked in Australia, the United States, and Britain, although it is also evident in Western Europe (with the general exception of Scandinavia) and East Asia. HRM strategies focused on the enhancement of human capital are conceived in individual terms and, in principle if not always in practice, have a negative impact on union organization. However, this focus on levels of union membership as a measure of union significance is misleading. Even where management adopts individualized HRM policies, this is partly in response to perceptions of the threat of union organization: improvements in the terms and conditions of employment are incorporated into HRM strategies to counter potential union influence (Bamber and Sheldon 2004). Hence British research has shown that HRM strategies are more likely to be adopted in establishments with union representation than in nonunionized establishments (Legge 1995:chap. 10).

The coverage of collective agreements remains wider than the scope of union membership, even in countries where the extended application of collective agreements is not legally required. In some countries (e.g., France) the application of the terms of collective agreements may be legally required even where employees are not union members, reducing the incentives for union membership and weakening the economic foundations of union organization, but extending union influence. The influence of union organizations politically exceeds their membership levels, especially in political systems in which union density is low, as in parts of Western Europe (especially France) and in Central and Eastern Europe. Unions also perform wider social roles, in association with other types of social organization. In socialist and former socialist societies, unions formed ancillary social organizations to political parties, while in Catholic regimes there has been a close association between unions and religious organizations. In such circumstances, unions may have little independent power but be important sources of social and economic benefits and thus maintain influence even if their membership has declined.

A main dimension of differentiation between types of union movement is the degree of focus on limited economic or broader political concerns. In this area, by using an integrated political economy approach, we can see unions both as a means of exercising economic power and as a means of political mobilization. In Marxist theory, unions are a means of political mobilization, whether on the shop floor or through the ballot box, or both. As Hyman (1989:221) argued, following a survey of European trade union movements in the 1980s, "the most successful of the union movements examined are those which have sustained a close articulation between the politics of production and the politics of politics." Union organizers may aim to mobilize workers for political objectives, even if the incentives for potential individual union recruits to join may be economic (Undy and R. Martin 1984:186–89). Union leaders and activists are disproportionately influential in the development of union strategies because rank-and-file union members have few incentives to participate in collective decisions and members' participation rates are low, except in decisions on pay awards and strike action. Political mobilization may be an intended outcome of union organization, as it was for the early Socialists in British unionism in the late 19th century, or may be an unintended consequence of union organization. Hyman's (2001) study of European trade unionism showed the close association between political movements and union organization in France, Germany, and Italy.

The Scope of Collective Bargaining

Collective bargaining has been central to most employment relations systems: "[c]ollective bargaining coverage is one of the essentials of organized industrial relations" (Traxler, Blaschke, and Kittel 2001:194). Employment relations systems differ in the levels at which bargaining occurs, the participants in the bargaining process, and the scope of the agreements or contracts made, as well as in the outcomes of the bargaining process. There have been major changes in the institutions of collective bargaining since the 1980s, for instance, in the United States, Britain, and Australia. Hence Katz and Darbishire (2000) identified an international trend toward decentralized enterprise-level collective bargaining. Many employers' organizations have redefined their roles to focus on providing consultancy, advice, technical support, and professional development for personnel professionals within enterprises rather than the conduct of multiemployer collective negotiations. Certain unions have changed in a similar way. Although collective organization remains a cornerstone of unionism, the growth of service-oriented unionism, whether based on providing individual benefits such as shopping discounts or insurance against arbitrary exercise of employer power, has tended to place relations between unions and their members onto a more individualized basis.

These and other changes have led researchers in the strategic choice tradition to emphasize the decline of collective organization and related collective bargaining. However, many of them have exaggerated the extent of the decline by focusing research on the English-speaking countries: United States, Britain, Australia, and New Zealand. In their study of employment relations in 20 countries, Traxler, Blaschke, and Kittel (2001:197) concluded that between 1980 and 1996 the coverage of collective bargaining increased in five countries (Finland, France, the Netherlands, Portugal, and Spain), declined in five (Australia, Britain, Germany, Japan, and the United States), and stayed the same in two (Belgium and Sweden), with incomplete data for three (Austria, Canada, and Denmark). Levels of collective bargaining remained high in the public sector, while even in the private sector the mean coverage of collective bargaining over all of these systems changed only from 69% to 61% of employees, with the largest changes being in the United States and especially Britain. The International Labour Organization remains committed to collective bargaining, while the European Union's social partnership arrangements institutionalize collective organization. The growth of collective bargaining in former socialist systems has increased the importance of collective bargaining internationally. It is also easy to exaggerate the extent of changes in the level of collective bargaining. Of 27 countries examined in 2002, only six (the Czech Republic, Hungary, Japan, Poland, the United Kingdom, and the United States) had company-level bargaining as the dominant mode, despite the presumed universal trend toward decentralized bargaining structures (Carley 2004).

Conclusion

This paper has characterized employment relations systems in terms of four touchstones: the role of the state, the degree of employer autonomy, the extent and type of union organization, and the extent of collective bargaining. We do not claim that these touchstones are the only possible ones, nor are they mutually exclusive (e.g., if union density is low, then it is likely that there will be relatively little collective bargaining). But they are among the key ones in most systems. This contribution has shown how three different theoretical perspectives—systems theory, strategic choice theory, and Marxist theory—have provided different views on the role of the state in employment relations, the level of employer autonomy, union organization, and collective bargaining.

Each perspective has highlighted different aspects of employment relations systems. Systems theory has highlighted how employment relations institutions, especially collective bargaining arrangements, may form an integrated system to accommodate employer–employee interests, provided there is consensus on procedural rules. The strategic choice perspective has highlighted the role of employers' initiatives, especially in developing employment relations responses to international product market competition. Marxist political economy theory has highlighted the role of political mobilization. These three perspectives, however, do not provide comprehensive analyses of the dynamics of comparative employment relations in the early 21st century. To provide a more comprehensive approach, the second section of the paper outlined an integrated political economy approach.

An integrated political economy approach provides a framework for analyzing international, national, sector, and enterprise-level influences on employment relations. We have sought to incorporate economic and political factors in this paper. But in reaction against deterministic approaches we have emphasized the "political" in the political economy approach, in three senses. First, *political* refers to fundamental social relationships, of which the most important are property relations and their importance for employment relations. The significance of such influences is especially evident once comparative employment relations research moves beyond developed market economies to focus also on developing economies. Second, the approach is political in its emphasis on the relationships between specific participants in employment relations and political actors, for example, in the relationships between business, unions, and political institutions. Third, it is political in that the relationships between participants in the employment relations system are based on power relations as much as on market relations.

Acknowledgments

We are indebted to Bruce E. Kaufman for patient and constructive editorship and grateful to Anamaria M. Cristescu-Martin for assistance and advice. Participants in seminars of the International Industrial Relations Association, Industrial Relations Research Association, International Labor Organization, European Foundation for the Improvement of Living and Working Conditions, and the University of Paderborn have made helpful comments at various stages in the writing of this paper.

References

Bain, George S., and Hugh A. Clegg. 1974. "A Strategy for Industrial Relations Research in Great Britain." *British Journal of Industrial Relations*, Vol. 12, no. 1 (January), pp. 91–113.

Bamber, Greg J., Russell D. Lansbury, and Nick Wailes, eds. 2004. *International and Comparative Employment Relations: Globalisation and the Developed Market Economies*, 4th ed. Sydney: Allen and Unwin; London: Sage.

Bamber, Greg J., and Peter Sheldon. 2004. "Collective Bargaining: Towards Decentralization?" In Roger Blanpain, ed., *Comparative Labour Law and Industrial Relations in Industrialized Market Economies*, 8th ed., The Hague: Kluwer Law International, pp. 509–48.

Baron, James N., and David M. Kreps. 1999. *Strategic Human Resources: Frameworks for General Managers*. New York: Wiley.

Beer, Michael, Bert Spector, Paul R. Lawrence, D. Quinn Mills, and Richard E. Walton. 1984. *Managing Human Assets*. New York: Free Press.

Belanger, Jacques, Christian Berggren, Torsten Bjorkman, and Christoph Kohler. 1999. *Being Local World Wide: ABB and the Challenge of Global Management*. Ithaca, NY: Cornell University Press.

Black, Boyd. Forthcoming. "National Culture and Comparative Industrial Relations Theory." *International Journal of Human Resources Management*.

Blyton, Paul, and Peter Turnbull. 1998. *The Dynamics of Employee Relations*, 2nd ed. Basingstoke, UK: Macmillan Business.

Boxall, Peter, and John Purcell. 2003. *Strategy and Human Resource Management*. Basingstoke, UK: Palgrave Macmillan.

Braverman, Harry. 1973. *Labor and Monopoly Capital: The Degradation of Work in the Twentieth Century*. New York: Monthly Review Press.

Budhwar, Pawan S., and Yaw Debrah. 2001. "Rethinking Comparative and Cross National Human Resource Management Research." *International Journal of Human Resource Management*, Vol. 12, no. 3 (May), pp. 497–515.

Burchell, Brendan, Simon Deakin, Jonathan Michie, and Jill Rubery, eds. 2003. *Systems of Production: Markets, Organisations and Performance*. London: Routledge.

Calder, Simon. 2003. *No Frills: The Truth behind the Low Cost Revolution in the Skies*. London: Virgin.

Carley, Mark. 2004. "Industrial Relations in the EU, Japan and USA, 2002." European Industrial Relations Observatory (EIRO) On-Line. <http://www.eiro.eurofound.eu.int/2004/01/feature/tn0401101f.html> [23 March 2004].

Crouch, Colin. 1993. *Industrial Relations and European State Traditions*. Oxford: Oxford University Press.

Crouch, Colin, and Alessandro Pizzorno, eds. 1978. *The Resurgence of Class Conflict in Western Europe since 1968*, 2 vols. London: Macmillan.

Dore, Ronald. 1973. *British Factory–Japanese Factory: The Origins of National Diversity in Industrial Relations*. London: Allen and Unwin.

———. 2000. *Stock Market Capitalism: Welfare Capitalism. Japan and Germany versus the Anglo-Saxons*. Oxford: Oxford University Press.

Dowling, Peter J., Denice E. Welch, and Randy S. Schuller. 1999. *International Human Resource Management: Managing People in a Multinational Context*. Cincinnati, OH: South-Western College Publishing.

Dunlop, John T. 1958. *Industrial Relations Systems*. New York: Holt, Reinhart and Winston.

Edwards, Paul, ed. 2003. *Industrial Relations: Theory and Practice*, 2nd ed. Oxford: Blackwell.

Ferner, Anthony. 1994. "Multinational Companies and Human Resource Management: An Overview of Research Issues." *Human Resource Management Journal*, Vol. 4, no. 3 (Spring), pp. 79–102.

———. 1997. "Country of Origin Effects and HRM in Multinational Companies." *Human Resource Management Journal*, Vol. 7, no. 1, pp. 19–37.

Ferner, Anthony, and Richard Hyman. 1998. "Introduction: Towards European Industrial Relations?" In Anthony Ferner and Richard Hyman, eds., *Changing Industrial Relations in Europe*, 2nd ed., Oxford: Blackwell, pp. xi–xxvi.

Ferner, Anthony, and Javier Quintanilla. 1998. "Multinationals, National Business Systems and HRM: The Enduring Influence of National Identity or a Process of 'Anglo-Saxonization.'" *International Journal of Human Resource Management*, Vol. 9, no. 4 (August), pp. 710–31.

Flanders, Allan. 1970. *Management and Unions: The Theory and Reform of Industrial Relations*. London: Faber and Faber.

Frege, Carola. 2003. "Industrial Relations in Continental Europe." In Peter Ackers and Adrian J. Wilkinson, eds., *Understanding Work and Employment: Industrial Relations in Transition*, Oxford: Oxford University Press, pp. 242–62.

Gall, Gregor. 2003. "Marxism and Industrial Relations." In Peter Ackers and Adrian J. Wilkinson, eds., *Understanding Work and Employment: Industrial Relations in Transition*, Oxford: Oxford University Press, pp. 316–24.

Gardner, Margaret, and Gill Palmer. 1997. *Employment Relations: Industrial Relations and Human Resource Management in Australia*, 2nd ed. Melbourne: Palgrave Macmillan.

Giles, Anthony. 2000. "Globalisation and Industrial Relations Theory." *Journal of Industrial Relations*, Vol. 42, no. 2, pp. 173–94.

Goldthorpe, John H. 1984. "The End of Convergence: Corporatist and Dualist Tendencies in Modern Western Societies." In John H. Goldthorpe, ed., *Order and Conflict in Contemporary Capitalism: Studies in the Political Economy of Western European Nations*, Oxford: Oxford University Press.

Gourevitch, Peter A., Andrew Martin, George Ross, Christopher S. Allen, Stephen Bornstein, and Andrei Markovits. 1984. *Unions and Economic Crisis: Britain, West Germany and Sweden*. London: Allen and Unwin.

Hall, Peter A., and David Soskice, eds. 2001. *Varieties of Capitalism: The Institutional Foundations of Comparative Advantage*. Oxford: Oxford University Press.

Hammarström, Olle, Tony Huzzard, and Tommy Nilsson. 2004. "Employment Relations in Sweden." In Greg J. Bamber, Russell D. Lansbury, and Nick Wailes, eds., *International and Comparative Employment Relations: Globalisation and the Developed Market Economies*, 4th ed., Sydney: Allen and Unwin; London: Sage, pp. 254–76.

Harris, Howell J. 1982. *The Right to Manage: Industrial Relations Policies of American Business in the 1940s*. Madison, WI: University of Wisconsin Press.

Hofstede, Geert. 1980. *Culture's Consequences: International Differences in Work-Related Values*. Beverly Hills, CA: Sage.

Hyman, Richard. 1975. *Industrial Relations: A Marxist Introduction*. London: Macmillan.

————. 1989. *The Political Economy of Industrial Relations: Theory and Practice in a Cold Climate*. London: Macmillan.

————. 2001. *Understanding European Trade Unionism: Between Market, Class and Society*. London: Sage.

Isaac, Joe. 2003. *Inter-cultural and Other Forces in the Transfer of Human Resource Management and Industrial Relations Practices under Globalisation*. Vienna: Austrian Institute of Economic Research.

Ishikawa, Akihiro, and Toshimasa Shiraishi. 2001. "Japanese Employees' Attitudes in Transition 1984–94." In Roderick Martin, Akihiro Ishikawa, Csaba Makó, and Francesco Consoli, eds., *Workers, Firms and Unions: Industrial Relations in Transition*, Frankfurt-am-Main: Lang.

Katz, Harry C., ed. 1997. *Telecommunications: Restructuring Work and Employment Relations Worldwide*. Ithaca, NY: Cornell University Press.

Katz, Harry C., and Owen Darbishire. 2000. *Converging Divergences: Worldwide Changes in Employment Systems*. Ithaca, NY: Cornell University Press.

Katz, Harry C., and Thomas A. Kochan. 2003. *An Introduction to Collective Bargaining and Industrial Relations*. Boston: McGraw-Hill.

Kelly, John. 1998. *Rethinking Industrial Relations: Mobilization, Collectivism and Long Waves*. London: Routledge.

Kerr, Clark, John T. Dunlop, Frederick H. Harbison, and Charles A. Myers. 1962. *Industrialism and Industrial Man: The Problems of Labour and Management in Economic Growth*. London: Heinemann.

Kitschelt, Herbert, Peter Lange, Gary Marks, and John D. Stephens, eds. 1999. *Continuity and Change in Contemporary Capitalism*. Cambridge: Cambridge University Press.

Kochan, Thomas A., and Harry C. Katz. 1988. *Collective Bargaining and Industrial Relations. From Theory to Policy and Practice*. Homewood, IL: Irwin.

Kochan, Thomas A., Harry C. Katz, and Robert B. McKersie. 1986. *The Transformation of American Industrial Relations*. New York: Basic Books.

Kuwahara, Yasuo. 2004. "Employment Relations in Japan." In Greg J. Bamber, Russell D. Lansbury, and Nick Wailes, eds., *International and Comparative Employment Relations: Globalisation and the Developed Market Economies*, 4th ed., Sydney: Allen and Unwin; London: Sage, pp. 277–305.

Lange, Peter, George Ross, and Maurizio Vannicelli. 1982. *Unions, Change and Crisis: French and Italian Unions and the Political Economy 1945–1980*. London: Allen and Unwin.

Legge, Karen. 1995. *Human Resource Management: Rhetorics and Realities*. Basingstoke, UK: Macmillan.

Leggett, Christopher J. 2003. "Strategic HRM and the Transformation of Singapore's Industrial Relations." In Michael J. Morley, Patrick Gunnigle, Noreen Heraty, Jill Pearson, Haaris Sheikh, and Siobhan Tiernan, eds., *Proceedings of the 7th Conference on International Human Resource Management: Exploring the Mosaic, Developing the Discipline* (University of Limerick, Limerick, Ireland, 4–6 June 2003). Dublin: Interesource Group, CD-ROM.

Locke, Richard M., and Thomas A. Kochan. 1995. "The Transformation of Industrial Relations? A Review of the Evidence." In Richard M. Locke, Thomas A. Kochan, and Michael J. Piore, eds., *Employment Relations in a Changing World Economy*, Cambridge, MA: MIT Press.

Martin, Roderick. 1999. "Mobilization Theory: A New Paradigm for Industrial Relations." *Human Relations*, Vol. 52, no. 9 (September), pp. 1205–16.

Martin, Roderick, and Anamaria M. Cristescu-Martin. 2002. "Employment Relations in Central and Eastern Europe: The Road to the EU." In Brian Towers and Michael Terry, eds., *European Industrial Relations Annual Review 2000/2001*, Oxford: Blackwell, pp. 169–86.

Martin, Roderick, Roger Undy, and John Gennard. 1999. "A Strategic Approach to Trade Union Behaviour." Unpublished paper, University of Strathclyde and University of Oxford.

Martin, Ross M. 1989. *Trade Unionism: Purposes and Forms*. Oxford: Clarendon Press; New York: Oxford University Press.

Millward, Neil, Alex Bryson, and John Forth. 2000. *All Change at Work? British Employment Relations 1980–1998, as Portrayed by the Workplace Industrial Relations Survey Series*. London: Routledge.

Mintzberg, Henry, and James A. Waters. 1985. "Of Strategies, Deliberate and Emergent." *Strategic Management Journal*, Vol. 6, no. 3 (July), pp. 257–72.

Moore, Thomas G. 2002. *China in the World Market: Chinese Industry and International Sources of Reform in the Post-Mao Era*. Cambridge: Cambridge University Press.

Murray, Gregor, Christian Lévesque, and Guylaine Vallée. 2000. "The Re-regulation of Labour in a Global Concept: Conceptual Vignettes from Canada." *Journal of Industrial Relations*, Vol. 42, no. 2 (June), pp. 234–57.

Park, Young-bum, and Christopher J. Leggett. 2004. "Employment Relations in Korea." In Greg J. Bamber, Russell D. Lansbury, and Nick Wailes, eds., *International and Comparative Employment Relations: Globalisation and the Developed Market Economies*, 4th ed., Sydney: Allen and Unwin; London: Sage, pp. 306–28.

Pontusson, Jonas, and Peter Swenson. 1996. "Labour Markets, Production Strategies and Wage Bargaining Institutions: The Swedish Employer Offensive in Comparative Perspective." *Comparative Political Studies*, Vol. 29, no. 2 (April), pp. 223–50.

Poole, Michael, Roger Mansfield, and Priya Mendes. 2001. *Two Decades of Management*. London: Chartered Institute of Management.

Porter, Michael E. 1980. *Competitive Strategy: Techniques for Analyzing Industries and Competitors*. New York: Free Press.

———. 1985. *Competitive Advantage*. New York: Free Press.

Purcell, John. 1989. "The Impact of Corporate Strategy on Human Resource Management." In John Storey, ed., *New Perspectives on Human Resource Management*, London: Routledge, pp. 67–91.

Purcell, John, and Bruce Ahlstrand. 1994. *Human Resource Management in the Multidivisional Company*. Aldershot, UK: Dartmouth.

Scott, W. Richard. 1995. *Institutions and Organizations*. Thousand Oaks, CA: Sage.

Sil, Rudra. 2002. *Managing "Modernity": Work, Community and Authority in Late-Industrializing Japan and Russia*. Ann Arbor: University of Michigan Press.

Smith, Christopher, and Peter Meiskins. 1995. "System, Society and Dominance Effects in Cross National Organisational Analysis." *Work, Employment and Society*, Vol. 9, no. 2 (June), pp. 241–67.

Tilly, Charles. 1978. *From Mobilization to Revolution*. New York: McGraw-Hill.

Towers, Brian. 1997. *The Representation Gap: Change and Reform in the British and American Workplace*. Oxford: Oxford University Press.

Traxler, Franz, Sabine Blaschke, and Bernhard Kittel. 2001. *National Labour Rela-tions in Internationalized Markets: A Comparative Study of Institutions, Change and Performance.* Oxford: Oxford University Press.

Undy, Roger, and Roderick Martin. 1984. *Ballots and Trade Union Democracy.* Ox-ford: Basil Blackwell.

Van Ruysseveldt, Joris. 1995. "Growing Cross-National Diversity or Diversity *Tout Court?* An Introduction to Comparative Industrial and Employment Relations." In Joris Van Ruysseveldt, Rien Huiskamp, and Jacques Van Hoof, eds., *Compar-ative Industrial and Employment Relations,* London: Sage, pp. 1–15.

Wailes, Nick. 2000. "Review of Katz and Darbishire, *Converging Divergences.*" *Rela-tions Industrielles/Industrial Relations,* Vol. 55, no. 3, pp. 540–43.

Wailes, Nick, and Russell D. Lansbury. 2003. "Integrating Interests and Institutions: The Case of Industrial Relations Reform in Australia and New Zealand." *British Journal of Industrial Relations,* Vol. 41, no. 4 (December), pp. 617–37.

Walker, Kenneth F. 1967. "The Comparative Study of Industrial Relations." *Bulletin of the International Institute for Labour Studies,* no. 3 (November), pp. 105–32.

Walsh, Janet. 2001. "HRM in Foreign Owned Workplaces." *International Journal of Human Resource Management,* Vol. 12, no. 3 (May), pp. 425–44.

Wever, Kirsten S. 1995. *Negotiating Competitiveness: Employment Relations and Organizational Innovation in Germany and the United States.* Boston: Harvard Business School Press.

Whitley, Richard. 1999. *Divergent Capitalisms: The Social Structuring and Change of Business Systems.* Oxford: Oxford University Press.

———. 2002. "Introduction: The Institutional Structuring of Market Economies." In Richard Whitley, ed., *Competing Capitalisms: Institutions and Economies,* Vol. 1, Cheltenham, UK: Elgar, pp. ix–xxvii.

Wilczynski, Jozef. 1983. *Comparative Industrial Relations: Ideologies, Institutions, Practices and Problems under Different Social Systems with Special Reference to Socialist Planned Economies.* London: Macmillan.

Zhu, Ying, and Malcolm Warner. 2000. "Changing Approaches to Employment Rela-tions in the People's Republic of China." In Greg J. Bamber, Funkoo Park, Changwon Lee, Peter Ross, and Kaye Broadbent, eds., *Employment Relations in the Asia Pacific: Changing Approaches,* Sydney: Allen and Unwin; London: Thomson, pp. 117–28.

CHAPTER 11

Toward an Integrative Theory of Human Resource Management

BRUCE E. KAUFMAN

Georgia State University

Human resource management (HRM) is a fast-growing area of academic research. The field remains weighted down, however, by a number of conceptual problems and shortcomings. Chief among these are the lack of theory and, in particular, absence of an integrative theoretical base, disagreements about the definition of the field and object of study, research streams in economics and the behavioral and administrative sciences that largely ignore each other, and a penchant to uncritically mix objective investigation of "what is" with normative and prescriptive commitments to "what should be." As a result, human resource management remains caught somewhere in the twilight between a science, an applied area of management practice, a heterogeneous collection of administrative tools, and a consulting or ideological statement about how companies should manage their employees.

In this chapter I endeavor to resolve or at least make progress on each of these problem areas. To do so, I bring together insights and contributions from history, economics, and industrial relations. The end product is unique in several respects. First, it suggests that many modern-day scholars have misapprehended and misspecified the concept of human resource management and the nature of the object of study; second, it provides the basis for an integrative theory of human resource management; third, it helps unify the economics and behavioral and administrative science wings of the field; and fourth, it helps ground prescriptive statements about best practice on a firmer base of theory.

HRM Problem Areas

By most accounts the field of human resource management in the academic world has made considerable progress in the last quarter century. But several significant problem areas remain that block a more rapid advance. In some cases these are well recognized, if disputed; in others cases they tend to lurk under the surface.

The Definition of HRM

A significant obstacle in the way of constructing a theory of human resource management is the plethora of alternative and partially contradictory definitions of HRM. Armstrong (2001), for example, surveyed the American and British literatures and identified nearly a dozen different conceptualizations or dimensions of HRM, while Strauss (2001) did the same and came up with five distinct definitions. A person setting off to construct a theory of HRM can thus legitimately ask: Will the real HRM please stand up?

Even if attention is restricted to America, a plethora of alternative definitions of HRM appear, sometimes in articles by the same authors. In the introductory chapter of the *Handbook of Human Resource Management* (1995), for example, Ferris, Barnum, Rosen, Holleran, and Dulebohn explicitly discussed the definition and conceptualization of the field. A careful reading of these pages yields at least three different conceptualizations of HRM.

The first definition visualizes HRM as a generic management activity or function in business firms. Ferris et al. (1995:1) state, "The utilization of people within an organization is a function of a broad range of dynamic factors. . . . However, the purposes of human resource management are more constant: getting and keeping the optimal quantity and quality of people needed to achieve the objectives of the organization." A second example is the statement of Beer, Spector, Lawrence, Mills, and Walton (1984:1) that "[h]uman resource management (HRM) involves all management decisions and actions that affect the nature of the relationship between the organization and employees—its human resources." A third example of a generic functional definition is by Wright and McMahan (1992:297): "The field [HRM] consists of the various practices used to manage people in organizations, and these practices commonly have been grouped into sub-disciplines of selection, training, appraisal, and rewards. . . . It is the sum of the technical knowledge within each of these functions that we refer to as the field of HRM." In this guise, HRM is largely equivalent to personnel management (PM) in that both are a generic functional management activity, although HRM is distinguished by a broader range of concerns and practices (e.g., self-managed work teams, work–family balance) that are sometimes considered at a higher management level in the firm (Schuler and Jackson 2001; Strauss 2001).

The second definition of HRM presents it as *one particular approach* to the management of people in organizations, an approach that is not generic across organizations and is clearly distinguished from and at least partially orthogonal to the approach of PM. Thus, Ferris et al. (1995:2) stated, "The term HRM reflects the evolution of a science and practice distinct from its predecessor label, personnel management. Personnel management implied that employees were an organizational expense. On the other hand, HRM emphasizes the potential of employees as organizational assets." Stated another way, in this view, personnel management regards employees as a factor cost to be minimized, while HRM regards employees as human capital to be developed and utilized for maximum performance. Storey (2001:5) also took this perspective:

> It is possible—and I would argue on balance more helpful than unhelpful—to conceive of HRM as one "recipe" among many others. . . . Some of these ways are distinctive and some [e.g., personnel management] are indistinctive and piecemeal. . . . Human resource management is a distinctive approach to employment management which seeks to achieve competitive advantage through the strategic deployment of a highly committed and capable workforce using an array of cultural, structural and personnel techniques.

Other authors emphasize different aspects of the HRM approach, although typically the human-capital dimension of human resources remains central. Nolan and O'Donnell (2003), for example, claimed that HRM is an application of what they call "high-commitment" and "high-involvement" approaches to people management. Even within the human-capital/high-involvement HRM construct, some authors have sought to introduce further qualifications. Brewster (1995), for example, attempted to differentiate between an American and European model of HRM, while some British writers (Armstrong 2001) distinguished between "hard" and "soft" HRM.

Ferris et al. (1995) offered yet a third conceptualization of HRM. This one is the broadest and most inclusive. They noted that the field has grown to cover an increasing range of topics and complexities, moving them to conclude, "Human resource management is the science and the practice that deals with the nature of the employment relationship and all of the decisions, actions, and issues that relate to that relationship" (pp. 1–2). They added, "This broad definition encompasses industrial relations," which they equate to labor relations (the study of unions and labor–management relations).Viewed from this perspective, HRM is not limited to the study of the employment management function in organizations but includes in its purview *all* aspects of the relations between employers and employees. Effectively, the positions of human resource management and industrial relations (IR) are reversed in this definition, given the position of most earlier writers that IR subsumed the entire employment relationship and HRM pertained to one branch of it: the management of people in organizations (Kaufman 2001a). For example, 25 years earlier, Heneman (1969:4, emphasis in original) stated, "Industrial relations is concerned with *employment relationships* . . . . [I]ts central focus is *employment,* in all aspects (micro and macro, individual and group): labor marketing, labor relations, personnel management, and the like."

This discussion thus raises a fundamental issue for theory building: Is the object of analysis the employment relationship, the employment management function in organizations, or a human-capital/high-involvement approach to employee management? Likewise, if an organization invests in its employees through additional training, does this make it part of HRM (augmenting human capital), but if it uses layoffs as part of downsizing or restructuring programs (cost reduction), is this personnel management? Obviously these ambiguities complicate theorizing.

Theorizing becomes even more complicated when a further development is introduced. The term "human resource management" first surfaced in the mid-1960s and gradually spread during the 1970s, slowly displacing personnel management. Then, in the early 1980s, HRM was further broadened and extended by the concept of *strategic* human resource management (SHRM). Wright and McMahan (1992:298) defined SHRM as "[t]he pattern of planned human resource deployments and activities intended to enable an organization to achieve its goals." An alternative statement was given by Delery and Doty (1996:802): "The basic premise underlying SHRM is that organizations adopting a particular strategy require HR practices that are different from those required by organizations adopting alternative strategies." Within SHRM, the two most important ideas that have emerged are *vertical fit* and *horizontal fit*. Vertical fit is the proposition that to maximize organizational performance, the firm should tailor its HRM program to achieve the closest alignment (fit) with its overall business strategy; horizontal fit is the idea that all HRM subfield activities (compensation, selection, training, etc.) should be jointly configured in order to develop an integrated package or "bundle" of HR practices that take into account and exploit all complementarities and synergies (Delery and Doty 1996). Schuler and Jackson (2001) described vertical fit as "adaptation" and horizontal fit as "integration."

SHRM has become a hugely popular research topic. But its implications for HRM theorizing are in some respects problematic. For example, if we accept the SHRM idea, does this imply that HRM by itself is *not* strategic? Some authors say yes (Storey 2001); others say no (Wright and McMahan 1992). Furthermore, if SHRM is defined as those HR practices that enable a firm to achieve its goals, then logic suggests HRM is not only nonstrategic but also divorced from corporate profit objectives. Then how is HRM different from PM? Likewise, if PM is defined as a cost-centered approach to people management, then is it possible for a firm to practice strategic PM (a long-range focus on minimizing labor cost) but not strategic HRM? Here are more troublesome ambiguities for theorizing.

Also present in the SHRM concept is the same split between a broad and narrow conceptualization of the subject domain of the field. Some authors treat HRM as the generic employment management function, and strategic HRM then becomes the study of alternative employment systems and the contingent choice of one system over another in the quest for maximal organizational performance. Thus, on the basis of their technology of production, market environment, and competitive strategy, some firms may find that a "high-road" human-capital/high-involvement HRM system maximizes performance, but others with different conditions may find that a "low-road" model using command and control management methods, little training, and minimal pay and benefits is the superior option.

If HRM is conceptualized as equivalent to a human-capital/high-involvement approach, however, the practice of SHRM then narrows to the study of *one particular model*. The epitome of the human-capital/high-involvement HRM model is the high-performance work system (HPWS), and the core object of study in SHRM often becomes the HPWS model (Kochan and Dyer 2001). By way of illustration, McMahan, Bell, and Virick (1998:197) stated, "Today, what we call strategic human resource management may well be 'second generation' employee involvement with a relationship to firm strategy and performance. In essence, we might have called this area of research 'Strategic Employee Involvement.'" An implication is that firms choosing an alternative employment system (e.g., a traditional command and control model, a secondary-labor-market low-road model) are not practicing SHRM and, indeed, may not be practicing HRM. This bifurcation was made explicit by Beer and Spector (1984), who defined HRM (and SHRM) as pertaining to those firms that pursue a unitarist, mutual-gains, high-involvement approach and defined PM and IR as including firms that pursue a pluralist, cost-focused command and control approach. Since the unitarist HPWS model by all accounts covers only a relatively small portion of the national workforce (e.g., Kochan and Dyer 2001), the generalizability and applicability of this version of the SHRM concept appear to be seriously limited.

Historical Misinterpretation

The evolution in the definition of HRM arises in part from and is abetted by the particular historical interpretation—or more correctly, misinterpretation—that many contemporary scholars give to the development of the field. In the standard account (Wren 1994; Dulebohn, Ferris, and Stodd 1995), HRM started out in the late 1910s as personnel management. Personnel management, as conventionally portrayed, was conceptualized and operationalized as a largely low-level, tactical, piecemeal, reactive, and cost-focused administrative function charged with hiring new employees, keeping employment records, handling the transactional activities associated with payroll and benefits, and organizing employee social and recreational activities. For example, Lawler (1988:24) stated, "Originally, HR management was handled by the personnel department, which made sure that employment records were accurate and that people were paid. These personnel departments often reported to the accounting department or to someone in charge of administration." In a similar vein, Ivancevich (1995:5) stated, "Until the 1960s, the personnel function . . . was viewed as a record-keeping unit that handed out twenty-five year tenure pins and coordinated the company picnic," while Wright and McMahan (1992:297–98) claimed that up until the 1980s "each of the various HRM functions have evolved in relative isolation of each other."

Beginning in the 1970s and then flowering in the 1980s was a major transformation, according to most historical accounts of the field. Dulebohn, Ferris, and Stodd (1995:29), for example, stated,

> Since the 1970s, the PM side of the HRM function has experienced an evolution from being a maintenance function, secondary to the IR function, to representing one of critical importance to the effectiveness of the organization. A number of environmental factors, leading to economic and structural upheaval, have resulted in this dramatic shift.

Among the environmental factors they cited are the end of America's post–World War II economic hegemony, intensified market competition, the influence of Japanese management, globalization, expanded employment law, and organizational restructuring. They then concluded,

> The HRM function has been called upon to foster a sense of mutuality and trust in the relations between managers and workers, to develop employees as assets with the view of increasing competitiveness, and to assist with the organization's compliance with government regulations. . . . [These] changes created organizational needs that required the HRM personnel function to emerge from being a low-profile and reactive maintenance activity to being a primary and strategic partner in organizations. The HRM transformation that has occurred has been such that today the HRM function is viewed as being essential for survival in today's competitive environment. (p. 30)

This historical portrayal of the HRM field is a convenient stylization because it gives credence to the view that the human resource function is of growing importance in business firms and supports the academic claim that the concepts of HRM and SHRM are substantively different from PM and IR. As described in the next section, however, a more in-depth examination of the history of the field reveals just the opposite—that IR and PM were practiced in a self-consciously strategic manner at leading firms from the very beginning of the field in the early 1920s. But if this is so, then how are HRM and SHRM conceptually different from PM and IR, and are HRM and SHRM really a fast-growing new development?

Lack of Theory and Theoretical Integration

A third problem area in human resource management research is the lack of a theoretical base for the field and lack of theoretical integration across the various HRM functional activities. The lack of theory and theoretical integration has been a long-noted feature of personnel and human resource management, as observed by Dulebohn, Ferris, and Stodd (1995:36): "In spite of these recent efforts [to develop theory], the academic side has been characterized by an absence of an integrative theory or conceptual system of HRM. . . . The failure of HRM researchers to develop a general theory of HRM is not a recent phenomena, but has been a persistent and enduring characteristic since the atheoretical beginnings of the field." In a similar vein, Delery (1998: 289–90) concluded, "[T]he conceptual foundations of SHRM have been relatively weak and many of the empirical investigations have made assumptions not driven by, or consistent with, the theoretical base," while Wright and McMahan (1992:297) provided this example of lack of theoretical integration: "[R]esearchers in the area of performance appraisal have become very adept at studying the various techniques that maximize the accuracy and effectiveness of the appraisal process, yet very little research attention has been devoted to understanding the relationship between appraisal systems and selection programs." A reason frequently cited for the lack of an integrative theory is that for much of the post–World War II era, PM and HRM were studied predominantly by researchers trained in the behavioral and administrative sciences (e.g., industrial or organizational psychology, organizational behavior) who took a mostly microlevel view and applied specific psychology-related theories to individual management practices and employee behaviors in relative isolation from the larger HRM system and competitive environment of the firm (Martell and Carroll 1995; Ferris, Hochwater, Buckley, Harrell-Cook, and Frink 1999).

By most accounts, research in the HRM field has gradually become more rigorous and theoretically informed, particularly over the last decade or so with the development of employment systems theory (e.g., Begin 1991; Marsden 1999). But to date the main body of HRM theorizing remains fragmented, underdeveloped, and often more taxonomic and descriptive than predictive. Illustrative of the fragmented nature of theory in HRM, Schuler and Jackson (2001) listed 13 theories that inform research in HRM. In the area of SHRM, McMahan, Virick, and Wright (1998) reviewed 10 different theoretical perspectives: behavioral, human capital, cybernetic, agency or transaction cost, resource-based theory of the firm, population ecology, resource dependency, institutional, Foucauldian, and strategic reference points or prospect. In yet another review, Delery and Doty (1996) distinguished between three theoretical perspectives on SHRM—universalistic, contingency, and configurational—while Lepak and Snell (1999) proposed a model of human resource architecture that yields four different employment modes: internal development, acquisition, contracting, and alliance. British authors frequently contrast the Harvard model and the Michigan model of HRM (Strauss 2001).

Certainly in terms of providing theoretical guidance to research in HRM, the strategy concept and theories of SHRM now play the dominant role. To what degree the SHRM literature actually provides a stronger theoretical base, as opposed to additional taxonomic frameworks, remains a matter of debate.

Wright and McMahan (1992:296) stated, "[A] good theory enables one to both predict what will happen given a set of values for certain variables, and to understand why this predicted value should result." They added, "Without good theory, the field of SHRM could be characterized as a plethora of statements regarding empirical relationships and/or prescriptions for practice that fail to explain why these relationships exist or should exist" (p. 297). Although opinions differ, in my judgment most of the SHRM literature does not qualify as bona fide theory when evaluated by these criteria.

One line of HRM/SHRM research follows what Delery and Doty (1996) called the universalistic model and others dub the "one best way" (Becker and Gerhart 1996). This theory, drawing on the human-capital/high-performance model and the resource-based theory of the firm, posits that there is a set of HRM practices that improve organizational performance across all firms. As an example, Pfeffer (1994) cited employment security, selective hiring, self-managed teams, high compensation contingent on performance, extensive training, reduction of status differentials, and sharing information.

The problem with a universalistic theory is that it lacks contingency and seems to contradict the underlying notion of strategy, given the hypothesis of this theory that a specific set of HRM practices maximizes profits across all firms regardless of industry, production technology, and state of the economy. The underlying justification for this bold proposition is the contention that "the human resources of the firm are potentially the sole source of sustainable competitive advantage for organizations" (Ferris et al. 1999:388), a perspective derived from the resource-based view of the firm (Barney 1991; Boxall 1998). While this theory certainly accords with many corporate mission statements that "people are our most important asset," it stands in sharp contradiction to most versions of economic theory, which posit that firms utilize different kinds and quantities of resource inputs in response to differences in input costs and productivities (a point developed later).

The alternative contingency and configurational models of SHRM address these conceptual weaknesses of the universalistic HPWS model but only at a significant cost. These models argue against a "one-size-fits-all" approach to HRM and claim instead that the optimal set of HRM practices is contingent on the firm's business strategy and should be configured in a way to exploit complementarities and synergy. One well-known example of this approach is Arthur's (1994) study of steel mini-mills, where he posited two alternative human resource systems: control and commitment, the former being characterized by HRM practices such as rule-bound procedures, output-based incentive pay, and low task scope and autonomy, and the latter by practices such as employee involvement, extensive training, and gain sharing. These theories solve the one-size-fits-all problem but suffer in other areas. For example, different authors have advanced divergent typologies of business strategies (defender/prospector, control/commitment, low cost/high service) with no agreement on their interrelation and why firms choose one versus another. Likewise, the notion that alternative HRM systems form around complementarities is an attractive and commonsense idea, but left largely unexplained are the origin and nature of these complementarities (the black-box problem) and how they vary across firms.

Lack of Interaction between the Economic and the Behavioral and Management Literatures

Unrecognized by most HRM scholars today, the academic roots of personnel management in the early years of the field (1915–1935) were in economics and industrial relations (Kaufman 2000, 2002). Indeed, personnel was considered "applied labor economics," economists of the institutional school dominated academic writing on employers' personnel and employment practices, and even into the 1950s the bulk of the best-known personnel textbooks were authored by people with an economics degree (e.g., Yoder 1962; Myers and Pigors 1961; Strauss and Sayles 1960). After World War II, labor economists lost interest in personnel and drifted away from it as their field increasingly came under the sway of the Chicago neoclassical paradigm and the study of labor markets. As the labor economists left, their place was filled by new faculty trained in industrial and organizational psychology, sociology, anthropology, organizational behavior, organization theory, and business administration, all of whom took a much more microlevel psychological and management approach to personnel and HRM issues.

From the early 1960s to the late 1980s, personnel and human resource management was largely the exclusive reserve of professors in industrial and organizational psychology, management departments, and business schools, while economists stayed away to study labor markets, and industrial relations researchers concentrated on unions and labor–management relations. But then the situation began to noticeably shift as economists and industrial relationists rediscovered personnel and human resource management (e.g., Kleiner, Block, Roomkin, and Salsburg 1987). During the 1990s a new subfield of labor economics, called the economics of personnel, emerged and quickly grew in numbers of participants and publishing activity. Using the tools of neoclassical microeconomics, these economists, led by Edward Lazear, developed a wide array of sophisticated models to explain a plethora of personnel practices, such as different forms of compensation, mandatory retirement rules, and screening models of employee selection (Lazear 1999; Gunderson 2001). Three economic theorists (Akerlof, Spence, Stiglitz) who made major theoretical contributions to this broad area of research received Nobel Prizes in 2001.

A significant source of missed opportunity in the personnel and human resource management field is that the two groups of researchers—from economics and from management—frequently ignore each other. Although it is an empirical proposition to be proved, one would think a priori that potential gains from trade between the two groups surely exist (Mitchell 2001) and that the research of economists would be strengthened by incorporating insights and ideas from management and the research of management scholars would likewise benefit from the incorporation of models and ideas from economics. Certainly a number of examples of intellectual exchange and integration can be found (e.g., Lepak and Snell 1999; Gibbs and Levenson 2002), but the dominant impression is that many potential gains from trade remain unexploited. A review of the two streams of literature reveals they are in many respects like the proverbial ships passing in the night. For example, in their major review of HRM research, management professors Ferris et al. (1999) provided a bibliography with 178 citations. Not a single citation is of an economics journal (three are of an industrial relations journal). By the same token, in Lazear's 1998 textbook *Personnel Economics for Managers*, the 172 end-of-chapter references included only one business or management journal (with an article by Lazear).

Mixing of Prescription and Prediction

A final problem area that impedes theorizing in HRM is the tendency of writers in this field to mix normative and positive, that is, prescription and prediction. By most accounts, HRM is a problem-driven field, so the desire to relate academic research to the solution of practical problems in organizations is understandable. But to have long-range value and to qualify as science, this research must be based on value-neutral concepts and reasoning and must endeavor to explain the world as it is and not how the analyst thinks it should be.

Perusal of the HRM literature reveals that normative considerations are woven through much of it, seriously compromising its scientific integrity. A normative statement typically includes the word *should* and expresses an opinion or judgment. These are examples frequently encountered in the HRM literature:

- People should be viewed as organizational assets, not expenses.
- HRM should take on the role of business partner in the organization.
- HRM should be a player in the corporate strategy process.
- Firms should be encouraged to move toward a high-involvement system of HRM.
- Human resources should be seen as the organization's source of competitive advantage.

Each of these statements may well be true. But their appropriate place in the scientific process is at the *end*, when the researcher, after an objective assessment of the evidence based on theory and empirical work, concludes that the weight of the facts supports these conclusions. Also important is recognition that in some situations these conclusions may not be true, thus keeping these statements in the realm of contingent implications rather than articles of faith or ideology.

Is a value-neutral, fact-based approach the way HRM research is conducted? Often times, clearly not. The modern literature of HRM is driven by an almost obsessive need to justify statements such as the ones just noted, even though common sense, empirical evidence, and the economic theory presented shortly suggest that often these statements not only are factually incorrect but, if followed by business firms, would in a number of cases lead to *lower*—not higher—profitability. For many firms in secondary labor markets, in times of economic recession and depression, or in lines of business where technology allows tight control and supervision, a HPWS approach to people management would be a large waste of money; instead, these firms are likely to make more profit by treating workers as commodities, managing in a traditional command and control mode, and using "hire and fire" personnel methods (Mahoney and Deckop 1986; Lewin 2001; Appelbaum, Bernhardt, and Murnane 2003). This reality is far too often ignored, however, in the modern literature of HRM.

Why does the field have such a slanted perspective? Part of the answer is that the very definitions and self-concepts of HRM and SHRM are normative propositions meant to support and promote a human-capital, strategic, HPWS approach to people management. Thus, in her review of HRM research, Fisher (1989:158, emphasis added) candidly observed, "A consensus seems to be emerging that most HRM activities can and should be matched to the organization's strategy. *Prescriptive articles to this effect abound;* empirical studies are substantially more rare." Another revealing statement is by Wright, Dunford, and Snell (2001:702, emphasis added):

> Growing acceptance of internal resources as sources of competitive advantage *brought legitimacy to HR's assertion* that people are strategically important to firm success. Thus, given both the need to conceptually justify the value of HR and the propensity for the HRM field to borrow concepts and theories from the broader strategy literature, the integration of RBV [resource-based view of the firm] into the SHRM literature should surprise no one.

The last quotation seems to hint at a normative factor that is driving a good deal of HRM research: the traditionally beleaguered, low-status position of HRM in the academic and business worlds and the consequent striving of HRM academics and practitioners to craft a theoretical rationale and body of empirical evidence that enhances the survivability, growth, and prestige of the field. In the last major article to appear in the *Harvard Business Review* on the HRM function, titled "The New Mandate for Human Resources," Ulrich (1998:124) told readers,

> Should we do away with human resources (HR)? . . . I must agree that there is good reason for HR's beleaguered reputation. It is often ineffective, incompetent, and costly; in a phrase, it is value sapping. Indeed, if HR were to remain configured as it is today in many companies, I would have to answer the question above with a resounding "Yes—abolish the thing."

One notes a strange discordance in this statement: the HRM literature for the previous 20 years had been extolling the virtues of taking a strategic, human-capital approach to people management and touting that the performance effects were superior to those of the old PM approach, and yet the actual record of HRM is (allegedly) so lackluster that unless completely transformed, the function should be abolished! Despite all the much ballyhooed talk about HRM's new role as a strategic business partner, in most companies is HRM still much like the (alleged) low-level, administrative practice of personnel management three, five, or seven decades earlier? Has Ulrich simply pulled the veil from all the normative posturing in the field and revealed that much of the literature is a fig leaf hiding HRM's continued marginal status? Apparently at least part of the answer is yes, per the statement of McMahan, Virick, and Wright (1998:100) that "[t]his evolution of what once was personnel management, is driven, among other reasons by a quest for a higher status that HR managers [and HR academics] have been trying to establish" and the statement of Rogers and Wright (1998:312) that "HR practitioners have become preoccupied with demonstrating the value of the HR function."

A Revised History of HRM

In overcoming these problem areas, the place to start is with the history of HRM. Most modern writers on HRM have followed an inaccurate historical portrayal of the origins and evolution of HRM, leading them to make incorrect inferences about the evolution and fundamental characteristics of HRM and the field's relationship to personnel management and industrial relations. A valuable contribution of historical analysis is that it helps point the way to a generic, value-free definition of the object of study, a prerequisite for fruitful theorizing.

The modern HRM concept originates, I believe (Kaufman 2001a), in economist E. Wight Bakke's 1958 published lecture *The Human Resources Function*. The use of the term *human resources* and its generic meaning as a human asset in production goes back, however, at least to economist John Commons' book *Industrial Goodwill* (1919).

I first highlight Bakke's definition of the human resource function because it demonstrates that nearly a half century ago he clearly articulated the modern concept of HRM. Bakke stated (1958:5–6, emphasis in original):

> The general types of activity in any function of management, whether it be production, sales, engineering, finance, or what you will, grows out of the fact the general job of management is to *use resources effectively for an organizational objective*. . . . The function which is related to the understanding, maintenance, development, effective employment, and integration of the potential in the resource "people" I shall call simply *the human resources function*. . . . The point of view expressed here is that "people" as an organizational resource is at least equally important with the others [finance, production, marketing,

etc.], and that ignorance, neglect, waste, or poor handling of this resource has the same consequences [loss of profit and potential bankruptcy] as ignorance, neglect, waste, or poor handling of money, materials, or market.

Bakke also makes this important point (p. 4, emphasis in original):

> The first thing that we ought to be clear on is that there is nothing new about the managerial function of dealing with people. Dealing with people, figuring out what makes them tick, arranging conditions and rewards and punishments so that they tick better, maintaining and developing their capacities, has been a part—an important and not neglected part—of the managerial function from the first day that some men tried to direct the activities of other men. Like other sub-functions of management, such as engineering, production, sales, finance, etc., it has been *carved out of* the *general* managerial function, not *put into it*.

The twin themes deserving emphasis from these quotations are Bakke's assertion that HRM is a generic management activity dealing with the effective utilization of people in organizations to achieve organizational objectives and his statement that as a generic activity HRM was present the first day an employment relationship existed and one person (the employer) directed the labor of another person (the employee). Bakke (1958:6) is quite explicit that the term *human resources function*[1] does *not* connote some activity different from personnel management or industrial relations but is simply in his view a more descriptively accurate and revealing name for this generic activity. If we follow Bakke, therefore, HRM (including variants such as PM and SHRM) is best defined as the generic function of managing people in organizations and the practices, activities, and outcomes that go with it.

Further insight is gained if we look back in time to the beginning of the fields of personnel management and industrial relations in the late 1910s and early 1920s. In 1919 institutional labor economist John Commons wrote *Industrial Goodwill*, described by a reviewer (*New York Evening Post*, April 26, 1919, p. 18) as "probably the most valuable book for intelligent employers that has been written since Taylor's *Scientific Management*." Here we discover that the concept of SHRM is not an idea of the 1980s or 1990s but was readily grasped, albeit in a more rudimentary form, at the very beginning of the personnel field (Kaufman 2001b). In his book Commons distinguishes five alternative models of labor management: commodity, machine, public utility, goodwill, and citizenship. In the commodity model, employers practice HRM as if the worker is a commodity traded in markets. In the machine model, the HRM system is configured and practiced with the assumption that the worker and work process can be engineered as a machine (scientifically managed). In the public utility model, employers practice HRM with the view that the worker is a valuable capital good or "human resource" (Commons 1919:130) and thus requires careful utilization and conservation. In the goodwill model, the employer practices HRM so as to gain high employee morale and performance through a mutual gain approach. And in the citizenship model, the employer views the firm as a form of industrial government and practices HRM in a democratic spirit so that workers have a voice and the protection of due process.

Contained in Commons's (1919) book is clear recognition of several of the key assertions of SHRM (Kaufman 1998). For example, Commons noted that the configuration of HRM practices varies with the strategic model of labor management chosen by the firm. For example, in the commodity model, wages are market determined, workers are motivated by fear of termination, and workers have no mechanism for voice; in the goodwill model, wages are set above the market level, workers are motivated by fair treatment and mutual gain, and workers have a formal mechanism for voice and dispute resolution. Commons also noted that while a goodwill model costs the employer money, the investment can more than pay for itself by creating higher productivity and giving the firm competitive advantage. (He stated on p. 74 that "goodwill is a competitive advantage.") Commons also clearly introduced the idea of contingency: "If the . . . employment manager looks upon labor as a commodity, then he weighs the facts according to the theory of demand and supply. If he looks upon labor as a machine he gives weight to the facts that get maximum output from the individual. If he entertains the goodwill theory then the facts that promote goodwill are looked for and get a proper emphasis in mind. . . . Only the foolish, the ignorant, the biased, or the arbitrary man ties himself up to a single theory [i.e., a universalistic or one-best-way explanation]" (pp. 166–67).

Commons was not the only writer in this earlier period to think about labor management in a strategic sense. Indeed, through the centuries all the way back to the early Greeks (who invented the strategy concept) we can find examples of strategy applied to labor, be it Robert Owens's advanced employment system in his British textile mill in the early 1800s or Xenophon's account of the wise management of labor in agricultural estates in pre-Christian Greece (Kaufman 2003e). Illuminating evidence on this matter is provided in the very first annual volume of the *Harvard Business Review*, published in 1923. Whereas Ulrich in 1998 proposed in the *Harvard Business Review* that the HRM function be abolished because it is value sapping, consultant and academic Willard Hotchkiss took a nearly opposite tack in his article "Industrial Relations Management" (1923), the first article in the *Harvard Business Review* on the subject of labor management. Hotchkiss observed that in the preceding 10 years (1912–1922) the practice of labor management had undergone a tremendous change—a change far more dramatic, it may be noted, than in the 1980–2000 period. Prior to the 1910s the idea of labor management as a functional business activity did not exist, even though all firms were practicing labor management in some form and often with a strategic perspective. (The decision of Carnegie and Frick to break the union strike at the Homestead steel mill by bringing in replacement workers was surely strategic, as was the decision of the McCormicks to start a corporate welfare program at International Harvester.)

About 1912 there appeared the first formal version of HRM, called employment management, followed in quick succession by personnel management (or personnel administration) and industrial relations (Kaufman 2004a). All three names connote a generic activity of labor management, but they differed from one another with respect to their range of activities and strategic focus—almost entirely parallel to the contemporary portrayal of the relationship of PM, HRM, and SHRM. Employment management was the narrowest version of HRM, largely concerned with hiring and staffing; personnel management was next, concerned with the full array of personnel practices (staffing, training, compensation, etc.). Industrial relations was the highest, broadest, and most *strategic* conception and practice of labor management. On the strategic nature of industrial relations, for example, Kennedy (1919:358) said, "[E]mployment management is, and always must be, a subordinate function to the task of preparing and administering a genuine labor policy, which is properly the field of industrial relations." Note that Kennedy used the term *industrial relations* to cover all business firms (not just unionized ones) and that the term *labor policy* was that era's conception of a long-range strategic orientation toward labor. (Business school courses called "strategy" today were commonly called "policy" until the early to mid-1980s.)

It is instructive to read Hotchkiss's (1923) article while keeping in mind the generalizations made by contemporary writers about personnel management and industrial relations. Hotchkiss observed that the fundamental factor that led business executives to become interested in the new field of industrial relations and "regard labor from a fundamental, long-term viewpoint" (p. 438) was the advent of a full employment economy during World War I. The sudden disappearance of unemployed workers from around the factory gates made the traditional commodity and autocracy system of labor management no longer effective, and to control turnover, elicit work effort, and maintain cooperative relations, employers had to find an alternative model. What they developed in the 1920s was an alternative to the largely external market-oriented commodity model in the form of an internal labor market–oriented goodwill and citizenship model that became the linchpin of the welfare capitalism movement of the 1920s (Jacoby 1985). With this in mind, Hotchkiss stated (pp. 439–40, emphasis added),

> Logically, the term "industrial relations" includes all of the contacts between individuals that come about in the process of operating a business. From this standpoint it would include relations between members of the management group, between members of the clerical force of the company or the supervisory force, or within the group commonly designated as labor. . . .
>
> Results obtained by giving expert analytical attention to industrial relations, whether directed to special phases of the task, such as selection and placement, or to the subject as a whole, have amply demonstrated the necessity and the fruitfulness of such an approach. It will not do, however, to jump to the conclusion that the setting off of industrial relations is merely a new step in the process of dividing management into departments and sub-departments. In many cases a separate department may help to give men who come into a business as industrial relations specialists a fitting place in management councils. This, however, is a question of expediency, the answer to which may wisely be sought in its relationship to local conditions and personalities rather than with regard to any governing principles. When, however, we pass from tactics to the question of major *strategy*, industrial relations management is essentially functional rather than departmental. A department tends to become self-centered. . . . But industrial relations management deals with a subject matter which pervades all departments and crosses all department lines. Whether organized as a separate department or attached to central management, it must to succeed exercise an *integrating*, not a segregating, force on the business as a whole.

Hotchkiss's emphasis on the generic, integrating, and strategic nature of industrial relations management was not unique. Chicago business school dean Leon Marshall wrote in the pages of the *Journal of Political Economy* (1920:730–31) that the job of personnel management is "that of getting men to work together effectively in terms of their work inside a plant," and if done properly "personnel work ceases to be a congeries of unco-ordinated, miscellaneous labor practices. . . . In relative importance it [personnel management] ranks second to none of the functions of business management . . . [and is] a pervasive, interweaving part of our whole social productive scheme." Or we can read the statement of economist William Leiserson (1929:139–40):

> When completely developed, then, Personnel Management not only integrates under centralized control the movement of the personnel, through its employment policies, and provides proper conditions surrounding the working force, through its welfare or service policies, but also makes provision for something like a bill of rights, with a legislative organization to represent the workers from all parts of the plant and some kind of judicial tribunal for the protection of the rights of workers and management [i.e., Commons's citizenship model].

Nor was the strategic thrust of industrial relations/personnel management merely academic opinion at this time. The nation's first major HRM consulting firm, Industrial Relations Councilors, Inc., stated in the first consulting report done for a corporate client (the Ohio Oil Company, 1926, quoted in Kaufman 2003b):

> From a technical standpoint labor administration has to do with the intricate and complex problem of obtaining the most effective use of the labor force or securing the maximum return from payroll expenditures. It ranks in importance, therefore, with production, finance, and other major functions of management. . . . As a result, labor administration takes on a special significance expressed by the term "industrial relations," which is defined as the direction and coordination of all human relationships for maximum necessary production, with a minimum of effort and friction and with the proper regard for the genuine well-being of the workers.

The report (300 pages long) then makes recommendations on establishing an overall labor policy and accomplishing this through a coordinated set of innovations in these areas (covered as separate chapters in the report): organization and administration, employment, wages and hours, training and education, accident and fire prevention, insurance and benefits, housing, sanitation, employee service activities, savings and investment plans, pensions, and joint relations (employee representation). The report concludes its recommendations to management by stating that the company should create a formal industrial relations department, noting that "the different activities of an industrial relations program such as employment, insurance, etc., are *so closely related to each other* as to require centralized control. Therefore, these activities come under one executive head, who, under whatever title, is the chief staff executive of industrial relations. *He assists in developing labor policies of the company* [i.e., helps develop HRM strategy] and supervises the execution of these policies" (emphasis added).

This evidence suggests that HRM and SHRM are not new ideas or practices suddenly discovered in the 1980s but stretch back many decades, even if practiced in only a distinct minority of firms (as is the HPWS today). Also largely unappreciated today is that the Japanese management methods (e.g., employee involvement) imported into the United States in the 1980s that helped engender the HPWS employment model were in large part American in origin, having been exported to Japan in the 1920s by leading American practitioners of industrial relations and welfare capitalism (Kaufman 2004a). The common portrayal of a reactive, piecemeal PM/IR model in the 1920–1960 period and an integrative, human-capital, strategic HRM/SHRM model in the 1970–2000 period does not, therefore, withstand careful historical scrutiny. Certainly the practice of labor management has expanded greatly in breadth, depth, and technical sophistication from 1920 to the present, just as automobile manufacturing and the practice of medicine have, but as a generic activity the essentials of labor management remain the same, and indeed, many current-day SHRM ideas and practices have their origins in this earlier era (Kaufman 2001b).

The last piece of evidence to present on this matter comes from the early 1930s. Canby Balderston, dean of the Wharton School at the University of Pennsylvania, canvassed academics, business groups, and consultants to identify those firms that were leaders in the practice of industrial relations. After on-site visits, he selected 25 (most had no union), wrote mini case studies of each, and then summarized lessons to be learned in his book *Executive Guidance of Industrial Relations* (Balderston 1935). It can be considered a 1930s version of *In Search of Excellence* (Peters and Waterman 1982), albeit with more critical detachment.

Balderston began the book with this warning, which has considerable relevance to a good deal of modern HRM/SHRM research written by management academics:

> To discuss industrial relations apart from the economic forces that affect them is one of our "pet" follies. Books and articles describe in detail the arrangements used by John Jones and his company. That the Golden Rule is his guide and Service is his motto is impressed upon us. He may even write and print a creed [corporate mission statement] to govern his dealings with associates and workers, and his personnel program, at least on paper, may be impeccable. But John Jones is not entirely his own master in dealing with his employees. He too has a "boss"— competition, usually harsh enough, but at times an inexorable tyrant demanding that he choose between his announced personnel policies and the survival of his business. The human relations that John Jones desires are turned and twisted by economic forces, and are attained only as the general management, aided by foresight, skill, and luck, is able to adjust to them. Thus a personnel program becomes understandable only as it is interpreted in the light of competitive and economic influences.

Balderston's important observation here is that a firm's business strategy and corollary HRM/IR practices must perforce be aligned with and take account of broader economic forces if the organization is to survive, and when the external environment changes in a fundamental way, so too must the business strategy and HRM/IR policy. This reality was all too evident at the time he wrote because the nation was in the midst of the Great Depression and many of the leading welfare capitalist firms of the 1920s were struggling to avoid being forced by the threat of bankruptcy to going back to a commodity or autocracy model. But the micro-focused, psychology-oriented management theorists of the 1940s to 1970s (starting with Mayo and the human relations group) largely ignored the economic environment, and this lesson remained fallow and was only slowly rediscovered as a new insight by macro HRM writers of the 1980s and 1990s.

Balderston also raised another oft-neglected idea about SHRM in contemporary research. He concluded, "In general, 'top' management devotes (or should devote) its attention chiefly to those items in which the most money is to be made or lost. The clue to many of its important problems can be ascertained by an analysis of the relative importance of labor, material, and overhead costs" (1935:230). Balderston's point here is that not all aspects of the business should be treated in a strategic manner, given that management's time, decision making, and available information are scarce and thus costly goods. Where alternative labor policies or practices have a significant potential impact on revenues and costs, therefore, they deserve strategic consideration; where they do not, it is the hallmark of good management to treat them as a tactical consideration and delegate these matters to a lower level of the organization, such as the personnel or HRM department. Seen in this light, the decision of companies to not have a personnel department, or to practice personnel management in a low-level administrative fashion, is not necessarily a sign of poor management or lack of strategic vision but may, quite the opposite, be the best strategy in light of economic conditions (massive unemployment as in the Depression) or the low return on investment from improved personnel and human resource management practices in that particular industry or line of business (Lewin 1987).

What did Balderston conclude about the nature of leading IR programs of the early 1930s? Based on the 25 companies, he put forward a "best practice" personnel program that contained 13 elements covering all aspects of the employer–employee relationship: fair wages and fair dealing (stated to be the foundation upon which all other elements rest); guidance of a definite policy; support of the chief executive and a well-organized personnel department; regularization of employment; unemployment reserves; insurance against death, illness, and sickness; pensions; standardization of base rates and salaries; financial and nonfinancial incentives; systematic promotion policy; a selection, placement, and training program; reduction of accidents and illness; and a program for joint relations. Balderston (1935:290) calls these elements a "composite program" and "integrated approach" for gaining and sustaining competitive advantage.

Theorizing HRM: First Principles

In this section I propose some first principles for theorizing HRM. The starting point is to write out the production function:

$$Q = f(K, e \cdot L) \tag{1}$$

Equation 1 states that the amount of output (Q) is a function of the amount of capital (K) and labor services $(e \cdot L)$, calculated as the product of the number of hours of work time committed to production (L) and the level of work effort (e) accompanying each work hour. If work effort is zero, labor services and production are also zero. I assume that production takes place in the short run, and thus capital and technology can be taken as givens.

The key insight from the production function is that through some human-engineered process, the factor input *labor* (or generically, "human resources") has to be acquired, coordinated, and effectively utilized (motivated) for production to take place. This process of acquiring, coordinating, and effectively utilizing labor is what Bakke (1958) called the *human resource function*. But this function can be operationalized in two different ways, only one of which involves human resource *management*. The other might generically be referred to as human resource *marketing*.

The dual nature of the human resource function is illuminated by the theory of institutional economics developed by Commons (1934), Coase (1937), and Williamson (1985). From their perspective, the study of economics is about how different institutions (or governance structures) coordinate economic activity and allocate resources. The two principal coordinating mechanisms are markets and hierarchical organizations. The former uses price and demand and supply to coordinate and allocate; the latter uses executive command and the management hierarchy. Often this distinction is framed as "make versus buy," connoting that a firm can either use management command to make the goods and services in-house or buy the goods and services through the market.

The implication for the concept of the human resource function is immediately evident. The only way positive output, Q, comes out of the production function is to put positive inputs of labor services, $e \cdot L$, into the production function. But this human resource function can be performed either by the market, management, or some combination thereof. For example, wage rates can be set by supply and demand in the external labor market, by the decision of compensation managers inside the organizational hierarchy (sometimes called the "internal labor market," albeit with considerable inaccuracy), or by some combination thereof. Similarly, workers can voice their dissatisfaction with aspects of employment by exiting into the external labor market (quitting) or by using a management-created employee involvement or dispute resolution process inside the firm. As a third example, firms can use the market to buy benefits administration for employees from another firm (e.g., a call center) or produce benefits administration in-house by hiring a benefits manager and supporting staff. And, finally, the market is one way to motivate employees to work hard through the carrot of a higher-paying job and the stick of unemployment, while management can also devise motivational carrots and sticks such as promotions and terminations.

From an institutional economics perspective, the fundamental object of theorizing is the human resource function. Theorizing about the human resource function proceeds in two logical steps in turn. The first and antecedent step is to determine the boundary between make versus buy in the human resource (HR) function, that is, the boundary between that part of the HR function done by the market and the part done by management. Knowing this boundary and the respective domains of HR marketing and HR management, the second step is to look at each domain separately from the other (a form of partial equilibrium analysis) and develop a theory that explains its operation and key outcomes. Presumably, however, the respective theories of HR marketing and HR management have some common points of intersection, for in an important respect they represent mirror images of each other, as illustrated by the fact that greater use of one necessarily implies lesser use of the other in any given production situation. Let us now look at the first of these two steps of theorizing (the boundary issue); I consider the second in the following section.

In institutional economics, the primary variable that determines the boundary between make and buy is transaction cost. The definition of transaction cost varies, but the version I find most useful is derived from Commons (Kaufman 2003d). According to Commons (1934), a transaction is a transfer of ownership, and thus transaction cost is the real resources used to effectuate this transfer of property rights. Since transfer of ownership involves some form of contracting (explicit or implicit), transaction costs arise at three steps of the contracting process: the negotiation of the contract, the creation or drafting of the contract, and the administration or enforcement of the contract.

In isolating the determinants of the market–management boundary, it is helpful to follow Commons and distinguish between three kinds of transactions. He argued that economic ownership rights can be transferred through either voluntary exchange in a market or through the command of a legal superior, such as in a government, business, trade union, family, or religious organization (Commons 1934). Voluntary transfer of property rights through a market is called a *bargaining transaction*, such as when an employee exchanges his or her property right over a certain number of work hours for the employer's property right in a certain amount of monetary compensation. Typically price is the variable that coordinates bargaining transactions.

The other way that property rights are exchanged is through the authoritative command issued by a legal superior to a subordinate. A government leader, for example, may direct that every able-bodied man provide two years of labor to the military services, or a chief executive officer of a company may direct that a profit-sharing bonus be distributed to all employees. Commons labeled transactions coordinated and consummated by command as *rationing transactions*.

Among rationing transactions Commons separated out one specific group for special treatment. These are called *managerial transactions*. With inanimate factor inputs such as coal and steel, once the entrepreneur obtains ownership rights over the input, it can be immediately put into the production function and will yield a determinate amount of output (based on BTUs, tensile strength, etc.). The factor input labor is fundamentally different, however, because it is embodied in human beings, and human beings volitionally determine the quantity and quality of the labor services provided. Thus, when an entrepreneur buys labor, what the firm really gets is ownership rights over a certain amount of the worker's time L, but time by itself produces nothing. The managerial transaction is, therefore, the use of management command in the form of carrots and sticks to acquire ownership rights over the worker's *effort* (labor power), e. It is labor power in terms of both quantity and quality of labor services that, multiplied by the number of work hours, represents the human resource input in the production function.

Commons's theory allows us to identify the two end points in the use of markets versus management in the human resource function (Kaufman 2003d). One end point is when only markets are used; the other is when only management command is used. First consider the market-only option.

The market-only option arises when bargaining transaction cost is zero. When the cost of transferring ownership rights through market exchange is zero, the market becomes the most efficient mechanism for coordinating and allocating resources. Zero transaction cost, in turn, is made possible by certain conditions, principally a human being with perfect rationality, an economic environment with perfect information, and a government with perfect (zero-cost) power of contract enforcement. Given these conditions, Coase (1937) deduced that with zero market (bargaining) transaction cost, all economic exchanges of property rights should take place through markets, including the exchange of labor services. A powerful implication is that no economic rationale exists for an employment relationship or multiperson firm. Thus, with zero bargaining transaction cost the economy's organization dissolves into a situation of perfect decentralization: an economy composed entirely of single-person proprietorships (e.g., family farms, owner–operator businesses, independent contractors) where price alone coordinates all economic activity.

What makes perfect decentralization and the absence of an employment relationship possible is the fact that with zero transaction cost, all contracts are complete, including the labor contract. With a complete labor contract, labor in effect changes from a human resource to a commodity, since every dimension of the quantity and quality of labor services can be costlessly written into a contract and costlessly enforced. Thus, the product $e \cdot L$ becomes a datum specified in the contract, eliminating the difference between labor time and labor services and making input of labor into the production function as determinate as the BTUs from a ton of coal.

The principal advantage of hiring employees is that the firm gains the legal right of control: the ability to continually redirect and revise the tasks and duties of the worker in light of unfolding developments and unforeseen contingencies. But in a world of zero transaction cost and complete contracts, control has no economic value, and all employees are thus "externalized" into independent contractors and self-employed firms. With all production taking place in single-person firms, there are no employees to manage, and the human resource function is effectively performed entirely by the market. That is, labor services no longer come from employees but are bought in the product market from other "workers" operating as independent contractors and self-employed entrepreneurs—implying that labor markets as such do not exist and the theoretical concept of a perfectly competitive (zero transaction cost) labor market is a logical non sequitur (Kaufman 2004b). Prices determined by supply and demand in perfectly competitive product markets in turn completely coordinate the exchange and pricing of labor services, although these labor services are now provided by firms in the guise of, say, John Smith Truck Driving, Inc., and the Sue Johnson Director of Marketing company.

The entire human resource function can also be performed entirely by management with no market involvement of any nature. This situation occurs in the polar opposite economic structure, perfect centralization. Where perfect decentralization is the ultimate form of economic disaggregation, perfect centralization is the ultimate form of aggregation. Perfect centralization occurs when rationing transaction cost is zero (executives have perfect rationality, perfect information, and costless and complete ability to enforce property rights) and bargaining transaction cost is nonzero (say, due to government law that prohibits market exchange). Rather than devolve into a myriad of single-person firms, the economy coagulates into one giant firm (possibly in the form of state socialism, directed by an omniscient central planner instead of an omniscient auctioneer à la general equilibrium theory) that covers the entire economy and coordinates through command all production and allocation decisions. With zero rationing transaction cost, the use of command to coordinate and allocate resources is frictionless and leads to optimal outcomes, causing the visible hand of management to replace the invisible hand of the market. In such an economy, all labor input is provided to the production function by executive command, and the human resource function is entirely contained within the domain of human resource management, including the setting of compensation, the acquisition of workers, and the coordination of job tasks. The job of human resource management is quite easy, however, because zero rationing transaction cost allows the central executive to craft complete contracts with each worker, thus eliminating the managerial transaction and any concerns about supervision, motivation, opportunism, and other principal–agent problems.

In the real world neither bargaining nor rationing transaction cost is zero, so the economy evolves into a "mixed" economy where economic activity takes place within an amalgam of markets and organizations and both price and command play a coordinating role. Important features of a mixed economy are multiperson firms, an employment relationship, and (imperfect) labor markets. Thus, in such an economy, labor input is provided to the production function through a mix of human resource marketing and human resource management; the exact dividing line is a function of relative transaction costs and underlying technological, psychological, informational, and political variables (e.g., the extent of complementarities in production, the cognitive and emotional attributes of people, gaps and holes in property rights, government laws and regulations, etc.) that influence the productivity and efficiency of alternative modes of production and coordination (Kaufman 2003d). Also of crucial importance in such an economy is the fact that contracts are incomplete, thus introducing the managerial transaction into all employment relationships and making it necessary that firms concern themselves and their human resource managers with the complex and difficult job of maximizing the worker's supply of labor power and minimizing all distortions that arise from principal–agent problems.

This theoretical framework has a number of implications for the study of human resources. At an intellectual level, it suggests that markets and management are both part of the broad field of (institutional) economics, and in a generic sense, labor economists and human resource management researchers are both *economists* (people who study the coordination and allocation of scarce resources). The skeptic may consider that the title of what is often considered the first scientific paper on the practice of management (Duncan 1989) is "The Engineer as an Economist" (Towne 1886). In the world of practice, this theory also helps explain the recent decision of many companies to externalize portions of their HR function. Companies, for example, have outsourced benefits administration, payroll, staffing, and training to third-party providers, in effect engineering a massive shift from "make" to "buy." A theoretical explanation for this shift rests on changes in the transaction and production costs associated with make versus buy. That is, new technologies (e.g., sophisticated software and personal computers), organizational forms (e.g., call centers), and changes in human resource services (self-administered benefit programs) have lessened the transaction cost of using the market and have lowered the relative cost of external production (e.g., because external vendors can reap economies of scale from higher-volume production), thus providing incentives for firms to externalize the HR function. Similar considerations help explain the decision of many firms to deconstruct portions of their internal labor markets and externalize certain types of jobs (Cappelli et al. 1997).

An Integrative Theory of HRM

Those firms that choose to internalize part of the HRM function must give attention to the functional business activity of human resource management. A number of choices must be made. For example, each firm must decide whether to set up and staff a formal HR department or, alternatively, delegate HR activities to other executives, departments, or the line managers in the firm. Another issue is the types and quantities of specific HRM practices and activities to provide. For example, should the firm invest in employee staffing, and if so, how many resources should be devoted to it? In making these decisions, strategic issues also must be considered. For example, presumably the breadth and depth of the HRM program depends on the firm's long-range competitive business strategy and the variables that underlie it. Also important is choosing the mix of individual HRM practices that produce the greatest synergy and contribute most to organizational performance.

Economics has a well-developed conceptual framework for answering these kinds of questions, and extending that framework to the case of human resource management is relatively straightforward. The conceptual framework is the microeconomic theory of production and derived factor demand. The basic idea is to consider human resource activities as similar in generic form to the services provided by other factor inputs, such as capital and labor.[2] This perspective leads to the augmented production function in equation 2:

$$Q = f[K, e(\text{HRM}_i) \cdot L, \text{HRM}_i] \qquad (2)$$

where HRM_i is the amount of the ith form of HRM practice (e.g., HRM_1 = recruitment, HRM_2 = training, etc.).

Equation 2 shows that investment in additional HRM services increases the amount of output Q in two ways. The first is the *direct effect*, representing the independent contribution that more units of input HRM_i have on production (the right-most term in the production function), holding constant the amount of labor and capital services. HRM_i might be employee selection, for example, and greater investment in selection activities, such as hiring tests, personal interviews, and psychological assessment, should presumably lead to greater output. Alternatively, HRM_i might be a turnover reduction program, such as a no-layoff guarantee and a just-cause termination policy. The second channel by which additional inputs of HRM_i affect production is the *indirect effect*. It enters the production function through the term $e(\text{HRM}_i)$. The indirect effect captures the influence that more HRM services have on output as they indirectly change the effective amount of effort e each worker provides. The indirect HRM effect can take a variety of forms, such as greater labor services due to the higher morale created by an employee involvement program or the extra work effort that comes from paying an above-market wage (the efficiency wage concept).

The existence of a direct and an indirect effect was well recognized in the early industrial relations literature, although I am not aware that this distinction has been formalized in the modern literature of HRM/ SHRM (but see Huselid [1995:637] for the idea in a suggestive form). For example, the report *Industrial Relations: Administration of Policies and Programs* by the National Industrial Conference Board (1931) classifies the impact of IR activities into two categories: "measurable results" and "indirect results." Examples of the former listed in the report are "better type of applicant," "decreased labor turnover," and "reduction in accidents," all of which fall under the rubric of direct HRM effects, while under indirect results are factors such as "improved morale" and "attitude of the community." It is worth noting that the report states, "Improvement in morale is the reason cited most often for the retention and extension of industrial relations activities" (p. 97).

The HRM Demand Curve

To derive predictions and hypotheses about firm behavior, some assumption must be made about the goal or goals of the firm. Economics is often criticized for making unduly simplistic assumptions, but the virtue of doing so is that it leads to concrete implications. The goal assumed here is that firms seek to maximize profit. Further assumed is that the firm operates in a competitive product market and faces a parametric price P for each unit of output. And finally, for the sake of simplicity, also assume that the cost per unit of providing HRM_i services is a constant amount V_i and the wage per unit of labor is a constant W. It follows, using standard marginal analysis, that additional units of each HRM practice should be devoted to production as long the extra revenue generated is greater than or equal to the extra cost (Jones and Wright 1992). Formally, if we drop the subscript i for the moment in order to focus on the composite HRM input, this conclusion comes from maximizing the profit function subject to the cost constraint as specified in equation 3:

$$\Pi = P \cdot f[K, e(\text{HRM}) \cdot L, \text{HRM}] - V \cdot \text{HRM} - W \cdot L \tag{3}$$

Solving for the first-order condition yields equation 4:

$$\frac{\partial \Pi}{\partial \text{HRM}} = P\left[\left(\frac{\partial Q}{\partial e}\frac{de}{d\text{HRM}}\right) \cdot L + \frac{\partial Q}{\partial \text{HRM}}\right] = V \tag{4}$$

The expression with brackets in equation 4 is the marginal revenue product (MRP) of HRM services. It is composed of two parts: the second term, $\partial Q/\partial \text{HRM}$, is the direct HRM effect (the extra product from more HRM services, holding labor services L constant), and the first term, $(\partial Q/\partial e)(de/d\text{HRM}) \cdot L$ is the indirect HRM effect (the extra product that comes from the positive effect that more HRM services have on employee work effort through morale, motivation, etc.). If labor were a commodity, the term $e(\text{HRM})$ would become a constant and fall out of the first-order condition, leaving only the direct effect. The larger the positive morale effect of HRM services, the greater is the indirect effect and the further to the right lies the demand curve.[3]

The right-hand side of equation 4, V, is the price per unit of HRM services. In words, equation 4 states that profit is maximized when the MRP of HRM services is equal to the per-unit cost, which is the marginal decision rule stated earlier.

As is well known, the MRP schedule also represents the demand schedule for a factor input. One such demand curve for HRM services is depicted in figure 1, denoted as D_1. Its position reflects the combined direct and indirect effects. The upward-sloping portion of the line shows that at first, additional units of the HRM practice have a rising MRP, indicating increasing returns in production; this is followed by diminishing returns and a downward-sloping MRP schedule. We can well imagine, for example, that at some point, adding additional training classes (or weeks of training) will, for a given size workforce, yield successively smaller increments to production and revenue. In figure 1, the optimal level of the HRM input is HRM_1 (point X), determined by the intersection of the marginal cost line V_1 and the HRM demand curve D_1.[4]

FIGURE 1

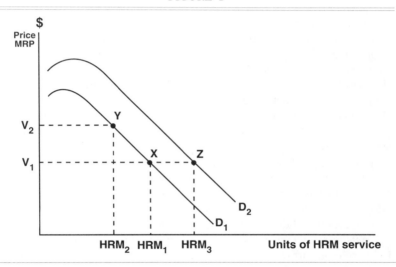

Figure 1 shows that a firm's use of HRM practices follows the law of demand, just as does its use of other factor inputs. Thus, a rise in the price of an HRM activity from V_1 to V_2 causes a movement up the HRM demand curve and a decline in quantity demanded, from HRM_1 to HRM_2 (from point X to point Y). If an occupational licensing law were passed, for example, that requires all HRM practitioners to have a university master's degree, firms would have to pay a higher wage (salary) to attract these more-educated workers. This higher labor cost would in turn increase the marginal cost of each unit of employee recruitment activity, or other such HRM input, leading to a movement up the HRM demand curve and a decline in the quantity demanded by the firm.

Firms' demand for HRM inputs is also influenced by all those variables that shift the HRM demand curve. These variables must affect one of the two determinants of the HRM input's marginal revenue product: the marginal physical product (the extra output produced) or the marginal revenue from this extra production (or both). The most important shift variables are a matter to be empirically determined. A sample of likely candidates, however, is available from Balderston's (1935) study of industrial relations programs. He identified 13 factors as among the most important determinants of the demand for HRM services, including industry profitability and concentration of control; relative share of labor, capital, and materials in total cost; stability of sales, production, and employment; age and rate of growth of the company and industry; intensity of competition and extent of overcapacity; level of unemployment; extent of unionization; quality of management; and the labor philosophy of management (pp. 223–24). Alternatively, a more recent study (Kaufman and Levine 2000) identified 11 shift factors that increase the demand for one particular type of HRM service: employee involvement programs. These factors are larger company employment size; production processes that are more complex and difficult to coordinate; interdependencies and complementarities among workers in production and social relations; employment situations in which working conditions and employment practices are subject to significant public-goods (free-rider) problems; firms where employees are viewed as a strategic asset; imperfectly competitive product markets; extensive internal labor markets; adoption of other high-performance HRM practices; full employment; macroeconomic stability; and extent of unionization.

Without reviewing each of these many shift factors, some (e.g., industry concentration) evidently affect the marginal revenue variable, while others (e.g., large size and complex production technology) affect the marginal product variable. A demand shift variable generally not included in the theory of factor demand is differences in employer preferences or "tastes." The presumption in standard microeconomic theory is that employers have only one preference—maximum profit. But Balderston's variable "management labor philosophy" may point to a taste factor unrelated to profit, particularly given his conclusion that leading personnel programs are "nearly always associated with a dominant personality or with a leader . . . intensely interested in the problems of the people associated with him" (1935:249). Alternatively, this variable may be consistent with profit maximization to the extent that it represents different labor strategies for gaining competitive advantage.

Variation in demand curves for HRM give rise to a similar distribution of HRM practices across firms and industries at a given point in time and to evolving patterns of HRM use over time. At the price V_1 in figure 1, for example, the firm with the HRM demand curve D_1 will demand only HRM_1 (point X), while the firm with the demand curve D_2 will demand the larger amount HRM_3 (point Z). Of course, in a complete model, variation in supply curves also needs consideration.

Approached in this manner, the object of study in human resource management takes on a generic and value-free quality and more readily yields testable hypotheses. To illustrate, in 1935 the National Industrial Conference Board (1936) surveyed the industrial relations practices used at over 2,000 firms employing 15% of the national labor force. Only 5% of firms with less than 250 employees had a personnel department, but 47% of firms with more than 250 employees had one. Among industries, the proportion of firms with a personnel department ranged from a low of 12% in the lumber industry to 72% in insurance, with the largest number clustered in the 20% to 35% interval. Other personnel practices exhibited similar dispersion (e.g., use of job evaluation ranged from none in mining to 28% in banking). Nearly six decades later, Freeman and Rogers (1999) asked 2,400 American workers and managers about the HRM practices at their place of employment. They formed an index of "advanced HRM practices" and plotted the distribution (p. 96). The data yielded a bell-shaped but distinctly skewed curve with a right-hand tail (representing the small proportion of firms with a highly developed HPWS).

The model of HRM factor demand provides a framework for explaining these patterns and suggests an empirical strategy and set of variables for testing the implications of the theory. I do not know of an alternative theory in the HRM field that approaches this level of generality, and indeed, the human-capital/HPWS conceptualization of HRM and SHRM prevalent in the field almost by construction limits theoretical and empirical attention to firms in the right-hand side of the distribution.

The Equilibrium Level of Several HRM Inputs

Equation 4 defines the profit-maximizing level of the composite HRM input. The next step is to consider the optimal level of each of the individual HRM practices, such as selection, training, compensation, and employee relations. It simplifies matters to work with only two of the HRM_i inputs, HRM_1 and HRM_2 (e.g., selection and training; note that HRM_1 and HRM_2 now refer to different types of HRM services, not different quantities as in figure 1). The per-unit cost of input HRM_1 is V_1; the per-unit cost of input HRM_2 is V_2. The profit-maximizing levels of HRM_1 and HRM_2 are analogous to equation 1:

$$V_1 = MRP_1$$
$$V_2 = MRP_2$$
(5)

Equation 5, in words, states that additional units of an HRM practice should be committed to production as long as the marginal increase in revenue exceeds the marginal increase in cost. Although simple, this idea has significant ramifications. For example, Delery and Doty (1996:807–8) claimed that "conducting more valid performance appraisals or using more valid selection devices should always be better than using less valid measures" and "There will be a positive relationship between financial performance and (a) the use of internal career ladders, (b) formal training systems, ..." Regarding the first point, assuming that performance appraisals and selection tests entail positive costs and diminishing benefits beyond some point, equation 5 suggests that this proposition is incorrect (assuming that the firm's goal is maximum profit). The second hypothesis also violates marginal reasoning unless one believes that an internal career ladder and training system provide greater benefits than costs in *every* firm (including fast-food restaurants?).

In much the same way as consumers maximize total utility by equating the marginal utility per dollar spent on each item consumed, firms maximize profit by equating the marginal revenue product-per-dollar cost of each input used in the production process. Thus, the equilibrium amount of multiple HRM inputs is given by equation 6:

$$MRP_1/V_1 = MRP_2/V_2$$
(6)

This equation states that the firm should adjust the amount of inputs HRM_1 and HRM_2 until the revenue gain per dollar of expenditure on each HRM service is equal. If, *ceteris paribus*, the MRP of the employee selection/recruitment function increases (say, due to a tighter labor market and scarcity of job applicants), the firm maximizes profit by reallocating HRM expenditures from training to selection/recruitment.

Strategic HRM

The final topic to consider is the application of this model to the theory and practice of SHRM. As cited earlier, a popular definition of SHRM is "the pattern of planned human resource deployments and activities intended to enable an organization to achieve its goals." From an economic perspective, this definition seems to be a straightforward paraphrase of the constrained maximization problem specified in equation 3 and the resulting equalities in equations 4 and 6. So viewed, it seems to lack independent intellectual substance. Economic theory, however, can rightfully be charged with so simplifying the strategy problem that it has little bearing to the real-world decision-making problems of managers. They live, after all, in a world of multiple organizational objectives and internal political struggles, bounded rationality, highly imperfect information, fundamental uncertainty, and constantly changing economic conditions. The implication of this thought, however, is not that we should give up on the economic model but rather accept it as the conceptual backbone for the study of SHRM and then try to incorporate these complexities and real-world features into the theory.

The two major principles that come out of the SHRM literature are the ideas of vertical and horizontal fit. Vertical fit is the contention that the organization's HRM practices and program should be crafted to align with and support the firm's overall business strategy and facilitate achieving the organization's long-range goals. Like the previously cited definition of SHRM, the concept of vertical fit seems to be another paraphrase of the structure and conclusions of the economic model, although the latter again portrays the decision-making problem in a highly simplified and deterministic way. Granting this, one must ask: isn't the obvious implication of equations 3, 4, and 6 that the firm should invest in the HRM function and align the different practice areas of HRM so as to achieve congruence with the global objective of maximizing profit? If so, what is new about the idea of vertical fit? This lacuna notwithstanding, the concept has interest because it leads the theorist to try to adapt the highly abstract model of economics to better match the actual decision-making problems of business executives. In this respect, SHRM—like industrial relations and personnel management of the 1920s—is a branch of *applied economics,* albeit with ample room for theories and concepts from the behavioral and organizational sciences.

In pursuing the idea of vertical fit, SHRM theorists have developed alternative typologies of business strategies, such as control versus commitment and prospector versus defender. Whether these particular typologies are robust is an open question, but the more general idea that firms pursue different strategies and thus adopt different HRM strategies seems an eminently reasonable and interesting proposition. Without too much effort and complication, the economic model presented earlier can be expanded to incorporate and explicate these notions. The model could, for example, compare the HRM investment decision for two firms in the same industry, one that is an established low-cost, high-volume producer and the other that is a new entrant seeking to exploit a product innovation. Differences in cost structures, elasticities of product demand, types of jobs and associated human capital, and other such factors could be introduced into the general model of equation 3. As long as these factors somehow affect the productivities, financial returns, and costs of HRM practices, they will lead the firms to adopt different HRM bundles. Another tack is to compare two production technologies and lines of business, one where workers have a large degree of discretion in job tasks and the product involves considerable face-to-face customer service (e.g., flight attendants) and the other one that features a tightly controlled production process and working with machines (e.g., auto assembly). We could reasonably hypothesize that the productivity gain from the indirect HRM effect (fostering greater morale and effort through HRM) would be considerably smaller in the latter firm, causing its HRM demand curve to lie further to the left and leading to a less HRM-intensive production process.

The model also sheds light on other propositions related to the vertical fit idea. As noted earlier, for example, some SHRM writers adopt a universalistic model in which they claim certain HRM practices (typically HPWS practices) improve organizational performance in *all* firms. The economic model provides a useful tool to evaluate this claim. On one hand, it is evident from equation 1 that this statement is correct in that more HRM inputs will increase output and (probably) labor productivity, as well as other intermediate measures such as retention and job satisfaction. Indeed, because of the incomplete nature of labor contracts, *anything* the firm can do to increase the flow of labor services from the employee time they have purchased will result in a gain of output. But the universalistic model has one large defect: it neglects the cost side of the practice of HRM. As long as HRM activities entail a positive cost and at some point encounter diminishing returns, there is always some upper limit to the amount that should be invested in HRM, and beyond this level the universalistic prescription is incorrect. Thus, one must regard the oft-stated universalistic claim that more firms should adopt the HPWS model as a normative proposition unless explicit consideration is given to the issue of its relative benefits and costs across *all* types of firms (e.g., not only Saturn and Hewlett-Packard but also McDonald's and Wal-Mart).

One contingency often noted in the early literature of industrial relations as having a substantial effect on HRM strategy is the macroeconomic and labor market environment, particularly the level of unemployment and the degree of cyclical instability in production and employment. An earlier quotation from Balderston (1935) speaks directly to this point, while Commons (1919; Kaufman 2003c) claimed that extensive unemployment and the boom and bust of the business cycle pattern are the single worst enemy of a high-performance "goodwill" work system. SHRM writers in the modern literature, on the other hand, generally give these considerations modest to negligible attention when they write about vertical fit. But clearly the state of the macroeconomy has a substantial effect on the type of business and HRM strategy a firm will pursue. The economic model of HRM described earlier helps explain why. The key consideration is that extensive unemployment reduces both the direct and indirect contributions of HRM. The direct effect of a unit investment of HRM services (e.g., recruitment and training) is much reduced when the firm has long lines of well-qualified job applicants, while the fear of job loss in a depressed labor market provides a substitute form of motivation, reducing the value of creating high morale and productivity via the indirect HRM effect. Seen in this perspective, the HPWS is far from being a universalistic, "one-best-way" employment model, as evidenced by the gutting of the mutual-gain welfare capitalist model during the Great Depression, while Karl Marx's "reserve army of the unemployed" is a very attractive HR tool for the individual capitalist because it stimulates employee work effort at much less cost than manufacturing it through high morale.

Finally, the vertical fit idea is used to criticize personnel management because it (allegedly) was operationalized in a low-level, nonstrategic way. This criticism is to a large degree misdirected, however, for it confuses the generic activity of HRM with the people who implement it and fails to consider that HRM decisions occur at different levels in the management hierarchy. Personnel and human resource managers may have no broader duties than handing out service pins and keeping employment records, but if the owner or CEO is endeavoring to maximize profits in some informed, systematic way, the presumption has to be that strategic, long-range (but not necessarily correct) decisions are being made about labor. This conclusion holds true even if the strategic decision is that labor is so cheap and plentiful it does not pay to strategize about it or that no business case exists for having a personnel department! The interesting issue is *why* personnel and human resource managers are not included in top-level strategy formulation. From an economic perspective, the most likely answer is that the CEO concludes that the contribution (marginal revenue product) of bringing HR to the table is less than the cost, leaving the personnel and human resource managers to work at a lower level in the organization performing tactical, administrative functions. Does this imply that personnel as a generic activity is unimportant? Perhaps, but not necessarily.

The second major principle of SHRM is the notion of horizontal fit. The idea of horizontal fit is that the individual HRM practices of selection, training, compensation, and so on should not be chosen in a piecemeal, isolated fashion but rather selected so as to craft a mutually supporting, consistent package. As recognized in the SHRM literature, the idea of horizontal fit rests on the proposition that there are complementarities among individual HRM practices. The notion of complementarities in production is an old one in labor economics (Hamermesh 1993) and has direct application to the theory of derived input demand, as developed here for the case of HRM services. Also, the concept of complementarities has become a key explanatory variable in the modern organizational economics literature (Milgrom and Roberts 1995). Two inputs are complements in production when adding more of one input increases the returns from adding more of the other, thus creating synergy. Complementarities arise from interdependencies and nonseparabilities in the production function, giving rise to team forms of production (Alchian and Demsetz 1972). In general, structuring production to take account of complementarities, such as forming employee teams around an interdependent production process, boosts output.[5] But exploiting interdependencies also has a downside (Becker and Gerhart 1996). Complementarities increase the interdependence of a production system, making it more prone to crashing when one part malfunctions or seriously underperforming when one function moves out of alignment. Thus, in an unstable, fast-changing economic environment (such as the pre–World War II era or 1990s), an additive (independently configured) HRM system may yield superior results.

The advantage of the economic model proposed here is that it allows inclusion of complementarities into the theory of HRM in a straightforward way, thus giving more formal and analytical content to the concept of horizontal fit. One can well imagine, for example, specifying a translog production or cost function with multiple HRM practices as separate independent variables and then using a large firm-level data set to empirically test for the presence of complementarities. I warrant that doing so will help put to rest the claim that horizontal fit is only a recent SHRM innovation. For example, although they did not use the production function framework and idea of complementarities, Baron, Dobbin, and

Jennings (1986) examined the 1935 NICB data set (National Industrial Conference Board 1936, previously described) and found evidence that personnel practices cluster into three different types of employment systems. And should we be surprised? I think not, since corporate executives and their top industrial relations managers in leading welfare capitalist firms recognized that to implement an employee representation plan (a 1920s version of employee involvement) without a supporting set of other HRM practices (e.g., employment security, above-market wages, promotion from within) was the epitome of shortsighted management and lack of strategic perspective. A number of more recent empirical studies have also found evidence that firms develop distinct bundles of HRM practices that can be grouped into a small number of separable employment systems (e.g., Baron, Burton, and Hannan 1999), and several studies by researchers from economics and industrial relations have incorporated in varying degrees the theory of production and input complementarity (MacDuffie 1995; Ichniowski, Shaw, and Prennushi 1997; Laursen and Foss 2003). I conjecture that further effort along this line, particularly in the management literature, would further advance this research, given the observation of Ferris et al. (1999:389) regarding horizontal fit that "there is little coherence among empirical results in the field."

Conclusion

By widespread agreement, the field of human resource management has been largely an atheoretic, problem-driven field characterized by a substantial element of description and prescription. The last decade has seen a welcome advance in theorizing, driven in substantial degree by new developments in the subfields of strategic human resource management and personnel economics. The extent of progress has been slowed, however, by a variety of problems, including disagreement about the definition and conceptualization of the object of study, an inaccurate portrayal of the historical development of the field, lack of theoretical integration across the practice areas of personnel and human resource management, the tendency of economists and management researchers to speak past each other, and a penchant to mix positive and normative premises.

Besides pointing out these problem areas, in this chapter I have also endeavored to improve upon them by drawing on insights from history, economics, and industrial relations. The brief review of history suggests that HRM and SHRM are not recent innovations that require a new or special theory but are extensions and developments of a timeless and generic activity that has existed for as long as employers and employees have worked together to produce economic goods. Likewise, strategic people management is not a new discovery of the 1980s and 1990s but was well understood and practiced at the dawn of the field in the early 1920s. Typically, the strategic conception of HRM went under the title "industrial relations" in those years.

In this chapter I have also drawn on the discipline of economics to lay the foundation for a more formal and integrative theory of HRM. Using ideas from modern institutional economics, I proposed that the core conceptual construct in the field is the *human resource function:* the process and activity used to acquire, coordinate, and effectively utilize labor input in production. Determined by the pattern of transaction and production cost, the human resource function can be performed by either markets, management, or a combination thereof. An implication is that with positive transaction cost, neither a purely economics (market) based theory or a purely organizational (management) based theory is adequate since the human resource function inextricably involves both markets and management due to the presence of incomplete labor contracts. A cross-disciplinary perspective and mode of theorizing are thus required at key points, a project that has been the traditional domain and raison d'etre of the field of industrial relations (also known as institutional labor economics).

For that portion of the human resource function performed by management, I then attempted to use the microeconomic theory of factor demand to develop an integrative model for analyzing and predicting HRM patterns and outcomes. The human resource function can be envisioned as a factor input into production, analogous to capital and labor, and the optimal level and mix of human resource practices are determined by the familiar marginal decision rules of neoclassical economics. This model is used to derive a demand curve for HRM services, to show that a firm's demand for HRM is composed of both a direct and an indirect effect, to predict the optimal mix of HRM practices, and to explain cross-sectional and time-series variation in HRM practices as an outcome of variation in firms' HRM demand curves. The model also suggests that the practice of SHRM is readily interpretable as a long-range profit maximization problem, subject to bounded rationality, imperfect information, and dynamic change in the environment. Differences in cost structures, market position, degree of competition, human-capital requirements of production, and management philosophy across firms in turn generate different business strategies and matching employment systems, while complementarities in production also give rise to distinct bundles of HRM practices, such as those associated with the high-performance HRM model.

Quite possibly neither economists nor management scholars will be entirely happy with the message of this essay, since it suggests that the theories and empirical work of both groups are incomplete and likely to suffer from misspecification and omitted-variables bias. Such is the sometimes uncomfortable but productive bridging role played by the field of industrial relations. Economists interested in personnel and human resource management would do well to further broaden standard microeconomic models to incorporate a richer set of behavioral and organizational theories and concepts, while management scholars would substantially strengthen their research by giving more attention to economic theory, the economics literature, and market forces as determinants of firm-level HRM practices. After stating this admonition to both sides of the house, I also have to state that it is my judgment that an integrative theory for the field will most certainly come from economics, although it will marry insights and concepts from neoclassical and institutional economics and incorporate ideas and empirical evidence from the behavioral and administrative sciences. I have endeavored to sketch the outlines of such a theory in this chapter and to point out interesting insights and implications. I hope others will find this exercise useful or at least thought provoking.

Notes

[1] Although Bakke used the plural term *resources,* I henceforth follow the mainline of the current literature and instead use the singular term *resource.*

[2] Illustrative of this perspective, Müller-Jentsch (1995:61) reports that a German consulting firm advised management "to consider the works council (a form of employee participation) as a 'factor of production.'"

[3] As an illustration, an executive at Delta Air Lines said "morale is everything in this business" (quoted in Kaufman 2003a), and not coincidentally the company invests huge sums in its HRM program, including an exceptionally advanced employee involvement program.

[4] Note that the subscripts on the HRM variable in the graph and surrounding text represent different *quantities* of a generic HRM input, not different *types* of HRM services as specified in equation 2.

[5] Thus, even if labor economists and management scholars are both "economists," as earlier suggested in the text, it is only productive to combine them in a team (e.g., a single university department or school) if significant complementarities exist in the research and teaching production functions.

References

Alchian, Armen, and Harold Demsetz. 1972. "Production, Information Costs, and Economic Organization." *American Economic Review*, Vol. 72, no. 5, pp. 777–95.

Appelbaum, Eileen, Annette Bernhardt, and Richard Murnane. 2003. *Low-Wage America: How Employers Are Reshaping Opportunities in the Workplace*. New York: Russell Sage.

Armstrong, Michael. 2001. *A Handbook of Human Resource Management Practice*, 8th ed. London: Kogan Pace.

Arthur, Jeffrey. 1994. "Effects of Human Resource Systems on Manufacturing Performance and Turnover." *Academy of Management Journal*, Vol. 37, no. 3, pp. 670–87.

Bakke, E. Wight. 1958. *The Human Resources Function*. New Haven, CT: Yale University, Yale Labor and Management Center.

Balderston, Canby. 1935. *Executive Guidance of Industrial Relations*. Philadelphia: University of Pennsylvania Press.

Barney, J. 1991. "Firm Resources and Sustained Competitive Advantage." *Journal of Management*, Vol. 17, pp. 99–129.

Baron, James, Diane Burton, and Michael Hannan. 1999. "The Road Not Taken: Origins of Employment Systems in Emerging Companies." In G. Carroll and D. Teece, eds., *Firms, Markets, and Hierarchies*, New York: Oxford University Press, pp. 428–64.

Baron, James, Frank Dobbin, and P. Devereaux Jennings. 1986. "War and Peace: The Evolution of Modern Personnel Administration in U.S. Industry." *American Journal of Sociology*, Vol. 92, no. 2, pp. 350–83.

Becker, Brian, and Barry Gerhart. 1996. "The Impact of Human Resource Management on Organizational Performance: Progress and Prospects." *Academy of Management Journal*, Vol. 39, no. 4, pp. 779–801.

Beer, Michael, and Bert Spector. 1984. "Human Resources Management: The Integration of Industrial Relations and Organizational Development." In K. Rowland and G. Ferris, eds., *Research in Personnel and Human Resource Management*, Vol. 2, Stamford, CT: JAI Press, pp. 261–97.

Beer, Michael, Bert Spector, Paul Lawrence, D. Quinn Mills, and Richard Walton. 1984. *Managing Human Assets*. New York: Free Press.

Begin, James. 1991. *Strategic Employment Policy: An Organizational Systems Perspective*. Englewood Cliffs, NJ: Prentice Hall.

Boxall, Peter. 1998. "Human Resource Strategy and Industry-Based Competition: A Conceptual Framework and Agenda for Theoretical Development." In P. Wright, L. Dyer, J. Boudreau, and G. Milkovich, eds., *Strategic Human Resources Management in the Twenty-First Century*, Suppl. 4, Stamford, CT: JAI Press, pp. 259–82.

Brewster, Chris. 1995. "Towards a European Model of HRM." *Journal of International Business Studies*, Vol. 26, no. 1, pp. 1–21.

Cappelli, Peter, et al. 1997. *Change at Work*. New York: Oxford University Press.

Coase, Ronald. 1937. "The Nature of the Firm." *Economica*, New Series, Vol. 4, no. 16 (November), pp. 386–405.

Commons, John. 1919. *Industrial Goodwill*. New York: McGraw-Hill.

———. 1934. *Institutional Economics: Its Place in Political Economy*. New York: Macmillan.

Delery, John. 1998. "Issues of Fit in Strategic Human Resource Management: Implications for Research." *Human Resource Management Review*, Vol. 8, no. 3, pp. 289–310.

Delery, John, and D. Harold Doty. 1996. "Modes of Theorizing in Strategic Human Resource Management: Tests of Universalistic, Contingency, and Configurational Performance Predictions." *Academy of Management Journal*, Vol. 39, no. 4, pp. 802–35.

Dulebohn, James, Gerald Ferris, and James Stodd. 1995. "The History and Evolution of Human Resource Management." In G. Ferris, S. Rosen, and D. Barnum, eds., *Handbook of Human Resource Management*, Cambridge, MA: Blackwell, pp. 19–41.

Duncan, W. Jack. 1989. *Great Ideas in Management*. San Francisco: Jossey-Bass.

Ferris, Gerald, Donald Barnum, Sherman Rosen, Lawrence Holleran, and James Dulebohn. 1995. "Toward Business–University Partnership in Human Resource Management: Integration of Science and Practice." In G. Ferris, S. Rosen, and D. Barnum, eds., *Handbook of Human Resource Management*, Cambridge: Blackwell, pp. 1–13.

Ferris, Gerald, Wayne Hochwater, M. Ronald Buckley, Gloria Harrell-Cook, and Dwight Frink. 1999. "Human Resources Management: Some New Directions." *Journal of Management*, Vol. 25, no. 2, pp. 385–415.

Fisher, Cynthia. 1989. "Current and Recurrent Challenges in HRM." *Journal of Management*, Vol. 15, no. 2, pp. 157–80.

Freeman, Richard, and Joel Rogers. 1999. *What Workers Want*. Ithaca, NY: ILR Press.

Gibbs, Michael, and Alec Levenson. 2002. "The Economic Approach to Personnel Research." In Shoshana Grossbard-Schechtman, ed., *The Expansion of Economics: Toward a More Inclusive Social Science*, Armonk, NY: Sharpe, pp. 99–139.

Gunderson, Morley. 2001. "Economics of Personnel and Human Resource Management." *Human Resource Management Review*, Vol. 11, no. 4, pp. 431–52.

Hamermesh, Daniel. 1993. *Labor Demand*. Princeton: Princeton University Press.

Heneman, Herbert. 1969. "Toward a General Conceptual System of Industrial Relations: How Do We Get There?" In G. Somers, ed., *Essays in Industrial Relations Theory*, Ames: Iowa State University Press, pp. 3–24.

Hotchkiss, Willard. 1923. "Industrial Relations Management." *Harvard Business Review*, Vol. 1 (July), pp. 438–50.

Huselid, Mark. 1995. "The Impact of Human Resource Management Practices on Turnover, Productivity, and Corporate Financial Performance." *Academy of Management Journal*, Vol. 38, no. 3, pp. 635–72.

Ichniowski, Casey, Katherine Shaw, and G. Prennushi. 1997. "The Effects of Human Resource Management Practices on Productivity: A Study of Steel Finishing Lines." *American Economic Review*, Vol. 87, no. 3, pp. 291–313.

Ivancevich, John. 1995. *Human Resource Management*. Homewood, IL: Irwin.

Jacoby, Sanford. 1985. *Employing Bureaucracy: Managers, Unions, and the Transformation of Work in American Industry, 1900–1945*. New York: Columbia University Press.

Jones, Gareth, and Patrick Wright. 1992. "An Economic Approach to Conceptualizing the Utility of Human Resource Management Practices." In G. Ferris and K. Rowland, eds., *Research in Personnel and Human Resource Management*, Vol. 10. Greenwich, CT: JAI Press, pp. 271–300.

Kaufman, Bruce. 1998. "John R. Commons: His Contributions to the Founding and Early Development of the Field of Personnel/HRM." In *Proceedings of the Fiftieth Annual Winter Meeting, Industrial Relations Research Association,* Madison, WI: IRRA, pp. 328–41.

———. 2000. "Personnel/Human Resource Management: Its Roots as Applied Economics." In R. Backhouse and J. Biddle, eds., *Toward a History of Applied Economics,* Raleigh, NC: Duke University Press, pp. 229–56.

———. 2001a. "Human Resources and Industrial Relations: Commonalities and Differences." *Human Resource Management Review,* Vol. 11, no. 4, pp. 339–74.

———. 2001b. "The Theory and Practice of Strategic HRM and Participative Management: Antecedents in Early Industrial Relations." *Human Resource Management Review,* Vol. 11, no. 4, pp. 505–33.

———. 2002. "The Role of Economics and Industrial Relations in the Development of the Field of Personnel/Human Resource Management." *Management Decision,* Vol. 40, no. 10, pp. 962–79.

———. 2003a. "High-Level Employee Involvement at Delta Air Lines." *Human Resource Management,* Vol. 42, no. 2, pp. 175–90.

———. 2003b. "Industrial Relations Councilors, Inc: Its History and Significance." In B. Kaufman, R. Beaumont, and R. Helfgott, eds., *Industrial Relations to Human Resources and Beyond: The Evolving Process of Employee Relations Management,* Armonk, NY: Sharpe, pp. 31–114.

———. 2003c. "John R. Commons and the Wisconsin School on Industrial Relations Strategy and Policy." *Industrial and Labor Relations Review,* Vol. 57, no. 1, pp. 3–30.

———. 2003d. "The Organization of Economic Activity: Insights from the Institutional Theory of John R. Commons." *Journal of Economic Behavior and Organization,* Vol. 52, pp. 71–96.

———. 2003e. "The Quest for Cooperation and Unity of Interest in Industry." In B. Kaufman, R. Beaumont, and R. Helfgott, eds., *Industrial Relations to Human Resources and Beyond: The Evolving Process of Employee Relations Management,* Armonk, NY: Sharpe, pp. 115–47.

———. 2004a. *The Global Evolution of Industrial Relations: Events, Ideas, and the IRRA.* Geneva: International Labour Organization.

———. 2004b. "The Impossibility of a Competitive Labor Market." Unpublished paper, Georgia State University, Atlanta.

Kaufman, Bruce, and David Levine. 2000. "An Economic Analysis of Employee Representation." In B. Kaufman and D. Taras, eds., *Nonunion Employee Representation: History, Contemporary Practice, and Policy.* Armonk, NY: Sharpe, pp. 149–75.

Kennedy, Dudley. 1919. "Employment Management and Industrial Relations." *Industrial Management,* Vol. 58, no. 5, pp. 353–58.

Kleiner, Morris, Richard Block, Myron Roomkin, and Sidney Salsburg. 1987. *Human Resources and the Performance of the Firm.* Madison, WI: IRRA.

Kochan, Thomas, and Lee Dyer. 2001. "HRM: An American View." In J. Storey, ed., *Human Resource Management: A Critical Text,* 2nd ed. London: Thomson Learning, pp. 272–87.

Laursen, Keld, and Nicolai Foss. 2003. "New Human Resource Management Practices, Complementarities and the Impact on Innovation Performance." *Cambridge Journal of Economics,* Vol. 27, pp. 243–63.

Lawler, Edward. 1988. "Human Resources Management: Meeting the New Challenges." *Personnel,* January, pp. 22–27.

Lazear, Edward. 1998. *Personnel Economics for Managers.* New York: Wiley.

———. 1999. "Personnel Economics: Past Lessons and Future Directions." *Journal of Labor Economics,* Vol. 17, no. 2, pp. 199–236.

Leiserson, William. 1929. "Contributions of Personnel Management to Improved Labor Relations." In *Wertheim Lectures in Industrial Relations,* Cambridge, MA: Harvard University Press, pp. 125–64.

Lepak, David, and Scott Snell. 1999. "The Human Resource Architecture: Toward a Theory of Human Capital Allocation and Development." *Academy of Management Journal,* Vol. 24, no. 1, pp. 31–48.

Lewin, David. 1987. "Industrial Relations as a Strategic Variable." In M. Kleiner et al., eds., *Human Resources and the Performance of the Firm,* Madison, WI: IRRA, pp. 1–41.

———. 2001. "Low-Involvement Work Practices and Business Performance." In *Proceedings of the 53rd Annual Meeting, Industrial Relations Research Association.* Champaign, IL: IRRA, pp. 275–92.

MacDuffie, John. 1995. "Human Resource Bundles and Manufacturing Performance: Organizational Logic and Flexible Productions Systems in the World Auto Industry." *Industrial and Labor Relations Review,* Vol. 48, no. 2, pp. 197–221.

Mahoney, Thomas, and John Deckop. 1986. "Evolution of Concept and Practice in Personnel Administration/Human Resource Management (PA/HRM)." *Journal of Management,* Vol. 12, pp. 223–41.

Marsden, David. 1999. *A Theory of Employment Systems.* London: Oxford University Press.

Marshall, Leon. 1920. "Incentive and Output: A Statement of the Place of the Personnel Manager in Modern Industry." *Journal of Political Economy,* Vol. 28, no. 9, pp. 713–34.

Martell, Kathryn, and Stephen Carroll. 1995. "How Strategic *Is* HRM?" *Human Resource Management,* Vol. 34, no. 2, pp. 253–67.

McMahan, Gary, Myrtle Bell, and Meghna Virick. 1998. "Strategic Human Resource Management: Employee Involvement, Diversity, and International Issues." *Human Resource Management Review,* Vol. 8, no. 3, pp. 193–214.

McMahan, Gary, Meghna Virick, and Patrick Wright. 1998. "Alternative Theoretical Perspectives for Strategic Human Resource Management Revisited: Progress, Problems, and Prospects." In P. Wright, L. Dyer, J. Boudreau, and G. Milkovich, eds., *Strategic Human Resources Management in the Twenty-First Century,* Suppl. 4, Stamford, CT: JAI Press, pp. 99–122.

Milgrom, Paul, and John Roberts. 1995. "Complementarities and Fit: Strategy, Structure, and Organizational Change in Manufacturing." *Journal of Accounting and Economics,* Vol. 19, pp. 179–208.

Mitchell, Daniel. 2001. "IR Journal and Conference Literature from the 1960s to the 1990s: What Can HR Learn from It? Where Is It Headed?" *Human Resource Management Review,* Vol. 11, no. 4, pp. 375–94.

Müller-Jentsch, Walther. 1995. "Germany: From Collective Voice to Co-management." In Joel Rogers and Wolfgang Streeck, eds., *Works Councils: Consultation, Representation, and Cooperation in Industrial Relations,* Chicago: University of Chicago Press, pp. 53–78.

Myers, Charles, and Paul Pigors. 1961. *Personnel Administration: A Point of View and a Method*, 4th ed. New York: McGraw-Hill.

National Industrial Conference Board. 1931. *Industrial Relations: Administration of Policies and Programs*. New York: NICB.

———. 1936. *What Employers Are Doing for Employees*. New York: NICB.

Nolan, Peter, and Kathy O'Donnell. 2003. "Industrial Relations, HRM and Performance." In P. Edwards, ed., *Industrial Relations: Theory and Practice*, 2nd ed., London: Blackwell, pp. 489–513.

Peters, Thomas, and Robert Waterman. 1982. *In Search of Excellence*. New York: Harper and Row.

Pfeffer, Jeffrey. 1994. *Competitive Advantage through People*. Cambridge: Harvard Business School.

Rogers, Edward, and Patrick Wright. 1998. "Measuring Organizational Performance in Strategic Human Resource Management Research: Problems, Prospects, and Performance Information Markets." *Human Resource Management Review*, Vol. 8, no. 3, pp. 311–31.

Schuler, Randy, and Susan Jackson. 2001. "Human Resource Management: Past, Present, and Future." In R. Blanpain and C. Engels, eds., *Comparative Labour Law and Industrial Relations in Industrialized Market Economies*, The Hague: Kluwer, pp. 101–31.

Storey, John. 2001. "Human Resource Management Today: An Assessment." In J. Storey, ed., *Human Resource Management: A Critical Text*, 2nd ed., London: Thomson Learning, pp. 3–20.

Strauss, George. 2001. "HRM in the USA: Correcting Some British Impressions." *International Journal of Human Resource Management*, Vol. 12, no. 6, pp. 873–97.

Strauss, George, and Leonard Sayles. 1960. *Personnel: The Human Problem of Management*. Englewood Cliffs, NJ: Prentice-Hall.

Towne, Henry. 1886. "The Engineer as an Economist." *Transactions: American Society of Mechanical Engineers*, Vol. 7, pp. 428–32. [Reprinted in Daniel Wren, *Early Management Thought*, Aldershot, UK: Dartmouth, 1997.]

Ulrich, David. 1998. "The New Mandate for Human Resources." *Harvard Business Review*, Vol. 76 (January–February), pp. 124–34.

Williamson, Oliver. 1985. *The Economic Institutions of Capitalism*. New York: Free Press.

Wren, Daniel. 1994. *The Evolution of Management Thought*, 3rd ed. New York: Wiley.

Wright, Patrick, Benjamin Dunford, and Scott Snell. 2001. "Human Resources and the Resource Based View of the Firm." *Journal of Management*, Vol. 27, no. 6, pp. 701–21.

Wright, Patrick, and Gary McMahan. 1992. "Theoretical Perspectives for Strategic Human Resource Management." *Journal of Management*, Vol. 18, no. 2, pp. 295–320.

Yoder, Dale. 1962. *Personnel Management and Industrial Relations*, 5th ed. Englewood Cliffs, NJ: Prentice-Hall.

ABOUT THE CONTRIBUTORS

Greg J. Bamber is professor and associate dean of the Griffith Business School, Griffith University, Queensland, Australia. He was formerly at Durham University (U.K.) and an arbitrator with the Advisory, Conciliation and Arbitration Service (U.K.). His (joint) publications include *International and Comparative Employment Relations: Globalisation and the Developed Market Economies* (Sage), *Employment Relations in the Asia Pacific* (Thomson), and *Organisational Change Strategies* (Longman). His publications have been translated into several languages. He is a past president of the International Federation of Scholarly Associations of Management and of the Australian and New Zealand Academy of Management.

Julian Barling is currently the associate dean with responsibility for the Ph.D., M.Sc., and research programs in the School of Business at Queens University, Ontario, Canada. Dr. Barling is the author of several books, including most recently *The Psychology of Workplace Safety*, and is the author or editor of well over 150 research articles and book chapters. Dr. Barling is the editor of the American Psychological Association's *Journal of Occupational Health Psychology*. In 2002, Dr. Barling was named as one of Queen's University's Queen's Research Chairs and elected as a Fellow of the Royal Society of Canada.

John W. Budd is an Industrial Relations Landgrant Term Professor in the University of Minnesota's Industrial Relations Center in the Carlson School of Management. He is the author of *Employment with a Human Face: Balancing Efficiency, Equity, and Voice* (Cornell University Press, 2004) and *Labor Relations: Striking a Balance* (McGraw-Hill/Irwin, 2005), and is coediting the 2005 IRRA research volume, *The Ethics of Human Resources and Industrial Relations*. He has received Excellence in Education and Outstanding Young Scholar awards from the IRRA.

Daniel G. Gallagher is the CSX Corporation Professor of Management at James Madison University. He received his M.A. and Ph.D. degrees from the Institute of Labor and Industrial Relations at the University of Illinois. His research has focused on psychological aspects of the employment relationship. Dr. Gallagher has been particularly involved in issues associated with the growth of alternative forms of employment contracts, as well as the dynamics of the union–member relationship. He currently serves on the editorial boards of *Industrial Relations, Journal of Organizational Behavior, Journal of Management,* and *International Journal of Conflict Resolution.*

John Godard (Cornell, 1989) is a professor in the Faculty of Management at the University of Manitoba, an editor of the *British Journal of Industrial Relations,* and president of the Canadian Industrial Relations Association. His main interest is in how institutional environments shape employer practices and ultimately worker, union, and societal outcomes, especially the role of national histories, state policies, and law in Canada, the United States, and the United Kingdom. His most recent publications appear in the *British Journal of Industrial Relations,* the *Industrial and Labour Relations Review, Industrial Relations,* and *Canadian Public Policy.*

Rafael Gomez is a lecturer at the London School of Economics and research fellow at the University of Toronto's Centre for Industrial Relations. He has recently published a book, in collaboration with Seymour Martin Lipset and the late Noah Meltz, *The Paradox of American Unionism* (Cornell University Press).

Richard Hyman is at the Department of Industrial Relations of the London School of Economics. He is editor of the European *Journal of Industrial Relations* and has published extensively on comparative industrial relations.

Bruce E. Kaufman is professor of economics in the Andrew Young School of Policy Studies and senior associate of the W.T. Beebe Institute of Personnel and Employment Relations at Georgia State University. He is the editor or coeditor of two previous IRRA research volumes, *Employee Representation: Alternatives and Future Directions* (1993) and *Government Regulation of the Employment Relationship* (1997). His most recent book is *The Global Evolution of Industrial Relations: Events, Ideas, and the IIRA* (2004).

E. Kevin Kelloway is professor of management and psychology and chair of the Department of Management in the Sobey School of Business at Saint Mary's University, Halifax, Nova Scotia, Canada. His research interests include occupational health psychology, leadership, the development and measurement of work attitudes and values, unionization, and the management of knowledge workers.

David Marsden is professor of industrial relations at the London School of Economics. Before joining LSE, he worked at the Laboratoire d'Economie et de Sociologie du Travail, CNRS, Aix-en-Provence. He has an enduring interest in comparative employment relations and employee management. This is encapsulated in his recent book *A Theory of Employment Systems: Micro-foundations of Societal Diversity* (Oxford, 1999).

Roderick Martin, professor and director of organizational behavior at the School of Management, University of Southampton, England, has had a long academic career, the greater part spent in Oxford. *The Effects of Financial Institutions and Investor Behaviour on Management Practice,* his current research contract commissioned by the U.K. Department of Trade and Industry for £161,000, is part of Dr. Martin's ongoing research interest in the sociological and comparative approach to organizational behavior as a counterweight to the economic rational-choice models dominating organizational studies, especially in the United States.

The late **Noah M. Meltz** authored many papers on industrial relations theory and comparative pieces on Canada–U.S. labor market differences. His last book, *The Paradox of American Unionism,* was published in 2004 by Cornell University Press. He was principal of Woodsworth College, professor emeritus at the University of Toronto, and the former director and cofounder of the Centre for Industrial Relations at the University of Toronto.

Walther Müller-Jentsch is professor emeritus at the Ruhr-Universität Bochum Social Science Department. He was Leverhulme Visiting Professor in European Industrial Relations at Warwick University, U.K. (1990), and member of the executive committee of the German Industrial Relations Association (1996–2003). He is editor of the *Schriftenreihe Industrielle Beziehungen* and coeditor of *Industrielle Beziehungen* (the German *Journal of Industrial Relations*). His main publications include *Soziologie der Industriellen Beziehungen* (2nd ed., Frankfurt-am-Main, 1997), *Konfliktpartnerschaft* (3rd ed., München and Mering, 1999; editor), *The Changing Contours of German Industrial Relations* (München and Mering, 2003; coeditor), and *Organisationssoziologie* (Frankfurt-am-Main, 2003).

Kirsty Newsome is lecturer in human resource management in the Business School at the University of Strathclyde, Glasgow, Scotland. Her research, writing, and teaching encompass industrial relations and industrial sociology. Her major research interest is exploring the impact of changing interfirm relations on the labor process of supply organizations.

Paul Thompson is professor of organizational analysis and vice dean (research) in the Business School at the University of Strathclyde, Glasgow, Scotland. He is co-organizer of the International Labour Process Conference. His research focuses on skill, control, resistance, and work organization issues, and his most recent publication is the forthcoming *Handbook of Work and Organization* for Oxford University Press (coedited with Stephen Ackroyd, Pam Tolbert, and Rose Batt).

Michael L. Wachter is the William B. Johnson Professor of Law and Economics at the University of Pennsylvania and codirector of the Institute for Law and Economics. His recent articles include "Judging Unions' Future Using a Historical Perspective: The Public Policy Choice between Competition and Unionization," *Journal of Labor Research* (Spring 2003); "Corporate Policy and the Coherence of Delaware Takeover Law," with coauthor Richard Kihlstrom, *University of Pennsylvania Law Review* (December 2003); and "Takeover Defense When Financial Markets Are (Only) Relatively Efficient," *University of Pennsylvania Law Review* (January 2003).

IRRA Organizational Memberships

The IRRA provides a unique forum where representatives of all stake-holders in the employment relationship and their views are welcome.

We invite your organization to become a member of our prestigious, vibrant association. The Industrial Relations Research Association (IRRA) is the professional membership association and learned society of persons interested in the field of industrial relations. Formed more than fifty years ago, the IRRA brings together representatives of labor, management, government, academics, advocates, and neutrals to share ideas and learn about new developments, issues, and practices in the field. Members share their knowledge and insights through IRRA publications, meetings, and IRRA listservs. In addition, the IRRA provides a network of 50 chapters where professionals meet locally to discuss issues and share information.

The purpose of the IRRA is to encourage research and to foster discussion of issues affecting today's workplace and workers. To that end, the IRRA publishes an array of information, including research papers and commentary presented at Association meetings; the acclaimed practitioner-oriented magazine, *Perspectives on Work*; a printed and online membership directory; quarterly newsletters; and an annual research volume. Recent research volumes include *Theoretical Perspectives on Work and the Employment Relationship*, Bruce E. Kaufman, editor; *Labor-Management Relations in Government Employment*, David Lipsky and Jonathan Brock, editors; *Collective Bargaining in the Private Sector*, Paul F. Clark, John T. Delaney, and Ann C. Frost, editors; and *The Future of the Safety Net: Social Insurance and Employee Benefits*, Sheldon Friedman and David Jacobs, editors. Other member publications and services include online IR/HR degree programs listings, an online library, job announcements, calls and announcements, competitions and awards for students and practicing professionals, and much more.

IRRA is a non-profit, 501(c)(3) organization governed by an elected Executive Board comprised of representatives of the various constituencies within the Association.

Organizational memberships are available on an annual or sustaining basis and include individual memberships for organization designees, a wealth of IRRA research and information, and numerous professional opportunities. Organizational members receive all IRRA publications and services. Your support and participation will help the Association continue its vital mission of shaping the workplace of the future. For more information, contact the IRRA National Office, 504 East Armory Ave, Room 121, Champaign, IL 61820. Visit the IRRA on the web at: www.irra.uiuc.edu.

The IRRA gratefully acknowledges the continuing support of its Sustaining and Annual Organizational Members

SUSTAINING MEMBERS
Sustaining Members provide a one-time contribution of $5,000 to $10,000.
AFL-CIO
The Alliance for Employee Growth and Development
Boeing Quality through Training Program
Ford Motor Company
General Electric
National Association of Manufacturers
National Education Association
UAW-Ford National Education, Training and Development Center
United Steelworkers of America

ANNUAL MEMBERS 2003-2004*
AFL-CIO Department for Professional Employees
American Federation of Teachers
California Labor Federation
Center for Human Resources, Wharton School, University of Pennsylvania
Centre for Industrial Relations, University of Toronto
Comey Institute of Industrial Relations, St. Joseph's University
Communications Workers of America
Department des Relations Industrielles, Université Laval
Department of Labor Studies and Industrial Relations, Pennsylvania State University
Division of Labor Studies, Indiana University
Erivan K. Haub School of Business, St. Joseph's University
George Meany Center for Labor Studies
Labor and Industrial Relations, Michigan State University
Lucent Technologies
Industrial Relations Center, Carlson School of Management,
University of Minnesota, Twin Cities
International Association of Machinists and Aerospace Workers
International Brotherhood of Teamsters
Institute of Human Resources and Industrial Relations, Loyola University of Chicago
Institute of Industrial Relations, University of California at Berkeley
Institute of Labor and Industrial Relations, University of Illinois at Urbana-Champaign
Las Vegas City Employees Association
Las Vegas Metropolitan Police Department
Master of Human Resources Program, Rollins College
Master of Human Resources Program, University of South Carolina
National Education Association
New York Nurses Association
Orange County Transportation Authority
Rollins College, Hamilton Holt School
San Diego Municipal Employees Association
School of Industrial and Labor Relations, Cornell University
School of Management and Labor Relations, Rutgers University
Sloan School of Management, Massachusetts Institute of Technology
Society for Human Resources Management
Working for America Institute, AFL-CIO

°Annual organizational memberships are available at the following levels:
Benefactor, $5,000 or more   6 employee members
Supporter, $1,000 to $4,999   6 employee members
Annual or Major University, $500   2 employee members
Educational or Non-Profit, $250   2 employee members

IRRA Chapters

Visit the IRRA website at www.irra.uiuc.edu for program and meeting information and to join a cjhapter in your area.

ALABAMA
  Alabama
ALASKA
  Alaska (Anchorage)
ARIZONA
  Arizona (Phoenix/Tucson)
CALIFORNIA
  Central (Fresno)
  Gold Rush (Oakland/San Jose)
  Inland Empire (Riverside/
    San Bernardino)
  Northern (Sacramento)
  Orange County (Anaheim)
  San Diego
  San Francisco
  Southern (Los Angeles)
COLORADO
  Rocky Mountain (Denver)
CONNECTICUT
  Connecticut Valley (Hartford/
    New Britain)
  Southwestern
DISTRICT OF COLUMBIA
  Washington, D.C.
FLORIDA
  Central Florida (Orlando)
  West Central Florida (Tampa/
    Clearwater)
GEORGIA
  Atlanta
HAWAII
  Hawaii (Honolulu)
ILLINOIS
  Central
  Chicago
  LIRA (University of Illinois)
INDIANA
  Delaware County (Muncie)
IOWA
  Iowa
MARYLAND
  Maryland (Baltimore)
MASSACHUSETTS
  Boston
MICHIGAN
  Detroit
  Mid-Michigan (Lansing)
  Southwestern (Kalamazoo)
  West (Grand Rapids)
MISSOURI
  Gateway (St. Louis)
  Greater Kansas City

NEVADA
  Southern (Las Vegas)
NEW JERSEY
  New Brunswick
NEW YORK
  Central New York (Syracuse)
  Hudson Valley
  Long Island
  New York Capital (Albany)
  New York City
  Western (Buffalo)
OHIO
  Central (Columbus)
  Greater Cincinnati
  Northeast Ohio (Cleveland)
  Southwestern (Dayton)
OKLAHOMA
  Greater Oklahoma
OREGON
  Oregon (Portland)
PENNSYLVANIA
  Central (Harrisburg)
  Northeast (Bethlehem)
  Philadelphia
  Southwestern (Pittsburgh)
RHODE ISLAND
  Greater Rhode Island
SOUTH/NORTH CAROLINA
  South Atlantic (Columbia/
    Charlotte)
TENNESSEE
  Tennessee Employment Relations
    Research Association (TERRA)
TEXAS
  Alamo
  Greater Houston
  North Texas (Dallas)
WASHINGTON
  Inland Empire (Spokane)
  Northwest (Seattle)
WEST VIRGINIA
  West Virginia (Morgantown)
WISCONSIN
  Wisconsin (Milwaukee)
CANADA
  British Columbia (Vancouver)
  Hamilton District (Ontario)
FRANCE
  Paris